COLUMBIA BIBLE COLLEGE
44 00037 3332

NO PLACE *for a Lady*

NO PLACE *for a Lady*

The Story of Canadian Women Pilots, 1928-1992

by Shirley Render

Dust jacket front:
L Helen Harrison, c. 1944.
C Jessica Jarvis, c. 1932.
R Ruthanne Page, c. 1984.

Back:
L Photo of Shirley Render by Bruce Barr.
R The author with Captain Alain Rioux, before a once-in-a-lifetime ride in a CF-18.

Canadian Cataloguing in Publication Data

Render, Shirley, 1943-

No place for a lady : the story of Canada's women pilots, 1928-1992

Includes bibliographical references and index.
ISBN 0-9694264-2-9

1. Women air pilots – Canada. I. Title.

TL539.R46 1992 629.13'0922 C92-098159 3

Design: Norman Schmidt

Printed in Canada by Hignell Printing Limited

Portage & Main Press
520 Hargrave Street
Winnipeg, Manitoba, Canada R3A 0X8

To my children

Kelly and Matthew

Follow your dreams

CONTENTS

Per Ardua Ad Astra was the motto of the Royal Canadian Air Force

FOREWORD

No Place for a Lady is the story of Canada's women pilots and how they progressed through the years to achieve recognition and qualify for airline and military positions of equal status with men. It is a story that has never been told before.

Shirley Render has done a tremendous job of research and followed it with interviews and personal contacts with women pilots all over Canada. She is a fully qualified pilot herself, with the ability to make her own observations on the factors that affected women's progress into commercial and military aviation.

This record of the experiences of pioneering women pilots will be of great value to present and future generations of women who take up flying seriously as a profession. The book is also a valuable contribution to the history of aviation in Canada, and I am privileged to have the honour of writing this foreword.

Punch Dickins
Toronto, 1988

PREFACE

"I didn't know we had our own pioneers," admitted Air Canada's first woman pilot, Judy Cameron. Indeed, how could she know? While dozens of books and hundreds of articles have told of the exploits of Canada's bush pilots and military heroes, the efforts of women pilots have gone virtually unnoticed. Yet there were women who flew in the early romantic days of flight, who wore the golden wings of the Air Transport Auxiliary, who penetrated the brass and brigade of the flight decks of the airlines and the military, and one who flew to the stars. *No Place for a Lady* tells their story.

Although it covers every aspect from 1928, when the first woman qualified for a pilot's licence, to 1992, when Canada's first woman astronaut rocketed into space, the book is much more than an historical account of the progress of Canada's female flyers. It is the inside story: a mixture of narrative and anecdotal history that reveals the women's hopes, dreams, frustrations, and accomplishments. I was entranced as I came to know so many of these women, and fascinated with the stories that they, their families, their flying instructors, their pupils, and their employers related. The women shared their experiences openly, as well as their photos and memorabilia, and the result is a colourful, poignant account that fills, I think, a long neglected gap in our aviation history.

It took Canadian women pilots more than fifty years to push open all the cockpit doors. Flying was simply a man's prerogative. I had no wish to write a book that moaned about discrimination, but it quickly became evident that women pilots were adversely affected by male prejudice — whether direct or stated as societal norms — although the women themselves only reluctantly admitted it. However, time and again the facts revealed that, until relatively recently, women were excluded from most areas of flying. Some were discouraged after gaining their first licence and either did not attempt a longed-for career in aviation or quickly gave up. Many hung in but remained on the periphery of the aviation industry. Consequently, the story of these women is not one of dauntless deeds but rather of their persistent struggle to gain admittance and acceptance into the world of flight. So discrimination is one of the most consistent themes although I have tried not to belabour the point. Interestingly, from a psychological viewpoint, another theme is also apparent and that is the type of woman who became a pilot. I found that women who flew, whether in the twenties, fifties or eighties had remarkably similar personality traits. The earliest women pilots, for the most part, usually had similar backgrounds as well, and were raised in an unconventional manner which allowed them to surmount the strictures of "proper behaviour" placed on women.

Research for this book was not easy. Information about women pilots was scarce, and about the early pilots it had all but disappeared. What was particularly frustrating was the inadequacy of official data — fifty years of government record keeping proved almost useless. For example, limited information on only seventeen of one hundred women licenced in the 1928 to 1945 period had been retained by the Public Archives of Canada. Fortunately, a list of the names, date of licence and licence number of these first one hundred women pilots had been retained (see page 361) and this gave me a starting point although, with no other identifying information, it was difficult to track down those who flew more than fifty years ago, often under a different (unmarried) name.

Transport Canada maintains the records dating from 1945 to the present, but again there were problems. Until the introduction of the computer in 1978 there was no breakdown by gender and therefore not even the name, type of licence, or even the total number of women flying were available. Scanning the lists of commercially licenced pilots, looking for women's names among the many thousand male pilots was not useful; too many individuals, both male and female, were listed by initials rather than first name. Finding the women for the most recent period, 1978 to 1992 was easier but it too was not without difficulty. Canada's privacy laws prevented Transport Canada from providing the names of the women currently flying, although total numbers for each type of licence were available. Those with the airlines, military, and Transport Canada itself were easily located, but women with the smaller charter companies or helicopter operators were more difficult to trace.

Surprisingly, I first thought, the women themselves knew little about other women pilots although, as their stories were revealed, I came to understand the isolation of each woman pilot. Finally, compounding the problem of incomplete or unavailable records, was the fact that there were few Canadian women pilots waiting to be found. Even in 1992 fewer than 150 women hold an airline transport licence, the highest rating that can be obtained.

To track down the women whose names I had found I

placed advertisements in newspapers and aviation publications, examined back issues of aviation periodicals, and wrote to former instructors, Department of Transport officials, airline, military and bush pilots, and others such as relatives and friends. Help also came from an unexpected source: publicity on the proposed book. I had received a Canada Council grant and the Amelia Earhart Research Award from the 99s (the International Organization of Women Pilots), and the grants and the project caught the attention of the media. As a result, in the fall of 1983 newspapers across the country ran articles on the proposed book, and national and local radio stations interviewed me. That publicity resulted in my receiving hundreds of snippets of information. In the end, having "found" as many female pilots as I could, I gathered most of the material in this book by interviewing the women themselves and others in the aviation industry. I found everyone, from World War I pilots on helpful and very interested in the task I had undertaken.

No Place for a Lady is arranged chronologically, with an emphasis on the women who were first to fly in each province and in each sector of aviation. To provide continuity and context I placed their stories within the framework of Canadian aviation history. As much as possible I used the words of the women themselves. Being both a woman pilot and an historian I had a delicate tightrope to walk: on the one hand not to be too subjective and, on the other, to bring a proper historical approach to the writing. Above all, I tried to write with insight and empathy and to give the aviation pioneers in this book their long-overdue recognition.

ACKNOWLEDGEMENTS

Writing a book is a solitary and often lonely experience. Although no one can do the writing for you there were, for me, many special people who were helpful, supportive, and caring. Indeed I owe deep gratitude to so many people for their help with *No Place for a Lady* that many pages would be required simply to list them all. Preeminent on my list are:

My children, my husband, and my parents for believing in me. In particular, I thank Doug, Kelly, and Matthew for holding the fort when I was away on research trips, for telling me not to worry about my hours spent hunched over the computer, and for their loving support throughout the years.

Keith Olson, Air Canada pilot and friend, has my eternal gratitude for his unfailing help, which included hundreds of hours of proof reading and constructive criticism of all drafts. Above all, I am thankful for his constant encouragement not to be discouraged when a chapter refused to be written, and his faith that I would complete the project and write "a good book."

Mary Dixon, my editor and publisher, approached the manuscript with creativity to produce a book different in format from all other aviation books. And most important, I enjoyed working with her; even in the final hectic phase as the book neared completion, Mary never lost her even temper and remained unflappable as I continued to add new information right up to going to press.

Many people read the manuscript in one draft version or another and made insightful suggestions. In particular, I thank Mary Hurst (my mom), Brenda Trevenen, Tannis Richardson, and Diane Rothberg.

Dr. John Kendle and Dr. Ed Rea, professors in the Department of History, University of Manitoba — having guided me through my Masters thesis, Western Canada Airways-Canadian Airways Limited: the development of commercial aviation in Canada, the research which gave me the necessary background to undertake *No Place for a Lady* — encouraged me in this project.

A very special thank you to Punch Dickins, member of Canada's Aviation Hall of Fame, winner of the McKee Trophy, World War I pilot, Royal Canadian Air Force, bush pilot with Western Canada Airways and Canadian Airways Limited, vice-president and general manager of Canadian Pacific Airlines, and executive with de Havilland, for writing the foreword. I consider myself honoured to have Punch, who has quite literally done everything and lived through all phases of Canada's aviation history, do this for me.

A book of this type requires getting to know the subjects and I very much appreciate the cooperation of Air Canada, Nordair, and Quebecair who provided transportation around the country so that I could do the necessary interviewing. Away from home, many kind people housed and transported me when I was in their city, in particular, Group Captain Arnie Bauer (Ret'd) of Ottawa, Ontario; Margaret and Keith Rutledge of Vancouver, British Columbia; Jack and Helen Reilly of Stony Plain, Alberta; Bruce Gowans of Calgary, Alberta; Barbara and Don Steeves of Moncton, New Brunswick; Shirley and Neil McDougall of Toronto,

Ontario; Isabel and Bill Peppler of Ottawa; Adele and Denis Stuber of Toronto; Tib Beament and her husband of Orillia, Ontario; France Gravel of Montreal, Quebec; Gina Jordan of Calgary; Rosella Bjornson and Bill Pratt of Edmonton; Phyllis Gaul, formerly of Montreal; Carole Morris of Toronto; Karen Brynelson of Vancouver; Ruth Stuart of Hamilton, Ontario; Gerry and Christine Burnett of Matane, Quebec; Eleanor and Bill Bailey of Calgary; and Louise Jenkins of Old Lyme, Connecticut. Many, many others extended their hospitality to me, and I would particularly like to thank the many 99s (International Organization of Women Pilots), especially Dorothy and Doug Renwick, who met me at airports and opened their homes to me.

The Sources (page 373) indicate the breadth of assistance I received from those in the world of aviation. So many people cheerfully searched their logbooks, and their memories, to give me starting points on my search for many of the "lost" pilots, and made the flavour of the era in which they were active come alive for me. Necessary factual information was provided by the Department of National Defence, the Directorate of History and Air Command, where Fran Burns and Major R.J. Butt of the Office of Information, CFB Winnipeg, and Tom Pollard of Air Command never failed to answer my seemingly endless questions. And Lieutenant General Fred Sutherland, former Commander of Air Command, ensured — to my everlasting delight — that I knew first-hand how the CF-18 Hornet performed.

Glenn Wright, formerly with the transportation section of the Public Archives of Canada and Gordon Howard of

Transport Canada were particularly helpful in locating long-forgotten records, as were librarians and archivists across the country who searched their records. I acknowledge with thanks the financial assistance towards research that I received from the Canada Council, Explorations Program, and from the 99's-sponsored Amelia Earhart Research Award.

Finally — and most important — this book could not have been written without the superb cooperation of the women pilots. They have given generously of their time over the years and still come forward with their support. Although it seems as if I have been writing this book forever — the idea came to me in 1979 — I would not have missed it for anything. To each and every one of these remarkable women I extend warm wishes; sharing your flying memories was an experience never to be forgotten. Thank you all!

PHOTO CREDITS

Photographs are identified by page number. All those not otherwise identified here are from the Western Canada Aviation Museum (WCAM), Canadian Women in Aviation collection, and are used with permission. Those identified "SR" are the author's; the donor's name follows.

The photographs on each chapter title page are of aircraft of the period. Aviation enthusiasts will undoubtedly recognize each one. For confirmation, they are identified at the end of this section.

Chapter One
1 K. M. Molson, with permission (A. G. K. Edward photo)
2, 3 National Aviation Museum, Ottawa

Chapter Two
11 National Aviation Museum, with permission
12 SR, F. Hollister-McQuin
13, 14 SR, Jack Herity
16 Public Archives Canada
20R Glenbow Archives, Calgary, via Bruce Gowans
20L SR, Elsie MacLean MacFarlane
21 SR, Don Miller
26 SR, Sandra Stewart
30 SR, Margaret Fane Rutledge
31 SR, Enid Norquay McDonald
32R WCAM, Father MacGillivray
35 Public Archives Canada

Chapter Three
37 K. M. Molson, with permission
38 SR, Jack Herity
39, 44 SR, Rolie Moore Pierce
42, 43 SR, Jessica Jarvis Hunt
44R Norm Scudellari photo, WCAM/CWA collection
45 SR, Ethel Croll
47 WCAM, Daphne Paterson collection
49 SR, Connie Culver Cubitt
50 SR, Eliane Roberge Schlachter
51 Canadian Pacific Railway photo
52 SR, Margaret Fane Rutledge
54, 56 SR, Jack Herity
59L SR, Margaret Fane Rutledge
59R Margaret Fane Rutledge, with permission
68 SR, Helen Harrison
71 WCAM, via Marion Orr

Chapter Four
77 Larry Milberry, with permission (Don Murray photo)
83, 95, 96, 104, 110 SR, Gerry Burnett
86 SR, Helen Harrison
91 Marion Orr, with permission
93, 105, 106 SR, Vera Strodl Dowling
99, 100, 103 WCAM, via Violet Milstead Warren
115, 116, 117 SR, Virginia Lee Warren Doerr

Chapter Five
125 K. M. Molson, with permission
133, 134L, 134R SR, Gerry Burnett
135 SR, Helen Harrison
138, 139L, 139R SR, Vera Strodl Dowling
141, 142, 143, 144 WCAM, Marion Orr
144 Toronto Star Syndicate, with permission

Chapter Six
147 Larry Milberry, with permission (Hal McCracken photo)
151, 152 WCAM, via Rolie Moore Pierce
161 SR, Phyllis Drysdale Lindsay
162 SR, Eleanor Jones Powers
166 SR, Gretchen Matheson
170 Mission Aviation Fellowship of Canada, with permission
174, 175, 176 WCAM, via Dorothy Rungeling
181L, 181R SR, Felicity McKendry
182 SR, Margaret Carson (photo from an undated reprint from *Canadian Flight*)
184L, 185R SR, Jack Reilly
185, 188 Lorna DeBlicquy, with permission

Chapter Seven
193 K. M. Molson, with permission
194 SR, Ruth Parsons Moore
197L, 197R, 198, 199, 201, 202 SR, Dawn Dawson Bartsch

204 Toni Ramsay, with permission
206L, 206R SR, Mrs. Lina Studer
208 Bob Grant photo, with permission
214, 215L, 215R, 217L Elizabeth Wieben Webster, with permission
217L Robbie Wieben Taylor, with permission

Chapter Eight
219 Larry Milberry photo, with permission
222 Darlene Tripp Simms, with permission
223, 224 Paula Matz, with permission
225 SR, Elaine Parker
227 SR, Jan Kuzina
229 SR, Karen Brynelsen MacGregor
232 Georgette Buch, with permission
234 Nicole Sauvé, with permission
237 SR, Mrs. D.C. Puttkemery
238 SR, Barb Warwashawski Kahl
242, 243 Kelly Hepburn Scott, with permission
244, 245 SR, Judy Adamson
246, 248 SR, Hella Comat
250 Susan Davis, with permission
252 SR, Margo McCutcheon
254 SR, Deborah McGrath
255 Bob Grant photo, with permission
256 SR, Diane Klassen

Chapter Nine
261 Jim Hawes, Custom Helicopters, with permission
262 SR, Dini Petty
266 SR, Diane Pepper
272L, 272R SR, Mireille Samson
273, 274L, 274R SR, Ruthanne Page
277 SR, Lois Hill
278 Suzanne Pomerleau, with permission
279 SR, Mary Ellen Pauli

Chapter Ten
281 Air Canada, with permission (photo by James Gregory)
287, 287L, 287R, 291 WCAM, CWA, via Rosella Bjornson
290 SR, Glenys Robison
294 SR, Barb Swyers
297 SR, Lucie Chapdelaine
298, 312 Canadian Airlines International, with permission
299 SR, Judy Cameron
301 SR, Gwen Grant
302 SR, Britt Irving
303, 304 Air Canada, with permission
305 Diane Rothberg, with permission
306 Paula Strilesky, with permission
309 SR, Kathy Zokol
311 SR, Stefanie Crampton
313 SR, France Gravel

Chapter Eleven
315, 317, 322, 332, 334, 336, 337, 339, 340, 342, 343, 348, 349, 350, 352 Canadian Armed Forces, with permission
319 SR, Wendy Clay
325 Dale Cumming cartoon, used with permission of *Winnipeg Free Press*
327 SR, Michelle Colton
329 SR, Mary Bryant
344 SR, Deanna Brasseur

Chapter Twelve
355 Canadian Space Agency, Ottawa
357 SR, Roberta Bondar

Aircraft pictured on chapter title pages
1 Elliot Air Service-built JN-4 Canuck
2 DH 60 M Gipsy Moth
3 Rambler I
4 Canadian-built Mosquito F.B.26
5 Fleet 80 Canuck
6 Stinson 108 Station Wagon
7 DHC 2 Beaver on Edo floats
8 Hawker Siddeley 748
9 Bell 206 Helicopter
10 Douglas DC9
11 CF-18
12 KC-135 Zero Gravity Trainer

NO PLACE *for a Lady*

CHAPTER ONE

The beginning

Madge Graham had never flown until she donned goggles, helmet, breeches, and a leather coat and climbed into the nose section of a Curtiss HS-2L, a war surplus wooden flying boat, on June 5, 1919.

MADGE WAS THE NAVIGATOR, her husband Stuart was the pilot, and with Bill Kahre as mechanic, they were ferrying the seaplane from Halifax, Nova Scotia to Lac à la Tortue, Quebec for the St. Maurice Forest Protective Association. With only the sketchiest of ground maps and engine noise preventing any conversation between Madge in the bow and her husband in the cockpit, it was not an easy trip. "I navigated by keeping a sharp lookout for contours of lakes and rivers," she recalled, "and I rigged up a small line on wheel pulleys, like a toy clothes line, and sent my messages back to the pilot on clothes pins." The flying boat carried three people: the pilot and mechanic side-by-side in an open cockpit and the navigator, Madge, in what had been the machine-gun position in the nose. All were exposed to the wind, rain, and cold and Madge, especially, got thoroughly soaked on every take-off and landing. The trip took over nine hours at an average speed of 66 miles per hour; a second ferrying trip took over twelve hours.

Madge's appearance caused a sensation at all the stops. While some admired her courage, most were aghast. Staying at the same hotel in Halifax was the famous Admiral Byrd, and his pronouncement — "Flying seaplanes over land is suicide and taking a woman along is criminal" — was typical of most public opinion and presaged the way women and flying would be viewed for another fifty years. Byrd's condemnation didn't faze the Grahams though. Madge continued to accompany her husband on forestry patrols and aerial surveys until her children were born.

Not surprisingly, Madge's flying was an exception rather than the rule. Commonly-held public opinion — the assumption that flying was a man's domain and woman's place was in the home — and male prejudice about women's abilities were strong factors against any women becoming pilots. However, unlike their counterparts in the United States, Great Britain, and Europe, Canadian women had another formidable barrier to overcome: the unique way aviation developed in Canada. While other western nations introduced air transport by establishing a network of airways between their major population centres, usually with government assistance, Canada's aviation industry was born "in the bush." It happened this way.

Launching the Curtiss HS-2L at Eastern Passage, Nova Scotia on 5 June 1919 for its flight to Quebec.

Prior to World War I, air transport as a commercial enterprise and official control of aviation did not exist. At war's end, there was little opportunity for anyone, man or woman, who wished to make a career out of flying. Some returning airmen tried to eke out an existence barnstorming. Others attempted to establish freight or passenger services. However, war surplus planes were not made for commercial purposes; they could not carry a sufficient payload to turn a profit, even if any business could be found, nor were the planes sturdy enough to withstand either the cold of winter operations or the ruggedness of Canada's terrain. As a result, few early aviation companies survived.

Perhaps the Canadian government of the early twenties was being fiscally responsible; both the war debt and the costs for

PAGE 16 June 1919 — THE DIGEST — 5

HYDROPLANES POUR GARDER LES FORETS

Le Base d'un Système de Patrouille Etablie au Lac à la Tortue — Le pilote habitera Grand'Mère

A sept heures du soir, le lundi 8 juin, le premier hydroplane qui ait jamais survolé Grand'Mère a passé sur notre ville à une hauteur de 2,800 pieds et, quelques minutes plus tard, est descendu au Lac à la Tortue, où il a été l'ancre pour la nuit.

Quelques minutes plus tard, l'hydroplane étant amarré, l'équipage a été conduit à terre en chaloupe. Il se compose du Lieutenant Stuart Graham, de sa femme, et de son mécanicien, M. Kehre. Ils ont été acclamés par la foule.

Cette envolée marque la première tentative de l'emploi des avions dans le commerce et c'est la première fois qu'un hydro-avion voie des provinces Maritimes à la province de Québec. Ce voyage qui marque une époque dans le développement de notre pays a été des plus heureux sous tous les rapports et Grand'Mère peut être justement fière de voir la part qu'elle joue dans le début de cette entreprise.

L'envolée s'est faite dans une machine prêtée par le ministère de la Marine à l'Association Protectrice des Forêts de la Saint-Maurice. Le Lt Graham est parti de Halifax le 6 juin et a fait son premier arrêt à St-Jean, N.B. Il devait ensuite descendre au lac Témiscouata mais un orage électrique l'a quelque peu dérouté et l'inexactitude de ses cartes lui a fait confondre Eagle Lake, Maine, avec le lac Témiscouata qui devait être son second arrêt. Il a ensuite pris la direction du lac Témiscouata puis, malgré un mauvais approvisionnement d'essence, il est arrivé à la Rivière du Loup le 7, à 6 heures et demie du soir.

La Tempête

Le Lt. Graham tenta de repartir le même soir pour Québec, mais une fois prêt, une tempête s'est élevée et l'eau devint trop agitée ce qui remit le départ au lendemain. Au moment du départ, la mer était encore telle-

THE PERSONNEL OF THE NEW AERIAL FOREST PATROL

LE PERSONNEL DE LA PATROUILLE AERIENNE DE NOS FORETS

Lieut. Stuart Graham and Mrs. Graham

M. Kehre
Lt. Graham's mechanic

MANY NEW VOLUMES PLACED ON THE LAURENTIDE BOOKSHELVES

"Hira Singh," by Talbot Mundy — A war story dealing with the experiences of an East Indian squadron in France.

"Little Journeys Toward Paris," by Simeon Strunsky —

the over-expanded railway system had to be dealt with and no doubt influenced the policy makers against early development of a national airways system. The fact that the Canadian population lay scattered along a relatively narrow band stretching some 3000 miles from coast to coast, and that the country was interspersed with formidable physical barriers and wide tracts of unsettled territory, were other factors. Whatever the combination of reasons, the government did little to encourage the development of an aviation industry. Its attitude was to let the commercial operators fend for themselves.

Parliament's apparent aversion to progress resulted, over the years, in a virtual military stranglehold on aviation. First, in

L *A 1919 newspaper article of the Graham flight.*

R *Madge Graham at the National Aviation Museum in front of the remains of Curtiss HS-2L, La Vigilance, in 1970.*

1919, all aviation was brought under government jurisdiction with the Air Board Act. One of the early actions of the Air Board was to commission the Canadian Air Force to attempt a trans-Canada flight from Halifax to Vancouver. The flight took place in 1920 and, though successful, it demonstrated the need to establish aerodromes and navigation aids across the country, an expensive and difficult undertaking. The Air Force, meanwhile, mostly to justify its existence, was handling work that could have gone to commercial companies. And there was also the spectre of heavy expenses to subsidize a trans-continental air service. All of these factors precluded the possibility of commercial endeavours being adequately promoted. Accordingly,

Sally Ross seated in a primary glider.

CANADA'S FIRST women fliers, "aeronauts" or "astronauts," as the newspapers dubbed them, were not licenced pilots but passengers, navigators, sky divers or glider pilots. The first Canadian woman to go aloft in a powered aircraft was Mrs. William Stark of Vancouver, British Columbia, who flew with her husband in his Curtiss biplane pusher on April 24, 1912. [Source: *125 Years of Canadian Aeronautics: A Chronology 1840-1965* by G. A. Fuller, J. A. Griffin, and K. M. Molson.]

SALLY ROSS (1910-1971)

Sally Ross was Canada's first woman glider pilot and the first woman to attend "an aero school for mechanics." In 1929 Harold Davenport and Art McCurdy formed the Aero School of Vancouver to teach engine maintenance, rigging, and theory of flight. Shortly after, they took over the Vancouver Glider Club and ran it as part of the school's operations. Sally was one of the first students and, according to Gordon Ballentine, another partner, was more than welcome because she brought some much needed publicity.

When reporters asked Sally if she were scared, she adamantly denied it. "The first time the boys let me fly the glider they were so worried I might break it that they spent all their time telling me how much repairs would cost. So when I started out all I could think of was care of the machine and I didn't have a chance to think of myself. After that it was easy." Ballentine remembered her as "a good glider pilot and an enthusiastic student who was well liked by the others."

THE VANCOUVER Glider Club, situated first at Lansdowne Field and then at what is now Vancouver International Airport, charged fifty cents per tow run or flight. Gordon Ballentine, Sally Ross's instructor, explained how it worked. "A run was one length of a field behind a 1918 Stutz Bearcat

the Canadian government balked at the cost and did nothing at that time, either to create a national, trans-continental airline system or to encourage commercial operators to do so.

In 1923 the Department of National Defence was created, and civil and military air services were grouped into one directorate in the Chief of General Staff Branch. This military grouping proved to be unsatisfactory and in 1927 a compromise was sought by creating a separate directorate for civil aviation; but it was still administered by the Department of National Defence. This arrangement continued until 1936, when the Department of Transport was formed, and civil aviation was at last separated completely from military control.

Left to their own resources, air operators, now with access to better aircraft, turned to the north where no airport construction was needed — hundreds of lakes and rivers provided natural take-off and landing areas for ski- and float-equipped aircraft. Thus most of Canada's aviation activity in the twenties and thirties was concentrated "in the bush" between Hudson Bay and the Mackenzie River basin and north 800 miles to the Arctic Ocean. The wealth in this remote region lay in its forests and minerals, its fisheries and furs. Aviation assisted in the development of these resources by providing fast, reliable, and relatively economical transportation.

By 1927 the demand by mining companies and others for air transportation exceeded the number of aircraft and pilots available. As well, the public was clamouring for inter-city air travel. The government, finally forced to admit that Canada lagged woefully behind other countries, decided to promote both inter-city airway development and pilot training.

First, to increase the number of qualified pilots and to promote the construction of airfields, the government assisted

Roadster. A 400 foot quarter-inch rope was tied to the tow car. At the glider end was an iron ring which was clasped by a jaw on the glider's nose. The jaw could be opened by the pilot pulling a cable which ran through a pulley and up to his seat . . ." Beginners did not get airborne on their first runs. First they were towed with only enough speed to give them coarse rudder control; then a little faster so they could ease the glider several feet off the ground. Harold Davenport and Ballentine took turns driving while the other would run alongside the glider shouting instructions. "We were in great shape in those days," recalled Ballentine, "It was amazing how well this primitive flying instruction worked!"

in the formation of "light aeroplane clubs" in the chief centres of population. It provided funds to purchase ten light aircraft as an initial issue to five clubs. In return, each club had to build an airfield and hangar, hire an instructor and mechanic, and assume responsibility for its own management. The government also gave the club a grant of $100 for each private pilot it trained. Second, the government approved an experimental airmail service on the prairies, which was expected to develop into a national airmail and passenger service. Trial flights took place in December 1928 and the service was inaugurated in 1930 by Canadian Airways Limited. Third, in response to the British government's promotion of airship travel as a way to maintain the links within the British Empire, the government constructed a mooring mast for airships at the airfield in St. Hubert, Quebec.

The public greeted all three schemes enthusiastically. Indeed, the response to the flying club plan was so great that by 1929 there were 23 flying clubs, 445 commercial pilots, and a total club membership (including social memberships) of 5,253, an increase from no flying clubs and only 43 commercial pilots in 1927.[1] The reaction was not surprising. The First World War had given an aura of romance to flying: pilots were heroes and the sound of an engine overhead caused people to stop whatever they were doing and rush outside to look skyward. Crowds assembled wherever there was any aerial activity and stories about flying were avidly consumed.

Women were not immune to what aviation could offer. Flying, more than any other activity, represented the ultimate escape from the considerable constraints of their everyday lives. It symbolized freedom and power and being in control of their destiny. In command of a plane a woman was master of her fate and had a sense of liberation that she might not experience elsewhere. For many flying was a passionate affair that they could not resist. They ignored the assumption that pilot

Canadian Airways Limited hangar, Winnipeg, with Fairchild 82A, CF-AXE, winter, 1936.

candidates should be male and signed up for lessons.

However, much to their chagrin, they found that they were not always welcomed. "A woman's only place in flying is as the mother of a pilot," was the reputed opinion of the president of the Regina Flying Club.

Even the government program, designed to encourage flying clubs to train as many pilots as possible placed women at a disadvantage. It was only for every male pilot who qualified for a private pilot's licence that the Department of National Defence gave a $100 bonus to the club. Another government directive gave the clubs an additional $4 per hour for first pilot (solo) flying time (up to a maximum of forty hours) for each *male* pilot training for his commercial licence.[2] With those kinds of financial incentives, it is little wonder that the clubs preferred to train men instead of women.

Easier to accept and to understand was why women were excluded from bush flying. In the simplest of terms, bush flying meant isolation, no facilities, little assistance in case of trouble, makeshift accommodations and being out of touch with civilization generally. Bush pilots flew north of steel (the railway) into undeveloped and often unmapped areas. They were frequently away for days or weeks at a time and accommodation was often a trapper's cabin or a tent. The planes carried machinery, livestock, men, and supplies, and it was the pilot's responsibility to load and off-load his cargo. Pilots were also expected to maintain their aircraft when away from the base. Mechanical know-how, strength, and bush survival skills were prerequisites for bush flying. Women were not considered because it was assumed that they lacked the physical strength to manhandle cargo or the ability to cope with conditions in the bush generally. Realistically, they also had not had the opportunity to obtain the necessary flying or mechanical qualifications. "We wouldn't have dreamed of sending a girl into the bush," said former bush pilot Z. Lewis Leigh. "Management was not about to lay itself open to the criticism that it was sure to receive if it sent a woman alone into the bush," explained pilot Ron Pickler of Canadair. "The bush was crude and rough even for a man." The widely-held assumption that women couldn't cope was a sensitive issue and was one of the strongest and most enduring arguments against women pilots. It was to keep many capable women pilots on the ground.

In 1930 the Canadian Flying Clubs Association (later the

Royal Canadian Flying Clubs Association) was formed to provide a central organization to help carry the clubs through the depression, to standarize procedures, and to publish a monthly magazine, *Canadian Aviation*. Armed with a permanent secretary in Ottawa and an annual government operating grant, the Association initiated such programs as the Trans-Canada Air Pageant and the Webster Trophy, a national competition for the best amateur pilot that continues to this day.

BUT THE EXCITEMENT and burgeoning activity were doomed and Canadians would wait until the end of the thirties for a trans-Canada airways system. Despite an auspicious start into civil aviation, the Great Depression of the thirties soon forced the government to cancel airmail contracts and to reduce subsidies to the flying clubs. Memberships in the clubs fell off and many were forced to shut down. Pilots, like others, were caught in the economic crunch. There were few flying jobs available for men and none for women. It's a wonder they learned to fly at all; but they did . . .

Notes

1, 2 *Report on Civil Aviation, Civilian Government Air Operators*, 1929. Departmenty of National Defence. — Public Archives of Canada.

CHAPTER TWO

"Can a girl learn to fly?"

Seventeen-year-old Violet Milstead was at a high school football game when a small plane "shot up" the field at intermission. "The sight of that airplane diving on the field, racing across it, then departing in a long, graceful climbing turn gave me a thrill I have never forgotten. I decided then and there that I would fly."

IN THE UNITED STATES, a woman was first granted a pilot's licence in 1911. By World War I there were eleven licenced women pilots and about two dozen others flying without licences. In comparison, Canadian women were late entrants into the world of powered flight. Flying instruction simply was not available to the general public; until 1927 only the military or the self-taught flew. In March of that year, J.V. Elliot's Flying Service and School opened in Hamilton, Ontario. It was the only civilian flying school in Canada at the time and, significantly, Canada's first licenced woman pilot was one of its first students.

In the sport aviation boom of the twenties and thirties Americans Amelia Earhart and Jacqueline Cochran, and Amy Johnson of England became heroic household names, but Canadian women had little opportunity to display their skills.

In the United States the twenties, with its air races and air shows, was known as the Golden Age of Aviation. Higher, faster, and farther were the goals of most pilots. In Canada there were few spectacular or record-breaking flights; the emphasis was on attempting to convince the public that air transportation had a role in peace time. Canadians rarely indulged in hero-worship or supported "frivolous" aviation activities. Canadian pilots had to prove the utilitarian, not the spectacular, function of the airplane. The bottom line was cost. Flying was expensive and Canadian businessmen were wary of investing in aviation companies, much less in sponsoring air racing — an activity of dubious financial benefit.

Eileen Vollick, 1928, the first woman to receive her pilot's licence in Canada. For her role in opening aviation to Canadian women Eileen was posthumously awarded the Amelia Earhart Medallion in 1975 by the First Canadian Chapter of the 99s, the International Organiztion of Women Pilots.

It was really the flying club movement, begun in 1927, that opened flying to the general public and put the spark into this wonderful new form of transportation. Women ignored the implied "for men only" rule and signed up for lessons. They learned, they flew, and they loved it. For many women — as well as men — the thrill of seeing an aircraft in flight captured their imagination and held it forever.

For other women flying was something they had long wanted to do. "I was always crazy about airplanes. I used to try and fly off the roof of the house in homemade contraptions," said Marion Powell Orr. "I knew when I was fourteen that I wanted to fly," recalled Rolie Moore Pierce. "I used to spend

EILEEN VOLLICK (1908-1966)

Eileen Vollick was Canada's first licenced woman pilot. A textile analyst from Hamilton, Ontario, Eileen avidly followed the construction of Hamilton Airport and the first flights of the JN-4s, open cockpit World War I biplanes, affectionately known as "Jennies." Intrigued with the idea of flying, she decided to learn. "Can a girl learn to fly?" she asked Jack Elliot, owner of J.V. Elliot's Flying Service. "I was fearful of being turned down or laughed at because women had not then entered this man's game in Canada," she later explained.

After sixteen hours of instruction, she took her private pilot's test on a ski-equipped Jenny. Eileen Vollick received Private Pilot's Licence (PPL) #77 on March 13, 1928: the first woman in Canada to earn a flying licence and the first woman in the world to be trained on a ski plane.

Realizing the publicity value of having trained Canada's first licenced woman pilot, Elliot presented her with a quasi-military uniform and called the newspapers. Soon her picture and story, complete with reference to Elliot's flying school, were featured in the local newspapers. Dressed either in her "uniform" or her fur-lined winter flying suit, the petite pilot was a fetching sight and the public greeted Canada's first aviatrix warmly. Eileen soon found herself deluged with requests to give speeches; she was also approached by American aircraft manufacturers to demonstrate their aircraft, which she declined. She endeared herself further to the Canadian public by taking up aerobatic training and skydiving; and in the summer of 1928, she claimed another honour when she became the first Canadian woman to parachute into water.

Her flying lasted for only a few years but was significant because it showed that women had the skill and aptitude to take up what was considered to be a man's sport.

CEREMONY

FOR THE UNVEILING OF AN HISTORICAL PLAQUE

IN HONOUR OF

EILEEN VOLLICK 1908–1968

SPONSORED BY

THE 99's INC.

AN INTERNATIONAL ORGANIZATION OF WOMEN PILOTS

EAST CANADA SECTION

AT

THE HAMILTON CITY HALL, MAIN ST. WEST

ON

SUNDAY, SEPTEMBER 19, 1976 – 1:30 P.M.

Program cover for the 1976 ceremonial unveiling of a plaque in honour of Eileen Vollick in Hamilton, Ontario, sponsored by the 99s.

every spare moment at Jericho Beach, the Royal Canadian Air Force base, or at Lulu Island airfield." And Vera Strodl Dowling said, "I had always longed to fly. I envied the seagulls. I used to watch them for hours on end. I tried jumping off roofs with umbrellas and built airplanes out of apple boxes and sacking."

For some an airplane ride was the start of a love affair with aviation. For her fifteenth birthday Marjorie Chauvin's father treated her to a ride in a Jenny with "Wop" May, a well-known bush pilot, at the controls. She found it so thrilling that she decided to learn to fly. Daphne Paterson was fascinated with engines and also with speed; she raced cars until she discovered airplanes. When, in 1929, she learned of the existence of the Montreal Light Aeroplane Club, she joined it, her interest in flying having been whetted ten years before when she had flown with world famous pilot, Bert Acousta, in New York.

Margaret Rankin-Smith, 1931, Ottawa's first licenced woman pilot.

Some women had relatives who were pilots. Margaret Rankin-Smith, Ottawa's first licenced woman pilot, grew up listening to airplane talk. As F. Hollister McQuin, her husband and former member of the Ottawa Flying Club, related, "Her uncle, a World War I pilot, lived with the family and used to take her to Rockcliffe airfield. She was so at ease in airplanes that he allowed her to solo when she was only fourteen. When he left Ottawa, Walter Deisher, Jack Charleson, and Jim Booth used to let her fly their planes. She didn't have a licence then because her father forbade her to try for it until she was twenty-one or had a hundred hours of experience." A charter member of the Ottawa Flying Club, Margaret eventually took her "official" training there and received Private Pilot's Licence #811 on April 4, 1931. Because of her years of experience, civil aviation officials endorsed her licence for the Avro Avian, DH 60 Moth, Fleet 2 and 7, Taylor Cub, and Aeronca on wheels, floats and skis; a Stinson 105 endorsement was added later.

"She flew all over, going as far as New Castle, Delaware and Richmond, Vermont and even to Winnipeg, Manitoba. Only her job — she worked in the Financial Division at the Post Office — kept her from going further afield," recalled Hollister McQuin.

Margaret was the only woman flying out of Rockcliffe until 1939, when she persuaded three friends, Gladys Smirle, Edith Treau de Coeli, and Muriel Munn, to take lessons. Reporters called them "Rockcliffe's Four Flying Ladies."

For other women, flying represented the ultimate escape from their humdrum small-town worlds. As a girl, Louise Jenkins had been raised in the cosmopolitan atmosphere of Philadelphia and New York; as a young woman she had skied in Switzerland, ridden camels in Egypt, played polo in England, and served in a world war. Life in rural, ultra-conservative, Prince Edward Island was too constricting for the sophisticated Louise. "I flew to cleanse the spirit and to get away from problems and to add excitement to my life."

Many of the women wanted to serve their country. War had not yet been declared when Ethel Higdon decided to take lessons in order to join the Royal Canadian Air Force. "I thought I stood a better chance if I proved that I could fly before I applied," she explained.

Marjorie Chauvin, 1929.

But how were the women greeted when they showed up for lessons? Connie Culver's instructor tried to make her sick on her first flight. "My first hour consisted of strenuous aerobatics. There I was on my back in a skirt. He laughed the whole time." In truth the reaction of the men varied. For the most part they accepted women as welcome social additions. However, some women were not even allowed to sign up for lessons while others found that the men applied a different set of rules or tried to scare them off.

Discrimination initially characterized the treatment Eileen Vollick, Canada's first licenced woman pilot, received. Jack Elliot, of J. V. Elliot's Flying Service, would not accept her as a student until the Department of National Defence approved her request. "No woman in Canada had previously made such application, and Mr. Elliot was doubtful of my success," explained Eileen. Officials took three months to endorse her application and did so only after checking with England and stipulating that she be nineteen years of age before a licence would be granted. The age requirement for men was seventeen. Even then her problems were not over. Her instructor, Earl Jellison, did not want to be bothered with a female student. "Although it was against the rules to stunt with a passenger, on my first lesson he did spins, loops and zooms thinking he could either frighten me or find out how much courage I possessed! I loved it and showed up for my next lesson." By contrast, her next two instructors, Dick Turner and Len Tripp, welcomed her, as did her classmates — thirty-five men.

Discrimination was certainly the name of the game for some

women. Marjorie Chauvin Herity, Canada's first woman demonstration pilot, was a native of Edmonton, Alberta. Former World War I pilot, Captain Moss Burbidge, the chief flying instructor of the Northern Alberta and Edmonton Aero Club, refused to accept her as a student. "Burbidge told her that if she wanted to fly she had better sprout wings because only men had the right temperament to pilot a plane," explained her husband Jack Herity. Marjorie took that as a challenge and continued to pester Burbidge. He finally told her he would hold a separate class for girls but only if there were a minimum of a dozen. Desperately wanting to fly, Marjorie begged her friends to sign up, but their answer was no. Unwilling to admit defeat and short of money, she nevertheless placed an advertisement in the *Edmonton Journal*. Only one woman, Elsie MacLean, replied. By now many months had passed and she seemed no closer to her goal. Discouraged but still determined, Marjorie checked the Civil Aviation Rules and Regulations. When she discovered that pilots did not have to be men she told Burbidge that she would sue him if he did not teach her and Elsie. Reluctantly he accepted them as students. However, their troubles were not yet over. As Elsie explained, "To make ourselves as inconspicuous as possible Marjorie and I wore men's riding breeks, a man's shirt, tie, leather jacket, and shoes. But it didn't help. We were the butt of many jokes and Burbidge used to call us *the snivets*, which meant 'insignificant birds.' We leaned on each other for support because the other students all followed his lead and made fun of us. We tried to ignore the worst of the remarks and to keep smiling."

Elsie MacLean (on the right) and Marjorie Chauvin, 1929, called the snivets.

As her husband Jack Herity explained, "It wasn't easy for Marjorie. She was on her own — her parents had died — and she was working at the Retail Credit. Twice she ran out of money before completing her training and twice she took the unprecedented step for a woman and applied for a loan. I think she got it because of her job and they knew she was a good risk." In December 1929 she took her flight test. "I didn't think I was going to pass," she wrote in her diary, "because on my first landing the tail skid broke. Inspector Howard Ingram allowed me to replace the skid and continue. Ingram was a good scout." She received PPL #480 on December 27, 1929.

"Marjorie knew from her first lesson that she wanted to make flying her life," stated her husband. "However, she realized from her experiences with Burbidge that she would never get a job in the west where most of the flying was in the bush." She wasted no time in applying for a company transfer and by January 1930, had moved to Toronto.

She joined the Toronto Flying Club to make contacts for possible employment. There she met Jessica Jarvis, Alex Samarow, and Tib Goulding. All good looking, the four women attracted the press when they flew together. According to her husband, Marjorie did not attend many of the Toronto Flying Club functions because "The club was very social and Marjorie could not afford to keep up with the group. She was not in flying just for fun but to try and make a career out of it." Marjorie's determination was formidable. Given the times, she managed quite a bit of flying, and her persistence surely made careers in aviation easier for those who came later.

Interestingly, Margaret Fane and Enid Norquay, who took instruction from Moss Burbidge a few years later, had nothing but praise for him. "I used to think that Captain Burbidge helped me more than some of the boys. He told me he liked my interest in flying and many times he would pick me up at 5:00 AM and take me to the airfield for my lessons," said Enid.

Finding an instructor or reaching the airfield were sometimes hurdles and some of the women went to extraordinary lengths to become qualified. For example, Ethel Higdon of Medicine Hat, Alberta rose at 3:00 AM every morning and drove a hundred miles to the Lethbridge Flying Club for lessons. When the club closed down she moved to Winnipeg to finish her training.

Gladys Graves Walker, an executive secretary with the provincial government and a well-known horsewoman, was in the first class of students at the Edmonton Aero Club and became Alberta's second licenced woman pilot. "There were fifty men and me," wrote Gladys. "Because there was only one aircraft, Wop May held the ground school course first and stated that the first ten people to pass the oral and written exams would be the first to fly. I was the ninth to pass." She took her training on a de Havilland 60 Moth, G-CAKJ.

"In those days the airport was just a field on the outskirts of Edmonton with three grassy lanes full of gopher holes and lumps. Getting my licence was slow going because the weather always left the field soggy and wet. Then Wop got an infected hand, which prevented him from flying for about six weeks. I would get up at 4:00 AM, take a streetcar as far as it went and walk the rest of the way, have my lessons, get back and go to work. After work I would exercise my horses. When the newspapers reported that there was a girl student I found myself simply invaded by insurance salesmen trying to sell me both life and accident. I took neither."

Her training was interrupted when she married George Walker, a Calgary lawyer, but she returned to Edmonton for instruction. "I was ready to take my test in the spring of '29 but had to wait until September when there were enough boys to qualify before they brought a government man up from Regina to give us the test." She received PPL #372 on September 27, 1929, the eighth woman in Canada to qualify.

Grace "Tib" Goulding, Toronto's first woman pilot.

ANOTHER PROBLEM, which continues to this day, was male jealousy of the publicity that the women received. "I think the men had the idea that we got too much publicity and that flying was their business, not ours," explained Joyce Bond. "There were five of us women flying out of Regina at the time and the men used to call us 'the flying quintuplets.' They used to tease us a lot. I won't say we were welcomed with open arms, but we were tolerated . . . well, not always tolerated."

Flying itself was glamourous enough to attract the attention of reporters but women pilots, particularly beautiful ones, were even more newsworthy. Grace "Tib" Goulding, Toronto's first licenced woman pilot, was a popular member of Toronto's younger set whose days were taken up with sports, charity, and social functions. A chance airplane ride in 1929 with family friend, Jim Crang, a former Royal Flying Corps pilot, led her into flying. Joining the very social Toronto Flying Club she took instruction from R. Carter Guest, Phil Hutton, and Ted Burton on a Cirrus Moth, G-CAJU. She received PPL #495 on January 15, 1930. Being a slim, pretty brunette, she found that reporters stalked her every move. Headlines like "Junior League Girl Goes Solo" or "Canada's Lady Lindy" were common. "It seemed that every time I turned around they were taking pictures of me," said Tib.

If more than one woman was flying from an airfield reporters had a heyday. Reporters inevitably exaggerated what the women did and made it sound as if they had performed some spectacular feats. For example, a short flight by four women pilots produced the headline, "Girls make a formation cross-country flight in Canada alone!" In the minds of the men the fact that four beautiful women had gone flying "alone" [that is, without a man] was an incredible happening. One woman flying alone was definitely newsworthy. A Toronto newspaper featured Marjorie Chauvin with this sub headline: "23-Year Old Pilot Has Exciting Experience in Toronto as Demonstrator with Manning Airways — Flies Solo to Ontario Meets."

Eileen Magill, 1928, Manitoba's first woman pilot.

EILEEN MAGILL (1906-1964)

Eileen Magill was Canada's second, Manitoba's first, licenced woman pilot. Born in Halifax, Nova Scotia, she moved to Winnipeg with her family in 1919 when her father became Secretary of the Winnipeg Grain Exchange. Her interest in flying was sparked by family acquaintance Jack McCurdy of Silver Dart fame. According to her brother and son, Eileen was no meek and mild girl. She was expected to go after what she wanted and to be good at what she did. She shocked her university classmates by smoking, wearing pants, and driving fast cars and, when the Winnipeg Flying Club was founded, she joined, not at all concerned that flying was considered unsuitable for young ladies.

The club's flying activities began on May 29, 1928, the day after Stevenson Field (now Winnipeg International

While women were called upon to add a touch of glamour to an occasion, what usually happened was that they stole the show. When Barker Field in Toronto was officially opened reporters focused on Tib Goulding. "Airport Opening Attraction" said a 1931 Toronto newspaper headline, with a photograph and the comment that she was "one of Canada's première pilots." Tib flew for about five years and would have enlisted in the RCAF in 1939 had it been open to women.

Being the centre of attention had its annoyances. "I was not just another pilot. Being one of only two girls had its drawbacks because everything you did was noticed and remembered," explained Dorothy Bell of the Winnipeg Flying Club. "One day I caught my ski in a snowbank while landing. The plane flipped over and I hung by my seat belt until I was rescued. Naturally there was a crowd around to see my inglorious landing and of course someone wrote it up and sent it in to *Canadian Aviation*."

Airport), was officially opened. The club's first instructor, Michael DeBlicquy, was described as "wonderfully unconventional . . . a marvellous man . . . and rumoured to be of Belgian royalty." Eileen and the rakish DeBlicquy were two of a kind and soon became inseparable. DeBlicquy later reminisced, "She was one of my first students. She did her first solo one summer evening and I guess she got carried away with being up by herself because all of a sudden it was dusk and she was still up there at 5000 feet. She put that damn Moth in a spin — to get down in a hurry — and recovered a bare 100 feet from the ground! I was really worried that she wouldn't be able to pull out in time. When she climbed out I gave her hell for doing such a manoeuvre on her first solo." Eileen Magill was an apt pupil; after ten hours dual instruction and five hours solo, she received PPL #142 on October 24, 1928.

Club members elected Eileen to the Board of Directors and she became the first woman in Canada to hold such a position. Out-spoken and photogenic, with dark good looks and a gleam in her eye, Eileen was also a favourite of reporters who featured her whenever they could. A flight to St. Paul, Minnesota warranted headlines in the *Winnipeg Free Press* boasting that she was the first Canadian woman to fly across the border.

Eileen tried very hard to obtain a position in aviation. Although highly recommended by the president of the Winnipeg Flying Club she was unsuccessful in getting even an administrative job. She flew only a few years before moving on to other challenges.

In addition to unwanted reporters, a few women encountered "unwanted advances" from the men. After earning a private pilot's licence, Marjorie Chauvin moved to Toronto and began working towards a commercial licence. Her personal papers, which contain all her ground school notes for a commercial licence and an application form for the flight test, dated May 19, 1932 and signed by Colonel Doug Joy, seem to confirm that she took all the necessary ground school and flying instruction at Century Airways and was considered ready for the flight test. However, when she showed up for the test, she discovered that the examiner had more on the agenda than flying. According to her husband, the examiner made "im-

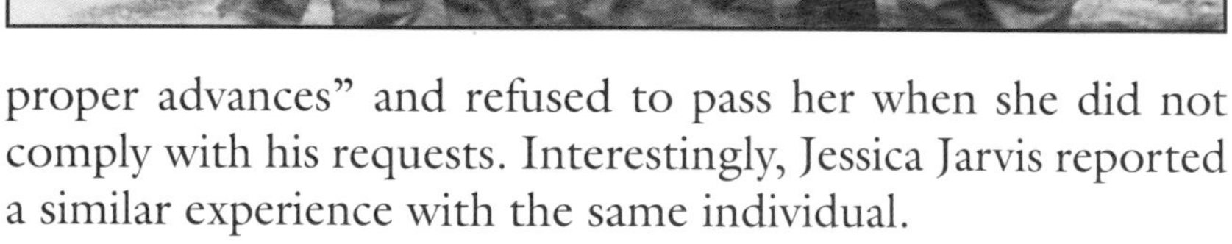
proper advances" and refused to pass her when she did not comply with his requests. Interestingly, Jessica Jarvis reported a similar experience with the same individual.

THE FLYING CLUBS were supposed to bring flying to the "man on the street," but, in reality, only the well-to-do could afford it. Instruction varied from $9 to $17 an hour whereas the average wage for women who worked outside the home was $13.50 a week. The cost of a private licence ran from $180 to $240 and a commercial licence from $500 to $600. The average working woman could not afford lessons "for the fun of it" and neither could she risk going after a commercial licence when there was little prospect of landing a job. Before

L *Members of the Winnipeg Flying Club, 1928, J.A. Sully, J.R. Morgan, Michael DeBlicquy, and Eileen Magill.*

R *Eileen Magill, on the right, with Mrs. Omlie on the left, the first woman to get a transport licence in the U.S., and Miss Klingensmith, from Fargo, N.D.*

she could even begin advanced training there were costs because she had to have a certain minimum amount of flying time. "Building time," as it is called, was almost as expensive as the actual training. Prices of $17 an hour dual (with an instructor) and $12 an hour solo (first pilot time), as they were at the Regina Flying Club in 1929, were not unusual. But they were simply too steep for most women whose wages were considerably less than those of the men. While the men often received free flying time in exchange for working in the hangar, this option was rarely open to the women. The idea of a girl cleaning oily engines or doing odd jobs around the club did not sit well with most men. Rolie Moore was an exception. Once

L *Elsie MacLean, 1929, standing beside a DH Cirrus Moth.*

R *Gertrude de la Vergne beside Great Western Airways DH 60X Moth.*

GERTRUDE DE LA VERGNE

Gertrude de la Vergne, Canada's third, Alberta's first, licenced woman pilot was raised on a ranch in Calgary and educated at private girls' schools. Gertrude returned to Calgary after college and became a free-lance writer. When the Calgary Aero Club was formed she signed up for lessons. As she explained, "To me flying was another way to experience the freedom of the skies and to get some more hands-on experience with engines. As a girl I loved to tinker with machinery. In fact, engines so intrigued me that before I began my lessons my father and I tore an engine apart and put it together again."

The Calgary Aero Club was "a little shack on the edge of a field with one instructor [Bill Rutledge] and two de Havilland Cirrus Moths,"KQ"and "LA." I was the first woman

she earned a private pilot's licence she spent every spare minute at the airport. "I was known as an 'airport rat.' I did anything they asked me in return for free flying time. I cleaned engine parts, washed airplanes, swept the hangar, and did fabric work."

In addition to their regular jobs, some were lucky to find "clean" jobs at the flying club to subsidize their flying. University graduate Florence Elliott took a job as a secretary at the London Flying Club. In addition to $60 per month she received a half-hour of free flying a week. "I couldn't borrow from my parents because I hadn't told them. I kept it a secret. I knew they'd disapprove. It was not the kind of thing you want your daughter doing, not in 1939 anyway. They'd worry."

Those who lived at home often received financial help from their fathers, if only the use of the family car to get out to the airfield for lessons. Elsie MacLean was raised in Edmonton, Alberta. "Airplanes fascinated me but I never thought of taking lessons until I saw Marjorie Chauvin's advertisement in the paper. My father had always encouraged me to try new things. He had taught me how to drive a car before I was the proper age and later, when I took flying lessons, he often gave me the family car so Marjorie and I could get out to the airfield for our lessons at six in the morning." A graduate of Alberta College and an employee of the Bank of Nova Scotia, she earned $75 a

student at the club and the first student Bill had ever sent solo. He was so nervous when I made my first solo flight that he kept lighting one cigarette after another, dropping lighted ones on the ground. By the time I landed the grass all around him was on fire!" Gertrude received PPL #157 on December 4, 1928.

Gertrude had fond memories of her flying days. "Even though I was the only girl the boys always included me in their discussions and activities. In fact, it was Wop May, a World War I pilot and the first instructor at the Edmonton and Northern Alberta Aero Club, who encouraged me to do aerobatics. I still vividly remember doing inside and outside loops with Wop." Despite her acceptance by the men and her skill as a pilot, they discouraged her from taking further training. "Flying was expensive and I knew if I were to continue I needed to find a job in aviation. The airmail service from Edmonton to Aklavik had recently been inaugurated and I inquired about flying the mail if I qualified for my commercial licence. They told me a woman would not be suitable. The commercial licence was too expensive to take without the assurance of finding work so I regretably gave up flying about a year later."

month. "That was a top salary for a girl in 1929. My father also helped me out." She received PPL #423 on November 12, 1929 but flew for less than a year after that.

For those on their own it was more difficult to pay for lessons. Jessica Jarvis was a bank clerk when she decided to qualify for a commercial licence. "It took me three years to build the necessary hours. Rarely could I afford more than twenty or forty minutes at a time. I earned only $28 a week and the club charged $12 an hour for dual and $8 an hour for solo time. I got no help from my parents who were divorced and I had only the interest from a $1500 trust fund to put towards flying."

Barred from the world of professional flying, Daphne Paterson was an enthusiastic supporter of the flying club movement and worked tirelessly to promote general aviation. Her determination to obtain every rating available and her skill as a pilot helped to pave the way for the next generation of women pilots.

DAPHNE PATERSON (1905-1982)

Daphne Paterson, New Brunswick's first woman pilot, was born in Saint John. A clever and ambitious woman who refused to be stifled by the lack of opportunities in the Maritimes, she attended McGill University in Montreal and graduated with a Bachelor of Science degree. Long fascinated with engines and speed, Daphne raced cars and held the speed record between Saint John and Montreal, some 800 miles apart.

In 1929 she joined the Montreal Light Aeroplane Club. Like Eileen Vollick, Daphne found her instructor less than thrilled at having a woman student. "My first lesson was with the chief flying instructor, Mr. Sparks. He believed that flying was for men only. To discourage me he gave me 'the works.'" The aerobatics had the opposite effect and Daphne appeared at the club the next day. Annoyed, Sparks turned her over to Captain Tony Spooner, a recent arrival from England. He encouraged her to continue for he had no objections to women pilots, his attitude no doubt influenced by the fact that his sister, Winnifred Spooner, had won the prestigious King's Cup Race in England. A natural pilot, Daphne soloed in seven hours and received PPL #327 on August 15, 1929.

Seven months later, after initial rejection of her test application, she received Commercial Pilot's Licence (CPL) #658, the first Canadian woman to obtain a commercial standing. An active member of the flying clubs in Montreal, Fredericton, and Toronto, she was a frequent competitor, and winner, in the Webster Trophy competitions.

Daphne was the first Canadian woman to obtain the highest Canadian rating then available — the Public Transport Licence. She received PTL #130 on August 9, 1938. With the possibility of war on the horizon, Daphne "...wanted to be as qualified as possible because I thought

Marion Powell Orr, an orphan at fifteen, left school to work in a factory. "I scrimped for six years, doing without little luxuries like lunch and makeup before I could afford to take lessons." She found it hard going as flying cost $9 an hour and she earned only $12 a week. "Often I could afford only fifteen minutes at a time." For Marion, the private licence was just the beginning; she knew more than ever that she wanted to fly professionally. To supplement her income, she became an aircraft inspector at de Havilland in Toronto. Even so it took another two years before she qualified for a commercial licence. "I had to fly in dribs and drabs; I missed meals, went without new clothes, walked instead of taking the bus and economized

women would be pilots in the RCAF." Unfortunately, despite her qualifications, it was not to be.

A Toronto newspaper quoted A. T. Cowley, Superintendent of Air Regulations, Department of Transportation, as saying that the only place for a woman who wished to fly professionally was instructing and "that women were not suitable to be commercial pilots."[3] Cowley, a personal friend of Daphne's, suggested that she obtain her instructor's rating but Daphne was not interested, saying that she did not have the patience to be a good instructor. Next, Cowley predicted a shortage of instructors when the British Commonwealth Air Training Plan was established, and promised her a job if she became qualified. Seeing it as a way to get into the RCAF, Daphne trained for and received an instructor's rating in May 1940. But Cowley's promises proved premature. "I was told there was no place for female instructors with the British Commonwealth Air Training Plan," she wrote many years later.

"I then decided to apply to the Air Transport Auxiliary but Cowley prevailed upon me to wait as something big was brewing for women pilots and he wanted me to be the head of it. I waited. By the time I realized that women were not going to be allowed to ferry aircraft and the newly formed Women's Division of the RCAF would offer ground assignments only, I was too old for the Air Transport Auxiliary."

As a last resort in 1942 Daphne wrote to Jacqueline Cochran, Director of Women's Flying Training, War Department, Army Air Force, USA, who replied saying that she would accept Daphne provided that she had American citizenship. She did not. Bitterly disappointed, Daphne spent the war years on the ground as a journalist. After the war she severed all aviation connections when she and her husband, pilot Tony Shelfoon, divorced and she realized she would never find a job flying.

in a dozen little ways to make my salary go further. It was a case of doing without, but flying always came first."

One enterprising young Winnipeg woman wrote to James A. Richardson, the president of Western Canada Airways, suggesting that his company teach her to fly and in return she would fly "anywhere and at any time that the company considered beneficial for advertising." She closed her letter saying that if he were not interested he need not reply. No reply was on file.

Nevertheless, the women had made a start. In 1928, a total of 111 private licences and twenty eight commercial licences were obtained through the flying clubs; of these, three private licences were issued to women.

The Brantford Flying Club.

FLYING in the twenties and thirties was vastly different from today. Aerodromes were often cow pastures, race tracks, and exhibition grounds. Air Regulations stressed that "pilots should carry hankies in a handy position to wipe off goggles . . . they should not trust the altitude instruments, and they should not wear spurs while flying." Women's standard garb, dictated by utility, not fashion, was a close-fitting leather jacket with a lambskin collar, tailored breeches, and high-laced boots, all crowned with the indispensable helmet and goggles.

The first flying club planes were generally the durable de Havilland Cirrus Moths, forerunners of the Gipsy and Tiger Moths. The Moth was a wood and fabric tandem two-seater open cockpit biplane powered by an 85 horsepower engine. Instructor and student sat in separate cockpits and normal conversation was impossible because of the noise. Communication was by the Gosport system, a rubber tube connecting a mouthpiece held by the instructor to the earphones in the student's leather helmet. "It was often a lot of yelling by the instructor," recalled Peggy Ricard, a student at the Halifax Flying Club in 1928. "Students were at a disadvantage with the Gosport system. When I made a mistake I almost got my helmet blown off, the air would turn blue but I couldn't answer back because the communication was only one way!"

Instruction was not standardized initially and training was often haphazard. Eileen Vollick received sixteen hours of instruction, which included "landings and risings" and a cross country flight from Hamilton to St. Thomas. What ground school classes the Winnipeg Flying Club held is not known but, according to Dorothy Bell, how Michael DeBlicquy handled flight instruction was most unorthodox. "He just put me into the passenger seat and told me to fly the damn thing. Mike told us all that we would be murdered if we smashed either of the club's two aircraft. After about 10 hours dual Mike was all for pushing us into the air solo — a growl from the front seat, 'You land it' indicated you were ready to go it alone."

Rolie Moore of Vancouver remembers her instructor, Des Murphy, making her practice spot landings "from different positions around the airport until I could land and stop, no brakes, and he could reach out and touch the wing tip from his position on the ground. He also made me practice figure eights in any wind conditions. His strictness paid off when I took up aerobatics." What loomed large in Enid Norquay's mind fifty years later were the three basic rules propounded by her instructor, Moss Burbidge: "One, make sure you have plenty of air speed. Two, make sure you have plenty of damn air speed. Three, make sure you have plenty of goddamn air speed. Happy landings and amen."

IN THE EARLY YEARS private pilot tests were casual affairs. For one thing, the examiner stayed on the ground. The applicant might be asked to climb to 5000 feet, do a spin to both left and right, make five figure eights, and complete five

Nellie Carson, 1929, Regina Flying Club.

NELLIE CARSON (1900-1949)

Nellie Carson was Saskatchewan's first (with Grayce Hutchinson) licenced woman pilot. She was also one of the original members of the Saskatoon Aero Club. Little is known about her personal life except that when she began flying in 1929 she was the credit manager for a Yorkton firm. She took instruction from Dick Mayson, I. Smith-Marriott, and Bill Windrum and received PPL #384 on October 12, 1929, the ninth woman in Canada to qualify.

In the early thirties, Nellie barnstormed in Saskatchewan for money to continue her flying lessons. She is best known for the altitude record she set in a Gipsy Moth. With no oxygen, considered necessary (in fact now mandatory) over 12,000 feet, Nellie tested both herself and her plane with this brave experiment. She took one hour and twenty minutes to reach a height of 16,000 feet by flying a series of circles over the airfield and was hailed by the aviation community and newspapers of the day for her success.

When war broke out Nellie tried to enlist in the RCAF as a pilot. Turned down, she served in the Women's Division of the RCAF. She died of tuberculosis in 1949.

landings "with no bounces" to within a certain distance from a designated mark on the ground. Some examiners parked their cars right on the flying field expecting the novice pilot to land and roll out accurately enough to allow him to get out of his car, take a step or two and touch the wing tip. More than one examiner ended up moving his car in a hurry when it appeared that a student might be a little too accurate!

In the late thirties, the commercial licence, officially called a "Limited Commercial Air Pilot's Certificate," involved a total of nine examinations. As Violet Milstead explained, "Application for the licence could be made when one had 50 hours first pilot (solo) time. However, the licence did not authorize the pilot to carry passengers for hire until he had 100 hours first pilot time. There were five written examinations: Theory of Flight, Airframes, Engines, Airmanship, Navigation and Meteorology. There were no multiple-choice questions and no navigation computers. There were two practical tests: swinging a compass and rigging a biplane. There were two flying tests: one a solo cross-country on which you carried a continuously

Grayce Hutchinson, 1929.

GRAYCE HUTCHINSON

Grayce Hutchinson, Saskatchewan's first (with Nellie Carson) licenced woman pilot, raced cars until she discovered flying. "My father was not pleased," said Grayce. "I don't know if it was his idea or instructor Stan McClennan's, but on my first ride I got `the works.' When we landed I was green at the gills and sick as a dog. He assumed that would be the last of me but I showed up the next day. When Stan and my father realized I was serious about flying there was no more opposition." Grayce received PPL #387 on October 12, 1929, the tenth woman in Canada to be licenced.

Flying the Atlantic Ocean was the rage in the late twenties, and Grayce was asked to be a co-pilot for one such flight. "I said `yes' but my father said `no.' I was crazy then. I wanted adventure and I would always take a dare. Nothing fazed me. I was caught in a bad storm once and the plane just fell apart on me. I don't remember much about the accident except the bawling out the mechanics gave me."

Grayce flew until she married a few years later, giving it up at her husband's request. While she settled into the routine of dutiful wife and mother, she secretly hoped to fly again. Once she thought her chance had come when the Chinese Air Force began recruiting pilots in Canada in the late thirties, but she was rejected. During World War II she attempted to join the RCAF and when rebuffed again, she gave up all thoughts of flying.

recording barograph. The test required landings at two intermediate airports. Signatures had to be obtained certifying your arrival at these airports. The second was a flight test around the airport, mostly a test of the pilot's ability to make engine-off 'forced' landings to a spot.

"In those years and until after World War II, the inspector did not ride with the pilot-candidate on any tests. He sat in a car facing the runway at right angles and off to one side. An imaginary line from the front of his car and across the runway was the pilot's target. He was supposed to land his airplane and stop rolling within one hundred feet of that line. The airplanes had no brakes, but they did have tail skids, which provided some drag after landing. The pilot being tested would take off and climb, circling the airport. On a signal from the inspector, he would close the throttle immediately and start a forced landing procedure from whatever position he might be in. The signal was when the inspector drove his car forward across the runway, then backed clear again. The airplanes had no flaps to assist in losing altitude. Excess height on approach was lost by sideslipping. If I remember correctly, four forced landings to the spot were to be made on signal. The fifth, and last, was different. The pilot climbed considerably higher, carefully selected a position on the leeward side of the field, entered a left hand spin of at least two turns, recovered, cleared his engine with one burst of power, entered a right hand spin of at least two turns, recovered, cleared his engine, and carried out a forced landing to the spot. Unofficially, the successful candidate was required to buy a case of beer for immediate consumption by the inspector and members of the flying and engineering staff. No exception was made because I was a girl."

"LEARNING TO FLY," educational movie, depicts in detail the strict

An educational movie, Learning to Fly, *being filmed, with Vi Milstead taking instruction from Pat Patterson.*

Violet's solo cross-country flight, from Barker Field to the old London Aero Club at Lambeth and from there to Jarvis, a grass field and back to Barker Field, involved more than flying.

"At Jarvis I had to shut down the engine, climb a fence and walk along a snow-covered country road to a farm house to find someone to sign my papers certifying that I had arrived."

It was not until 1933 that the Department of National Defence specified special licences for flight instructors. Two years later it offered instructor's training (to men only) at Camp Borden. By the early forties, instructing was open to women but flight tests for the instructor's rating were still conducted by the military. This placed the women at a decided disadvantage because they had to take their tests on an aircraft that they had never flown before. Margaret Littlewood found the experience disconcerting. "I'll never forget it. I had to take time off work

Jeanne Gilbert.

JEANNE GENIER GILBERT (1902-1986)

Jeanne Gilbert, British Columbia's first woman pilot, was born in Kamloops, British Columbia. Jeanne discovered airplanes during World War I and yearned to fly. Earl McLeod, a World War I pilot and a Department of National Defence flight examiner, said of Jeanne, "I remember when she was a high school student she would rush out and refuel my plane whenever I landed in Kamloops. She was so eager to be around airplanes."

In 1928 Jeanne moved to Vancouver and signed up for lessons at the BC Aero Club. That year she also married Walter Gilbert, whom she had met at the BC Mountaineering Club. Gilbert, then with the RCAF, was to become one of Canada's most famous bush pilots. Unfortunately for Jeanne, her husband's constant transfers made it difficult for her to learn to fly. Just before her first lesson Walter was transferred to Winnipeg. The Winnipeg Flying Club did not yet offer instruction so Jeanne, impatient to start, talked Floyd Bennett (Admiral Byrd's pilot who was in Winnipeg at the time) into taking her up in the Ford Trimotor. Thus, her first logbook entry shows her as a passenger with Bennett at the controls of the Trimotor on April 7, 1928 at the St. Charles Airfield. Her next flight, again as a passenger, was on May 30, 1928 in "ZM," a Vickers Vedette from the RCAF's Red River base. Jeanne received only a few hours instruction from Mike DeBlicquy before Walter was transferred again, first to Dryden, Ontario, then to The Pas, Manitoba, and finally to Pelican Rapids, Saskatchewan. Temporarily abandoning all thoughts of formal lessons, Jeanne bent all her energies to keeping up with her husband. They lived in tents and back rooms of Hudson's Bay Company trading posts and hitched rides in canoes and planes. In this way she acquired many unofficial flying hours in Fairchilds and Fokker Universals.

and go to the RCAF base at Trenton and then I ended up sitting in a hotel room for a couple of days waiting for the weather to clear and getting more and more nervous as time passed." To make matters worse, she could not see out of the plane properly. "The seat-pack parachute in the airforce plane was not 'up' enough for me and I had to do a lot of stretching to see around the squadron leader sitting in the front seat. He wore the most beautiful skunk mitts but he kept holding the helmet earphones closer to his ears with both hands and almost completely blocked my vision. However, I managed to pass."

Along with flight training the clubs offered social memberships and a special camaraderie developed in the cozy club

In the fall of 1928, Walter moved to Vancouver to work for Western Canada Airways. Trailing him once more, Jeanne arrived only to find that he had been transferred to Stuart, BC (on the border of Alaska). Discouraged, she followed him but not before obtaining a few more hours of instruction. A year later, when Walter returned to Vancouver, Jeanne hurriedly signed up for more lessons. "But flying time was hard to get," she wrote, "as everyone was trying to become another Lindbergh." To make matters worse, her instructor, Percy Hainstock, was killed and Walter was transferred again. This time Jeanne remained in Vancouver long enough to complete her training. She received PPL #479 on November 10, 1929, the thirteenth woman in Canada to be licenced.

Home for the Gilberts for the next seven years was Fort McMurray, about 240 miles northeast of Edmonton. Energetic and sociable, Jeanne hated the isolation and forced inactivity. "It is cold and dreary in this place," she wrote to her aunt. "Absolutely nothing to do and it has rained so much . . . I am so glad I am going out of here. I simply could not face another winter of this solitude . . . that 50 below stuff . . . and the days and days with Walter away . . . alone in this little shack." Relief from boredom came only when she could snatch bits of right seat flying in Western Canada Airways' aircraft. Enjoying the feel of heavy aircraft, she decided to take her commercial training in the hope that she might be allowed to fly with her husband.

In 1939 Walter was again based in Vancouver and once more Jeanne renewed her membership at the BC Aero Club. She also joined The Flying Seven, an all-women's flying group, took a 10 hour refresher course and acquired her Radio Operator's Licence. Unfortunately, she never finished her commercial training because the government, with war declared, attempted to ration gasoline and forbade all unnecessary civilian flying. She then tried to enlist in the

Walter and Jeanne Gilbert, believed to be the only husband and wife to hold pilots' licences in Canada, in 1930.

lounges where pilots could sit around "hangar flying." As longtime pilot Arnold Warren recalled, "There was a feeling of intimacy in the aviation community of the thirties. Everybody knew, or knew of, everybody else, and contact with the Department of Transport was likely to be a very personal thing." The thirties were also the day of the "Rumble Club" — whose membership was open only to those who were caught making foolish flying mistakes. As Joyce Bond of the Regina Club explained, "An unlucky pilot caught doing an uncorrected bounce was fined ten to fifty cents; for a downwind take-off or landing, twenty-five cents; sneaking in over the fence, ten cents; getting stuck in the mud, twenty-five cents; and erasing fines, twenty-five cents." Fines went into the club's social funds.

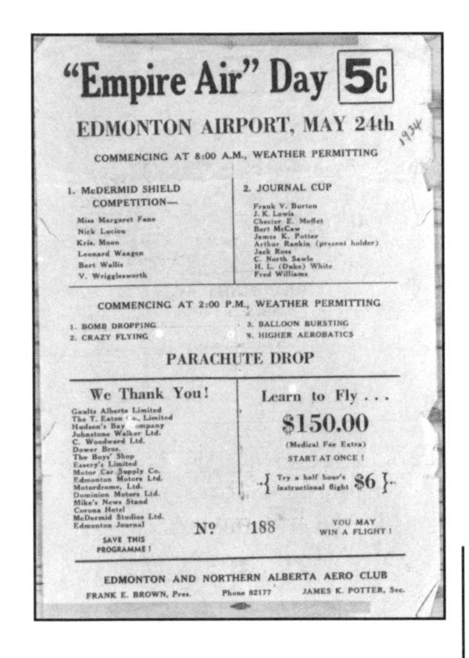

"Empire Air" Day 5c

EDMONTON AIRPORT, MAY 24th 1934

COMMENCING AT 8:00 A.M., WEATHER PERMITTING

1. McDERMID SHIELD COMPETITION—
Miss Margaret Fane
Nick Luciou
Kris. Moon
Leonard Waagen
Bert Wallis
V. Wrigglesworth

2. JOURNAL CUP
Frank V. Burton
J. K. Lewis
Chester E. Moffet
Bert McCaw
James K. Potter
Arthur Rankin (present holder)
Jack Ross
C. North Sawle
H. L. (Duke) White
Fred Williams

COMMENCING AT 2:00 P.M., WEATHER PERMITTING

1. BOMB DROPPING
2. CRAZY FLYING
3. BALLOON BURSTING
4. HIGHER AEROBATICS

PARACHUTE DROP

We Thank You!
Gaults Alberta Limited
The T. Eaton Co., Limited
Hudson's Bay Company
Johnstone Walker Ltd.
C. Woodward Ltd.
Dower Bros.
The Boys' Shop
Essery's Limited
Motor Car Supply Co.
Edmonton Motors Ltd.
Motordrome, Ltd.
Dominion Motors Ltd.
Mike's News Stand
Corona Hotel
McDermid Studios Ltd.
Edmonton Journal

SAVE THIS PROGRAMME!

Learn to Fly . . .
$150.00
(Medical Fee Extra)
START AT ONCE!
Try a half hour's instructional flight $6

No. 188

YOU MAY WIN A FLIGHT!

EDMONTON AND NORTHERN ALBERTA AERO CLUB
FRANK E. BROWN, Pres. Phone 82177 JAMES K. POTTER, Sec.

Promotion of aviation through flying clubs, 1934.

WOMEN WHO FLEW in those early days came mainly from upper-middle to upper class families, which was not surprising considering the expense. Most had a better than average education and many held a university degree — a most uncommon achievement for women. As children they did not follow the usual pattern of tea parties and dolls but rough-housed with boys and tinkered with engines. Their upbringing could hardly be considered conventional for the times. While they were raised strictly, in the sense that manners and respect for elders were stressed, they were rarely discouraged from trying anything as long as they stayed out of trouble.

RCAF to no avail. As her flying ground to a halt, so did her marriage. Unable to fly and soon to be divorced, she bitterly turned her back on anything to do with aviation.

Jeanne Gilbert's logbook shows less than 50 hours on light aircraft, but as the wife of one of Canada's leading airmen, she logged many hours in commercial aircraft over country unseen by most Canadians. On many of Walter's epochal voyages Jeanne acted as navigator or spotter and their logbooks hold the romantic story of Canada's retreating frontiers. When the Gilberts flew, commercial flying was in its infancy and every flight was an adventure. Undoubtedly Jeanne saw herself as another Anne Lindbergh, whom she had met in 1931 when the Lindberghs had landed in Aklavik. Jeanne took flying seriously, remarking that "flying was no trivial sport but a tremendous field for women if the stubborn prejudice of the average man could be overcome." This was not to be, and thirty more years would pass before a woman flew down the Mackenzie River as a pilot in command of an airplane.

Many had fathers who spent time with their daughters and whom the women later described as "progressive," resulting in a different home atmosphere from what most girls experienced. (A supportive father is a common theme in the lives of women achievers.) Eileen Magill's father, for example, was an academic who pushed her to achieve excellence at university. Isobel Whitaker was raised in the wilds of British Columbia and often accompanied her father into logging camps. "She had a well-developed sense of adventure and was never concerned with the social niceties of the day," said her son Nicholas Gilbert. Joan Bonisteel helped her father, a World War I pilot, build an airplane. "No one was surprised when she announced she was going to learn to fly. She was a tomboy, always playing hockey, soccer, and football," recalled a childhood friend.

Enid Norquay, 1931, in the driver's seat. "This was the little car that my sister and I owned and used to drive to the airport for my lessons. This car also had to be cranked to start it as did the Cirrus, Gipsy, and Tiger Moths."

ENID NORQUAY, of Edmonton, Alberta said, "I was born into a family of achievers and raised to do things." Her paternal grandfather was a former premier of Manitoba, her maternal grandfather was the first mayor of Edmonton, her father was a magistrate for the Northwest Territories, and her mother was a well-known horsewoman. Enid used to accompany her father on trips to the Territories and was as much at home on a horse and carrying a gun as she was in a drawing room entertaining government officials. As a girl she was active in all sports and was particularly interested in anything that flew: birds, bees, and butterflies. "When the prairie airmail service began in 1930 I used to go to the airport to watch the planes. I was so enthralled with the whole idea of flying that I asked my parents if I could go to Winnipeg on one of the airmail planes." Her parents agreed and off she went. She never forgot that flight.

"I took off from Edmonton with a bad cold, a box of chocolates, and a big bag of cherries. Taking off was the most wonderful feeling — I felt like a bird. I was so happy, I ate the box of chocolates. During the first landing the wonderful feeling left. When we took off again I began feeling sick. Next thing I knew I was ill, just sick, sick, sick. Used all eight paper bags on the plane! At Moose Jaw the pilot put me off the plane saying that I would never make it by air to Winnipeg. I was mortified, humiliated, and disgraced. Then and there, as sick as I was, I decided to learn to fly. I would show the boys that girls were not sissies. I was determined to be a good pilot." Unlike Marjorie Chauvin and Elsie MacLean, she had nothing but praise for Moss Burbidge. She found him patient but strict and on November 23, 1931 received PPL #928.

In 1932 Enid toured England and met Lady Hay-Drummond, president of the Women's Institute Association of Aeronautics, whose motto was *Air-mindedness destroys narrow-mindedness.* "She offered to finance my commercial training because she believed that the only way women would be accepted by the male flying community was by becoming highly qualified. I was tempted. However, I was engaged to be married that year and I knew that my fiancé would not approve of my flying after we were married." When Enid returned to Canada she never flew again.

L *Louise Jenkins, 1932, the first woman pilot in Prince Edward Island.*

R *The Puss Moth that Louise Jenkins flew. Note the registration, CF-PEI.*

LOUISE JENKINS (1890-1986)

Louise Jenkins, Prince Edward Island's first woman pilot was born in Pittsburgh and raised in Philadelphia and New York. Louise met her husband-to-be, Colonel Jack Jenkins, a medical officer from Prince Edward Island, in England, where she was serving in the Voluntary Auxiliary Division. Married in England after the war, they settled in his home, Upton Farm, near Charlottetown, where he practiced medicine. Her new home held no charms for Louise. "In the twenties PEI was no idyllic Eden but an isolated and primitive spot, approached only by ice breakers during the long winter," she recalled. This slow unreliable method of transportation to the mainland was unsatisfactory for a doctor treating critically ill patients and because of their wartime experiences the Jenkins knew how valuable aircraft

THESE EARLY WOMEN PILOTS wanted to live beyond traditional expectations. They liked a challenge. The lure of accomplishing an unusual and risky endeavour intrigued them. As a young woman Isobel Secord skied and climbed mountains in Canada, the United States, Europe, and Asia; toured China on foot; and worked as a nurse in South Africa. By 1933 there was little that she had not tackled except flying. "I flew simply for the challenge of learning another sport which promised to provide some thrills and adventure," she explained. (When I interviewed Miss Secord in 1984 she had just taken her first hot air balloon ride.) That flying was considered unsuitable for women was of no consequence. "I fought to be different,"

could be. However, the conservative Islanders were not receptive to change and did not accept the Jenkins' offer of land for a municipal airport until 1929. Upton Field, as it was called, opened in 1930 and served as Charlottetown's airport until 1941.

"Almost immediately the house was full of pilots and their gear. I used to feed them and put them up for the night and in return they took me flying. I soon became airplane crazy and decided that I had to learn to fly," explained Louise. She chose the Curtiss-Reid Flying School at Cartierville Airport in Montreal for her training. With her children in boarding school and her husband busy with his work, she had little compunction about moving temporarily to Montreal. Her logbook shows that she began flying on December 2, 1931 and flew every day until the 21st, when she returned home for Christmas. Her daughter, Joan Stephenson, remarked in later years that it seemed as if her mother could not wait for the holidays to be over and her children gone so that she could return to flying. Louise received PPL #973 on March 8, 1932.

"She was a natural pilot," recalled her instructor Gathen Edward, "and a beautiful lady whom we all treated with extra care." Her daughter also commented that her mother could make anyone do anything once she made up her mind. (When I met Mrs. Jenkins she was over ninety but her charm and beauty were still apparent and one could understand how she made things happen.) At one point she talked Gathen Edward into flying to New York and to the Maritimes with her, and later she requested him to assist her in buying a plane. Settling on a de Havilland Puss Moth, she then prevailed upon the Prime Minister of Canada to help her obtain the airplane registration "PEI" in honour of her adopted province.

Although she did not know it, her flying days were numbered. Perhaps she suspected as much, for she flew

Hers First Plane
To Make Landing
On Beach in P. E. I.

CHARLOTTETOWN, P. E. I. July 11 — (Special) — The first plane to make a landing on a Prince Edward Island beach was the privately owned machine CF-P.E.I., piloted by Mrs. J.S. Jenkins, who accompanied by her husband, Dr. Jenkins, flew from this city to Tracadie yesterday afternoon. They were accorded a rousing reception by the crowd of Sunday visitors. Mayor Stewart and Mrs. Stewart drove Dr. and Mrs. Jenkins to their summer cottage for lunch.

Newspaper article about Louise Jenkins.

recalled Grayce Hutchinson, and Joyce Bond commented, "I never really cared what other people thought of me." These women carried their disregard for "proper" womanly pursuits into other aspects of their lives as well. In an era when marriage was considered to be a woman's ultimate goal and spinsterhood was shunned, these women did not rush to the altar at age twenty-one, if at all. At a time when home and motherhood were expected to consume all of a woman's energies, very few confined themselves solely to their families.

DOROTHY BELL, a university graduate, became secretary to the president of the University of Manitoba and Manitoba's second woman pilot. She fell under flying's spell after a number of flights with pilots of the RCAF and Western Canada Airways and, when the Winnipeg Flying Club was formed in 1928, she was one of the first to sign up for lessons. A longtime acquaintance described her as "an extremely vivacious girl with a total disregard for other people's opinions." After instruction with

almost every day until the end of that fair summer. "I'd take up government dignitaries for hops around the province or I'd drop off my children's clothes at their boarding schools," she said. Her daughter recalled her mother dropping bundles of clothes in the school yard from her plane. Her husband became seriously ill, and the good times came to an end on November 8, 1932 when Louise made her final flight in the Puss Moth. "When I sold the plane I felt that I had lost something very special," she remarked. She went flying a few times in 1933 but even that she gave up because of her husband's illness. "I was heartbroken because I couldn't fly anymore."

Her motives for flying in no way detract from the very real contribution that she and her husband made. The Jenkins brought aviation to Prince Edward Island. Louise's graciousness and her enthusiasm for flying were an inspiration to others, among them the well-known Father MacGillivray of Nova Scotia, who also flew Puss Moth "PEI." On a more personal level her attitude was typical of other women pilots. She cared not a whit for the opinions of others and defied social conventions. It took courage and determination for this forty-year old mother of three to leave home, husband, and children to take lessons in another province and to commute between PEI and Quebec in the dead of winter, when transportation was at its slowest and worst. After her husband died and her children were grown she left the Island for good, settling in Old Lyme, Connecticut.

the flamboyant Michael DeBlicquy, Dorothy took her test on a ski-equipped Cirrus Moth from Air Vice Marshall Lee Stevenson and received PPL #220 on February 16, 1929.

Marriage and children eventually ended her piloting days but not her association with flying. Married to a cousin of James A. Richardson, president of Western Canada Airways-Canadian Airways Limited, she was on a first-name basis with many of the company's pilots and, when the spirit moved her, would leave her family in the care of a nanny and fly into the North. An unscheduled night stop in the bush or flying over uncharted territory did not bother her at all. "Unconventional" continued to describe her lifestyle until she died; at well over seventy she might have been found on a safari in Africa or tracking caribou in the barren lands of northern Canada.

WHILE HEREDITY and family and cultural influences are said to shape the personality and behaviour of an individual; birth order is another factor. Firstborn and only children are said to have certain characteristics, such as competitiveness, aggressiveness, self-confidence, and high levels of achievement. Interestingly, well over half of all women pilots right up to the present day were firstborn or only children.They could be single-minded too. Dorothy Bell recalled, "I lived for flying. It

Dorothy Bell, 1929. She was one of the first people to sign up for lessons when the Winnipeg Flying Club was formed in 1928.

GERTRUDE DUGAL

Gertrude Dugal of Montreal was the first francophone woman pilot trained and licenced in Quebec. Although French and Roman Catholic her upbringing was not typical of most French Canadian girls. Her father encouraged his daughters to look beyond the home for satisfaction and Gertrude, a journalism graduate fluent in French, English, and Spanish, worked as a translator and ghost writer. A flight on a commercial aircraft in 1946 so thrilled her that she decided to take flying lessons. She enrolled at Laurentide Aviation at Cartierville Airport and took her training from Jack Scholefield, receiving PPL #5666 on March 11, 1947.

Quebec newspapers loved having their own heroine and referred to her as "une Canadienne française qui a des ailes" and "la première Canadienne française a obtenir un brevet de pilote...un titre de gloire." Unfortunately family problems forced her to abandon her dream of flying professionally. "I knew for a short time the great thrill and freedom of taking off in the air, leaving everything behind," she remembered wistfully.

became an obsession with me. I'd leave home at 4:30 in the morning to fly before work. My friends thought I was crazy because I spent all my money on flying instead of new evening gowns and I never cared if I was asked to the next dance. All I ever worried about was my next flight." Florence Elliott elaborated, "I had tunnel vision. I didn't care what else was happening in the world, so long as I got flying time in each week. I went without clothes and food and every other interest in life, working toward that Limited Commercial Licence. It was like the Holy Grail." Women pilots were independent, determined, and strong-willed. They had to be to overcome resistance to receive training or to cope with negative attitudes from friends and neighbours. As Louise Jenkins' daughter Joan (Tony) Stephenson explained, "My classmates were impressed that I had a mother who flew, but the women of Prince Edward Island thought it was disgraceful."

FINALLY, FLYING WAS an emotional experience. Perhaps Violet Milstead described it best when she said, "I felt alive in a way I had never before imagined. Flying, as a vocation, is in a class by itself. It is the very greatest. It affords satisfactions — intangible ones — available in no other line of work and, after the hangar doors are closed, fellowships of the finest and most enduring kind. I seem to be blessed with a temperament which has enabled me to delight in the challenges of flight, to love its freedom, its self-sufficiency, its splendid loneliness, to marvel at the awesome beauty of skyscapes, to pity the earthbound."

Note
3 Daphne Paterson Shelfoon, letter on file.

"*Have you an opening for a lady pilot?*"

"I took the commercial licence to prove to myself that I could do it. The licence itself was a farce because I could do nothing with it." — *Jessica Jarvis*

FOR MANY OF THE FIRST WOMEN who discovered the joy of flying a plane, there were exciting, yet idyllic times. Edina Newlands, daughter of Saskatchewan's lieutenant-governor, who flew out of the Regina Flying Club, wrote, "Flying in the thirties was a comparatively safe and pleasant pastime; the sky was ours from the zenith to the horizon. The airfields in the small prairie towns were all the same; a small huddle of planes neatly parked on one side, some well-worked runways or landing strips, and high on its pole in the middle, the wind sock gently giving the wind direction."

For the most part the men accepted the women as welcome social additions to the flying clubs. F. Hollister McQuin of the Ottawa Flying Club fondly remembered Margaret Rankin-Smith, "I can still see her in the club house when the weather was bad — the only girl and a bunch of boys — sitting on the edge of a table blowing her head off on a harmonica or a slide whistle. The boys all liked her and seemed to enjoy having her around. Marg was good at everything: singing, playing musical instruments, sports. She was very outgoing and very beautiful."

Many women flew "for fun," which meant air shows, competitions, and social events. Fly-in garden parties were the rage in the Toronto area. The most famous was held each spring by the Norman Irwins at their home, Stonehaven, in Whitby, Ontario. Formal invitations were issued and the guest list read like the Social Register of Toronto.

Most of the early women pilots took part in airshows. They were opportunities to meet other pilots as well as to test their own skills. Grayce Hutchinson of Saskatoon recalled, "I used to fly a lot with Smith-Marriott and Buck Buchanan. Flying with

AVIATION GARDEN PARTY AT "STONEHAVEN" BRINGS SEVENTEEN PLANES

Toronto Mail + Empire 6-15-1931

venteen planes were piloted to Whitby on Saturday for the jolly aviation garden party given by Mr. and Mrs. Norman Irwin at their home, "Stonehaven". On the left, in
cture above, are C. C. Bogart and Miss Lorene Regan, who were compelled to make a forced landing in a field near Wexford, on their way to the party, because of engine tro
e pilot soon adjusted the difficulty, and they arrived at "Stonehaven" before five o'clock. In the centre are four others who flew out: Mr. and Mrs. James, Miss Chase Atki
standing in front of their respective planes. On the right is Miss Marjorie Chauvin, the only lady who flew solo to "Stonehaven"; and below is a view of

Smith-Marriott, whom we called 'Smudge,' was never dull. We used to go to all the air meets around the province and his favourite stunt was to knock over a bottle of beer with his wing tip. We always entered the flour bombing contests and I became quite an expert at it."

The women were not shy about becoming involved in flying club events. Enid Norquay, for instance, spent all her free time at the Edmonton Aero Club. "It was an exciting place to be in those days," she recalled. "I remember interviewing Wiley

A 1931 newspaper article about one of the famous springtime fly-in garden parties at Stonehaven.

Post and Harold Gatty when they landed in Edmonton on their flight around the world. I was a reporter for the club *Bulletin*. I used to pester other pilots to take me flying. I remember looping and spinning with Grant McConachie [later president of Canadian Pacific Airlines] and flying with Wop May and Andy Cruickshank, pilots with Canadian Airways."

If there was no special flying event planned, they organized their own. Barely three weeks after she received her licence, Louise Jenkins of Charlottetown, Prince Edward Island persuaded her instructor, Gathen Edward, into accompanying her on a trans-Canada flight. She had just purchased her own aircraft, a de Havilland Puss Moth, registered "PEI" after her province, and she wanted to test her flying skills. Armed with road maps and a bag of sandwiches, she was actually climbing into her aircraft when a call from home (which was never explained to the author) put an end to her trip before it had even begun. "I shall never recover from the disappointment," she wrote in her logbook.

Rolie Moore of Vancouver concentrated on improving her

Rolie Moore in the mid 1930s.

ROLIE MOORE BARRETT PIERCE

Rolie Moore Barrett Pierce of Burnaby, British Columbia was Canada's first woman aerobatic pilot. "When I was eighteen I earned my first flight by sketching Maurice McGregor's Waco," she recalled. After high school Rolie attended the Vancouver School of Art and graduated in 1931. Another four years would slip by however before she could afford flying instruction. She took lessons at the Columbia Flying School at Sea Island because it offered the best deal: $400 to obtain a licence, which she received (PPL #1737) on October 7, 1935.

From the start Rolie wanted flying to be an integral part of her life. With that in mind she qualified for her commercial licence (#C-1609 July 19, 1939). Although she was an active member of The Flying Seven, finding a job was not easy and more than a year passed before something came her way. The BC Aero Club asked her to ferry a plane from the Piper factory in Hamilton to Vancouver. She leapt at the chance even though it meant leaving her baby behind in the care of her mother. (Rolie was now Rolie Barrett, having married her fiancé just before he went overseas.) "The trip never materialized. It kept getting postponed. I waited around for three months 'hopping passengers' to earn money until I was finally told the flight was cancelled. When I returned to Vancouver, all civilian flying had stopped and I did not get back into the air until 1945."

flying skills by taking up aerobatics and entering flying competitions. Rolie, who would become Canada's first woman aerobatic pilot and the second woman to earn the coveted Public Transport Licence (in 1949), was so "hooked on flying" that when her mother took her and her sister to Europe in the mid-thirties to tour the continent she stayed in England to join the Brooklands Flying Club. There she began cross-country flying, instrument work, and aerobatics with Ken Waller, a well-known instructor. She also entered her first competition, the Lord Northesk Trophy. Rolie so enjoyed the precision of instrument and aerobatic flying that, when she returned to Canada, she continued her training at the BC Aero Club with

FLORENCE ELLIOTT WHYARD

Florence Elliott Whyard was just a little girl when she went flying with World War I pilot, Tom Williams, of Woodstock, Ontario. "It was a marvellous ride until Tom got a little too fancy and I threw up all over the plane!"

Despite this inauspicious beginning she took up flying after graduating from university in 1938, doing odd jobs around the London Flying Club in return for lessons. Despite an "incident" — when Flo wrecked a club plane (see page 44) — she received her licence on November 16, 1939. "I began working on my commercial licence immediately. It was like climbing the rungs of a ladder; once you started you kept on going. I borrowed clothes from my sorority sisters and scrounged meals from everyone so I could use all my earnings for flying." She received Commercial Licence C-1846 on October 31, 1940, the fourteenth woman in Canada to earn one, and immediately applied to the RCAF.

"They gave me a flat `no' unless I was willing to sit and type, thus releasing some man to fly. I thought, `In a pig's eye.' I was damned if I would sign up to bang a typewriter just so some man could get all that lovely air training and go flying off at my expense." So incensed was she at being turned down by the RCAF that she refused to join the Women's Division and enlisted instead in the Women's Royal Naval Service, where she served as an information officer.

Flo did not renew her licences after the war. Marriage, and a lack of money and opportunity prevented her from pursuing flying, but she never lost her love of aviation. After a term as Mayor of Whitehorse and as a Member of the Legislature for the Yukon, she wrote a book on Ernie Boffa, a Yukon bush pilot, and helped establish an aviation museum in the Yukon.

Hal Wilson. She became so proficient that Wilson asked her to perform on behalf of the BC Aero Club at the 1937 Vancouver Air Show. A modest, gracious woman, Rolie insisted that it was nothing fancy. "I did a routine which consisted of inverted spins, Cuban Eights, slow rolls, flick rolls, whip stalls, loops, bunts and finished with a falling leaf." Nevertheless, her performance caught the eye of well-known American stunt pilot, Tex Rankin. "He asked me to join him on the airshow circuit. I reluctantly declined but it was very flattering that the great Tex Rankin had noticed me."

George Ross, the executive secretary of the Canadian Flying Clubs Association, recognized Daphne Paterson's skills

GIRL PILOTS ANXIOUS TO BE USEFUL

Girl pilots across Canada are discussing ways and means by whic
hey may be useful to the department of national defence. Eliann
Roberge, president of the Flying Seven (LEFT), who came from Ottaw
o discuss the matter with Toronto girl pilots, believes that some coul
e employed by manufacturers to ferry planes to airfields. She is show
vith Florence Elliott, one of the Toronto pilots anxious to see
ational organization of girl pilots formed. Beryl Armstrong, Vancouve
ice-president of the Flying Seven, proposes the girls start schools t
rain girls in aeronautics.

Eliane Roberge (on the left) and Florence Elliott, pictured in an article. Although both had commercial pilot's licences, they could not obtain flying jobs.

as a pilot and organizer, and asked her to fly in the first Trans-Canada Air Pageant — quite an honour considering how few women flew — and to serve as the vice-chairman of the permanent contest committee for the Maritimes. A year later she also helped to organize the First Annual Maritime Goodwill Tour. Louise Jenkins of PEI was also involved. "I flew around the province dropping off posters which advertised the airshow and I entered some of the events too. The one I remember the best was a 'rat race' which was a sort of a follow-the-leader flight. They gave me the honour of leading the air pageant fly-past over Halifax," recalled Louise.

The two outstanding women competitors in the thirties were Daphne Paterson and Rolie Moore, who regularly scored well in the Webster Trophy competition. In 1931 Daphne, a member of the Montreal Light Aeroplane Club and the Fredericton Flying Club, entered the first Webster Trophy

Jessica Jarvis, c. 1932.

JESSICA JARVIS

Jessica Jarvis was the first woman pilot in Toronto to receive a commercial licence. Despite a privileged background that included private schools in England and Canada, Jessica described her childhood as lonely and unhappy. "I flew to do something to justify my existence and to stand out from the crowd." A member of the Toronto Flying Club, she received PPL #860 on August 21, 1931.

Uncertain as to what direction her life should take, Jessica went to London, England for a year. There she joined the London Aeroplane Club and obtained the British Empire Aviator's Certificate #4932. When her money ran out she returned to Toronto and worked as a bank clerk. She began working towards her commercial licence but a shortage of funds dictated a time span of three years before she received CPL #1161 on August 23, 1934 — the fourth woman in Canada to qualify.

For Jessica, attaining the commercial licence represented a personal achievement. "I took it to prove to myself that I could do it. The licence itself was a farce because I could do nothing with it. Women were not wanted on the field by some of the men because they detracted from the mystique of the male pilot. If a mere woman could fly an airplane then the man slipped a notch or two in the girlfriend's estimation."

Marriage, followed by a divorce, left her with a child to support. Knowing full well that she had no hope of ever finding a flying position and wishing to get out of her clerical dead-end job, she attended university and earned a

Star Weekly cover, 1940.

degree in Home Economics. Despite limited finances and time, she maintained her membership at the Toronto Flying Club and managed to stay current, "passenger hopping" to help cover costs. Rarely, however, did she attend any of the club's social functions. Former Toronto Flying Club president Mel Alexander described her as a loner, "She didn't hang around the club to socialize; she just wanted to fly."

When war broke out Jessica was sure that the RCAF would accept women but of course discovered otherwise. "I was so incensed that I refused to consider the Women's Division when it was formed and I joined the Navy instead and spent the war years as a dietician. When Canada wouldn't make use of women during wartime, I knew there would be no place for them in peacetime so I didn't renew my membership at the club and never flew again."

competition. Flying a Cirrus Moth, G-CAKK, she won the Maritimes zone elimination trials and the coveted de Havilland Trophy. As the top amateur pilot in the region she represented the Maritimes in the finals, placing second overall. Twice more in the thirties she was runner-up for the Webster Trophy. Rolie Moore entered her first Webster Trophy competition in 1938 and placed second in the western division, which qualified her to represent western Canada in the finals. For Rolie, it was an exciting time. "The competition itself was a good one. I placed second in the general flying and seventh overall." The following year she won first place in the western eliminations and again went to Ottawa for the finals. However, just before she was to compete she received a telegram from home notifying her that her four brothers were to be shipped overseas imminently. "I wanted to see them before they went off to war, even if it meant that I didn't compete; so I returned home."

L *Rolie Moore during the 1939 trials for the Webster Trophy.*

R *The de Havilland Trophy.*

THE WOMEN also had their share of misadventures. Dorothy Bell once ran out of gas in southern Manitoba. "Mike DeBlicquy had to rescue me. He was not pleased with me nor did he think much of the cow pasture I had landed in because the cows were trying to lick the wing. They liked the dope [aircraft finish] and he was afraid they would damage the plane." Florence Elliott of the London Flying Club recalled an inglorious landing, "There was a pile of rocks in one corner of the field and I landed in it, nose first, after half stalling all the way across the field, too stupid to put the nose down and gain flying speed. I remember sitting there while bits of fuselage fell quietly around me in the great silence after the crash. I hoped that I would be killed or at least have two broken legs to justify wrecking the poor little plane." Florence had nothing worse than a few bruises and a broken heart because the plane was not insured. The crash came back to haunt her a few weeks later when, after her flight test, she and Inspector Joy were walking through the hangar and he spotted the wrecked Taylorcraft, which had been pushed into a corner. "The club had not got around to reporting it and Joy was furious. He told me he never would have tested me if he had known."

The effervescent Helen Harrison, who would spend over thirty-five years in aviation, also had "incidents" throughout her career. Shortly after she earned a commercial licence, she decided to "passenger hop" to build time. "I bought myself a three-place plane called a Spartan and set myself up in a farmer's field. I almost put myself out of business before I began," Helen recalled. "Hoping to entice the locals to take a flight, I planned

MARGARET CLEMENTS (1902-1960)

Margaret Clements scandalized the ladies of Regina, Saskatchewan when she appeared at the airfield in men's clothes and announced that she was going to fly. They were aghast that the matron of the hospital would do such a thing but defying social custom was not new to Margaret. She had initially intended to be a pharmacist and, contrary to all advice, had enrolled in the University of Saskatchewan's Faculty of Pharmacy. She was the only woman in the class. She made it through the first year but then was forced to drop out because no druggist would allow her to do a summer apprenticeship with him. As her sister Edith Croll explained, "Prohibition was in effect in those days and many druggists acted as bootleg dealers and only wanted strong young men who could deliver (illegally) medicinal spirits. Her only alternative was nursing."

To Margaret flying was a way to escape the tea parties and cliquish atmosphere of a small town. "She felt stifled by the social conventions of the day and enjoyed the companionship of the pilots at the Regina Flying Club more than the ladies of her acquaintance," explained her sister. Long-time friend Maurice McGregor of TCA-Air Canada, described Margaret as "one of the most personable, energetic, capable, and versatile women I have ever known and I could understand why she would not have been happy sipping tea and gossiping." Margaret received PPL #1517 on October 9, 1934. She continued to fly until she moved to New Westminister, British Columbia a few years later to accept the position of superintendent of nurses. She joined the BC Aero Club but found it too distant, and herself too busy, to keep up her proficiency and regretfully she allowed her flying to slip away. When war was declared she tried to enlist in the RCAF and, when rejected, joined the Army instead and attained the rank of captain as a nursing sister.

Margaret Clements, 1934.

to do a few flips around the town to attract their attention. When the engine did not start on the first few swings of the propeller I advanced the throttle. It caught on the next swing and as I started to climb in, the darn thing began to move. I had forgotten to chock it!" Shouting for help, which never materialized although an interested audience soon gathered, Helen tore off after the plane. "Fortunately it did not pick up enough speed to take off, but it did nose over and break the prop. I don't think I impressed anyone that day."

A few women attempted and set flying records. The best known was Nellie Carson of Saskatoon, who in 1931 set a Canadian altitude record. Flying a series of circles over the

Joyce Bond in the 1930s.

JOYCE BOND

Joyce Bond of Regina, Saskatchewan became western Canada's first woman skydiver. She achieved PPL #1092, on December 8, 1936 and then sought new challenges. "I wanted to skydive because that seemed to be the ultimate adventure." Instruction was sketchy — Joyce simply went up in a plane a few times with a friend and watched what he did. On September 25, 1937 she made her first and only jump. "Jack Hames, flying instructor at the Regina Flying Club, flew me in one of the club's Fleets. I jumped from a height of 4000 feet, free-falling until 2500 feet when I opened my first chute. Then I dropped another thousand feet and opened a second chute. It was exciting."

In pursuit of further thrills she took aerobatic instruction at the BC Aero Club when she visited Vancouver the following year. She also joined The Flying Seven but lost contact with the group once she returned to Regina. "I tried to join the Chinese Air Force too, and when Canada declared war, I tried to enlist in the RCAF, but they told me they wouldn't take a woman." By this time Joyce had heard rumblings that civilian flying would be curtailed and, desperately hoping that she could find her niche in aviation before this happened, she left Regina. "I moved to Hamilton to apply for a job at the Cub factory, testing aircraft. I couldn't get anything except an office position so I took it to be close at hand. I managed to do a little ferrying of aircraft and also dropped pamphlets promoting war bonds." Even this petered out and, after spending a winter hoping for something else, she gave up and returned to Regina in 1944 having abandoned all hope of flying. "I knew that at war's end, with all those returning airmen, I stood very little chance of being hired as a pilot and I was not prepared to remain on the edge of flying any longer."

field, she took a Gipsy Moth to a height of 16,000 feet.

Jessica Jarvis became active in international aviation circles and was the first Canadian woman to obtain licences in three countries: the British Empire Aviator's Certificate No. 932, the Republique Française Brevet et License de Pilote d'Avions de Tourism No. 1439, and the Federation Aeronatique Internationale License No. 10878.

BUT IF MEN generally accepted women who looked no further than a private licence, the attitude that professional flying was a man's domain remained firmly entrenched. The five women who earned commercial licences before 1940

found that, while men might be charmed by their presence in the flying clubs, it was a different matter once they tried to move into paying positions.

Compounding the problem was the poor economic situation of the thirties. The optimistm of the late twenties and the government initiatives regarding flying, begun in 1927-28, fell by the wayside as the Great Depression took hold.

The government's decision to pull the rug out from under Canadian Airways Limited in 1932 spelled disaster for pilots. A national airways system supported by the government meant jobs and the hope of expansion but a company relegated to the bush held little promise. For women pilots it held none. While a company flying from city to city *might* hire women pilots, a

Canadian artist Don Connolly's rough sketch of Gipsy Moth CF-AAA "Landing at The Webster." Commissioned by Daphne Paterson, 1980.

company operating north into the bush would not.

In fact, discrimination towards women who wanted to make flying their career became apparent before they even asked for a job. In 1930 government officials told Daphne Paterson, the first woman to apply for a commercial licence, that she was unsuitable because she was female. Having been encouraged by her instructor Tony Spooner to qualify for a commercial licence, she was surprised and angry when the Department of National Defence (which issued all licences) rejected her application for a flight test on the grounds that the commercial licence could be granted to men only. Spooner went to bat for her, pointing out to officials that the word "pilot" was used throughout the Civil Aviation Rules and Regulations and nowhere did it say that a pilot must be male. Reluctantly the Department of National Defence allowed her to take the test and she received Commercial Pilot's Licence #658 on March 24, 1930, the first Canadian woman to obtain a commercial standing.

With the issue of her commercial licence officialdom added a new rule. In 1930 Civil Aviation Rules and Regulations made no mention of pregnant commercial pilots; after all, until Daphne, all commercial pilots had been male. This clearly concerned the Department of National Defence because written on her licence was the directive to report for a medical every three months instead of the six month interval required for men. As it happened officials need not have worried because no one would hire her.

Daphne did not abandon her goal. Supporting herself as a journalist, she threw herself wholeheartedly into all flying club activities in order to publicize her name and flying skills. She hoped that in time something somewhere would break in her favour. She continued to fly for fun and was an active member of the Montreal Light Aeroplane Club, the Fredericton Flying Club and, in later years, the Toronto Flying Club.

In the mid-thirties Daphne married Tony Shelfoon, a pilot, which temporarily curtailed her own flying. Although it was a struggle financially — "All our spare money went towards Tony's training," she wrote — she maintained her flying proficiency and, in 1938, with war a possibility, and thinking she could be an RCAF pilot, she trained for the Public Transport Licence. This licence had been recently established by the Department of Transportation and was the highest Canadian

Daphne Paterson.

rating obtainable. Daphne received PTL #130 on August 9, 1938, the first Canadian woman to do so. It too contained the stipulation that a medical examination was required every three months.

Newspapers in Toronto, Montreal, and Saint John made much of the fact that Daphne was qualified to fly for the airlines and quoted Daphne as saying, "Women pilots certainly should be able to find their place in aviation in Canada." Headlines such as "Place in Flying For Fair Sex Asserts Noted Woman Pilot" were common. But the transport licence was as worthless a ticket to employment as the commercial licence had been. None of the bush companies or the recently formed Trans-Canada Airlines had any intention of hiring a woman.

THE LACK OF JOBS open to them, while demoralizing, did not deter these determined women. Some tried to create their own opportunities. For instance, Eileen Magill applied to John A. Wilson, Controller, of the Department of Civil Aviation, for an administrative job, hoping to use that as an entry into the flying world. Supporting her application was Mr. J. Sully, President of the Winnipeg Flying Club, who wrote to Wilson that Eileen had all the necessary qualifications plus a "pleasing

Connie Culver, lounging in the hangar doorway.

CONNIE CULVER

Born in Simcoe, Ontario, Connie Culver had her first plane ride when she was eight, when a barnstormer landed on the family's tobacco farm. As soon as she graduated from high school and went to work, she began saving towards flying lessons. "Once I'd saved $50 I went to Tom Senior of the Brantford Flying Club. He told me that $50 was not enough. Finally we struck a deal for I convinced him that the publicity of a woman pilot would bring lots of business." Soloing in 3 hours and 25 minutes, she received a private licence on February 21, 1939. Connie and her brother, also a pilot, bought a J-3 Cub, CF-BBY. Using it to build time, she worked towards a commercial licence, which she received on May 17, 1940, the twelfth Canadian woman to qualify.

"I continued to clerk at Woolworths but I tried to find a job flying. Tom Senior let me give check rides and do some unofficial instructing. I thought of getting my instructor's rating but Tom could not promise me a job because most of the flying clubs were being converted to training schools for the war effort. I also applied to Austin Airways at Sudbury but they were not interested in hiring me." A year later gasoline rationing put an end to her flying.

personality and lots of tact and common sense." Nothing came of it and Eileen eventually left flying for other challenges.

Some women cashed in on their femininity and good looks to obtain free flying time. Grayce Hutchinson of Saskatoon dropped pamphlets for the Budweiser Beer Company. Tib Goulding's appearance and social standing in Toronto made her an attractive publicity gimmick and in 1931 Jim Crang and Earl Hand, distributors of the Buhl aircraft, asked her to demonstrate the Buhl. "The premise was that if a mere woman could fly it then anyone could," explained Tib. "The Parker Pen Company also approached me to fly an aircraft with its marking on it. My father would not allow me to accept any of

Eliane Roberge, 1930.

ELIANE ROBERGE SCHLACHTER (1909-1981)

Eliane Roberge was born in Prince Rupert, British Columbia of French Canadian parents. Her father died when she was very young and her mother supported the family by mining for gold in the Yukon. "Eliane saw her first plane when she was just a schoolgirl," said her husband Fred Schlachter, "and from that moment on she wanted to fly. Her mother however insisted that she get an education and sent her to Montreal to stay with her grandparents and attend Beaux Arts." It was there that Eliane took flying lessons. Unfortunately her logbook reveals little, only that she was a member of the Montreal Light Aeroplane Club at St. Hubert Airport and also flew out of La Salle with a Mr. Dewar and with Stuart Graham, a civil aviation inspector. She took her flight test from Graham in a Gipsy Moth, CF-ADA, and received PPL #678 on October 18, 1930, the third woman in Montreal to be licenced.

Eliane, a commercial artist, remained in Montreal for about five years, obtaining her Commercial Pilot's Licence, A-1028 on October 12, 1932, the third Canadian woman to qualify. Her logbook shows that she flew with Gathen Edward in a Rambler and Bluebird at Cartierville Airport and with Captain Finney and Captain Spooner at St. Hubert Airport, flying Aeronca CF-AQC and Moth CF-ABY. Likely she knew Daphne Paterson and Louise Jenkins. She returned to the west coast in 1935 or 1936 and set her sights on a job in the aviation industry.

Since Grant McConachie of Yukon Southern Air Transport seemed to make his own rules, she settled on him as the most likely prospect. Well aware that women were not considered suitable for flying jobs, Eliane did not apply for one. Instead she used the strategy that a secretary who could fly was far more valuable than one who could not. A master salesman himself, McConachie recognized a good

pitch when he heard one and hired her. Once she got her foot in the door she then convinced him to check her out on all of Yukon Southern's aircraft and to let her fly the right seat as required. Tall and strong, Eliane had no problem handling the heavier aircraft. Officially she was the secretary and dispatcher; unofficially she served as co-pilot or spotter for search and rescue and fire fighting missions. Her logbook shows that McConachie himself checked her out on the Fokker Standard Universal CF-CAFU, the Waco CF-BBP, the Norseman CF-AZE, a Fairchild 71, a Barkley-Grow, and the Ford Trimotor CF-BEP. Most of her flights were with McConachie, the majority of them in the Barkley-Grow on the Vancouver to Fort St. John or the Vancouver to Edmonton routes.

Eliane Roberge's flying activities were a well-kept secret. While most of the aircraft did not require a co-pilot, the fact

A Yukon Southern Air Transport Barkley-Grow on floats, an aircraft Eliane Roberge was checked out to fly.

the offers, saying that they were unsuitable for his daughter."

During the summer weekends of 1930 and 1931, Nellie Carson of Saskatoon tried unsuccessfully to raise money by barnstorming so that she could qualify for a commercial licence. She would fly into farmers' fields and when a crowd had gathered she would canvass the onlookers and charge a cent a pound for one five-minute circuit.

MARJORIE CHAUVIN of Edmonton was one of the most determined and ambitious women of the early thirties. She firmly believed that women could contribute to Canada's aviation development and she wanted to play a part. She

Eliane Roberge ready for takeoff in an Aeronca, Montreal, 1930.

that Eliane was often along was unusual. McConachie, never one to let convention stand in his way, unless it affected his profits, nevertheless took a risk when he allowed her to fly right seat because he knew that the public "down south" would look askance on a female bush pilot. Normally a publicity hound, he covered his tracks well on these occasions by not allowing Eliane's flying to be leaked to the press. She herself never spoke of it except to her husband, whom she married twenty years later.

When war was declared Eliane applied to the RCAF. When she was rejected she went to Ottawa to apply in person, to no avail. She then tried to get her instructor's rating in order to teach at one of the flying schools operated under the British Commonwealth Air Training Plan. Here too she got nowhere. No one in Vancouver could tell her how to go about qualifying. Finally, in exasperation she wrote John A. Wilson, controller of civil aviation, on September 21, 1940. "I have inquired at our airport but everyone seems very vague as to what procedures a girl should take." Wilson replied on September 26 that she could take her training at one of the civilian schools, but it would not do her much good as the RCAF could not test her because it was wartime. The last statement was incorrect and inexcusable. Until gasoline rationing forced the closure of the civilian flying schools, pilots were permitted to qualify for their instructor's ratings. In fact, six other Canadian women did just that in the 1940-1942 period, taking their categorization tests at the RCAF base in Trenton. In the same letter, Eliane also asked about the possibility of being employed by the Department of National Defence in a "flying capacity" such as instructing or ferrying aircraft. Again Wilson cut her off saying that "no arrangements have been made to employ women pilots for the duration of the war."

Frustrated, she left Yukon Southern in 1941 for a position with the British Air Commission in Washington, DC,

aggressively pursued her goal and did, in fact, become Canada's first woman demonstration pilot. Although it was an unpaid position, she clearly showed that women could cope with the irregular hours and variety of aircraft that were the lot of a "demo" pilot. Marjorie earned a private pilot's licence in late 1929 and, after assessing the situation, came to the realization that she would never obtain a job in the west, where most of the flying was in the bush. She decided to move east where there was some inter-city flying. She applied for a job transfer and by January 1930, she was in the Toronto office of the Retail Credit. "That was a brave thing for a girl to do in those days," her husband recalled. "She had no relatives or friends and was

hoping that she might have more luck with the Royal Air Force. She fared no better. Even the opportunity to fly as a civilian came to an end. "Grounded — Pearl Harbour," she wrote in her logbook on December 7, 1941. Over the next two years she continued to bombard the Department of National Defence with letters but the response was always the same: negative.

In December 1943 Eliane tried one last time. Hearing that a women's ferry group was being proposed she wrote an acquaintance, Major Grahame E. Joy, on December 29th asking if she would be eligible. He ducked the question and passed her letter onto his brother, Colonel Doug Joy, Acting Superintendent of Air Regulations. Colonel Joy, in his reply to his brother's letter, confirmed that the RCAF was indeed planning on training women pilots and said that it was such a recent decision that Eliane should "make application for service with the Department of National Defence for Air" herself. Unfortunately, the rest of the correspondence is missing; it is not known what reply Eliane received and a women's ferry group was never formed.

The brush-off by the military and the reorganization of the major bush companies into Canadian Pacific Airlines during the war spelled the end of Eliane's flying ambitions. Whether she ever approached McConachie after the war for a job with CPA is not known. Likely he would have found a place for her — at a desk. Raised in the north and able to handle herself in the wilderness, Eliane was no lightweight, physically or mentally. A strapping woman with a friendly no-nonsense manner, she was perfectly capable of moving freight, spending the night in the bush, or throwing a drunk off a plane. But the social conventions of the day ruled out any flying opportunities.

all on her own. But she wanted to fly and was determined to break into aviation."

To make contacts, Marjorie joined the Toronto Flying Club and then made the rounds of the aviation companies at Barker Field to inquire about work and instruction. Manning Airways, which called itself "an aviation college" and company providing "air transportation," sent her a standard letter explaining its program: "Dear Mr. Chauvin" it began. Marjorie set them straight about gender and, shortly after, on February 24, she received an acceptance into the "Ladies Class." As it turned out, no other "ladies" materialized, and she was the only woman in the class. Her next step was to build flying time, preferably at no cost to herself. To do this, she approached aircraft dealers with the pitch that a woman demonstrating aircraft would be good for sales. A natural saleswoman, she expounded on the publicity benefits of being the first company in Canada to have a woman demo pilot. Attractive, persuasive and charming, Marjorie soon won over "Red" Murray, the general manager at Century Airways.

Her life became unbelievably hectic. Because she needed the assurance of a steady income, she continued to hold a responsible full time office position while attending, twice a week, ground school for her commercial licence and demonstrating or ferrying aircraft around the province on weekends. When she finally had the required hours to begin her commercial flight instruction she still did not have the money. In June 1930 she tried another angle. She wrote to Fairchild Aircraft Limited in Montreal.

"Have you an opening for a lady pilot or a secretarial position in your Company?" she asked. "I obtained a Private Pilot's Licence last September in Edmonton, Alberta and desire to continue training for a Commercial Licence, but have no funds. I came East from Edmonton in the hope that I might secure a position with an Aviation concern who would be

Century Airways, Toronto, with two Aeroncas and a DH Cirrus Moth.

interested in helping me to fly, allowing me to pay part of my salary in each week or month, to help offset the expense." She then gave her age and business experience and stated that she was "confident" that she would give "satisfaction" in any type of office work. She closed by saying, "I believe I could be of advertising value to your Company as I understand there is not yet a lady Commercial Pilot in Canada." Clearly Fairchild did not think much of the idea for they did not reply.

Discouraged but ever optimistic, Marjorie approached the Aero Corporation of Canada, suggesting that they hire her as a secretary and in return for free flying, she would demonstrate aircraft. She argued that the Corporation had nothing to lose

ALMA GAUDRAU GILBERT

Alma Gaudrau was one of eleven children born in a little village in northern Quebec. She attended a school run by the nuns until she dropped out after grade nine. "I left to get away from Quebec where girls couldn't do very much. I didn't want my life like that so I went to the United States to learn English." In 1921 she returned to Canada and settled in a small town in Ontario where she worked as a telegraph operator. Five years later she pulled up stakes again and travelled west to Vancouver where she met and married pilot Frank Gilbert in 1928.

In 1930 Frank and Alma formed Gilbert's Flying Service at Sea Island Airport. They started with one aircraft, an Aeronca, CF-AQK, and one instructor, Hal Wilson, and offered instruction and charter services. Alma's place was on the ground doing the books. Unhappy with that arrangement she told her husband she wanted to learn to fly. He did not share her sentiments and made her wait until October 2, 1933 for her first lesson. She flew between paying customers and finally received PPL #1303 on April 7, 1934. Now she wanted a commercial licence. Not unexpectedly her husband said "No" and refused to discuss the matter further. "He didn't want a woman to be equal," explained Alma. He limited her flying to pleasure trips or the occasional ferry flight. With no one to back her, or money to go elsewhere, Alma had no choice but to comply with Frank's dictum.

Two ferry flights however were significant because of the distances involved, the lack of navigational aids available, and her relative inexperience. The first trip occurred in September 1935 when she flew an Aeronca, CF-BPW, from Cincinnati, Ohio, through the northern States to Vancouver. The trip took eight days and almost 39 hours of flying. Four years later she ferried another Aeronca, CF-BTR, from Middleton, Ohio via the Canadian prairies to Cranbrook, BC,

Alma Gaudrau seated in aircraft.

and everything to gain: an experienced executive secretary and the publicity of having a woman pilot. This time she was hired — as a secretary!

Being a demo pilot was neither an easy nor a secure way to make a living, particularly in the economic uncertainty of the depressed thirties. Certainly the life style was unconventional for a woman. Her hours were irregular as she would often be called upon, at a moment's notice, to ferry an aircraft to Montreal or to Toronto from the United States. A Toronto newspaper described Marjorie's job as follows:

"An important part of Miss Chauvin's duties is the putting through the Customs of planes coming in from the States. Over

Marjorie Chauvin and Jack Herity, Toronto, c. 1930.

south back to the States to by-pass the Rockies and north again to Vancouver.

During this period Alma also met the other women who, with her, would form The Flying Seven. In essence the group offered her a lifeline: the companionship of women who enjoyed flying and who shared her dream that women be allowed to fly professionally. For Alma, who had been on her own since her mid-teens and whose life had been one struggle after another, it must have been a satisfying moment when the six other women chose her as their first president.

Perhaps because of their encouragement, Alma took her commercial training even though it meant openly defying her husband. She received Commercial Licence #C-1974 on September 26, 1941. Immensely proud of her accomplishment at age 46, she made plans to obtain her instructor's rating. Unfortunately gasoline rationing came into effect and she was not allowed to begin. In fact, she never flew again. "I then tried to join the RCAF but they didn't want women." In 1945 Frank Gilbert sold the company to Al Michaud, who renamed it Vancouver U-Fly (it later became West Coast Air Services and then Air BC). Her rebellion against her husband, however, spelled the end of their relationship and a few years later, they were divorced.

Alma Gaudrau Gilbert was the first Canadian woman to be actively involved in an aviation company, albeit in a behind-the-scenes role. Nevertheless, she was a well-known figure in the field. Indeed, no one could miss her; petite with dark flashing eyes, a beguiling French accent, and a white flying suit topped off with a French beret, Alma caught everyone's eyes.

this portion of the work she is not enthusiastic, as often a whole afternoon is spent registering a single plane. Nor is hers a leisurely life, for in busy seasons she is at work at half-past eight, and her day frequently includes a morning of office duties, an afternoon of battling with customs officials, followed by an evening spent demonstrating planes at the flying field."

Marjorie thrived on the challenges that her job provided and accepted the misadventures that came her way with good humour. For instance, one ferry trip from Montreal to Toronto took three days because of strong headwinds. Looking for ways to make the trip enjoyable she followed the train tracks and, when the chance arose, "raced" the train. As her husband later

Alma Gaudrau Gilbert was hard to miss on the flying field, wearing a white flying suit topped off with a French beret.

related, "She could not keep up with it on the straight-away but would catch up with it on the curves. The engineer would toot his whistle whenever he caught sight of her." As it turned out, her husband's poor health made it difficult for Marjorie to continue her pursuit of a career in aviation. She stopped trying to combine an office job with flying and chose to give up flying and its irregular hours to devote more time to looking after her husband and to establishing herself in the business world.

Two women, Eliane Roberge and Margaret Fane, used their commercial licences to obtain office jobs with bush companies. Once their feet were in the door, they talked their bosses into checking them out in the company aircraft and allowing them to fly right seat as spotters in search and rescue missions. While neither woman had a paid flying position, they flew and had long and rewarding jobs in aviation.

MARGARET FANE of Edmonton, Alberta began a life-long love of aviation with her first airplane ride in 1928. Three years later the Trans-Canada Air Pageant appeared in Edmonton and that event inspired her to learn to fly. "My parents were both very air-minded; they flew in the first aircraft to arrive in Edmonton and my father helped to build a glider. He owned an auto repair shop and he encouraged me to take an interest in mechanical things." After two years of saving money she enrolled at the Northern Alberta and Edmonton Aero Club and received PPL #1317 on October 12, 1933. Of her instructor she said, "Moss Burbidge was terrific. I got nothing but help from him."

About this time she also began working towards her ham radio operator's licence and her air engineer's licence. Next she decided to improve her flying by taking her commercial training. That required another two years of saving. "I earned $22 a week and lessons were $12 an hour," said Margaret. "I used to do the club's bookkeeping and cover wings [stretch fabric over the wooden ribs] in return for free flying time." It took Margaret more than two years to accumulate enough time to take her commercial training but she received Commercial Licence A-1236 on August 29, 1935, the first woman in western Canada to do so.

In the fall of 1935, the Fanes moved to Vancouver and Margaret sorrowfully bade her friends at the flying club goodbye. They threw a going-away party and as a farewell gift to one of its most popular and enthusiastic members, the Edmonton Aero Club presented her with a watch on which was inscribed "We miss you. From the boys of the Northern Alberta and Edmonton Aero Club. Commercial Pilot 1935."

Once settled in a new job as a secretary/bookkeeper she headed for the airport where, to her delight, she discovered six other licenced women pilots — and helped to found The Flying Seven (see page 64). During the next busy years she divided her time between her job, the airport, and Flying Seven activities.

In 1935 Margaret knew that she stood no chance of being hired as a pilot. Instead she concentrated on improving her flying, obtained her ham radio licence and her radio operator's licence, perfected her technique in aircraft fabric work, and continued to work towards her mechanic's licence. In 1938 she got her first big break.

Ginger Coote of Ginger Coote Airways, a small bush company, needed a radio operator for his base at Zeballos, a mining town some 200 miles north of Victoria on Vancouver Island. Grant McConachie of Yukon Southern Air Transport recommended Margaret, whom he had known for many years. McConachie had just taken over Ginger Coote Airways as a subsidiary of Yukon Southern and set up a meeting between them. Coote was impressed with the stocky, efficient woman and hired her on the spot.

McConachie, who had a nose for publicity, informed the newspapers that Ginger Coote Airways had just hired the world's first female radio operator for an airways company. Whether that was correct (likely it was) did not concern him; business was business and Ginger Coote Airways needed publicity. Reporters loved the story and pictures of Margaret seated beside the radio set in Zeballos were splashed across the newspapers of western Canada.

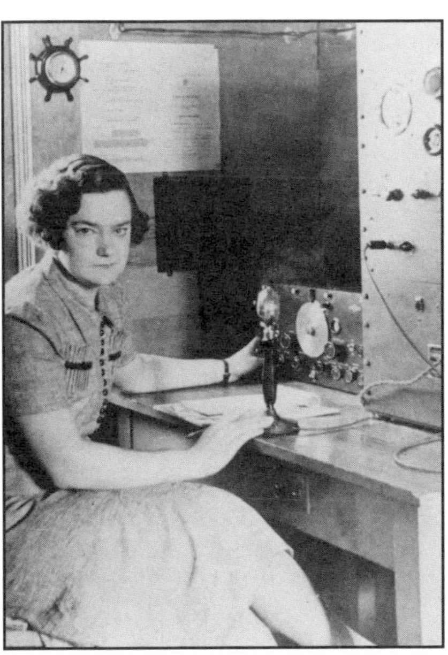

Margaret Fane was likely the first female airways radio operator in the world.

Although Margaret was one of three unmarried women among 1500 or so men in the town, neither Coote nor McConachie had any concern about her safety. Neither did she. With a no-nonsense manner and an easy sense of humour; she got along just fine. Hired as the radio operator, Margaret in reality was Ginger's girl Friday. As she explained, "I was supposed to be the radio operator but I also dispatched, did the waybills for the freight, tied up and fuelled aircraft, and herded loggers and miners on and off the planes. I took a dunking more than once while trying to push a drunk logger onto a plane. I also flew right seat in the Norseman when required." There were non-aviation duties as well. "Ginger used to bring 'the girls' in from Vancouver to Zeballos. Often I was the one sent to round them up for the trip. 'You will volunteer,' said

Ginger and, of course, I did. We used to call it the 'goat ranch!' For this I received a navy blue uniform with gold braid, brass buttons, and a set of wings. He paid me peanuts, sometimes bought me lunch, but I loved it."

Margaret handled nine "skeds" (scheduled flights) a day between Vancouver, Fort George, Fort St. John, and Zeballos. "I had to be in constant touch with the pilots, giving them on-route weather, information regarding passengers, cargo, and so on. When the company was short a pilot I flew, unofficially, as co-pilot. Most of my time was in the Norseman although I flew right seat in Grant's Barkley-Grow." Working for Ginger Coote, whom Margaret described a "real character," was never

ETHEL HIGDON

Ethel Higdon was born on a ranch in Medicine Hat, Alberta. War had not yet been declared when she decided to take lessons because she wanted to join the RCAF. The closest flying club was at Lethbridge, over one hundred miles away. "The instructor, Austin Currie, was amused when I showed up for lessons. He thought I was simply a girl with money looking for a thrill." When the club closed down she moved to Winnipeg to finish her training and received a private licence in August 1939. At the Winnipeg Flying Club she became close friends with Iva Coutts and they took their commercial training together. Ethel received Limited Commercial Licence C-1657 on January 8, 1940. Armed with two licences she applied to the Department of National Defence for pilot training. "I was informed that there was no provision for women pilots. I decided to become an instructor, but by then all the training was to be geared towards the war effort and I didn't get anywhere." The war marked the end of her flying but not her association with aviation because she married her former instructor, later a radio announcer, Austin Currie.

IVA COUTTS

Iva Coutts of Winnipeg, Manitoba, began flying lessons on a whim. She took instruction from Charlie Graffo of the Winnipeg Flying Club and received a private licence in June 1939 and a commercial licence in February 1940. "There were no grants for women so even if I was booked for a lesson and some man came along he got the lesson. I tried to get into the ATA (Air Transport Auxiliary, England) but they told me I was too short — I'm only five feet. I also tried the military but Cowley [A.T. Cowley, Superintendent of Air Regulations] said 'no women.' I managed to keep flying throughout the

dull. "I remember the day we went to Gun Lake to put in a radio station. He told me to fly the Norseman while he went back to read the newspaper. When we got there I called back to him to take over as I had never landed it by myself. He was sound asleep and too groggy to wake up — he liked his liquor. When we docked he fell off the float and I had to jump in after him. What a man!"

In 1941, the Canadian Pacific Railway bought ten bush companies, including Ginger Coote Airways, and amalgamated them to form Canadian Pacific Air Lines. Margaret was sent to the Vancouver office to handle the reservations, eventually becoming superintendent of reservations and traffic train-

war years. It was mostly ten minutes here and another ten minutes there — testing flying aircraft. Charlie Graffo had a contract to train TCA pilots for their instrument ratings and he let me check out the aircraft and also ferry planes to Fargo, North Dakota where they were serviced."

In 1935 Iva acquired her instructor's rating and worked part-time for Charlie Graffo while maintaining her position as an executive secretary. "I could not make a living flying. I got along well with everyone because I was not a threat; I was not after the airline jobs. Instructing was as far as a woman could go in those days. I remained in aviation as long as I did because I didn't make waves and I got along fine with the fellows because I proved I could fly. You had to earn their respect. The aviation community in those early years was very closeknit and I considered the airport my second home." Iva flew until 1968.

Ethel Higdon and Iva Coutts.

ing, the first woman to hold such a position. Being with Canadian Pacific Air Lines spelled the end of her flying days although, thanks to McConachie, she once flew as co-pilot in a passenger airliner, a Lockheed 14. It was during the war years. "One day he walked into my office and asked me what I was doing the next day. 'Nothing,' I said, 'It's my day off.' 'Good,' said Grant, 'then you can work for me. I need a co-pilot on the 14 to Edmonton.' It was not a passenger run but a test flight with Lockheed's test pilot. Grant and one test pilot took one of the Lodestars, and the other test pilot and I flew from Vancouver to Edmonton."

Margaret remained with Canadian Pacific Air Lines for twenty exciting years, travelling extensively over its routes, checking the reservations system, and implementing new systems. "Sometimes it seemed as if I was never home. Keith [Rutledge, her second husband. Her first husband, Gordon Scott of CPA, died in the 1950s] was with Okanagan Helicopters and sometimes we didn't see each other for weeks." Retired and living in Vancouver, Margaret is still a well-known figure in aviation circles. A member of the Quarter Century Club and other aviation groups, she remains almost as vigorous as she was fifty years ago.

ABOUT NINETY WOMEN received licences in the late twenties and thirties and of these, five qualified for their commercial licence and one obtained a public transport licence. Certainly those with commercial licences would gladly

Betsy Flaherty in The Flying Seven "uniform."

BETSY FLAHERTY (1891-1961)

Betsy Flaherty was the manager and buyer for The Flapper Shop at the exclusive David Spencer Store in Vancouver and travelled extensively with her job. She took her instruction at Minoru Park and received PPL #942 on December 19, 1931, the second woman in BC to become qualified. Although she was a well-liked member of The Flying Seven, the others always referred to her as "Mrs. Flaherty," probably because she was a fair bit older.

Gasoline rationing during World War II cut short her flying although she remained an avid air traveller until she retired. She was a member of United Air Lines 100,000 Mile Club, the first woman in Canada to be so honoured. She was also chosen to be the first woman passenger on Trans-Canada Airlines inaugural west to east flight across Canada in 1939.

have supported themselves by flying but no one would hire a woman pilot. Indeed many women who held private pilot licences would have gone to the expense of earning a commercial licence if there had been any indication of employment. In Canada not a single qualified woman pilot was hired as a pilot before World War II. It would take a world war to break down some of the barriers of discrimination against women pilots.

The only Canadian woman to be paid for actually flying before 1940 was Helen Harrison, who had moved to Cape Town, South Africa in the late thirties just when the Pretoria Flying Club was looking for someone to instruct reserve pilots for the Royal South Africa Air Force. Helen arrived at an opportune moment with all the desired qualifications: instructor's, multi-engine and instrument ratings and the latest instructor's "patter." She was too good a bargain to ignore and the club hired her. "All the instructors wanted to fly with me before taking their check rides. Even the chief flying instructor flew with me. He wasn't too pleased when I failed him though — he attempted to turn back on a simulated engine failure on take-off." She was South Africa's first woman flying instructor. What happened next was even more remarkable.

The Royal Air Force check pilot allowed Helen to take the military instructor check ride. "I was amazed that he would test me and even more amazed when he told me I could take the

Jean Pike, a member of The Flying Seven.

JEAN PIKE

Jean Pike was about nineteen when she joined The Flying Seven and records show that she received PPL #1844 on January 3, 1936. Very little is known about her. She and her brother ran a flying school in Vancouver until financial problems forced them to close it in 1937 and they left the city.

TOSCA TRASOLINI (1916-1991)

Tosca Trasolini was a charter member of The Flying Seven. According to her brother Norm, "She excelled at whatever she did, whether it was at school or in sports. She won gold and silver medals for running, discus, javelin, shotput, and broadjump and was a Canadian Women's Champion." Norm described her as an outgoing adventuresome person who looked upon flying as another challenge to meet. Tosca, a legal secretary, worked for one of the foremost criminal lawyers in BC when she received PPL #1942 on August 12, 1936.

refresher course at the Air Force base in Pretoria and be checked out as one of the civilian instructors for the Air Force. I was the only woman on the base and the first woman in the British Empire to fly and instruct on military aircraft. I flew the Avro Tutor and the Hawker Hart." Helen also filled in as a charter pilot for Airtaxi Limited. "She was quite a character and got along well with everybody," recalled K. Weinstein, an Airtaxi pilot. Fifty years later Helen said, "South Africa was the only country where I didn't have to battle to get ahead. I was accepted as a pilot."

If the women could not find jobs they could find support and comfort in each other's company, so they organized. On

The Flying Seven: (from left) Jean Pike, Tosca Trasolini, Eliane Roberge, Alma Gaudrau Gilbert, Betsy Flaherty, Margaret Fane, and Rolie Moore.

the west coast seven women pilots, all business women, organized themselves in 1936 into Canada's first all-female flying club. They called themselves The Flying Seven. The group was loosely organized and backed by little other than their love of flying and their wish to promote women in aviation. The seven charter members were Margaret Fane, Betsy Flaherty, Alma Gaudrau Gilbert, Rolie Moore, Jean Pike, Eliane Roberge, and Tosca Trasolini. They remained active until 1941.

THE FLYING SEVEN was the brainchild of Margaret Fane and was modelled roughly on its American counterpart, the 99s, the International Organization of Women Pilots, begun by Amelia Earhart in 1929. Since she had received her private pilot's licence in 1933, Margaret had been interested in getting together with other women pilots. As the Edmonton Aero Club's reporter for the Canadian Flying Clubs Association, her name was known to George Ross, executive secretary of the Association, who agreed with her interest. On December 13, 1933 he wrote to Margaret that he was sending a copy of the December issue of *Canadian Aviation*, which contained an article on the 99s, to every woman pilot in Canada. He suggested that if there were any interest in forming such a group in Canada that she lead it and offered help from the Canadian Flying Clubs Association. Nothing came of this initial attempt to organize but the idea was rekindled in 1935 when, on a visit to California, Margaret met Amelia Earhart. When she inquired about establishing a Canadian 99s chapter the Americans were lukewarm because of the small number of Canadian pilots. Once again the idea was put on hold. The following year the Fanes moved to Vancouver and when Margaret discovered six other women pilots at the airport, she broached the concept to them. They were interested and on October 15, 1936, The Flying Seven was born, with Alma Gaudrau Gilbert as the first president.

VANCOUVER, BRITISH COLUMBIA, THURSDAY, JUNE 20, 1940

'Flying Seven' Stages 'Bomphlet' Raid

While their aim was to encourage other women to fly and to promote higher flight standards within the aviation community, The Flying Seven was primarily a social group, having no constitution, bylaws, or formal structure. Members met once a month, usually for lunch or dinner, and were distinguished by their "uniform" — gray silk blouse, gray culottes, gray wool jacket, a gray Glengarry hat, and a Flying Seven pin. They even had their own logo, designed by member Rolie Moore, and it appeared on their stationery, briefcases, and Christmas cards.

For publicity they staged a novel "Dawn-to-Dusk" flight, an exhausting all-day flying rally in which one member was always in the air. The idea was Margaret's, who had taken part

A newspaper article about The Flying Seven activities in 1940.

in a similar event with the Edmonton Aero Club. Held at Sea Island airfield, each woman flew for about 25 minutes and, as her plane glided to a landing, another was waved for take-off. This venture was an ambitious effort for seven women who owned no aircraft and had little money. However, they did their homework well and found sponsors to cover the costs and donate aircraft. The day of the rally was bitterly cold and grey, but the public turned out in full force to watch Vancouver's aviatrixes perform. The press hailed The Flying Seven as "the forerunners of a splendid air movement that may some day give Canada its Mollison and Earhart." Over the next few years the group sponsored flying competitions and other events to improve pilot proficiency. A rosebowl, trophy, and cup, donated by others, added spice to winning.

Despite its small size, The Flying Seven was well-known in the area and was often asked to perform in airshows such as the 1938 Seattle airshow. In a letter dated March 27, 1940, the President of United Airlines expressed United's appreciation for "the splendid activities of your group in promoting the use of air mail and scheduled air transportation."

When Canada declared war members were prepared to fly for their country, and when The Flying Seven received a telegram from the Canadian Flying Club Association (which participated in the British Commonwealth Air Training Plan), asking for the names of the pilots with a commercial licence and more than 250 hours, it looked as if their chances had come. However, when Margaret promptly replied that three of the women had commercial licences and more than 250 hours and would be pleased to serve, the Association was no longer interested. ("Men only need apply" was the between-the-lines response.) Two members, Eliane Roberge and Jeanne Gilbert, did not accept the rejection without a fight and individually they appealed to the RCAF. Eliane went so far as to go to Ottawa to plead her case. Their efforts were unsuccessful.

In Vancouver the others realistically turned their energies in other directions and took part in various community projects to help the war effort. One of their most publicized events was the "bomphlet raid," as the newspapers termed it, in which they dropped over one hundred thousand pamphlets in the Vancouver area appealing for "dimes or dollars to buy our boys more planes." However, they realized their contribution would be minimal unless they could involve more women. They therefore sent out questionnaires in the Vancouver area asking women whether they would be interested in learning aviation-related skills. The response was so overwhelming that they quickly organized The Flying Seven Auxiliary (1940) to train women, with or without a pilot's licence, in parachute packing, fabric work, and theory of flight.

They also rented the Model Arts Building from the Vancouver School Board, obtained instructors, such as Terry Finney (chief flying instructor at #8 Elementary Flying Training School), and advertised their ground school courses in the newspapers. The Flying Seven was deluged with applications from women eager to learn and prepared to pay the $3 fee. Fifty women from over three hundred applicants were chosen for the first course. Carter Guest, a civil aviation inspector, was the featured speaker for the opening night. In true military fashion a half hour of drill preceded the lecture. The first session was so successful that The Flying Seven made plans to offer another. But, as it turned out, further courses were unnecessary because the Women's Division of the RCAF was formed in July 1941 and instituted similar courses. The *raison d'etre* of The Flying Seven Auxiliary was wiped out. In later years reporters would call The Flying Seven an advance wave of the women's liberation movement. This was denied by Margaret and Rolie who would not admit to prejudice against them. Asserted Margaret, "If we were discriminated against we didn't realize it at the time."

After the war the original members of The Flying Seven dispersed and the few who remained in Vancouver made no attempt to regroup. If they had been able to expand their membership significantly before the war The Flying Seven might have survived. However, only five other women (Beryl Armstrong, Jeanne Gilbert, Dorothy Renton, Joyce Bond, and Iva Coutts) had joined the original seven and two of them were from out of province. The Flying Seven had tried to become national by writing to other Canadian women pilots but the great distances and the small number of women pilots worked against the group's expansion and war spelled its ultimate demise.

The Flying Seven existed for a scant five years but it should not be lightly dismissed. Through their competitions that promoted flying skills, their support of general aviation and the war effort, the women showed that they could be more than mere decorative additions to airfields. It was the first time in Canada that women pilots had formally organized themselves and they certainly raised the profile of women in the aviation world.

WHILE THE WEST COAST WOMEN found only support roles, five women in Toronto were in the right place at the right time. In the early forties, until the British Commonwealth Air Training Plan was fully operational, flying instructors were desperately required. Helen Harrison, Marion Powell Orr, Marion Gillies, Margaret Littlewood, and Violet Milstead were qualified and on the spot. All were hired.

Helen Harrison, for example, returned to Canada from

Helen Harrison, c. 1933.

HELEN HARRISON

Helen Harrison, born in Vancouver, British Columbia, had an undisciplined childhood. The Harrisons moved to England when she was in her early teens and, in an attempt to control their unruly daughter, her parents sent her to boarding school. After graduation, Helen drifted aimlessly until a handsome young soldier caught her eye. They married and Helen soon had three babies. Unhappy with her situation at the age of twenty-four, a chance joy ride in the summer of 1933 so thrilled her that she knew she had to make flying her life's work. Telling no one, she enrolled for lessons and received her "A" Licence (private pilot) on March 4, 1934. "I learned more than flying. The day I passed my test the other students and instructors took me to the local pub and gave me my first drink. It was a Pimm's No. 1. I soon learned to drink, smoke, and swear!"

The next year, leaving her children in the care of her mother and a nanny, Helen took off for Singapore to visit her instructor. While there she qualified for her seaplane rating on a Gipsy Moth, possibly the first woman in the British Empire to do so and certainly the first Canadian woman. On her return to England she began working towards her "B" Licence (commercial), which she received on November 12, 1936, with the proviso that she have a medical every four months (it was six months for men). For the next ten months Helen "built time" and on September 10, 1937 flying a de Havilland Dragonfly, she qualified for her instructor's, multi-engine, and instrument ratings, the first Canadian woman to receive these licences. Shortly after, she moved with her family to South Africa (see page 63) and became the first woman in the British Empire to fly and instruct on military aircraft, flying the Avro Tutor and the Hawker Hart.

England in early 1940. Without a doubt she was one of the most experienced pilots anywhere. She held commercial, instructor's, multi-engine, and instrument licences from England, South Africa, the United States and Canada and had accumulated over 2600 hours on a variety of civilian and military aircraft. She was likely the first woman in the world to hold a commercial licence in four countries. However, as qualified as she was, she found it tough to find work. "I couldn't find anything in Toronto or Ottawa so I hung around the Cub factory in Hamilton until I was hired as a test pilot," recalled Helen. "The test flying wasn't much. All I did was put the aircraft into a spin and do a few other checks on it." She next instructed provisional pilot officers at the Kitchener-Waterloo Flying Club. Doubtless her colleagues and students have some vivid memories of their vivacious blonde instructor.

"She could swear like a trooper," recalled Florence Elliott, who was the club's secretary. "We used to sit outside the hangar while she glided a student in and we could hear her yelling, 'Keep your bloody nose on the horizon!'" Said Helen, "Those RCAF officers kept me on my pins with all their questions. I'd be rough and tough with them. Once in the air I wasn't male or female; I was an instructor. We got along fine." Already Helen was beginning to build a reputation, one that would remain with her during her thirty-five years in aviation. Interestingly, her manner did not appear to affect her popularity as an instructor.

Years later one of her students recalled his time with her. "I'll never forget my first flight. If there was anything that could be done wrong I did it. In fact, I probably invented a few new wrong things right on the spot. When we landed Miss Harrison let me have it. I hadn't exactly lived a cloistered existence but I wasn't quite used to hearing ladies use such colourful language. It was a classic performance. Never before, nor since,

Helen Harrison, c. 1933.

had I been so roundly roasted. She finally said, 'Now taxi back and try it again.' I did everything right this time. I went solo with a grand total of 4:35 hours of dual instruction. To this day I don't know if I would have made it with two or three times that amount of dual had she not chewed me up in little pieces and spit me out. I still fly and of all the people I've come across in my long, long, love affair with aviation, none is remembered so well, nor with such special affection, as I remember Helen."[3]

Helen's next position was as chief flying instructor at the Air Transport and Training Company Limited at Toronto Island Airport until it closed in late 1941. Then, in her usual style, she seized the initiative and entered the most exciting and challeng-

Marion Powell Orr, c. 1940.

MARION POWELL ORR

Marion Powell Orr was born in Toronto. Her father died when she was two and her mother when she was fifteen, forcing her to leave school. She worked and saved for six years before she could afford her lifelong dream — flying lessons. Like Violet Milstead she took her instruction from Pat Patterson of Flyers Limited at Barker Field. Marion found it hard going with lessons at $9 an hour and her salary at $12 a week, but she received her private pilots licence on January 5, 1940. She supplemented her income working as an aircraft inspector at de Havilland, and after two years had enough hours to qualify for her commercial licence, (C-2029) which she received on December 12, 1941. Marriage to Doug Orr, her instructor, an instructor's rating, and a job at the St. Catherine's Flying Club followed shortly after. Unfortunately a fire at the club six months later destroyed the hangar, the aircraft, and her job.

Flying positions were scarce in 1942; gas rationing was in effect at the civilian flying schools and other schools were converting to the needs of the British Commonwealth Air Training Plan. Marion was able to get work at Goderich Airport as an air traffic control assistant, the second woman in Canada to qualify. "Air traffic control was pretty primitive but we were busy because No. 12 Elementary Flight Training School was operating at Goderich," she said. For awhile it looked as if that was as close to flying as she was going to get until the war ended. Frustrated to see men with little or no experience being accepted for pilot training while she was grounded, Marion jumped at the chance when Vi Milstead told her about the Air Transport Auxiliary and within two months they were on their way to England.

ing flying of her career — as a ferry pilot with the Air Transport Auxiliary.

In Toronto, longtime friends Marion Gillies and Margaret Littlewood were instructing at Gillies Flying Service. In fact, Fred Gillies, owner of the company and Marion's father, had placed the management of the flying school in the hands of Marion and Margaret. They remained there until gasoline rationing shut the flying school down. As Canadian men were eager to qualify as pilots, there was no lack of students for Marion and Margaret. When asked how women flying instructors were accepted in the early forties, Margaret's answer, tactfully phrased, summed up what the others generally experienced. For the most part the men accepted them as capable. "An occasional student would be shocked when he saw his instructor was a women, but once I got him up in the air it was okay. Besides, there was a war on and men wanted to learn to fly to get into the RCAF easier. Only one man refused to fly with me, until one day he came in without an appointment and had to take me if he wanted a lesson. After that he always asked for me because he felt I had more patience and explained things better. I think the men were less averse to displaying fear or relief to a woman instructor." As an example, Margaret told of the time she and a student had an engine-failure on a cross country flight. "I turned around to tell my student that I had control and it was something to see. There he was, feet and hands in the air and saying, 'It's all yours, Margaret.' When we landed and rolled to a stop I felt two arms go around my neck from the back seat!" Margaret and Marion were so popular they often received presents from their students. "It was mostly boxes of chocolates but sometimes jewellery, which I never had a chance to wear. I hardly ever got into girl-type clothing. We were working twelve to sixteen hours a day, seven days a week and I never went anywhere but to the airport. I hardly ate, I was so busy."

Margaret Littlewood and Marion Gillies.

Violet Milstead received her commercial licence in April of 1940. She then owned and managed her family's wool shop in Toronto, but managed to fly regularly. This is her own story of those exciting early war years.

"Organization and construction work were rushing ahead to get the great British Commonwealth Air Training Plan producing aircrew. Flight training airports were being built from coast to coast at a fantastic rate. Pilots would be needed to staff them. But where could they be found? Once the plan was rolling, the RCAF would be able to train all the pilots it required, but it was not yet rolling. To get it going, the RCAF looked to the civilian flying schools. About the first of June 1940, a telegram was sent out from Ottawa. It must have gone to just about every man who ever held a commercial licence in Canada, inviting him to enlist in the RCAF as a flying instructor. After a quick, intensive instructor's course at Central Flying School, Trenton, he would be posted to one of the rapidly opening Elementary Flying Training Schools. These schools would be civilian-operated for some reason best known to the powers-that-be. The instructors would be on leave of absence from the Air Force, in civilian clothes, in the pay of the civilian schools. So the exodus began. It thinned the ranks of my friends

Margaret Littlewood going for instructors "ride" at CFB Trenton.

MARGARET LITTLEWOOD

Margaret Littlewood of Toronto began flying lessons quite by chance. At the time she was working full-time at Eaton's Mail Order and part-time writing a sports column for a Toronto newspaper. The year was 1938 and Fred Gillies and his wife and daughter had just moved to Toronto. Gillies, a World War I pilot and well-known barnstormer, had just formed Gillies Flying Service and wanted the publicity of having a girl take flying lessons. His daughter Marion agreed provided he also teach her friend Margaret. "I thought the idea was great," recalled Margaret.

They trained on a Piper Cub and received their licences on August 3, 1938. Both were such good pilots that Gillies asked them to take their commercial and instructor's training and work for him. Margaret continued working at Eaton's and it took her two more years to qualify. She received CPL, C-1840 on October 31, 1940. A few months later she completed her instructor's training and went to the RCAF Base at Trenton where she was required to take her flight test. After a traumatic test (see page 29) she received her instructor's rating in January 1941 and began teaching full-time at Gillies Flying Service.

around the flying school but the obvious opportunities for pilots which it revealed brought in many new people and business was booming.

"What the Americans called the 'phoney war' had been going on for some months with nothing much happening . . . Then, early in May 1940, all hell broke loose. Blitzkrieg! A British army was soundly defeated in the field, the miracle of Dunkirk, the fall of France, the retreat to the British Isles and, that summer, the Battle of Britain with all its horrors, not the least of which was the distinct possibility that Britain, too, would fall. No doubt this new view of the war was responsible for a great expansion in the already vast plans for air training in Canada. At some point it became apparent to the Air Force that their supply of potential flying instructors, young men who were taking flying training at the civilian schools at their own expense, was drying up and that they, the Air Force, were not yet ready to pick up the slack from their own resources. So they began enlisting potential flying instructors and contracting with the civilian schools for their training. More business. Bonanza!

"The Air Training Plan had pilot requirements other than flying instructors. Air Observers Schools were opening across the country to train navigators and bomb-aimers. They also were civilian-operated and most of their flying staff was in training at schools like P & H Aircraft during 1940-1942. A frantic ferment of activity was going on in all branches of the aviation industry from one end of the country to the other, and this was not an unqualified joy to the civilian schools. For example, the North Atlantic Ferry Command was recruiting pilots to fly bombers overseas; the Air Observers Schools were flying all twin-engine equipment and paying good money. Some of the lads were leaving flying instruction to take on these different challenges. It was this fluid situation that created my next objective.

"Some time during May 1941 Pat Patterson of Patterson and Hill Aircraft suggested that I go for an instructor's licence. He would underwrite the training and I would pay him back from my earnings while instructing for P & H Aircraft. Pat was my friend. But he was not being altruistic. By this time I had about twice the flying hours required for an instructor's licence, but there were other considerations. Girls simply did not become RCAF elementary flying instructors; girls did not fly for the Air Observers Schools or with the North Atlantic Ferry Command. Therefore, Pat would be acquiring an instructor who would be expected to stay with him as long as needed. How long might that be? All of us understood very clearly that civilian flying training would cease as soon as the Air Force could produce its own pilot requirements. We were flying on borrowed time.

"Needless to say, my answer was never in doubt. I accepted Pat's offer. However, it would mean that I would be employed full time at the airport. What about my wool shop? Looking back, it is quite remarkable how things worked out. A friend of mine gave up her job to enter a partnership with me in the wool

VIOLET MILSTEAD WARREN

Violet Milstead was seventeen when she decided to fly. Captivated by her dream she read everything she could find about flying and worked at her mother's wool shop to earn money for lessons. In September 1939 she enrolled at Pat Patterson's Flyers Limited at Barker Field in Toronto. "Pat encouraged anyone with two feet and the money," observed Vi, "he was looking for business." Patterson became her friend and mentor. Learning on a 40 horse-power Piper Cub, CF-BIT, she received her private pilots licence on December 20, 1939.

Flying was everything she dreamed it would be. "I felt alive in a way I had never before imagined." She obtained a commercial licence in April 1940, the eleventh woman in Canada to do so. "My objective in learning to fly was mostly to gratify a totally absorbing interest in flying . . . but after the commercial licence, then what?" Vi knew that there were no professional women pilots in Canada and that women were ineligible for the RCAF.

A solution came when Patterson asked her to instruct for him. With the war machine gobbling up flying instructors a woman instructor would be a valuable commodity since she would not leave for the military. Vi went to the RCAF base at Trenton for her instructor's flight test and took her test on an aircraft that she had never flown before. "I can state very definitely that the experience was unnerving in anticipation . . . However I was treated with every courtesy, even gallantry, by all I met there. The officer conducted the test in a very professional manner . . . and contrived to make me feel that he was privileged to be picked for it." Vi earned the following written commendation from RCAF examiner Tony Shelfoon, "A smooth pilot who should do well as an instructor." She received her instructor's rating in July 1941, one of five women to do so before the end of World War II.

shop. We ran it until wartime shortage of materials compelled us to close it.

"So once again, I was striving towards a flying licence. It was by no means all new work. Immediately after I had completed my commercial licence I had taken some dual instruction on 'patter,' that is, learning to synchronize the form of words used to teach a flying lesson with the actual demonstration of the manoeuvre, and I had flown a few times practising patter with another student-instructor. For financial reasons I had given up any idea of obtaining an instructor's licence. I had, however, kept a copy of the 'patter book,' officially known as 'The Sequence of Flying Instruction.' The first logbook entry for

GIRL FLIER TAUGHT BY GIRL WINS INSTRUCTOR RANK IN R.C.A.F. TEST

...PT SHE WON an instructor's rating after a gruelling ...A.F. test flight. Instructor Margaret Littlewood is ...ed from the plane by Wing Commander Carling-Kelly.

FIRST GIRL PILOT in Canada to be trained by another girl for her instructor's qualifications, Margaret Littlewood, 24, Toronto, is congratulated by Flight Lieut. D. F. McTavish, left, and Flying Officer J. F. Reid.

SUCCESS CROWNED the efforts of Marion Gillies a qualified instructor who taught the same course to Miss Littlewood. This is Miss Gillies in the cockpit of her plane.

PLUGS 4 YEARS IN A.M.'S
COACHED BY GIRL FRIEND
NOW AIR INSTRUCTRESS

Vi worked full-time at Patterson & Hill Aircraft Ltd, instructing from dawn to dusk. P&H trained pilots going into the service and many of Vi's students became staff pilots at the civilian-operated Air Observer Schools. In November of 1942 civilian training ceased. At loose ends, Vi was open to suggestions when Jack Ball, another P&H pilot, told her about the Air Transport Auxiliary. Marion Orr was interested too and the three of them applied. With close to 1000 hours, Vi had no problem meeting the minimum requirements or passing the flight test on the Harvard. "This was the first flight for either Marion or myself in an airplane with so much power and performance, not to mention retractable undercarriage. I don't recall any problems; there was just a little more plane in front and back of me. It was a joy to fly and the RCAF instructor was satisfied with us." Vi and Marion sailed for England on April 19, 1943.

L *A newspaper article about women pilots' involvement in the war effort.*

R *Violet Milstead.*

this new era was June 6, 1941, 1 hour 10 minutes dual on patter in a Fleet biplane CF-CHE. In July I joined the ranks of professional pilots as an instructor for P & H Aircraft, Barker Field. A few of my students were women — Mary Spearing, Dorothy Craw, Sally Kerton (Wagner) and Flight Officer Molly Beall, RCAF, Women's Division. Molly Beall became Molly Reilly, probably Canada's outstanding woman pilot of her generation."

During the next year Patterson turned more and more of the school's management over to Vi, who soon found herself working from dawn to dusk. "The pace was fast and the news from overseas added a sort of charged-up urgency to the air. Then things began to wind down. In November 1942 our civilian flying training ceased. I was in the air five times during December, test flying five RCAF Tiger Moths after overhaul in P & H Aircraft shops. It was nice of Pat to give me these lollipops. There were no more. The month of January 1943 appears in my logbook as one lonely entry. On the 29th I flew Stinson CF-BLD cross-country from Toronto to Windsor. I can't remember what for, except that Marion Orr was on the expedition so there were two airplanes. This flight closed my civilian logbook for the duration." However, like Helen Harrison and Marion Orr, Vi did not remain grounded for long.

CHAPTER FOUR

World War II

"When I applied to the RCAF I was rejected because I wore a skirt. I was furious. I just couldn't believe it. I had 2600 hours, an instructor's rating, multi-engine and instrument endorsements, a seaplane rating, and the experience of flying civil and military aircraft in three countries. Instead they took men with 150 hours." — *Helen Harrison*

WORLD WAR II BEGAN, as usual, as a man's war, but manpower shortages eventually forced the three Canadian services to accept women for war work. Forty-five thousand women served in support groups: the Women's Division of the Royal Canadian Air Force, the Canadian Women's Army Corps, and the Women's Royal Canadian Naval Service. However, despite the severe shortage of pilots, the military refused to consider women for pilot training. Indeed, women in the RCAF in any role were anathema to its tradition. It took more than three years before the Women's Division was established — and flying was not on the agenda.

The Department of National Defence (DND) did not keep records of the number of women who applied for pilot training. "The idea of women in the RCAF was such a preposterous notion that there was no need for any documentation on it.

Everyone knew that women were too high strung, came apart under stress, and were too weak to fly the big planes," was a DND official's tongue-in-cheek explanation in 1984. It seems likely that hundreds of women tried to get on as aircrew. Rejected, they sought, individually and in groups, to change the RCAF eligibility requirements or, alternatively, to form a civilian organization. But to no avail. The following excerpt sums up the military's attitude. ". . . the present policy does not allow the use of women ferry pilots, nor for any other RCAF flying duties," wrote Group Captain M. Costello, on behalf of the Chief of Air Staff, DND, to Eliane Roberge, who had written on May 27, 1943 to inquire about a women's ferry group. He added, "It would not be feasible to use women as much of the ferrying would be done over isolated territory, such as in northern Ontario and Quebec and in the event of a forced landing special accommodations for women would have to be made." This response was typical of military thinking but interestingly, it was not unanimous, for the letter arrived with an unsigned memorandum, which stated another officer's viewpoint. "I personally don't think Group Captain Costello's excuse for not using women pilots is a good one. True, ferrying in northern Ontario and Quebec may be difficult, but there still remains a good deal of country which could be considered safe for women pilots. Also, regarding special accommodations for women — neither the U.S.A. nor England had these facilities previous to the women who took over their ferry duties."

For the women already licenced it was a frustrating time. As instructor Margaret Littlewood bitterly commented, "I had worked and studied for five years and then I found my country couldn't or wouldn't make use of what I had learned."

Consideration may, in fact, have been given to the recruitment of women for pilot training in the winter of 1943-44. Margaret Rankin-Smith and Daphne Paterson, who had reliable contacts in DND, were told that a special women's pilot group would be formed, and a letter from Doug G. Joy, Acting Superintendent, Air Regulations, Department of Transport, dated January 6, 1944, stated that arrangements had recently been made for training women pilots. The fact that nothing concrete materialized was likely due to the late date; by 1944 the urgency of the military situation had lessened and additional pilots were simply not required.

Very few options were open to women who wanted to fly

for the war effort. In Canada, officially, nothing was available. In actual fact, one woman, Margaret Littlewood, was hired as a Link Trainer instructor at one of the civilian schools operated under the authority of the British Commonwealth Air Training Plan. Four Canadian women managed to fly for Great Britain's Air Transport Auxiliary (ATA), a civilian organization formed to ferry aircraft, and Virginia Lee Warren of Winnipeg, who had dual American/Canadian citizenship, flew with an American civilian organization called the Women's Airforce Service Pilots (WASPs).

There was so little publicity about the ATA and WASPs however that most Canadian women were unaware of the existence of these opportunities. Those who wished to serve in a military capacity enlisted in one of the three women's service groups. Many joined the Women's Division of the RCAF, but some were so angry at being rejected by the air force for pilot duties that they joined the army or the navy or turned their backs on the military altogether. Pilots and aspiring fliers could hardly be content with the Women's Division motto: "We Serve That Men May Fly."

MARGARET LITTLEWOOD found herself out of a job in the fall of 1942 when the flying school where she had been instructing closed because of gas rationing. "I didn't bother to apply to the RCAF because I already knew the answer. Vi Milstead, Marion Orr, Helen Harrison, and I had met earlier to see if we could come up with a plan to get the RCAF to use women pilots, but nothing came of it. I didn't want to let all that training and knowledge go to waste so I wrote to all ten of the Air Observer Schools (AOS), which were run by civilians. I said that I could relieve a man for other duties and suggested that I could be a flying instructor or a Link Trainer (instrument flight simulator) instructor. I received nine refusals: reading between the lines I could tell it was because I was female. However, Wop May, the manager of No. 2 AOS Edmonton, telegraphed me and told me I had a job as a Link Trainer instructor if I were interested. He was not a man to dilly-dally with problems. He thought I was qualified and he didn't care that I was a woman. He had always been an aviation pioneer and proved it again by hiring me: the only woman Link Trainer instructor in Canada during the war."

Margaret arrived in Edmonton February 1, 1943 and

immediately began training for the examination in March. "Even though I had 1000 hours flying time, I had no instrument time so I found it difficult at first." Added to the stress of learning to operate the Link was the strain of being the only woman pilot on the base. "I knew everyone was watching every little move I made. I found out later there had been a lot of talk when Wop had hired me. The men had laid bets that I was some old dame with a hatchet face and size twelve shoes!"

Margaret taught 140 men radio range procedures and advanced instrument flying. "I thought I would be teaching elementary Link Trainer work and when I learned I'd be working with airline and senior pilots with thousands of hours I felt overwhelmed. Wop had smoothed the way for me by saying that I was a highly qualified pilot although most of my students knew more about flying than I did and it was a learning experience for both of us. I found most of the men willing to share their knowledge with me. They often took me flying and I got in a lot of unofficial hours on Ansons." Likely the fact that Margaret was a good-looking twenty-four year old with sparkling eyes, a ready smile, and an agreeable disposition helped. She had the utmost respect for Wop May. As she said, "I'm proud to have been associated with such a great person. He was a stickler for perfection and it paid off as No.2 AOS won the Efficiency Pennant for all ten schools most of the years they were in operation."

Margaret Littlewood at No. 2 Air Observer School, Edmonton, with an unidentified student, c. 1943. Margaret was Canada's only female Link Trainer instructor.

All pilots and instructors were required to take courses in astro navigation and aerial photography, and to drop one incendiary bomb. "After the classroom session we were assigned to an Anson V for the practical portion. I hadn't got too much out of the classroom part and worried that I might drop the bomb on someone's house. One of the senior pilots told me not to fuss, that he would help me. I don't think I impressed anyone that day. I could barely move in my quilted flight suit, which was too big. I also had on big boots and the only way I could climb into the plane was by belly-flopping across the wing. When it came my turn to drop the bomb the other pilot and I could barely squeeze into the bubble compartment that held the camera and bombsight. Words can't describe both of us trying to slide into the compartment. I never did see the target but found out the next day I was only 140 yards off."

One of the few times Margaret ran afoul of Wop May was over the question of her uniform. "I was supposed to wear a flannel jacket with pocket crest and a medium gray straight skirt. But I decided to wear gray serge slacks since I had to climb up on the trainer and skirts were not practical. I had quite a job convincing Mr. May that I should wear slacks but after some arguing he said I could when I dropped the subtle hint that I may as well go back to Toronto." Evidently Wop was pleased with Margaret for he often recommended her to speak at various functions. Reporters were also pleased to feature her and often billed her as the "Queen of the Link."

In May 1944 No.2 AOS closed and Margaret, at the request of Ferry Command, went to Dorval to instruct on the new Link Trainer on order. With over 1200 flying hours and approximately 250 hours on Ansons, not to mention her time on the Link, she was well qualified. However, when she arrived she found that the order for the new trainers had been cancelled. "I was really disappointed. I'd come to love that little airplane on the pedestal." Margaret remained at Ferry Command in the Crew Assignment Office until war's end.

The Air Transport Auxiliary

THE ATA MOTTO WAS "Aetheris Avidi" — Eager for the Air. But Don Miller, a former Royal Air Force (RAF) pilot recalled, "We called them 'Ancient and Tattered Aviators.' They flew everything with wings from factory to active squadrons." The Air Transport Auxiliary was a civilian organization formed in 1939 to fly support roles in order to release servicemen for other duties. Too old, physically disabled, female, or otherwise ineligible for the RAF, ATA pilots were drawn from Britain and twenty-two other countries. What began, in 1939, with twenty-seven male pilots flying Tiger Moths grew to 1318 pilots, 166 of them women. They flew ninety-nine different types of aircraft from twenty-two bases in the United Kingdom. At its peak ATA staff totalled 3555, including aircrew, ground staff, and RAF attached personnel. The immensity of its wartime operation can be summarized in two statistics: 309,011 aircraft ferried and 414,984 hours flown.[4]

Although 154 ATA personnel were killed on active duty, as civilians they were ineligible for military medals. Operational pilots surely won the war but just as surely ATA pilots sustained them. In fair weather and foul, these civilians ferried airplanes to and from the squadrons. ATA pilots flew with little fanfare and went almost unnoticed; twenty-seven of them were Canadian, and four of these pilots were women.

The ATA was conceived in the months immediately preceding the war. The plan was to use civilian pilots who were ineligible for the RAF for duties such as the transport of mail, news, dispatches, and medical supplies. However, by September of 1939 the military was asking the ATA to ferry service aircraft and this soon became its main function.

In the beginning there was virtually no organization or training. Potential ferry pilots were simply checked out on light aircraft and off they flew. But, when given the task of ferrying more complex service aircraft, the necessity for training *on type* became apparent. What evolved was a unique training system and the formation of an Elementary Flying Training School (the "infants school") at Barton-in-the-Clay, an Initial Flying Training School at Thame, and an Advanced Flying Training School at White Waltham. By the early forties, when the Canadian women arrived, all schools and ATA itself were in full operation.

The ATA was controlled functionally by the Ministry of Aircraft Production, operationally by #41 Group RAF, and administratively by the British Overseas Airways Corporation. Entirely self-contained, ATA had its own medical staff, engineers, transportation, training, taxi aircraft, and pilots. Initially applicants had to be male, twenty-eight to fifty years of age, and have a minimum of 250 hours of flight time. In November 1939 the Air Ministry allowed the entry of eight similarly-qualified women pilots for limited flying duties. In time, more women were added but their entry was gradual, with die-hard resistance to be overcome at every step. (A witticism of the day was "the hand that rocks the cradle wrecks the crate.")

The pressure on these first eight women was great. Although all were commercial pilots, each with over 1000 hours' experience, they felt treated like beginners. They flew knowing their every action would be closely scrutinized and their performance would determine whether more women would be recruited. In that first long dreary winter the women were restricted to flying Tiger Moths and they moved over 2000 without an accident. It was cold monotonous work but occasional humour was also memorable. They were required to fly in "gaggles" (groups of four) — to make it easier for the Observer Corps. "Four of us," recalled one of the women, "were flying up the Severn Valley, when we got caught in a snowstorm. When we came out, we were seven, having some-

A typical between-flights ATA scene.

how picked up three more Tiger Moths in the middle of it!"

The fall of France in 1940, the step-up in aircraft production, and the desperate need for more service pilots, some of whom were tied up with ATA-type operations, forced the ATA to recruit more pilots. Officials had little choice but to consider more women. But it was with reluctance, for they had intended to limit the women to flying only non-operational aircraft. Even so it was a welcome step forward for the women because until then they had been allowed to fly only Tiger Moths. Now they could tackle Oxfords, Dominies, Magisters, and Masters and, within the year, they were also flying such obsolete military aircraft as the Battle and the Lysander.

Ferry pilots wore a distinctive uniform, which had to be

tailor-made. When in 1941 British pilots Margot Gore and Phillippa Bennett walked into the tailor shop selected by the ATA, they found that they were the first women to cross its threshold. Its tailors had never made a garment for a woman, much less measured one, and their appearance caused much consternation. Two old gentlemen retired behind a screen and after a whispered debate emerged to say that they would see what could be done. Two different elderly gentlemen were brought out to take measurements. They started with Margot and as Allison King described the process, "Length of sleeve, both from shoulder to elbow and elbow to wrist, had gone swimmingly, but his approach to the bust had, they thought, been unusual. He would take a few quick steps, throw the tape measure round her back, catch it in mid-air and, turning his head away as if he couldn't bear to look, wait until the two ends met before giving a fleeting glance to the number of inches it recorded. Then he whispered his findings into Mr. Hix's hairy ear, as if they were too awful a secret to bear alone. Waist and hips again went swimmingly, although the secret numbers were again imparted in a whisper." When Margot and Phillippa told them they needed trousers as well as a skirt, there was another consultation and more eye-rolling before the two decided they could tackle the lower female form with a tape measure.

The result of all this was a dark blue uniform that was the same cut and style as the RAF Officer's uniform but different in colour, rank insignia, pilot's wings, and buttons. For flying duties all pilots, women and men, wore regulation navy blue overalls without flying badges but with rank stripes. On ceremonial occasions — Helen Harrison didn't remember any ceremonial occasions except funerals — women had to wear skirts with plain black stockings and low-heeled shoes, and their hair could not go below the collar.

A pilot was classed as "Cadet" until graduation from Initial Flight Training School and then might move through Third Officer, Second Officer, First Officer, Flight Captain, Captain Commander, Senior Commander, and Commodore. By the time the Canadians arrived pilots were being promoted more slowly with the result that none advanced beyond First Officer. Only British women pilots progressed to the higher ranks.

Good friends, Marion Orr and Violet Milstead c. 1943, in brand-new ATA uniforms.

IN 1941 THE EXIGENCIES OF WAR again forced authorities to make more use of women. The general war outlook remained gloomy. Good weather in March resulted in renewed attacks by German bombers and Britain was once again reeling under the effects of the Blitz. Service pilots were so desperately needed that the RAF withdrew entirely from ferry operations and the ATA assumed the task of flying aircraft from the maintenance units to the squadrons. It quickly became evident that *all* ATA pilots had to be used to their maximum potential and that meant using the women to fly operational aircraft.

Finally, in July of 1941, authorities allowed four of the original eight women to take the conversion course for operational aircraft. All passed easily. As luck would have it however one of the women almost immediately blew a tire landing a Hurricane and serious discussion once more ensued as to whether women were, after all, suitable. But the dust eventually settled and all of the women with the ATA completed their training.

The Trans-Atlantic Ferry Organization was formed in November 1940 to facilitate the transport of men and aircraft to Europe. No women pilots were permitted.

While converting to the Hurricane was the breakthrough, flying the Spitfire was every pilot's "dream come true." For the first time women were on their way to working on an equal basis with the men. Still, the women had to fight for each new type of aircraft. Sometimes it seemed as if past performance didn't count. For example, the women were told that they had to make *ten* satisfactory solo landings in the Halifax for their four-engine checkout; men had to make six. Even when they proved they could fly the heavy bombers the women often heard, "You'll never be able to hold'em dear if one engine cuts."

In November of 1941 further changes occurred. No. 6 Ferry Pilots Pool at Ratcliffe was opened to four women. For Lettice Curtis, one of the original women pilots, it was an intimidating experience. As related in her 1971 book, *The Forgotten Pilots*, "No. 6 Pool had collected a band of relatively young, tough, and self-assured pilots, many of them American, who liked to think of themselves as the dead-end kids who could deliver their aircraft when even the birds were walking . . . Ratcliffe was no place to which to be posted for the first time in the fogs of winter." Her first assignment came when the weather was poor. Unwilling to be seen as "chicken" she took off. "The cloud was low, the visibility poor and the Spit was not the easiest of aircraft to see from in such conditions . . . had I got lost, even for a short time, darkness would have fallen, and in the wartime blackness there would have been no chance of making a safe landing. I have often wondered

Helen Harrison as an ATA pilot, about to climb into the cockpit of a Spitfire.

HELEN HARRISON

When England declared war in 1939, Helen Harrison returned from South Africa to enlist in the RAF but was rejected. She next attempted to get on as a civilian instructor for the military. Turned down again, she accepted the position of chief flying instructor (CFI) with the Sheffield Aero Club and remained there until returning to Canada. "I stopped off in Virginia and got my American licences and as soon as I got to Toronto I picked up my Canadian licences. I think I must have been the first woman in the world to hold a commercial licence in four countries." Helen assumed that Canada would not be like stodgy old Britian. She was wrong. "When I applied to the RCAF I was rejected because I wore a skirt. I was furious. I just couldn't believe it. I had 2600

whether Ursula [another ATA pilot] was as shattered by the trip as I was; one didn't discuss these things too much at the time, partly out of a reluctance to admit to others, all apparently radiating confidence, that one had frightened oneself and partly because once safely back on the ground, anxiety would give place to a heady exhilaration at having completed one's task under adverse conditions. On this occasion, however, I did not pride myself on my judgement in taking off."

In 1942 the first Canadian woman, Helen Harrison, joined the ATA and in 1943 four more Canadian women signed up: Gloria Large, Violet Milstead, Marion Orr, and Elspeth Russell. By then the whole operation had become streamlined.

hours, an instructor's rating, multi-engine and instrument endorsements, a seaplane rating, and the experience of flying civil and military aircraft in three countries. Instead they took men with 150 hours."

Helen tested Cubs in Hamilton and instructed at the Kitchener-Waterloo Flying Club where her students were provisional pilot officers. She also worked as chief flying instructor at the Air Transport and Training Company Limited at Toronto Island Airport until it closed in late 1941. Meanwhile she was still trying to get into the military. "I had a friend, an air vice-marshall, who tried to pull some strings for me, but even that didn't help. I was madder than heck. I tried to get a women's auxiliary air force group going but there just weren't enough qualified women pilots to make any sort of impression on the military or government." Hearing about the ATA she jumped at the chance to join. "I flew to Washington and met Jackie Cochran and she took one look at my logbook and said, 'Come along with me.' I was sent to Dorval for the check ride on the Harvard." She found herself back in England in April 1942. "I remember my first night back. Jackie had put three of us up in a hotel and the air raid siren went off. We were the last ones down to the shelter because we stayed behind to fix our hair and put on our make-up. We learned not to do that again."

Helen quickly became known to her commanding officers. Engine problems on one of her first ferry assignments forced her to land in a farmer's field and brought her to official attention. Investigation cleared her and she received her first commendation. Unfortunately her next visit to the CO's office was less than pleasant. "I ran my plane off the runway. I was flying a Hurricane and couldn't get the flaps down on the downwind leg." As she explained she should have then decided to land without flaps. Instead she circled to make another approach and ended up doing . . ." a real greaser, except I overshot the active runway

The British Commonwealth Air Training Plan was one of the most important wartime organizations devoted to the Allied cause. It was devised by Britain, Canada, Australia, and New Zealand to train aircrew. Canada was selected as the training location because of its space, resources, and climate. It was also secure from attack yet close enough to the battlefields to keep transportation costs to a minimum. The Plan began in June 1940 and continued through the war years. It was a group effort in which the RCAF, in cooperation with the flying clubs and airlines, trained over 130,000 Commonwealth airmen (pilots, navigators, radio operators, etc.) in all aspects of flying.

Despite the desperate need for instructors and ferry pilots, there was no place for qualified women pilots.

Each base or pool had its own pilots, maintenance staff, and inspectors and, with new bases established throughout the UK, ferry trips had become shorter. The pattern of war was changing too. Britain was no longer looking solely inward to her defence but outward as the aggressor. The Allied forces had sufficient aircraft to enable them to begin wholesale bombing of German military and industrial areas. In early 1944, the whole ATA operation moved into high gear as new aircraft poured out of the factories at an average rate of 2400 a month, with an additional 500 being returned to service after repair. Total deliveries reached 6000 per month, about 200 a day. (On February 21, 1945 the ATA moved a record 570 aircraft.)

and landed on the wrong one, which was too short. I ran off the end and into the mud and put the plane up on its nose.

"When I got back to White Waltham I was called up on the mat — 'Well Miss Harrison,' said my CO, 'I would think with your experience you would have known better what to do. What is it, 2000 hours?' I told him in no uncertain terms that of course I knew what I should have done, that of course I was sorry; no one could have felt worse than I did. I think he was quite shocked that I spoke to him like that instead of 'No sir, Yes sir.' I didn't hear anymore about it and shortly after I got my Second Officer stripe and was posted to Ratcliffe, No. 6 Ferry Pool, north of London."

Another incident occurred while she was flying a Lysander. "I was taking it to the graveyard to be broken up. I broke it up for them. I had been told it would leap off the ground, but I had difficulty and once airborne, I couldn't get the trim handle to move and had to struggle to keep the nose up. As soon as I could, I turned back — thinking at least the crash wagon would be there to pick up the pieces. I had one hell of a job keeping the thing in the air and didn't dare throttle back or the nose would go down. I knew I couldn't land with all that power on so, on final approach, I took a deep breath, throttled back and just before touching down I heaved back on the control column as hard as I could and put a burst of power on. I hit at 110 mph. Everything collapsed. No prop, no undercarriage. I slid off the runway and then dead silence. No crash wagon and the stink of gas. The door wouldn't open. I wondered if I would end up in the graveyard with the plane. Finally a mechanic came, broke the perspex and hauled me out. A transport car came and took me to the hospital. All I had were some bruises and one hell of a scare. Next time I was on leave I sure celebrated!" The Board of Inquiry cleared Helen, when the investigation revealed that the previous pilot had removed the ballast from the tail and not reported it.

"Anything to Anywhere" — as ATA came to mean — explains the organization's success and uniqueness. The ATA made every member versatile; a senior pilot could fly any one of more than fifty-two main types of aircraft and sixty-five Marks (variations). This was achievable because of the unique training system based on the rationale that, once pilots were trained on one aircraft of a particular type, they should, without further instruction, be able to fly all other similar types. To attain this level of expertise the ATA ran its own flying school, classified aircraft in order of difficulty of operation, and grouped them according to type. (See page 371.)

There were six classes of aircraft. Class I signified light

In August 1943 Helen returned from leave in Canada in the right seat of a Mitchell bomber. "When I was on leave I had taken a course on the Mitchell — I went out with an officer here and there," she explained in her offhand way. At 4:00 AM on the morning of her departure she was informed that a Mitchell was taking off that morning and she was to be on it. "I thought I was going to be a supernumerary passenger but the captain needed a co-pilot and I was the only passenger who happened to be a pilot. He wouldn't let me do a take-off or landing; it was mainly gear up and gear down and doing the fuel consumption calculations. The most difficult part of the flight was using the tube to go to the bathroom. I got a little damp! The captain and I had a laugh about that."

The bomber landed at Goose Bay, Labrador and at Reykjavik, Iceland, where they spent two nights. "As I was the only female there the RAF had to rig up accommodations for me — some old radio shack with an old coal stove which didn't give out much heat, a cot with a couple of blankets, and a toilet which didn't flush. I was so cold I went to bed with my flight suit on over my uniform and my boots and gloves on. I grumbled about the RAF food and accommodations and asked why they didn't have a base like the Americans. I was told that while the Americans were flushing their toilets the RAF were sinking German subs. I didn't complain again."

On her return to England she completed the Class IV course and over the next year she ferried mostly Defiants, Spitfires, Wellingtons, Blenheims, Dominies, Hamdens, Beaufighters, Barracudas, and Warwicks. "I remember one of the Spits I flew. It had a Priority 1 chit. When I collected it from the maintenance unit to take it to a fighter squadron it had a sign on the control column which said, 'Guns loaded.' I was sure tempted to give just a little burst but managed to control myself."

single-engine types, such as the DH Moth and Magister. Class II aircraft were divided into two sections: advanced single-engines such as the Harvard, Spitfire, Mustang, and Typhoon in Section 1, and the Airacobra and Helldiver in Section 11. Class IIIs were light twin-engines such as the Oxford and Anson, (Class III+ pilots were cleared to fly passengers in a taxi Anson, used to "taxi" ferry pilots). Class IVs were advanced twin-engined aircraft with the Wellington, Beaufighter, and Mosquito in Section 1, and the Hampden and Whirlwind in Section 11. Class Vs were four-engine aircraft including the Halifax, Lancaster, and Fortress. Class VI was the seaplane category with aircraft such as the Catalina and Sunderland. Woman flew all but Class VI aircraft.

ATA pilots flew alone except in the four-engined aircraft and some of the twins. In the Hudson, for instance, an Air Training Corps cadet was taken along to help with lowering the undercarriage in the event of failure in the normal and reserve methods. Nine types, such as the Stirling, Halifax, Lancaster, and Liberator required a flight engineer.

All pilots, regardless of their prewar experience, began at the Class I level and worked their way through the conversion courses according to ability. At each stage the pilot received technical information and dual instruction. Once checked out on type pilots were expected to be able to fly any other aircraft

In March 1944 Helen requested a leave of absence because of family problems. When she was ready to return she was told she was no longer needed. "I was devastated," she recalled. "I knew I would never get another chance to fly those fast military planes. I also was due for the Class V conversion course and lost out on that too. My time with the ATA was the most exciting and interesting of my career." In total Helen flew thirty-four different types, not counting the different Marks. Her favourite was the Mosquito. "You could control it nicely; it was a fast airplane — for those days. The Spit was a nice airplane but it could be tricky on a crosswind landing. The Mustang was a real dandy."

Helen flew about 500 hours with the ATA; a considerable time when most flights were 20-30 minutes in duration. It was mostly take-offs and landings. She left with the rank of First Officer and the written comment from her CO that she was "a good Officer and sound pilot: flies with accuracy and care."

in that class without further instruction. After each conversion course they were sent back to their ferry pools. Upgrading to the next level of classification occurred after completion of a certain number of ferry trips and upon recommendation by the commanding officer.

The ATA pilot learned only enough to get the plane from A to B safely. As Vi Milstead explained, "There were a lot of knobs and dials you ignored. The progression from type to type without further training was made possible by the ATA policy of feeding the pilot with aircraft types of higher performance as she demonstrated ability and by a very special set of notes called the Ferry Pilot Notes."

In fact there were two sets of notes available for each aircraft. First devised were the comprehensive "Handling Notes," (or "White Notes" because of their covers). Twenty to thirty pages per aircraft type, they were designed to enable the ferry pilot to deliver a type of aircraft she may never have flown before. The information in all the notes was arranged in exactly the same order and produced in the same style. Vi Milstead recalled, "Mechanical details such as cockpit controls, undercarriage, retractable gear, fuel system, and so on were given first. These were followed by instructions for starting the engine, preparation for take-off, cruising, landing, etc. There were carefully written instructions on emergency action to be

Marion Orr, with Spitfire, c. 1944.

MARION ORR

Marion Orr logged her first flight with the ATA on June 2, 1943. "It was a good life for someone who liked to fly. It was a continual challenge to fly so many different types. But an airplane is an airplane; maybe different speeds, different knobs, heavier, but that didn't bother me at all; it was a thrill. My favourite was the Spitfire. It was a pilot's dream. It was very manoeuverable, light, and sensitive. I remember my first flight in one. I added power and was pressed right back in the seat as I went screaming down the runway, shot off, and was 5000 feet up before I knew it!"

Like other Canadians, Marion found navigation difficult. "When I first went over I was lost all the time. Here the roads run north and south; there, it was like spaghetti — roads all over! It was hard to read a map unless you were going up the coast. The weather was the biggest hazard because we didn't have any instrument training." She remembers one trip in particular when she was assigned to take a Spitfire to Scotland. Marion left England in poor

taken in the event of such things as hydraulic failure. These notes were available on loan to pilots from the Engineering Library at each ferry pool. We borrowed them and studied them in our spare time." The Handling Notes covered all Marks of a particular aircraft and also pointed out any unusual features, such as pronounced trim change when flaps were lowered.

However, as the ATA network expanded, these notes proved to be impractical, for a pilot often found herself away from home base with orders to ferry a different type of aircraft or one which she might not have flown for weeks or months. What was needed was a compact reference covering all types

weather and it became progressively worse. "I took off because I had made the trip many times; it was a milk run. But rain and low cloud put me off course and before I knew it, I was lost. Just when my fuel was almost gone, I saw a river through the haze and decided to ditch in it, rather than take a chance and land on a house. I said some prayers and prepared to go in, but at the last moment I spotted orange lights — runway lights and slipped safely to the runway below. When I crawled out, the RAF crew greeted me with the comment that they knew it had to be an ATA pilot because no one else would fly in such bad weather." On another trip up the coast she lost visual contact with the ground and found herself out over water and so low that "I could taste the salt and feel the spray. I quickly turned back and picked my way back to the base."

Marion had her share of mechanical problems and others of a less serious nature — like the first time she donned her winter flying gear. Dressed in the "Teddy Bear" suit, big boots, and mitts she had a hard time climbing up the slippery snowy wing to get into the cockpit. "I had thrown my parachute up ahead of me and had finally crawled up to the cockpit of the Hurricane when my foot slipped and off I fell. I was so bundled up I couldn't move. I just lay on the ground and laughed. The guys gave me a boost up."

For Marion ATA life meant not only the challenges of flying and the close comradeship of other pilots but also the pain and sorrow of visiting the wounded in nearby hospitals. "Often on my days off I would visit pilots who had no one. I was so lucky that I never had an accident that I felt the least I could do was visit those who had been hurt."

Marion went on leave in October 1944 but found her services were no longer required when she prepared to return to England. Honourably discharged she left the ATA with the rank of Second Officer and close to 700 hours on sixty-seven different types and Marks of aircraft.

that a pilot could carry with her at all times. What evolved were the "Ferry Pilot Notes" or the "Blue Book."

Everything that a ferry pilot needed to know about a plane was on one 4x6 inch card. (There were a few exceptions: the Wellington with its four possible engine types, and the twenty-four Marks of the Spitfire/Seafire required two cards.) The cards making up the Blue Book were arranged in alphabetical order by aircraft and held together with rings so that a pilot could lay the book flat on her lap open at the appropriate page. The information was so comprehensive that pilots often did not bother with the White Notes. "We called it our 'Blue Bible,'" said Helen Harrison. "With it you could fly anything. It told us how to inspect the aircraft, the procedures for take-off and landing, how to fly straight and level, and so on. You'd be up there and think, 'Now, how do you land it. Well, I'll look in my Blue Book!'"

"What you were really studying were the numbers: RPM, take-off and landing speeds, cruise . . . ," added Vi Milstead. "After all, a plane is a plane; what's a few extra feet in front of you or behind you. If you can fly at all, your hands and feet will

ATA pilots at an "all girl" ferry pool.

do the right thing. We did not try to memorize the data. We looked it up. It became routine to climb into the cockpit of a new type, get out our Notes, find everything in the cockpit, check engine starting procedures — take-off, climb, cruise, landing numbers — then start the engines and go. We could take-off, cruise and land with the best of the boys — perhaps even a little better than some. Their job was to fight with the airplane, with taking-off and landing merely a means to the end. Our job was limited to flying the airplane, and we worked at it. The system worked beautifully. But we really couldn't blame the air force boys for finding it hard to understand.

"It was amusing to watch the shock on the faces of the RAF

ELSPETH RUSSELL BURNETT (1922-1974)

Born in the little lumber town of Matane, Quebec on the shores of the St. Lawrence River, Elspeth, an only child with an invalid mother and a busy father, led a quiet and lonely existence. When her father died in 1933 she was sent to an exclusive girls' boarding school in Montreal. Exposed to the stimulation of good teaching and sports Elspeth bloomed, excelling both academically and in sports. At McGill University she proved to be a brilliant, all-round student and completed a Bachelor of Arts degree at the age of nineteen.

Then out of the blue she decided to take flying lessons in the hope that she could fly for the ATA. "She saw herself playing an active role in the war. She refused to consider the Women's Division of the RCAF. In her mind they were stepping back to allow the men to fly. That was not for Elspeth," her husband Gerry Burnett explained later. The British Commonwealth Air Training Plan was in full swing and flying schools were busy training men for military service. However, as Gerry remarked, "If Elspeth thought there was a possibility of doing something, then she would try. It was definitely a challenge for her to find an instructor who was prepared to give her flying time as fuel was rationed."

Finally she persuaded "Fitz" Champagne of the Curtiss-Reid Flying School at Cartierville Airport to give her lessons. He could only fit her in between flights and she spent a lot of time hanging around the airport waiting for a lesson that could be ten minutes or forty-five minutes and rarely on the same aircraft. Learning on Reid-Ramblers, Tiger Moths, Taylorcrafts, and a Stinson 108, she received a private licence in June 1941. Because of gasoline rationing it was another year and a half before she had the required time to take the ATA checkride. Finally, in November 1943 she was on her way to England.

pilots when one of us climbed out of one plane and into another type," Vi Milstead continued. "At first they wouldn't believe us if we said we had never flown that aircraft before. It was utterly baffling to military pilots accustomed to air force procedures for qualifying pilots on new types. 'No problem,' I would say, 'It's all in my book.' 'Good God, girl,' exclaimed one RAF pilot, 'You can't fly this plane (a Beaufighter) from a book!' And I answered, 'I can from *my* book.'"

If pressed for time, experienced ATA pilots thought nothing of climbing into the aircraft without first referring to their Blue Book — they did that as they went along. "As I was taxiing I would read the recommended take-off and climb speeds and

Classmates renamed the shy Elspeth "Russ." This masculine nickname did not prevent one Gerry Burnett, also on course, from noticing the small woman with the sparkling eyes. Elspeth was not immune to the ebullient Gerry and seeing each other soon became their secondary duty. Unfortunately, he was stationed at No. 8 Ferry Pilot Pool in Belfast, Ireland, and Elspeth was successively posted to Luton, Hamble, and Cosford in England and Prestwick, in Scotland. Gerry, however, became ingenious at finding opportunities to court Elspeth and one of his best allies was the weather over the Irish Sea. This phenomenon often kept him weatherbound at Elspeth's ferry pool. Indeed, help for the pair was all around. As Gerry explained, "Everyone knew about us and tried to make things easier for us. Whenever possible, they even gave us aircraft to ferry when we were going on leave so we could meet each other." Gerry eventually managed to get himself posted to Prestwick.

One shared ferry trip was almost the end of them. "I'll never forget it," recalled Gerry. "Elspeth was delivering a Boston and had arranged to pick me up along the way. I was sitting in the back in the navigator's seat, cut off from Elspeth by the bomb bay and the fact that the radios weren't working. I got bored and when I spotted the socket for a control column — but no stick — I wiggled it, hoping to get a reaction from Elsepth. I did. She thought I wanted to fly the plane and let go of the stick, assuming that I had control. We were out over the Irish Sea and the aircraft first turned out to sea and then began turning to the left, towards what initially looked like a hill, except that it kept getting bigger and bigger. I finally realized that neither of us had been flying the plane for the last ten minutes and we were about to fly into a mountain! Elspeth, as I found out after, was day-dreaming and not watching. I wiggled the socket as vigorously as possible to get her attention. Finally, at what was literally the last moment, she took control and

Elspeth Russell, ATA.

when I was at my cruise altitude I would see what speed I let down and land at," remembered Helen Harrison. "That wasn't always the wisest thing to do because sometimes you were so busy map reading and trying to figure out where you were that you arrived at the airport before you had the numbers for landing!"

Sometimes, the steps into progressively bigger and more sophisticated aircraft were almost overwhelming. As Lettice Curtis wrote, "Constant speed propellers, retractable undercarriages, cooling gills and a host of other items were things that only weeks ago we hadn't known existed and, as for coming in to land at 90 mph, this was as high as the cruising

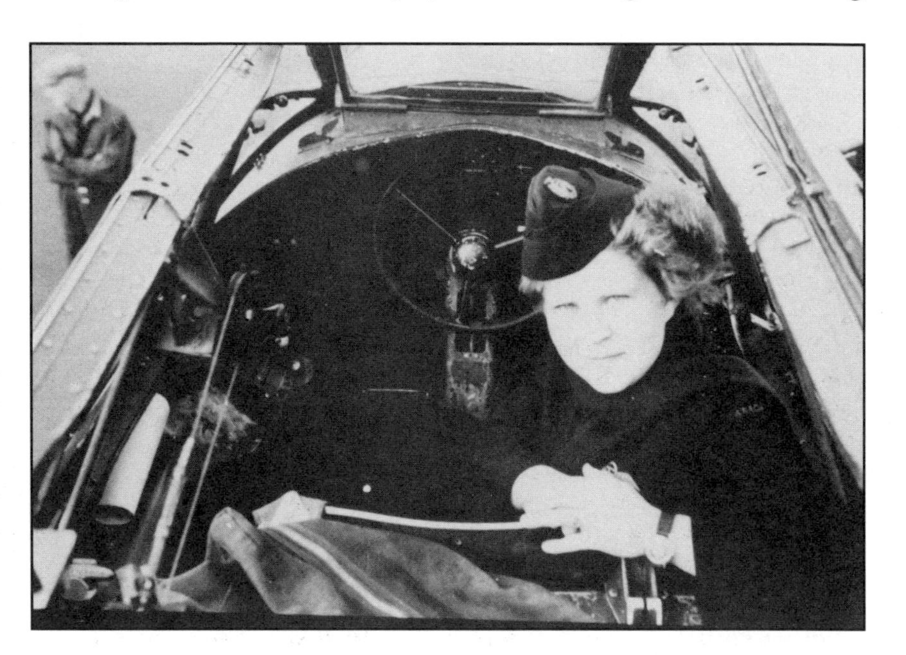

turned away from the mountain. We had a few words for each other once we were safely on the ground."

Elspeth was barely five foot two and with her short legs had difficulty reaching the rudder pedals of some aircraft, such as the Mustang. Her commanding officers were aware of this but because she proved so competent they were prepared to work around the problem. As one CO wrote on her General Record on September 9, 1944, "She has made excellent progress throughout her training and on the whole proved an above average pilot and a good officer. One trouble has shown up . . . and that is her short stature . . . If she had not had good ability this difficulty would have proved insurmountable but so far she has coped with all situations well . . ." He did express the concern that her shortness might make Class IV difficult, but Elspeth proved

Elspeth Russell.

speeds to which we were accustomed. On top of this we had to learn to cope with two engines . . . We were just shown the various gauges and devices and told what they ought to read, or how they ought to look, and this we memorized blindly . . . The Oxford training followed much the same pattern — a couple of trips dual . . . and then two or three solo flights . . . This was hardly enough to leave us brimming over with confidence but somehow we all seemed to cope."

Pilots also faced the challenge of adapting to a plane with continental instrumentation, such as the Tomahawk, which had a throttle that operated back for OPEN and forward for CLOSED — a bit like suddenly driving on the wrong side of the road. As Lettice Curtis described it, "I managed to bring myself to 'shut' the throttle for take-off and found I had covered the short distance to my destination before I had finished sorting out the readings on the various unfamiliar gauges. The landing was accompanied by an even-greater-than-usual bout of mental activity. In the circuit I kept reassuring myself by calculating five-eighths of the indicated airspeed, to translate it from kilometres per hour, to a scale I could better understand. In fact it was quite extraordinary how readily one adjusted to the 'backward' throttle, nevertheless I had the greatest difficulty in ridding myself of the idea that if I undershot on final approach, I would be unable to overcome the instinct to push the lever forward, closing the throttle with no doubt disastrous results."

Contrary to general military practice, ATA pilots were taught to do a three-point landing because so many of their trips were into grass airfields and short dispersal strips. That

him wrong. By using pillows or her parachute she managed to complete the Class IV conversion course just fine. On April 9, 1945 the CO wrote, "This pilot has completed a very satisfactory course and, considering her small stature, she has shown herself to be a very capable pilot who should very quickly become above average." A couple of months later, the CO of No. 12 Ferry Pool wrote, "An excellent ferry pilot in her Class. Hardworking and ready for any job allotted to her."

Elspeth was honourably discharged on October 31, 1945 with the rank of Second Officer, having flown 548 hours in 34 different types of aircraft, including Spitfires (her favourite), Barracudas, Mustangs, Hudsons, Hellcats, Wellingtons, Mosquitoes, and Corsairs.

there were few if any accidents from holding off too high, in a tail-down attitude on the heavy aircraft, is remarkable.

Another important part of the ATA scheme was the taxi system. Ferry Control tried to allocate jobs to the various pools so that pilots could fly themselves back to their home pool. When this was not possible pilots were picked up at the various aerodromes by taxi aircraft, such as the four-place Fairchild 24 or the Avro Anson that could seat more than ten pilots plus their parachutes. There were no designated taxi pilots; all qualified pilots shared the work. "It was a real pleasure at the end of a long, hard day to see the taxi Anson waiting for you with a familiar figure at the controls, to take a seat among a

VIOLET MILSTEAD

Violet Milstead arrived in England on May 9, 1943 and she and Marion Orr were soon at the ATA Elementary Flying Training School at Barton-in-the Clay. Vi flew her first military aircraft, a Miles Magister, on June 2. After training they were posted to the Initial Flying Training School at Thame where her first flight was on a Hawker Hart, a big biplane that had been a prewar fighter/bomber. Training continued through July with the emphasis shifting to cross-country work. "Our cross-country flying was done in the lower altitudes and we were never permitted to use our radios. Navigation was entirely by dead reckoning, compass and map reading. Accurate navigation was essential with military airports, barrage balloons, anti-aircraft batteries and other defence installations all over the place, along with a great deal of poor visibility."

There were two separate ATA units at Thame: the Initial Flight Training School and No. 5 Ferry (Training) Pool. At the end of July Vi and Marion were transferred to No. 5 Ferry Pool for a two week intensive ground school course to prepare them for Class II ferrying. "We learned about such things as hydraulic systems, retractable undercarriages, flap systems, braking systems (including pneumatic), different kinds of constant speed propellers and superchargers." On September 1 after 45 minutes dual instruction Vi flew solo in a Miles Master. "This aircraft had a Rolls Royce Kestrel liquid cooled engine of 585 horsepower and was an excellent stepping stone to the British fighters. On the same day I also flew my first service type aircraft, a Hawker Hurricane." By September Vi's formal Class II training was over; she had flown five flights in a Master, five in a Hurricane, four in a Harvard, and three navigational flights as second pilot in the twin-engine Oxford. Both Vi and Marion started Class II ferrying duties at No. 5 Pool. In January 1944 they were

group of girls from your own pool amid an exchange of good-natured nonsense, and take-off for home," said Vi Milstead. "It was all very normal to us, but a girl once remarked as we droned along, 'I suppose the people down there look up and say, 'There go our bomber boys to blast the enemy.' What would they say if they could look inside and see a woman up front flying the thing, and a bunch of women sitting in the back knitting?'"

Sometimes the flights could be dovetailed so nicely that there was no need for taxi service. For example, on March 30, 1945 Vi Milstead's logbook read: "Ferried an Oxford from Cosford [her base] to Prestwick, Scotland (terminal of the North Atlantic ferry flights), 1 hour 50 minutes. Carried a

posted to No. 12 Ferry Pool, Cosford, one of two "all girl" pools; the other was at Hamble.

"We shared the field with a Spitfire assembly plant and clearing this plant provided us with part of our work. I went on to fly about fifteen different Marks of Spitfires and such performers as the North American Mustang, the Vultee Vengeance, the US Navy's Vought Corsair, the Grumman Wildcat, and the much more powerful Grumman Hellcat, the Hawker Typhoon with its 24 cylinder H-type engine developing almost 2400 horsepower, and finally, the ultimate — the Hawker Tempest with another 24 cylinder H-type engine developing more than 2800 horsepower."

Back in Cosford after her Class III twin engine course in White Waltham, Vi was kept busy flying fighters to the south coast. "It was an interesting and exciting time as the Allies were building up for the invasion of Europe. We knew what the fighters were for. That was no secret. We didn't know when they would be used. Obviously it would be soon. The fighters I delivered were mostly Spitfires and all were painted with the black and white 'invasion' stripes on the wings. I suppose this was because the skies over the invasion beaches were going to be very crowded. The stripes made the aircraft both easy to see in the air and easy to identify. The organization was excellent. As soon as we landed there would be airmen at our wing tips guiding us to dispersal points. These might be in such unlikely places as among the trees of an orchard. They were thrilling, nerve-tingling days. Everyone was affected by the feeling of momentous events pending. But when the great day came on June 6, the air belonged exclusively to the Allied Air Forces. We were grounded. We sat, listened to the news broadcasts, talked quietly or moved restlessly about, and I suspect that most of us offered silent prayers for the boys on beaches."

Like other pilots, Vi had difficulty with the weather. "I remember taking off from Cosford in a Warwick, a great,

Violet Milstead, ATA pilot.

Flight Engineer (a girl) with me for the next trip which was to ferry a Dakota from Prestwick to Kemble, 2 hours. Left the Flight Engineer at Kemble to be picked up by taxi aircraft and completed the day's work by ferrying a Typhoon from Kemble to Cosford, 20 minutes (I believe the ATA speed for the Typhoon was 300 mph)."

Central Ferry Control was the heart of the ATA organization. It plotted the movement of aircraft for the pilots of all the ferry pools. The trips criss-crossed all over England, Scotland, Northern Ireland, and much of Wales. The whole system of matching pilots to aircraft and to the needs of the squadrons required skill and memory on the part of the director of operations and his assistants. They had to know the exact situation each day, what type of aircraft had to be moved between which locations, the number of pilots available at each ferry pool, and what they were capable of flying. It was like a game of chess.

The day of the ferry pilot officially began at 9:00 AM when she received her ferry chits, which gave aircraft type, pick-up point, and destination. "The chit was our authority to collect the aircraft and its equipment," explained Vi

Vi Milstead and a de Havilland Mosquito, RAF Station, Hullavington, England, c. 1944.

lumbering twin-engine bomber. Immediately after take-off I encountered very poor visibility, so poor that I would have returned to Cosford if I had dared. But I couldn't see enough to risk it. The weather was supposed to be improving ahead so I kept going. There was nothing else to do. The visibility was worse in the Midlands where great quantities of industrial smoke mixed with the vapour in the air. I knew that my course would take me quite close to an enroute ferry pool and I would have landed there if I could have found it. The Warwick and I were well into Scotland when the weather changed. Eventually I landed at Kinloss and parted company from my Warwick."

Vi was only five foot; nevertheless she managed to reach the controls. "If the seats were not adjustable I simply used my little black leather overnight bag to sit on. The first time

Milstead. "It gave full details of its present location, its Mark, and its destination. It included a form of receipt for the aircraft which the ferry pilot was required to give to the authority from whom she collected it, a 'signal of delivery' to be sent to Central Ferry Control immediately after arrival at the aircraft's destination, and a report sheet on the state of the aircraft as she found it. If you got an aircraft you didn't like, you thought, 'Oh God, one of those.'"

With chit in hand, she then went to the Met (Meteorology) Office. The ATA had developed its own weather service to suit the special requirements of ferry pilots whose flying was strictly VFR (Visual Flight Rules) and without radio. "Once the pilot

I flew an Avenger I thought, 'How do I get up there with my parachute and overnight bag?' I can remember only once when my length of leg, or lack of it, was a problem. This was in the Lockheed Hudson bomber (the military version of the Lockheed 14). The TCA [Trans-Canada Airlines] pilots were taught to land on the main gear with the tail up. But not us. We were taught to land the Hudsons on three points for this would allow us to land the plane more slowly and use smaller fields. By the time I had enough cushions behind me to get full rudder travel, it was almost necessary for me to exhale to get the wheel back far enough to make a three point landing!"

A Class IV course began on September 5 and Vi trained on the Lockheed Hudson and the Albermarle before being posted back to Cosford. "From the Class IV group I flew mostly Wellingtons, Whitleys, Blenheims, Bostons, Mitchells, Mosquitoes (my favourite), and the very challenging Beaufort and Beaufighters. I also flew a Welkin. I am proud of that. It was a rarity. I think there were only one or two of them made.

"After the Allied invasion of Europe in June 1944, enemy aircraft intrusions were few, although buzz bombs and V-2s kept us a bit thoughtful before their launching sites were found and blasted. But by the spring of 1945 we knew that the end of the war was approaching. The steady, triumphant advances of the Allied armies into Germany from the west and the east, made it inevitable." Her last flight in wartime was May 4 to ferry a Typhoon from Lichfield to Milfield.

Vi could not recall much about VE-Day (Victory in Europe Day, May 8, 1945). "No doubt I reported for flying as usual, learned that there was no flying to be done and, with some of the other girls, wandered back to the village. I saw no wild rejoicing and dancing in the streets such as were reported, for example, from London. My next flight was May 10, two days after the war in Europe had ended; I flew a

was airborne," Vi explained, "she had no one to help her decide what to do if she encountered bad or unexpected weather conditions." The exacting task of the Met Office was to reduce to a minimum the number of occasions on which pilots ran into unexpected weather — a real challenge as, in wartime, ships in that vast area of ocean west of the British Isles were not permitted to radio weather information. At any rate, ATA's weather information needs were different from those of the military pilots; what was required was detailed information over a comparatively small area. In Vi's words: "Met presented this in two standardized forms: forecasts and actuals. Maps of the British Isles were covered with transparent plastic on which

Beaufighter from Weston to Cosford, 50 minutes. The next couple of weeks were very busy but pilots were resigning and Cosford closed May 24. In those three weeks of May I ferried seven Spitfires, three Barracudas, two Typhoons, one Mustang, two Hellcats, two Tempests, four Fairchilds (taxi), one Hurricane, five Mosquitoes, three Beaufighters, one Beaufort, two Warwicks, one Anson (taxi), two Wellingtons and one Welkin."

When Cosford closed Vi was posted to one of the "invasion" pools: No. 1 Ferry Pool, White Waltham, just west of London. After VE-Day ATA pilots followed the different squadrons with new aircraft, delivering aircraft to Europe and bringing back unserviceable airplanes. They flew into France, Germany, Belgium, and Holland, landing on whatever was available. "Everyone wanted to get over to the continent," said Vi. "It was something that was dished out to the more senior pilots. The forward boys were operating off mesh runways which were rolled down on fields in advance of the planes. The problem was not the actual landing on these make-shift runways but finding them in the first place; they weren't marked on the map. In Holland it seemed as if everything was flooded. I remember landing at an American field in Holland and asking a pilot which way to the girls' room. He pointed up a path saying, 'You have to drop your pants under the wing at the dispersal hut.' It was pretty primitive! However, there were always separate accommodations if we were overnighting. The military would have taken over the local hotel and we would stay there."

Vi logged approximately 700 hours on 29 different single engine aircraft and 17 different twin-engine aircraft, not including the different Marks of aircraft. For example, she flew 15 different Marks of Spitfires. "My favourite aircraft was the twin-engine Mosquito. I guess because I flew it so much. It was the most common ferry job for No. 1 Ferry

Year 1944 Month	Date	AIRCRAFT Type	No.	Pilot, or 1st Pilot	2nd Pilot, Pupil or Passenger	DUTY (Including Results and Remarks)
--	--	—		—	—	— Totals Brought Forward
OCT.	3.					
	3.	FAIRCHILD	HB601.	SELF	TAXI.	COSFORD · CRANWELL · WITCHFORD · HENLOW · COS
	4.	BARRACUDA	MX 578	SELF	-	COSFORD · KIRKBRIDE
	4.	ANSON	NK. 754	SELF	-	BILLOTH - COSFORD
	5.	SPITFIRE V.B.	EP250	SELF	-	COSFORD · CRANWELL.
	6.	FAIRCHILD	FV768	SELF	TAXI.	COSFORD · ANSTY · HOMRECROSS · COSFORD
	6.	ANSON V	RK 810	SELF	TAXI.	COSFORD - RATCLIFFE · ELSHAM · COSFORD
	7.	SPITFIRE IX.	RX808	SELF	-	COSFORD - DUMPHRIES
	7.	OXFORD	DX138	SELF	-	KIRKBRIDE - U HERTON - ASTON.
	10.	SPITFIRE II.	SM141	SELF	-	COSFORD · LICHFIELD
	12.	ANSON	NK 861	SELF	TAXI	ANSTY · COSFORD
	12.	FAIRCHILD	EV 768	SELF	TAXI	COSFORD · WALSALL
	12.	HARVARD	FX 407	SELF	-	WALSALL · KIRKBRIDE
	12.	FAIRCHILD	EU 356	SELF		KIRKBRIDE - DUMPHRIES
	12.	WELLINGTON XIV	NB 966	SELF	-	DUMPHRIES · HIGH ERCALL
	12.	FAIRCHILD	HB631	SELF	TAXI	HIGHERCALL · COSFORD
	15.	SPITFIRE	R.R. 193	SELF		COSFORD - LICHFIELD
	15	SPITFIRE	R6694	SELF	-	DARLEY MOOR · COSFORD
	16	BARRACUDA	MD913	SELF	-	WOLVERHAMPTON · WROUGHTON
	16	BARRACUDA	MX631	SELF	-	WROUGHTON · COSFORD
	17	FAIRCHILD	EU 768	SELF	-	COSFORD · HIGH ERCAL · WROUGHTON - COSFORD
	18	BARRACUDA	MX654	SELF	-	COSFORD - KIRKBRIDE
	18	MASTER II	DM275	SELF	-	KIRKBRIDE - COSFORD
	19	BARRACUDA	MD917	SELF	-	WOLVERHAMPTON · COSFORD
	19	ANSON V	NK 901	SELF	TAXI	COSFORD - LICHFIELD · COSFORD
				GRAND TOTAL [Cols. (1) to (10)] ....Hrs. ....Mins.		Totals Carried Forward

A page from Vi Milstead's logbook while with the ATA, 1944.

Pool, where I was stationed much of the time. This pool was close to the factory where some 7000 of them were produced. I ended my career in the ATA in style — my last three deliveries were a Tempest, a Mosquito, and a Spitfire."

Once her resignation was accepted there were final medical examinations and other formalities and eventually she was sent to a hostel in London to await embarkation. "I waited and waited. I was still waiting when Japan surrendered and the whole, long war came to an end. August 10. A date which would go down in history. And there I was, alone in London with nothing to do. I couldn't just sit there . . . On that so-special day I had to do something. I took what was, for me, an uncharacteristic step and went, by myself, to a big old home in London which had been turned into a meeting place for Canadian Air Force officers. I was of course in uniform. There I met, or perhaps I should say, there I was found by Jack Reilly, the same Jack Reilly whom I was to meet a couple of years later at Leavens Brothers Air Services Ltd., the same Jack Reilly who, still later, married Molly Beall. Jack, a boisterous Irishman and highly gregarious, tells of finding this little person wearing Wings and with Canada badges on her shoulders standing by herself."

On August 18 Vi was assigned to a ship and arrived home August 28, 1945.

was shown, in coloured chalk, any areas in which conditions were below ATA minimums of 800 feet and 2000 yards [800 foot ceiling, 2000 yards visibility]. In addition a chalkboard showed actual conditions at a large number of airfields around the country. Each pilot made her own "go, no-go" decision, taking into consideration the weather, the type of aircraft, and the route. Each pilot was required to sign a book in the Met Office certifying that she had obtained the met information necessary for her flight. It worked well but, when dealing with the weather, no system could be perfect. Sometimes we had anxious minutes or hours."

Although enemy action was a threat, the real danger for

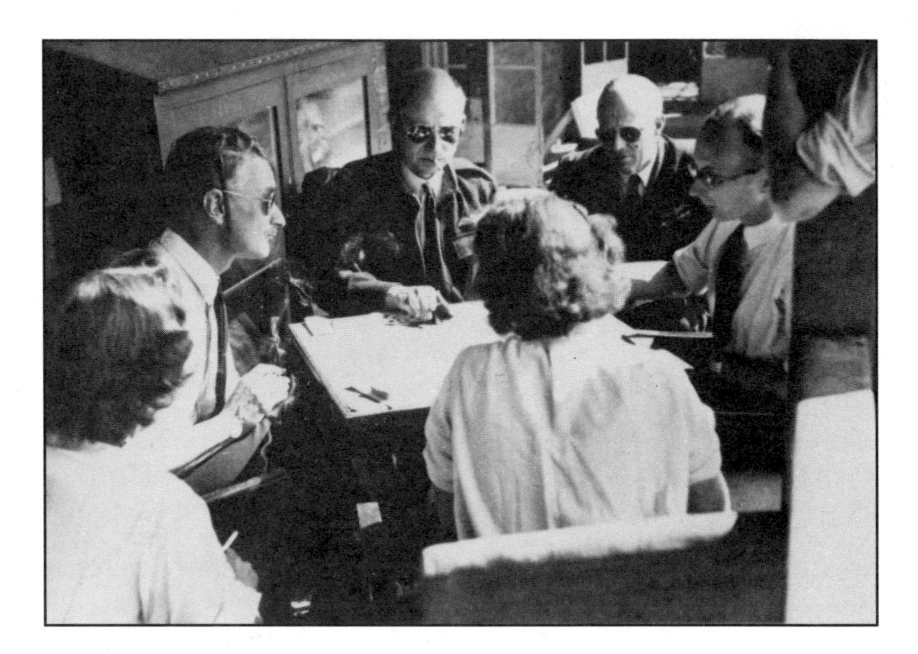

ATA pilots — waiting for the weather to lift.

VERA STRODL DOWLING

Vera Strodl was born in England of British and Danish parents, raised in Denmark and became a Canadian after the war. Vera always longed to fly. "When I was seventeen I left home for England to learn to fly." She scrubbed floors and washed dishes in a restaurant to pay for her lessons. "I had to work six and a half days a week and could afford only twenty minutes flying every two weeks. It took me two years to earn my "A" Licence." Vera took her lessons on a Gipsy Moth at the Sussex Aero Club and received her licence in 1937.

Anxious to learn everything she could about aviation, she took gliding lessons (Glider's Licence #1224 in 1938) and worked in an aircraft factory, becoming a qualified inspec-

ATA pilots was the weather, particularly in the short days of winter when it could change quickly because of a fast-moving depression coming in from the ocean. Cross-country flying was done at low altitudes and navigation was by dead reckoning, map reading, and a constant eye on the compass. Flying with no radio or other navigational aids (navaids) was difficult enough; any poor weather, such as fog or cloud, that hindered visual contact with the ground, meant trouble.

"We flew below, between, and above the clouds. In the fast fighters it was easy, we went above the cloud and then prayed for a hole to get back down," described another ATA pilot, Vera Strodl. "It often seemed that Providence helped, for time after

tor (PR# 79). When her employers found out she had an "A" Licence they asked her to test fly the Auster. "The Auster Company had received the contract for an army spotter aircraft and the Auster was designed as an observer aircraft for World War II. I was flight testing a newly-designed aircraft and what I did was mainly take-off tests, angle of descent tests, stalls and turns, aerobatics, and learning how to get out of unusual attitudes. I also demonstrated it around the country."

What she really wanted to do was to fly for the ATA and as soon as she had the required 250 hours, she applied. Accepted in 1941 Vera remained with the ATA until the end of the war. She said little about her ATA experiences, preferring to talk of her faith in God, for it was while flying for the ATA that she became convinced of Divine Intervention. She spent her ATA years based in Hamble, White Waltham, Bristol, and Prestwick. "I lived mostly in Nissen huts which had condensation dripping down the walls; it was always damp and I was always shivering. At Hamble I became used to the constant 'ack ack' and the fluff of explosions." Listening to Vera one could easily get the impression that the flying was very routine and to her it was; but many of her flights were anything but normal. "I had one tight landing. A total engine failure forced me to land in a field studded with poles and barrels — placed there to prevent enemy aircraft from landing! I glided to a stop with only two feet clearance on either side of the wing tips."

Vera encountered enemy aircraft more than once but her greatest fear was the weather. "When we were asked to deliver a Priority 1 aircraft we often felt pressured to start out in marginal weather. But even taking-off in good weather was no guarantee that we might not encounter deteriorating conditions. Vicious cold fronts came in from the ocean. On one of my trips I was flying a Hellcat along the coast from Scotland to England and I suddenly flew into

Vera Strodl, ATA.

time when things were looking bad and fuel was getting low a momentary break in the cloud would appear and we could slip through to safety."

"It was always the pilot's decision to fly," recalled Vi Milstead. "The pressure was your own; no one could make you fly. But you didn't say 'no' too often, particularly if you had received orders for a Priority 1 aircraft, for that meant it was to be delivered to its destination that same day if possible." When pressed, Vi admitted that she had problems because of weather but typically understated them. "You got into difficulties and you got out of them and there wasn't much to tell. Or, you don't get out of them and someone else did the talking." The

Vera Strodl ferrying a Spitfire.

a wall of solid murk. When I tried to turn back I lost control of the airplane, and by the time I had regained control I had lost altitude. I was so low I could almost taste the spray, and it was raining so hard I couldn't even see the wing tips. I was cold and then hot and I was dripping with perspiration. I was seized by the most awful fear. Just when I thought all was lost I heard an 'inner voice' and I knew that God was my copilot. He guided me to safety on earth. I promised that one day I would preach the gospel."

On one trip she twice lost control of an aircraft because of bad weather. "I was delivering an Oxford and I flew into cloud. With no instrument training I lost control and got into a spiral dive. I recovered barely 1000 feet above the ground. But I couldn't get out of the weather; I couldn't get above it and I did not dare go any lower. I ended up in cloud

knowledge that the plane was urgently needed often pushed the pilots to fly in hazaradous weather conditions. As Vera Strodl said, "We had to remind ourselves that we were paid to deliver aircraft safely, not to be heroes." (Not without cause was the unwritten ATA motto, "better late than never.")

After checking with Met the pilot went over to Maps and Signals. This was operational intelligence. All flights made by ferry pilots came under the category of non-operational flying in wartime. To keep out of trouble, the ferry pilot had to pay attention to the rules and regulations for non-operational flying. "That was to avoid interference with or confusion among the active and passive defences of the country, to avoid the risk of false air raid alarms, and to avoid being shot down by our own defences. There were areas which a ferry pilot could not enter without advance routing because Fighter Command reserved the right to 'shoot first and ask questions afterwards' in the case of unidentified aircraft," explained Vi Milstead.

The ferry pilot needed current information about the condition and regulations of the airfields into which she would be flying. She also had to concern herself with the location of defence installations, such as anti-aircraft batteries, practice ranges and barrage balloons and any corridors through which she might be flying. A flight into an aircraft factory usually meant an approach through a "corridor" clear of barrage

again and lost control once more. I was sure I was going to crash. At the last moment God guided me to safety."

Another close call came as a result of her flying an unserviceable aircraft, which she was delivering to the graveyard for scrap. An inflight fire forced her to make an emergency landing, but when she attempted to get out she found the canopy jammed closed. Unable to extinguish the fire or escape, she thought she had "bought it." At the last possible moment the canopy gave way — proof to her again of Divine Intervention — and she quickly climbed out. "I believe that many pilots have a belief in God. As a pilot you get a bird's eye view of life and living. It makes you realize what a speck you are and that you can't do anything alone. You realize you are at the mercy of the elements; the weather is the biggest problem for a pilot and, to face it, you need faith."

A skillful pilot and competent officer, she gained the rank of first officer and attained the Class V level, flying approximately 1000 hours on 65 aircraft types, including heavy four-engine bombers.

balloons, which were erected to protect sensitive areas from low level air attacks. These balloons presented a hazard to the pilot, especially if visibility was reduced.

"It went without saying that your navigation had to be accurate," said Vi. "I found it difficult at first, coming as I did from Canada where cities were often hundreds of miles apart and the country was not as built-up as Britain. At first I found myself overshooting my destination. I had to learn not to look for far horizons but just to look over my nose!" The other Canadians also commented on how England seemed like a maze of railways going in every direction except the one they wanted.

The pilots' last stop was to study the taxi sheet to learn who would pick them up, where, and approximately when. As Vi observed, "It was always comforting to see in black and white the plans made for bringing us back home."

FLYING FOR THE ATA was no sinecure. Vi Milstead summed up their duties and potential dangers, "Our job was to move aircraft from factory and repair depot to operational fields and back again, and between one operational field and another. Add together the urgency of the times, the well-known British weather, the crowded skies, the barrage balloons, the occasional intrusion of enemy aircraft, and the work could become, well, interesting."

Flying in conditions that would make anyone sweat with anxiety was only one facet of being an ATA pilot. Being female was another, particularly in the first few years. The women knew if they messed up the men would say, "I told you so." Initially, a shake of the head and a patronizing remark —

GLORIA LARGE (1924-1989)

Gloria was born and raised in Charlottetown, Prince Edward Island. "Flying was in my blood," she stated. "My father was a World War I pilot and an airline pilot and I grew up listening to his stories about flying. It seemed natural that I should fly and my father supported me all the way." After high school she moved to California to attend university. "I wanted to get out of PEI and I had relatives there," she explained. "One day I skipped classes and went out to one of the little airports and signed up for lessons. That was the end of university." She completed her training in Hamilton, Ontario, and received a private licence on June 4, 1942.

"I tried to enlist in the RCAF and was rejected. It was then that I heard of the ATA. When I took the flight test on

"You're just a little girl!" — were common male reactions to a woman climbing into a military aircraft. To prove themselves the women had to maintain a balance between being overly cautious and being reckless. They learned to ignore a lot and to cultivate a sense of humour. They became used to reading articles on themselves that spoke of "neat nylon legs" or "though they flew bombers and fighters they still used lipstick." Inevitably the girl who landed a Spitfire "took off her helmet, glanced fearlessly (or shyly) around, and [invariably] shook out her 'golden' curls." If she was married then the press gleefully used such headlines as "Mother Knits While Waiting For Her Bomber."

the Harvard I had never flown anything bigger than a Cub. I was so scared of that big machine that even the instruments frightened me. I think if the men hadn't been so disparaging I might have backed down, but it seemed as if they all lined up to watch me kill myself and that gave me the determination to go through with it. One thing stuck in my mind and that was the horrible landing speed of the Harvard, and when I saw the runway dashing up at me and felt the ground I closed my eyes for a second." She passed the checkride and went to England. There appears to be some question as to whether she actually served with the ATA. Only one of the three books on the ATA show Gloria as being with the organization. *The Forgotten Pilots* states that she arrived in England in May 1942 and left in September 1942 with the rank of Cadet. Why she was released is not known.

On her return to PEI she married but shortly after was divorced. In 1947 she moved to Montreal where she enrolled with the Scholefield brothers of Laurentide Aviation at Cartierville Airport and qualified for her commercial and instructor's licences. "We hired her. She was a good instructor and it was good PR for us," recalled Jack Scholefield. Gloria was the first woman instructor in Montreal and newsmen flocked to the airport to photograph her. Although newspaper articles stated that Gloria flew bombers across the Atlantic, this was not correct; women were not part of Ferry Command.

After about a year of instructing, Gloria returned to PEI where she tried to make a living by barnstorming, crop dusting, and flying charters. "I tried TCA and Maritime Central Airways but they weren't interested in hiring a woman pilot." In the early fifties she remarried and gave up flying. This marriage also ended and Gloria supported herself and her children by operating a tourist camp on the Island.

Gloria Large, ATA.

When the war reached its climax so did the scope of the ATA. As the Allies advanced deeper into Europe, so too did the ATA, and selected pilots flew into France, Belgium, Holland, and Germany. It was not the first time that the ATA had ventured onto the continent. In May 1940 ATA pilots had flown Battles and Hurricanes to rural France prior to the Dunkirk evacuation. Then they had gone without life-jackets or maps to fields towards which the Germans were drawing closer hour by hour. In September 1944 they were properly briefed and equipped. To handle the overseas assignment, No.1 Ferry Pool at White Waltham and No. 9 at Aston Down were designated "invasion" pools. Initially women were not

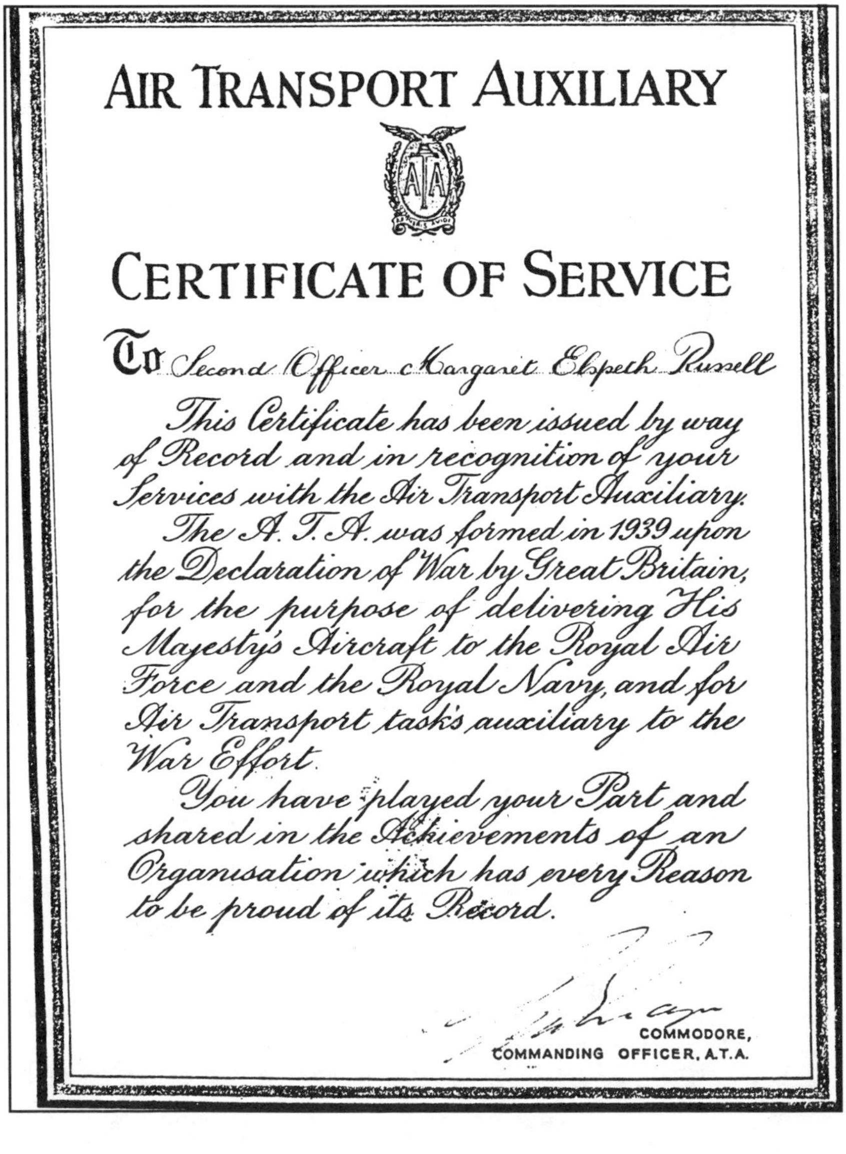

AIR TRANSPORT AUXILIARY

ATA

CERTIFICATE OF SERVICE

To Second Officer Margaret Elspeth Russell

This Certificate has been issued by way of Record and in recognition of your Services with the Air Transport Auxiliary.

The A.T.A. was formed in 1939 upon the Declaration of War by Great Britain, for the purpose of delivering His Majesty's Aircraft to the Royal Air Force and the Royal Navy, and for Air Transport tasks auxiliary to the War Effort.

You have played your Part and shared in the Achievements of an Organisation which has every Reason to be proud of its Record.

COMMODORE,
COMMANDING OFFICER, A.T.A.

ATA certificate of service.

accepted. But, as the Allies advanced deeper and deeper into Europe the ferry trips grew longer and longer; RAF and male ATA pilots could not keep up with the demand and female pilots flew into Europe in January 1945.

ATA pilots flew Mitchells and Bostons to Brussels, Mosquitoes to Amiens and Rosieres, Dakotas to Courtrai, and Spitfires to Brussels, Everes, Nijmegen, Ghent, Luxeuil, and Colmar and, just before VE-Day (May 8, 1945), to Stuttgart. Pilots were greeted with France's coldest winter in years and those who landed in Paris — with no overcoats — found the city without coal, and electricity cut off at dawn each day. Navigation was difficult with rivers and other landmarks all but invisible under ice and snow. At the beck and call of Transport Command, ATA pilots often flew beyond their original destination and were away for days at a time. They supplied needed aircraft and nurse-maided unserviceable ones back, brought the "walking wounded" back to England, and took VIPs or supplies to far-away places like Berlin, Rome, Norway, even Algiers and Cairo.

In 1945 the war was winding down. In April Mussolini was captured and shot, and Hitler committed suicide; on May 7th Germany signed an unconditional surrender. On August 6th the first atomic bomb was dropped on Hiroshima, and on the 9th the second was dropped on Nagasaki; Japan surrendered on the 14th. The war was over. Yet still the ATA flew, although its end was near. November 30th was set as the day for its termination. Those remaining cleared out their lockers and handed in equipment. In return they received an envelope that contained their ATA report cards giving hours and types of aircraft flown, a letter from the founder and commanding officer of the ATA, Gerard d'Erlanger, thanking them for their services, and, as official record of their participation, blue and gold Certificates of Service. Then the flag at White Waltham was lowered for the last time and this unique organization ceased to exist.

The women came out looking good. They took no longer to train and, in terms of aircraft deliveries, they held their own. They ferried ninety-nine different types and Marks of aircraft, from the most elementary civilian types to the most sophisticated military ones. Commanding Officers found that the women took more care with their cockpit drill, always checked the weather, and were less likely to show off. Their "wastage rate" — those who left the ATA — was somewhat higher than the men (but less than 5%, according to Vi Milstead), but their safety record percentage was better and fewer were killed on duty: 4.9% of the women compared to 8.1% of the men. The women of the ATA did their work efficiently and performed a task of supreme importance.

For all who had been involved it was an emotional time; for many there was a feeling of loss. It was, wrote Lettice Curtis, ". . . something of an anti-climax, taking away incentive, our very *raison d'etre,* and putting nothing in its place . . . . To those of us who had nothing to go back to and nowhere particular to go, the end of the war was about as climactic an experience as the outbreak." For the pilots, the days so filled with flying now seemed like a dream, as if they had never existed. Indeed it was almost so, for there was little tangible recognition, no honours or awards or ceremonies to acknowledge the task they had performed so well. ATA passed into history as it had begun — almost without notice.

We live in the wind and sand and our eyes are on the stars.
— WASP motto.

The Women's Airforce Service Pilots

IN THE UNITED STATES women were given the opportunity to earn their wings only after the supply of eligible male applicants had trickled to nearly nothing. Two organizations sprang up almost simultaneously: the Women's Auxiliary Ferrying Squadron and the Women's Flying Training Detachment. These two groups merged in 1943, becoming the impressive organization of accomplished women aviators known as the Women's Airforce Service Pilots. The women were hand-picked to perform a variety of non-combat flying assignments at US Army Air bases and training fields to relieve male pilots for combat duties. The image of the aviatrix captured the imagination of many adventuresome young American women and reportedly 25,000 applied to fly for their country. Only 1,074 won their wings; one of them was Virginia Lee Warren of Winnipeg, Manitoba.

The Women's Auxiliary Ferrying Squadron was formed in September 1942 after more than two years of lobbying by pilot Nancy Harkness Love. It was an experimental unit, established within Air Transport Command, Army Air Forces, to utilize women pilots. Applicants had to be high school graduates between the ages of twenty-one and thirty-five, have a commercial licence, and a minimum of 500 hours on aircraft of at least 200 horsepower. Nancy Love was appointed squadron commander and she directed the ferrying activities until the program was disbanded in December 1944. She chose twenty-three women to begin ferrying duties.

Meanwhile, well-known pilot Jacqueline Cochran had been agitating for the use of women pilots for the war effort since September 1939. She foresaw that the United States would be drawn into war and believed that women should be trained and ready. Nothing came of her efforts until after the US had entered the fighting and the shortage of male pilots became evident. But Cochran had not been idle; she had been recruiting American women to fly with the ATA in Great Britain and had examined that organization as a possible blueprint for what she hoped to organize in the US. She argued that the twenty-three WAFS were but a drop in the bucket and what was needed was a training program to bring American women pilots up to Army Air Force service standards. What Cochran was permitted to form was the Women's Flying Training Detachment, or "Woofteddies," as it was popularly called.

Applicants to the Training Detachment had to be high school educated, American citizens between the ages of twenty-one and thirty-five (later lowered to eighteen), five feet tall (later raised to five foot two and a half and then to five foot four, as the women began flying the big four-engine aircraft), and have 200 hours flying time (dropped to 100, then to 75, and finally to 35 hours). In addition, all applicants had to undergo an Army flight medical and personal interview with Cochran.

When the first Woofteddies reported for training in November 1942 there was no organized housing or messing. Instead they were billetted all over Houston and transported to and from the airfield in what became known as "cattle trucks." Many did not get breakfast and had to go the whole day without eating. This happened because some of the landladies, suspicious of what the women were doing, refused to feed them before they were picked up at seven in the morning. Since the trainees were not permitted to enlighten their doubting guardians, this went on until alternate arrangements were made. The second and third classes were billetted in tourist courts, which were not much of an improvement. Often they slept two to a bed and showered in cold water because the hot water supply was insufficient to handle a flock of women.

In December a mess hall was erected on the field. It was a long three-quarters of a mile away and trainees were required to march and sing to and from meals. To the tune of the Notre Dame fight song they composed the Army Air Forces Flight Training Detachment song, the first verse of which was:

We've gotten zoot suits, jackets and stuff
Now we are drilling, boy are we rough
Calisthenics make us sore
Still they will give us more and more
Plenty of ground school, no time for flight
Long waits for mail, no letter in sight
That's AAFFTD
Some life we all agree.

The WASPs had their own mascot. Walt Disney was so impressed with their work that he created a character just for them; "Fifinella," sister of another Disney character, "The Gremlin," was a dainty kind-hearted little elf who helped the WASPs out of tight spots.

The "zoot suits" referred to in the song were what the Woofteddies called the Army issue of flying overalls. Made to fit the average-size man, they were far too large for the women and made them look like clowns. Typically, the women saw the humour and immortalized the zoot suits in the first verse of another of their songs. Sung to the tune of *The Man On The Flying Trapeze*, it went like this.

Once we wore scanties, but now we're in zoots
They are our issued GI flying suits.
They come in all sizes, large, large and large
We look like a great big barge.

The WAFS and WFTDS each wore their own unofficial uniform until their merger in August 1943, when a special women's uniform was designed for the newly-formed Women's Airforce Service Pilots (WASPs). The uniform consisted of slacks with no pockets — it was considered undesirable to add to the natural female hip-breadth — an oxford cloth blue shirt, an Eisenhower-type battle jacket plus heavy dark blue cotton flight coveralls. The dress uniform was a "Santiago Blue" skirt and jacket, white shirt and black tie topped with a beret emblazoned with the seal of the United States. Upon completion of training each woman received a set of wings, which were modified Army pilots wings with a diamond symbol in place of the shield.

AS LEE WARREN, the only Canadian WASP, remembered, "I was told that you had to have 200 hours and be twenty-one to join the WASPS, whereas the ATA required only that you be eighteen and have at least 50 hours on a 100 hp machine. I couldn't do anything about my age so decided to concentrate on becoming eligible for the ATA. That wasn't easy; all the higher horsepowered aircraft were only for military training. I didn't have a licence either even though I had completed my training. Konnie Johanneson of Winnipeg told me that I had to have an employer before I could get a Limited Commercial Licence. I wrote all over the country trying to find someone who would give me time on a 100 hp aircraft. Finally I found someone in Superior, Wisconsin, who would give me lessons. While I was there a letter from the WASPs caught up with me, saying that they were waiving the age limit and for me to report as soon as possible to Minneapolis. They also waived the required flying time because I had only 75 hours."

The program quickly outgrew the facilities at Houston and arrangements were made to relocate at Avenger Field, Sweetwater, Texas in February. When the class of 43-W-4 (1943, women, fourth class) arrived, the eighty-seven women were delighted to find a group of male cadets who were just finishing their training. This was undoubtedly the only co-educational military flight training in the history of the American armed forces until the mid-seventies.

Lee had an Army medical, an interview with Jacqueline Cochran, and was told to report to the Women's Flying Training Department at Avenger Field, for the October class. "I only had time for a brief visit home: barely enough time to unpack, re-pack, say hello and goodbye. I was airsick most of the way to Dallas. It was my first time in a large aircraft. I was ready to walk back home, anything to get off that plane! When I arrived, the hotel was so full that I slept on a couch in the

WASPs.

lobby. The next day a bus picked us up and took us to Sweetwater."

Texas was a shock to her system. "As excited as I was, I was appalled by the barrenness of the place and the dearth of trees. The wind seemed to blow most of the time [note the WASP motto]. You could see forever when the dust wasn't blowing too much. 'Desolate' describes it. On the base it was strip after strip of stark one-storey buildings. There was a six- to eight-bed hospital, an administrative wing, a ground school building, and the barracks. Our quarters were a series of bays; each bay had a concrete floor, six beds, six lockers, a window, a few desks, and a central pot-bellied stove. In between each bay there was a bathroom also with a concrete floor, two sinks, two showers, and two toilets. Outside was a 'green area' although I never saw any green. There was another building which housed the lounge, snack area and dining room; we called it the feeding station because it had trestle tables seating twelve to sixteen. It was nothing like home. It was an experience being on a base with three hundred women a long way from home. I found out that I wasn't as mature as I thought I was."

The weather was no help to morale either. That year Texas was unseasonably cold and had one of its rare snowfalls. "Many

Lee Warren, Women's Airforce Service Pilot.

VIRGINIA LEE WARREN DOERR

Lee Warren was born in Winnipeg, Manitoba, the only child of American parents. Her family settled in Winnipeg where her father opened Breslauer & Warren Jewellery Ltd. Lee had many friends but her closest buddy was her father. "He took me hunting and fishing, taught me to drive a car before I was twelve and used to let me help out at the store. He was very determined that I would do something with my life." She attended Wesley College [now University of Winnipeg] preparatory to going to University of California for law school but was bored with the whole university setting.

"I was over at Sally Perrin's one night and heard her father [John Perrin, owner of the San Antonio Gold Mine at Bissett, Manitoba] talk about his problems getting bush pilots for the mine. I thought, 'Why not become a bush pilot?'" Lee soon talked Sally into taking lessons with her and Mr. Perrin agreed to hire them. As soon as university examinations were over they signed up for instruction at Konnie Johanneson's at Stevenson Field. That was in 1942 and gasoline rationing was already in effect so flying time was hard to get. "I took my lessons on a Taylorcraft, Piper Cub and Gipsy Moth — anything that was available. My

in our class got the flu and missed too much flying to keep up with the rest of the class. I was off sick a lot but I managed to survive both the civilian and army check rides. Only sixty-five out of one hundred and twenty-five girls finished in my class. My class was part of the 'guinea pig program' — we jumped from primary to advanced, missing basic training; and that put a lot of stress on us. The biggest problem for me was going from a 120 hp to a 600 hp aircraft with retractable gear. We had the normal amount of washouts in primary but the largest in advanced. We jumped from the PT-17 (Stearman) to the AT-6 (Harvard)."

If the weather was good trainees flew in the early morning, early afternoon, and at night; when not on the flight line, they were in ground school. "We spent about four or five hours a day in class, though if the weather was poor and then improved, we flew a lot and doubled up on ground school. We did calisthenics if the weather permitted and we marched even if the weather was rotten." Their instructors were civilians under Army supervision. After each phase of training candidates took a civilian and army check ride. At any time a student could be sent for a ride with the Army check pilot and if she did not pass, out she went. "They were tough. They weren't going to waste money on questionable pilots. We lost a lot.

"Our social life was very limited — despite what the book *Santiago Blue* says. In theory we were allowed into town one night a week, either Friday, Saturday, or Sunday, but we had to be back by nine. Once a month we could stay out till one. If the weather had been poor and we were behind schedule and the weather cleared over the weekend, then we could not leave the

mother wasn't very happy with my flying and I wasn't allowed to hang about the airfield." Then tragedy struck. Sally and her instructor were killed when another student flew into them. Shaken, but encouraged by her father to keep flying, Lee continued but the purpose was now gone. "When Sally died Mr. Perrin gave up the idea of having me fly for him."

Lee looked around for another job, and that was when she heard of the ATA and the WASPs. Her career with the American Women's Air Service Pilots ended in 1944 when the organization was terminated.

Lee married pilot Lou Doerr, who she had met in the WASPs, had children, and she and Lou managed Breslauer & Warren in Kenora until 1964, when they moved to Arizona.

Lee Warren and unidentified co-pilot, c. 1943.

base; just fly, fly, fly. A big night out was a steak dinner and a movie."

Poor weather often threw the flight schedule out of kilter and trainees soon learned that old military virtue of patience, and the practice of "hurry up and wait." They waited for the weather, for the planes, for meals, and for the single latrine! If the weather was good on Sunday, their "free" day, they flew. The notoriously poor weather inspired another song:

> We get up at six in the morning
> Regardless of where we have been.
> But at quarter past eight
> It won't hesitate
> The fog rolls in!
>
> We hurry our eating at lunch time
> Get out our 'chutes,' check the pin.
> But exactly at two
> We've nothing to do
> For the fog rolls in.
>
> At dusk when the daylight is waning
> 'Tis then at the end of the day
> That you'll hear us all sigh
> That it's too late to fly
> And the fog rolls away!

The program grew by leaps and bounds. Initially intended to train 122 students every four and a half weeks, it was increased to 750 and then to 1000. The flight program was also expanded, from 115 hours to 210 hours. Each girl accepted for training received $150 per month (later increased to $172.50), from which $15 was deducted for quarters. Meals and uniform were extra. Each paid her own way to Texas and, if she washed out, she paid her own way home.

The women's program was grueling: a stepped-up version of the nine-month course developed for the male aviation cadets. It covered everything except gunnery and formation flying. Their day started at 6:30 AM and finished at 10:00 PM. The flight program was a thirty-week course divided into three 70 hour segments: primary, intermediate, and advanced. Instrument and navigation training were emphasized in the last two phases. They flew BT-13s, AT-6s (Harvards), PT-17s, and PT-19s (Cornells). The ground school program, initially 180 hours, was increased to 560 hours and included 309 hours academic subjects, 137 hours military training, 10 hours (increased to 24 hours) aero equipment maintenance, 81 hours physical training, and 23 hours medical training. This was an intense curriculum for a civilian program. In early 1944, when it appeared that the WASPs would be militarized, a twenty-day military course was added for those WASPs with at least three months of operational duty. Additional subjects included military law, base and staff functions, and technical and tactical aspects of Army Air Force operations, such as electronic aids to flying, air-sea rescue, and radar. Designed to prepare WASPs to become Army officers, the course ran from April 1944 to October 1944 when the decision came down to deactivate the entire WASP program.

A FEW INCIDENTS kept Lee Warren's training from being purely routine. One occurred in her last month at Sweetwater. "I was flying an AT-6 and had a fire on take-off. I had smoke and oil on the windscreen and couldn't see anything. When I reached altitude for my first turn I called the tower, who misunderstood me and told me to bail out. I told them I was still in the circuit and I wanted to land. I managed to make a great navy 360 approach, landed on the runway and was met with fire trucks. It all happened in about ten minutes but it seemed like ten hours. The Board of Inquiry cleared me."

On another occasion, while flying a PT-17 on her short cross-country, Lee was overtaken by a terrifying dust storm. "When I finally was able to land at Oklahoma City all the airport trucks were lined up on the field with their lights on to give me enough illumination to land. That was at four in the afternoon." Lee's long cross-country did not go exactly as planned either. The women were required to fly from Texas to California. She set off knowing that five of her classmates had died because they flew into weather crossing the mountains. "I ran into weather problems right away so went south of the usual route. I also discovered that my radio wasn't working. I didn't want to turn back so I just kept going, navigating by railway tracks, roads, and mountains. Unfortunately I also had compass problems and ran into strong headwinds. I finally saw a small airfield. I knew it was the wrong one but I was running low on gas. I circled three times, trying to get the wind direction. When I landed I was met by three jeeps with machine guns on the back and five military personnel with guns ready. When I stepped out there were a lot of surprised looks. I had landed at an abandoned civilian field, then part of a Japanese Internment Camp in New Mexico. They told me that if I had circled around once more they [American military] would have shot at me!"

As soon as WASPs earned their wings flying duties commenced; they ferried light aircraft from factories to training bases and quickly progressed through all aircraft classifications, including pursuit and bomber aircraft. In fact, the women flew pursuit aircraft so impressively that a women's detachment was stationed at the Republic factory to fly P-47s (Thunderbolts). And fly them they did. Two thousand P-47s were delivered by WASPs. Ferrying the P-39s (Airacobras), nicknamed "the

flying coffins," the WASPs had a lower accident rate than the men. In all, 303 WASPs were assigned to Ferry Command and they delivered 12,652 planes with only three fatal accidents, none in the big bombers or cargo aircraft.

In addition to ferrying duties, WASPs were assigned to almost every stateside command, where they flew a variety of missions. They towed targets for live air-to-air gunnery and ground-to-air gunnery practice. They flew simulated strafing missions, smoke laying exercises, and radio control or drone (unmanned aircraft) experimental flights. They also instructed at both the basic and advanced levels and served as test pilots.

Molly Beall, refused for pilot training, joined the Women's Division of the RCAF. She requested photographic duties — the only trade open to women where flight time was possible. After the war she had an illustrious career in aviation.

Despite their proven capabilities, they were restricted to domestic ferry duties and were not permitted to fly across the

Atlantic. Two WASPs almost made the history books by attempting to do exactly that, but they were reined in at the last, crucial moment. Nancy Love and Betty Gillies were both checked out and cleared to fly a B-17 Flying Fortress to Scotland. They, along with three male aircrew, had already reached Goose Bay, Labrador, where weather grounded them. By chance this information was passed to General "Hap" Arnold, Chief of the US Army Air Corps and organizer with Cochran of the WASPs. He promptly radioed Labrador, where he caught the women already on the runway ready for take-off, and ordered the flight to be held. He then issued a statement that no women were to ferry aircraft across the ocean.

Lee Warren received her WASP wings in April 1943 and was posted to Romulus, Detroit, Ferry Command Base. All psyched up to fly fast aircraft, she found her first assignment a letdown. "I had to fly a Piper Cub to the scrapyard. Twenty of us, the rest men, civilian pilots, had to pick up twenty Piper Cubs in Kansas and fly them to the graveyard in Rome, New York. The Cubs, which had been sitting unprotected in a field, were in terrible shape. The fabric was full of holes and they had no instruments. It took us almost three weeks to move them. My Cub gave up on me just before Newark. There was no place for me to make a forced landing. There were mountains on the right, hydro lines, and the Hudson River. I managed to nurse it almost onto the runway, landing on the grass and then blowing a tire when I hit the concrete runway. I dinged a wing. I was called to explain what happened and told by the military officer I should have landed it in the river. What a way to start."

The WASPs based at Romulus flew everything from Cubs (L-4s) and AT-6s to Flying Fortresses (B-17s) and Liberators (B-24s). In a typical day Lee might fly a B-24 from Detroit to St. Paul, pick up another to fly to Norfolk, Virginia and then return to base by commercial airline. Trips often averaged 500 to 1000 miles. Except for the twin and four-engine aircraft WASPs flew without radio contact. "It was a grueling pace at Ferry Command. Our schedule was seven days a week twenty four hours a day if the weather was good. My favourite trips were to Dorval, Montreal to pick up Harvards. It was nice to return to Canada. We'd take the Harvards to Newark, New Jersey, turn over all the documents, be cleared, and catch an Air Force flight back to the base; all in the same day — except that the days were thirty to thirty five hours long for we'd start at

5:00 AM and finish at 8:00 PM the next day."

Despite her tiny size Lee had little trouble handling the large aircraft. "I often needed up to five cushions to reach the controls and see out but I didn't have too much difficulty with the actual flying. I had more problems just walking out to the plane with all my pillows and my parachute."

Enemy fire was never a threat to the WASPs but sabotage was. Twice Lee experienced engine failure because of it. "I was taking an aircraft from Rome to Newark and couldn't stay airborne. I'd just get off the runway and boom, back down I went. After two more attempts I taxied back to the hangar where a mechanic's cap was found wedged into the carbeurator. The second time it happened was because someone had put sugar in the gas tank. Again it was on take-off; fortunately there was a long runway and I got back down safely."

Lee almost got her wish to fly fighters in July 1944 when she was posted to Dallas, but her father became seriously ill and she returned to Canada. "When I returned, the class for fighters was full so they posted me to Orlando, Florida for Officer's Training. It made a nice break from the hard pace at Ferry Command. At least I knew where I would be sleeping each night. I remember the session on survival procedures in case you landed on a tropical island. We were told what we could and could not eat. Some of the things I was familiar with, but 'fillet of sheepshead, morsels of rattlesnake steak'?"

From Florida Lee went to Greenville Army Air Base, North Carolina, as a test pilot. "Greenville was a basic training field and the aircraft were BT-13s, 15s, and UC-78s. It was a very routine job. We were to flight check the aircraft after any mechanical or airframe work was done, before the students and instructors flew them. I used to try and take the mechanic who worked on it with me. I found out that if the mechanic knew he had to fly the aircraft he had repaired he did a good job. We cleared them or sent them back to the shop." It was at Greenville that Lee met her husband, Major Louis C. Doerr, US Army Air Corps, chief of flying advisory board and safety officer for the base. "I checked out his plane and then gave him a thorough briefing on it. Lou and I made several trips together."

The WASPs were unexpectedly relieved of flying the B-29 Superfortress. The two women who had already been checked out and had flown numerous demonstration flights for training purposes were informed their services were no longer needed. According to Dora Dougherty Strother, Lt Col, U.S.A.F. Reserve, the reason, revealed in a later interview, was that the girls were doing a fine job but they were ". . . putting the big football players to shame."[5]

PRAISE FOR THE QUALITY of flying done by the WASPs came from all quarters. Commanding officers usually preferred to have a WASP ferry an aircraft because she reached her destination a day or so ahead of a man doing the same flight. (They thought that perhaps it was because the WASPs did not carry little black books full of addresses.) Official commendation came from General Arnold on December 7, 1944: "It's on record that women can fly as well as men. Certainly we haven't been able to build an airplane you can't handle. From AT-6s to B-29s, you have flown them around like veterans. We of the Army Air Forces are proud of you."

Then without warning came the death blow. Despite the promise of militarization, the program was terminated in December 1944. Political pressure and a well-organized lobby effort by male civilian pilot instructors blocked the passage of the 1944 bill to give the WASPs military status. Apparently instructors feared that expansion or militarization of the WASPs could end their contract flying with the Army Airforce and make them eligible for the draft.

As Lee Warren remembered that time, "We were given three weeks notice. It was the abruptness with which we were told that was a real jolt. Many of us had just finished our officer's training and we assumed we would be in until the war ended. Aircraft were stranded all over the country. There we were, trained to fly with nothing to fly and the war still on. Some went home. Others of us, who had been test pilots, were valuable to the small aircraft manufacturers." Lee received offers from Beech and Piper and was also asked to fly the mail from Seattle to Alaska but she couldn't pass the medical. "I had about 400 hours with the WASPs and didn't want to let all that training go to waste." Lee however did not fly professionally again.

The women had taken a military oath to defend their country, were subject to military discipline, served in uniform, and handled all Army Air Force non-combat flight missions around the clock from 1942 to 1944. In return they were abruptly disbanded and received neither military status nor benefits. Thirty-eight WASPs died on active duty and their families had to pay to have their daughters' bodies shipped home. Adding insult to injury was the knowledge that when WASP and male aircrew died in the same crash the man's family received military benefits; the WASP's family received nothing.

In 1977, after much lobbying — and the passage of thirty-two years — WASPs were finally accorded "official recognition" by the US government; but, even then, they were allowed only limited veterans' benefits.

THE WOMEN ATA PILOTS AND THE WASPs were pioneers in every sense of the word and their very existence raised issues about the exclusivity of the male military. They accomplished far more than the safe and efficient delivery of hundreds of vitally needed aircraft. They proved that they could handle the most challenging assignments and that nations could call upon their women with complete confidence. They left behind them an impressive and unprecedented record.

Notes

4 Statistics cited in "The Epic of ATA," by Basil Clarke, in *History of Aviation*.

5 Information from former WASP Dora Dougherty Strother, Lieutenant Colonel, USAF Reserve.

CHAPTER FIVE

The war pilots' return

"I felt so empty. It was as if my whole life was behind me. I knew I would never get near a military airfield again, never get a chance to fly those fast planes. I had all that experience and I knew I couldn't put it to use in Canada." — *Marion Orr*

FOR THE CANADIAN WOMEN who had flown some of the world's fastest and largest aircraft and had climbed "almost to the top" there was, after the war, an emotional letdown almost too great to bear. Each returned from Air Transport Auxiliary duty in England hoping for a continuation of her career but surely knowing that the "chance" she had had in wartime would not occur again. For these committed women, however, flying could not be denied and for the next twenty to forty-five or more years it continued to be a part of their lives.

Vi Milstead's return to flying coincided with the appearance of the Fleet Canuck, a trainer, just off the assembly lines at Fort Erie. The distributor, Alex Hennessey, asked Vi if she would be interested in promoting the aircraft — "the girl pilot thing," explained Vi. However, when no contract materialized she looked for something else. In the end she applied for a position at Leavens Brothers in Toronto. “I was interviewed early in May 1946 by that so-conservative, so-gentlemanly pair, Walt and Clare Leavens. They offered me a job as a flying instructor. I was hired on their terms. The base pay was not good but the pay per flying hour was — if I could get students to come to me — they were not gambling that much. I was back in the air on May 6, working for Leavens' chief flying instructor, Arnold Warren.” The post-war flying boom was in full swing and instructors worked all day every day, including summer evenings. “Every Sunday, weather permitting, there was a breakfast flight somewhere for the entire fleet. I have been at the airport before dawn, about 4:30, starting airplanes, and not finishing until after dark, about 10:00.”

That winter was a lean time financially for Leavens and for Vi. The highlight was a snow storm which swept through south-western Ontario bringing highway and railway traffic to a complete halt. “For a few days we were very busy flying newspapers into the area and flying yeast to the villages so they could make bread. I spent one day flying diesel fuel from Orangeville to Shelburne to get snow ploughs moving. This, believe it or not, was in a tandem two-seater 65 hp Aeronca Champion.”

Meanwhile, a romance between Vi and Arnold Warren was flourishing. “We were planning a life partnership. This required a sound economic base, hard to find in the aviation business. What we saw at Leavens Brothers made us uneasy. There was plenty of activity but senior staff were not being made to feel they were making a contribution.” Then in the late winter of 1947 two things happened which combined to affect their lives: Leavens Brothers bought Barker Field and Nickel Belt Airways was formed. “Barker Field was becoming too valuable to continue for long as a small airplane airport.” Vi related, “Nickel Belt appeared very aggressive and progressive with plans for expansion across Canada. The backbone of its equip-

It was a welcome diversion from instructing when Violet Milstead was asked to fly Miss Canada of 1946 around to publicize Canada's first International Air Show held at Downsview airport that year. They even went to Washington, DC on one of the first Fleet Canucks. As Vi related, “Marion Saver, Miss Canada, and I were well entertained on that trip, particularly in Washington.”

ment was the new Canadian Fairchild Husky bush freighter for which Nickel Belt was the distributor. Jimmy Bell, chief pilot and partner, appeared at Barker Field one day with a beautiful new Husky. Tempting bait." A couple of weeks later Bell contacted Vi and Arnold again and asked them to meet him at the Walker House Hotel. With him was the legendary aviator, Johnny Fauqier, a pioneer bush pilot, "King of the Pathfinders," and Canadian commander of the famous RAF "Dambusters" Squadron. "We spent a wonderful evening together. Johnny did most of the talking, telling hilarious war stories in which he was never the hero. No business was discussed." Some weeks later Bell and Vi and Arnold did talk business with the result that Vi and Arnold agreed to join the fledgling Nickel Belt Airways.

Theoretically Arnold was hired as chief flying instructor and Vi as a flying instructor. In practice, Arnold flew charters and Vi handled the school. She also did some charter work, the first time in Canada that a woman was hired to fly in the bush. This attracted so much attention that *Chatelaine*, the most widely read women's magazine in Canada at the time, sent writer June Callwood to do a story. Titled "The Bush Angel, the Only Lady Bush Pilot in the World," tales of Vi's exploits reached all corners of Canada.

Vi and Arnold used the Fleet Canuck mainly for instructing and the Husky for bush flying, although on occasion they also flew a Seabee. The Husky, a high wing monoplane powered with a 450 horsepower Pratt and Whitney engine, could carry a crew of two plus eight passengers or freight. Most pilots considered it underpowered although both Vi and Arnold had good things to say about it. To fly an aircraft of that weight class, Vi needed permission from the Department of Transport. She had no problem receiving it. Indeed, Stuart Graham, superintendent of air regulations, was so impressed with her ATA record that he wrote, "In recognition of your flying record during the past seven years I am endorsing your licence for all types, single and multi-engine, up to the DC-3."

Float flying was a novelty to her. "I had my share of falling into the water! I enjoyed learning how to dock and beach the aircraft. The Husky had a rear-loading capacity so it was a matter of finding out how to manoeuvre it to the shoreline to use that rear hatch. I also had to learn how to do a glassy water landing." Flying floats in the summer and skis in the winter, Vi flew as far south as Muskoka and Toronto, east beyond North Bay, north to Folyet and Kapuskasing, north-west to Biscotasing and Chapleau. The work involved forest fire suppression, supplying bush lodges, flying fishermen, hunters, and prospectors, carrying Indian trappers to and from their trap lines, and timber cruising. "I even flew Lester Pearson when he was stumping for elections. It was wilderness, unspoiled wilderness, and I loved it."

Initially, navigation was a problem for Vi, partly because of the maps she and Arnold were issued and also because she had been used to flying in built-up areas, using power lines, railway tracks, and towns as landmarks. "Now I had only waterways in

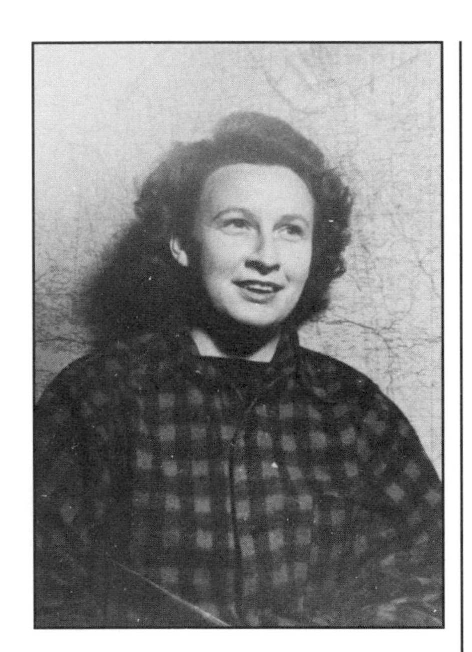

Vi Milstead, when she worked for Nickel Belt Airways, 1947-1950.

VI MILSTEAD related this incident while flying her boss in northern Ontario. "He had owned a plane for many years and could fly it after a fashion. He had no licence and needed considerably more training. He was a strong, hard-driving man, likeable in many ways, and utterly exasperating in a few others. He was the force behind Nickel Belt Airways and, probably, its fatal weakness. His most dominant characteristic was that wherever he was, he was in charge. As far as he was concerned, the pilot was his employee and did what he was told. He merely announced where he wanted to go and when, and expected it to happen. Some of the stories the boys brought home from such trips were, well, interesting."

Vi had one of these experiences when she flew him to Parry Sound for a business trip and he decided to return to Sudbury just before dusk. "I knew that it would be dark long before we arrived and it was going to be a dark, moonless, starless night. The Canuck had no blind flying instruments, instrument lights, or nav [navigation] or landing lights and there was no way of lighting a landing path on the lake at Sudbury. As captain I should have said, 'It's too late now . . . Not only would it be unsafe, it would be illegal.' But I didn't say anything. As usual, when we were in the Canuck the boss did the flying. I was worried what might happen if I allowed him to land the aircraft. The only way to land safely in the dark was to do a glassy water landing, a technique used for setting a seaplane down on a mirror surface, that is, a surface you cannot see. What you see is a reflection, mostly of the sky. It is totally deceiving and a deadly trap for the unwary . . . The glassy water technique requires delicate control of attitude and power during the landing procedures. My boss had no idea of airspeed control. His usual approach for landing took lots of room and his control handling was anything but delicate. I knew that one brutal jerk on the elevator at the wrong time

rough, rocky terrain. On my first trip into the bush I actually got lost. I started from Sudbury one morning to fly to Mississagi Lodge, a hunting and fishing lodge on Upper Green Lake. There was no town or village anywhere near it. The trip should have taken about one hour. I arrived in the area but couldn't find the lodge, tried systematic search procedures without success, then flew to Bisco and taxied into the Forestry base there. When the boys got over fainting spells from seeing a girl, they became very helpful. When one of the pilots saw the map I was using he laughed. 'No wonder you couldn't find the lodge. You can't navigate in the bush with that map.' He handed me his, a Department of Lands and Forests map. After that I had no more trouble."

Like all bush pilots Vi had her share of forced landings and unexpected nights in the bush. "Once I was alone with a man who was not my husband. The Husky was on skis and there was a sudden change in weather — a thaw which produced slush — which made it impossible to take off. The skis just stuck to the snow. I spent the night in the plane with my passenger. No excitement, but grounds for much good-natured teasing."

Her students also provided some interesting moments. "They were all men; not a girl among them. Sudbury was a mining town and most were connected to the mining industry.

and we'd be in the lake, not on it. I couldn't let him attempt the landing; but how was I to stop him? I finally told him very firmly, in my best professional manner that I was taking over. He gave me a very surprised look but let go, reluctantly, and said in a gruff, injured voice, 'What's the matter, don't you trust me?'

"I swung well back for a long approach, picked a small cluster of lights on the west shore of the lake, pinned the airspeed on 70, adjusted power so the lights held steady in the lower part of my windscreen. The lights held their position in my windscreen, getting steadily larger as we descended towards them. When I judged it proper, I eased the nose up into the 'step' attitude and made a power reduction. The lights passed beneath the keels of our floats and we swept out over the black hole of the lake. I picked the lights of the air base as a direction reference. Then I sat quietly and waited. The feel of the seat told me that the plane was sinking slowly. Slowly enough? Too slowly? Suddenly, without warning, there was the sound and feel of water under the floats. I closed the throttle. We scooted forward on the step, then settled comfortably in."

They were a very different group than at Barker Field — a little rougher. Some were shocked to find a woman for their instructor. One of my students was Dr. Stanley Davidson, who developed the principle of the flying magnetometer for aerial prospecting.

Unfortunately the company was heading for trouble (as it turned out, Austin Airways took it over) and Vi and Arnold began looking elsewhere for work. Salvation came in 1950 when the Department of Transport asked them to take over the management of the bankrupt Windsor Flying Club. "We accepted because it was a way to get back south. It was not easy to find a place that needed two pilots, one of them female,"

explained Vi. "Officially Arnold was the chief flying instructor and I was an instructor. Unofficially I was also bar maid, cleaning lady, cook, etc., etc., and etc." In less than two years the Warrens turned the club around, making it a financially solid operation, but they had had enough.

When, in 1952, the Saskatchewan Government Air Service offered Arnold a job, they were tempted, but there was nothing for Vi, except a job running the flying club at Prince Albert, which she did not want. Instead they chose something which took them much farther afield, to Indonesia, where Arnold had been selected to be the first chief flying instructor of the Indonesian Aviation Academy in Djakarta, Java. "That was part of a United Nations Technical Assistance Mission to train the

Vi with the Husky, shown here on floats. Sudbury, Ontario, 1947.

newly liberated Indonesians to fly their own national airline and for the Indonesian Air Force," explained Arnold. Again there was no place for Vi. Although she received an Indonesian instructor's licence, the first ever granted to a woman in Indonesia, she could do little with it. The Moslem religion forbade a Muslim from taking instruction from a woman. "I accepted it," Vi said, adding, "I don't know how gracefully. But there was really nothing I could do. I gave the occasional lesson to a non-Muslim, using a J-3 Cub which belonged to the defunct Dutch Flying Club."

On their return to Canada in 1954 they worked at Orenda Engines at the Avro plant in Toronto. "We were still in aviation,

but not flying. Arnold was a public relations officer and I was a librarian. We remained there until 'Black Friday,' the day the Avro Arrow was cancelled [1959].

Vi then became a librarian for the Ontario Water Commission, and in 1973 the Warrens retired and settled in Les Îles de la Madeleine in the Gulf of the St. Lawrence. "We bought a souped-up PA-12 and later upgraded to a Mooney. We made many trips back and forth between the Islands and Ontario and enjoyed the challenge of the 100 miles of open water." In the late seventies they moved to Colborne, Ontario, where they currently reside, restoring a beautiful century-old home.

Vi Milstead in a de Havilland Chipmunk, RCAF, Air Reserve training at the Windsor Flying Club, 1951.

Vi Milstead Warren was a credit to her profession. She flew over 7000 hours on 60 different types of aircraft. Throughout her career she maintained a level of competence and professionalism that won her the admiration and respect of her colleagues. One of her former students, de Havilland's former chief test pilot, Bob Fowler, summed up Vi with the compliment, "She was a peach of a pilot and a peach of a girl."

ELSPETH RUSSELL married pilot Gerry Burnett within a week of their discharge from the ATA. They spent the next two years trying to settle upon a way of life and finally decided to move to Elspeth's home town, Matane, Quebec, to start a flying service. Flying had brought them together and since neither of them could shake the flying bug, they decided not to fight it any longer. From the start it was understood that Elspeth would be a working partner, but it was not easy for her to buck society's rules and to work, particularly in conservative Quebec, where wives typically stayed at home.

Together they formed Matane Air Service in 1947 to provide service to the communities along the St. Lawrence River. Matane Air began operation with one aircraft, a Stinson 108, and two pilots, Elspeth and Gerry. Initially business was slow and to subsidize the company both obtained their instructor's ratings and offered flight training in addition to charter work. After the excitement and pressure of the war years, they found peace-time flying and living difficult to get used to. "It was a real let down for us to go from flying fast and powerful warbirds to the slow aircraft. But it was better than driving a truck," said Gerry.

Although Matane was the hub of air activity for the lower St. Lawrence and only Quebecair and Rimouski Airlines were operating in the area, the Burnetts found it a long uphill battle to secure a foothold. At first they were limited to the south shore of the St. Lawrence where business was slow. "Quebecair, which was really Canadian Pacific Air Lines, had an air mail contract. It was using ski planes, Dragon Rapides. When CPA left the east and concentrated in western Canda all the licences were up for grabs. Rimouski Airlines took over CPA's routes. It was using Ansons and later, DC-3s. We had trouble getting a licence for regular transport."

The restrictions about not paralleling existing commercial services slowed their growth, but later, as Gerry explained, "We were allowed to parallel but only in the non-busy season so we were no threat, but we became known. There was really only

Rimouski Airlines that we had to watch out for; there was someone up at Gaspé and there was Northern Wings flying on the north shore, but we were not in conflict with them. I kept my eye on future developments — iron ore production was just beginning, the lumber industry — and when it seemed the right time we expanded across the St. Lawrence. For that we needed twin-engine aircraft. We obtained concessions slowly. By the mid fifties we were operating three DC-3s and a couple of Lockheeds and we had a Link Trainer. Our operation was VFR [Visual Flight Rules] but all our pilots had instrument ratings."

According to Gerry there was no real airport in Matane, just

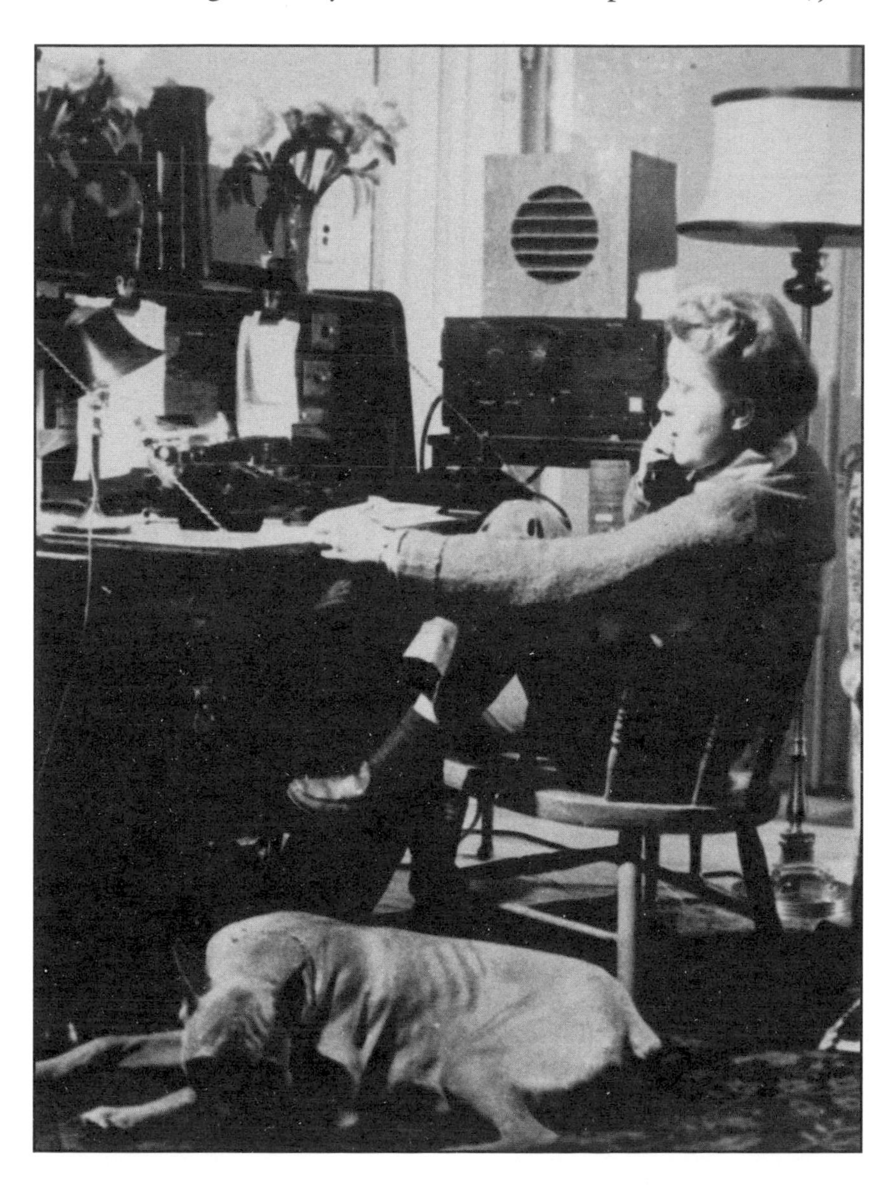

Elspeth handling Matane Air Service air radio operations.

a rough gravel strip, and air strips elsewhere were not maintained by the government. "We had problems operating off the primitive air fields that were in use in northern Quebec. We began in a farmer's field near the house. The snow was not removed but compacted with rollers. But if the snow hadn't 'cured' enough then the wheels of the plane would sink two to four inches. Then you would spend hours digging the plane out."

Matane Air Service thrived under the energetic Burnetts and grew into a company of twenty-eight employees offering a scheduled network of services all over northern Quebec. Their fleet included a Fairchild 24, a Cessna Crane, DC-3s, and

Lockheed Electras. "It was a hub-and-spoke operation; the spokes going north-bound to a half-dozen strips along the coast of the north shore and inland about 130 miles to the hydro project." However, by 1963 success had brought them into conflict with Quebecair. As Gerry recalled, "We had reached our potential and had started cutting back. Our entire operation was geared for the Matane area and we had been serving six companies on the north shore and five of them ceased their lumber operations completely — became ghost towns. Fortunately we had the hydro project and Baie Comeau. But we had to tighten our belts. We weren't prepared to fight Quebecair and when they approached us to sell, it seemed the sensible thing to do." They sold out to Quebecair in 1965 and

L *Elspeth and Gerry Burnett with a Matane Air Service DC-3.*

R *Elspeth took part in all activities at Matane Air Service, including wing repair.*

with that act, closed the aviation chapter of their lives.

Elspeth worked side-by-side with her husband to develop Matane Air into a thriving business. She washed aircraft, did minor repairs, and helped build the hangar. She also flew as an instructor and charter pilot on anything from Fairchild 24s to DC-3s and, along the way, she soothed startled miners and lumberjacks who had never flown with a woman pilot, much less heard of one. Her logbook shows relatively little time in the air for the years she flew but her 1200 hours were painstakingly accumulated in flights that averaged only 40 minutes. As the years went on and three sons claimed her time, she eased out of flying and took over such ground activities as radio communications, dispatching, and bookkeeping. But she remained current, flying mostly during their busy season, right up to the time the company was sold, making fourteen charter trips in May-June 1964. Elspeth Burnett was the first professional woman pilot in Quebec and marked the way for the next generation of women pilots in that province.

—*Photo by Rapid Grip and Batten*

A CASUAL "FLIP" with an air-minded friend started Helen Harrison into the sky-lanes. Vancouver-born, she has spent most of her life in other parts of the globe, and has had a spectacular career. Photo taken on start of a hop from Toronto to Vancouver. With her is John Carrol, manager of the Percival Proctor Co. of Canada. One of many well-wishers is bidding her adieu.

Helen Harrison.

THE ONLY JOB Helen Harrison could find when war ended was driving a cab at Dorval Airport, Montreal. One night a passenger recognized her and asked, "What are you doing driving a cab?" When Helen explained he was incredulous that someone with her flying experience could not find work and he promised to find her a job. Her passenger was Buzz Beurling, a famous World War II ace, and he soon got her a job demonstrating the Percival Proctor aircraft across Canada.

Fully aware of the publicity value of a good-looking woman, the company made sure that the newspapers were alerted to Helen's arrival in each city. No shrinking violet, Helen posed obligingly for pictures. However, when that demonstration trip ended, so did her job and she again found herself at loose ends. Finding nothing in the east, she and her three sons headed to Vancouver in 1947.

Recognizing that most British Columbia flying was on floats, Helen obtained a float rating (from Rolie Moore) before she went job hunting. Not unexpectedly, the only thing she could find was instructing — the only flying position open to women — with the Duncan Aero Club on Vancouver Island. Two years later, in 1949, Kent Logging Company of Vancouver hired her to fly lumbermen and company officials in its Cessna 170. Based at Galiano, she was the only woman pilot in the area. Extremely voluble sometimes, Helen could be exasperatingly closed-mouthed at other times and she said virtually nothing about her experiences during this period, only that, "I had no trouble. I had my share of sweeping snow off the floats and flying drunks." When this job came to an end, she spent the next twenty years or so instructing or acting as interim manager at flying clubs wherever she could find work. She said very little about the years 1950 to 1969.

"I can't tell you how many clubs I've cleaned up the mess

A student of Helen Harrison immortalized her in a poem:

ODE TO HELEN

Now have you ever been
With an instructor so mean
And your temper is really on fire,
And she hollers "you know
That your left wing is low"
But it's just that the right wing is higher.

So you trim up the ship
And you button your lip
Thank God for a minor correction.
She screams "You'll never learn
Now you've started to turn
And I told you to watch your direction."

So you swing the thing back
And get on your track
You are happy. It worked out so neat.
But with scorn in her tone
That cuts right to the bone
She says "You lost damn near five hundred feet."

for. I was often hired to get a club out of a financial jam and add a little life to it, but as soon as the club was prospering the Board of Directors would put a man in as chief flying instructor/manager. It was frustrating, always having to step back and let a man do the job when I had already shown that I could handle it." Nevertheless, she earned the reputation as the best float instructor in the province. According to Helen, even BC Airlines sent their new pilots to "Floats Harrison" as she was known. "Yet they wouldn't hire me," reported Helen bitterly.

It was the same with the airlines. "I applied at Trans-Canada Airlines, Pacific Western Airlines, and Canadian Pacific Air Lines. The answer was always the same. I was either 'too weak to handle the controls' as one TCA captain told me or 'the public wouldn't accept a woman' as Grant McConachie said. It didn't matter that I had thousands of hours experience flying heavy twins and floats in BC. I couldn't overcome my sex. I even checked out helicopter flying when helicopter pilots were in demand. But Carl Agar of Okanagan Helicopters said, very

You turn right around
Wish you're back on the ground
But your troubles are not over yet.
With a lead heavy heart
Your landing you start
And she wonders how dumb you can get.

She says "My God Don
If you just carry on
I will be a complete nervous wreck.
I beseech and implore you
Now this one will floor you
You forgot the whole pre-landing check."

Now you're down and you're glad
Cause it wasn't so bad
You really did take lots of pains
She says "We arrived
And I'm glad we survived.
You poor guy, you've got sawdust for brains."

There are some good teachers
Professors and preachers
Who'll give a thing all that they've got
And in spite of her yellin'
When you're taught by Helen
You'll sure as hell know you've been taught.

nicely, that he would not hire a woman to work in the bush."

On August 26, 1969, she closed her logbook forever. There were over 15,000 hours recorded. Recognized for her flying achievements, Helen was named to the Order of Icarus in 1963 and to Canada's Aviation Hall of Fame in 1973. "Floats Harrison" was an unforgettable woman. As an instructor she was a tough, no-nonsense type who did not believe in mincing words. A former student wrote, "Helen was a terrific person, a terrific instructor and a terrific aviator whose whole life was flying."

AFTER THE WAR, Vera Strodl was first a charter pilot in Sweden and then an instructor in England, eventually becoming chief flying instructor at one of the flying clubs. Vera probably would have remained in England if, in 1952, an advertisement for an instructor at the Lethbridge Flying Club in Alberta had not caught her eye. Believing that Canadians were more progressive in their thinking than the British, she responded because she assumed that she could move into an airline position. Instructing was simply her ticket to a better job — she thought.

"I arrived in Canada with four English pennies in my pocket," she said. She also brought over 3600 hours in her logbook, most of it on heavy twins and four-engine aircraft. It was that experience that got her the job. Vera later found out that the club had chosen her because she was the most qualified — a logical decision not taken by other clubs later. The Department of Transport also recognized her experience and asked her to be one of the instructors at the 1952 government sponsored Instructors' Refresher Course held that year at Lethbridge.

Unfortunately, Vera found that Canadians were even more

VERA STRODL DOWLING loved her adopted country — Canada. "I thought the Rockies were the most beautiful, awe-inspiring range of peaks imaginable and I used to tell my students, 'Pick yourself a mountain peak on which to keep straight.' I was amused with their comments on visibility, which was excellent, seldom less than a hundred miles. When on rare occasions it was reduced to eighty miles, pilots would say, 'My what a dreadful haze this morning; can't see very far!' I don't know how they would find their way in England's murk."

Vera Strodl, c. 1960.

conservative than the British when it came to women pilots. Thinking she might stand a better chance of being hired by the airlines if she were better known to the companies that operated out of Edmonton's Municipal Airport, she applied to the Edmonton Flying Club. But more than 4000 flying hours could not overcome the fact that V. E. Strodl was female. Speaking thirty years later Vera said, "I found it difficult to get a job at times because men were considered more reliable; they didn't have periods or babies." It took five years before the manager of the Edmonton Flying Club finally hired her. "He told me he did not think that the students would accept a woman instructor. I told him they would once they knew my

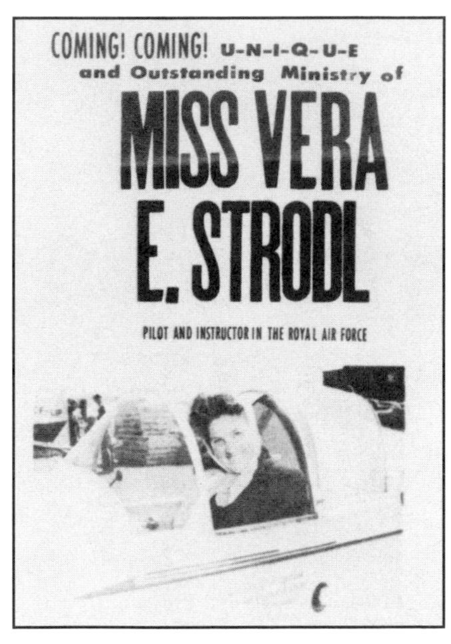

background. When he finally hired me he told me to keep a low profile. I felt like something the cat dragged in. I was treated like a junior instructor." Contrary to the manager's predictions, Vera found her students very accepting of her position.

In the early sixties Vera left the flying club and used her savings to buy a Mooney Mite, a single seat aircraft. On it, she painted religious quotations such as "God is a Good God" and spent the next few years flying into Indian reserves and other isolated areas in Alberta and Saskatchewan carrying the gospel. "I figured I owed the Lord something for saving my life," she explained, referring to incidents that occurred during her wartime work with the ATA. She returned to instructing only when she ran out of money, then with a new "nest egg"

L *Vera Strodl and her missionary plane, a Mooney Mite.*

R *One of Vera's posters advertising her ministry.*

accumulated, she would continue "spreading the word." Unfortunately a fire in 1967 destroyed the Edmonton Flying Club hangar and with it her plane, which was uninsured. The following year she was injured in a car accident and lost her commercial medical. Trained for nothing but flying, she was literally down and out. However, she never lost her faith and, characteristically, turned to helping people less fortunate than herself, serving in the soup kitchens of the Salvation Army and going to Malaysia to work with lepers. During this period she married but was widowed a few years later.

In 1971 her luck changed when the Northern Alberta Institute of Technology offered her a position as a ground school instructor and she re-entered the aviation world. The following year she regained her medical and returned to flying. Shortly after the Canadian Forces commissioned her to design and teach ground school courses for the air cadet program and, in 1982, Transport Canada appointed her a designated flight test examiner. She also began free-lance instructing, and soon she was putting in sixteen hour days and coaching students on the side. The pace proved too much and, worn out, she retired in January 1987.

In her long and colourful flying career Vera logged 23,000 hours on more than 160 types of aircraft. With her usual optimism she accepted that only instructing was open to her and enthusiastically taught for over thirty years. Her dedication to flying was recognized by the British in 1971 when she received the prestigious "Master Pilot's Award" from the Guild of Air Pilots and Air Navigators for her outstanding service to Great Britain as a pilot and instructor. She was the first Canadian pilot, and only the ninth woman in the world, to be so honoured. In 1972 the Alberta Government also recognized her years of dedicated instructing by presenting her with the Award of Achievement. In 1989 the Western Canada Aviation Museum in Winnipeg awarded her its Pioneer in Aviation Award. To all this, Vera disclaims any credit, saying "Give God the Glory." Master Pilot accurately depicts this gracious lady and skillful aviator.

MARION ORR SPENT the first few post-war years bouncing from one company to another: Gillies Flying Service, Aero Activities, Savage Air Service, back to Gillies and to Aero Activities, where she stayed until it folded in 1949.

Working twelve to fourteen hours a day, Marion decided if she was going to put out that much effort it might as well be for herself. Since she had always dreamed of having her own company, she bought the bankrupt Aero Activities at Barker Field. Actually all she purchased was the name, the licence to run a flying school, an office, and a sign saying "Aero Activities." She kept the name because it came first in the telephone book. To finance the purchase of aircraft and the construction of a hangar, she optimistically went to the bank for a loan. However, banks in the forties were not interested in loaning money to women, particularly for a flying school. "Thank heavens for friends," recalled Marion. "I was able to scrape together enough money to buy a couple of planes and get going." In 1949 she was in business, the first Canadian woman to own and operate a flying school.

A year later Marion moved Aero Activities from the Dufferin Street side of Barker Field to the Lawrence Street side. Not wanting to leave her office behind — it was a sturdy brick building — she took it with her. She and fellow pilot Helen Wilson (Hems) took it apart brick by brick and rebuilt it at the new location. "I was so busy trying to run the school and get resettled that I slept in my office. It seemed as if I didn't leave the field for months. I sold my car and most of my personal things — I even sold pop bottles — to raise money to buy a Chipmunk for instrument training. While Helen and I were building the office we dropped a tarp over the open end and had a little stove for heat and cooking. For awhile I even operated out of a booth!"

Enthusiasm for flying was high in the early fifties and Marion and her school were in demand. For the first time in her life, the future looked good. Then in 1951 the bottom fell out. Barker Field was sold to a housing developer and Marion was given twelve months to vacate the premises. Determined to stay in business, she began looking for a place to relocate, finally

Marion Orr, taking the tarp off her de Havilland Chipmunk, 1950.

finding suitable property in the little town of Maple, just north of Toronto. However, local residents, enraged at the prospect of an airport in their town, blocked her application for rezoning. She spent almost a year trying to get approval, speaking to people individually and attending council meetings to try to convince them of the potential benefits. But townspeople wanted sleepy little Maple to stay as it was. "I asked everyone what I should do. Someone told me to go to the Department of Transport, but when I did, they said they couldn't do anything; only the prime minister could help me. They snickered when they said that. But that's exactly what I did. I went to Ottawa to see Prime Minister St. Laurent!

"'Do you have an appointment?' asked his secretary. I said 'no.' 'Well, you cannot see the prime minister.' I said that I would wait until I could see him as it was very important to me. I couldn't afford to leave. I had borrowed money to make the trip. I had only one chance and that was it. I missed lunch and remember thinking how hungry I was but I didn't dare leave to get something to eat. Around four o'clock the secretary asked me why I wanted to see the prime minister. I explained how I had put more than $5000 into developing an airport and how the townspeople had waited until I had put in the runway before they told me they were going to block it. About a half hour later the secretary told me the prime minister would see me. Mr. St. Laurent was very kind. He listened to me and then smiled and said, 'People should not try to stop progress and anyone with your determination deserves an opportunity. You go home now, you'll get your airport.' A few days later I got a letter from Prime Minister St. Laurent saying that he was pleased to help me. My application to operate an airport went through with no more trouble."

Marion Orr was the first woman pilot in Canada to own and operate an airport and flying school. Reporters loved the fact that she had built her own airfield and was the owner, manager, chief flying instructor, and mechanic all rolled into one. They splashed her story on front pages with such headlines as, "She Runs a School in the Sky" and "Flying Is Her Business, Canada's Only Woman Airfield Boss."

The year had gone by in a blur of hard work. As soon as she was through for the day at Barker Field she hurried out to

Maple, rarely taking the time to eat properly. With the help of friends and students, she cleared and graded the land for the runway, dug drainage ditches, and built a combination hangar, office, and small apartment. "I sunk all my energy and money into Maple. I never dared to ask myself if I was doing the right thing. I'd go out at night with a pick and shovel, working by car lights. It was hard work clearing the land of stones and stumps. My students and friends helped me; we did everything ourselves. I even built a furnace room myself out of cement blocks. Helen and I built the office. I'll never forget the day the building inspector showed up — he took one look at the wall and said it had to come down. I was heartbroken. All that work

Maple, Ont.

Canada's Future in the Air

Only woman in Canada to own and operate a flying school, Marion Orr of Maple, Ontario, passes on much of her zest for flying to the young men and women who come to her for training.

Sunday picnic flights, overnight hops and competitions keep enthusiasm at a high pitch. There are over 8,350 civilian pilots in Canada; more than 250 of them are women. National Film Board Photos by Chris Lund.

In her office at Aero Activities, Marion Orr plots a cross-country flight. Each flight is planned in minute detail before take-off. Accidents and mishaps are kept to

Well-paid jobs in civil aviation await commercial pilots! In 1955 Canada's 45 flying schools and 37 flying clubs trained 183 pilots to commercial standards, but the supply

Publicity, c. 1954.

for nothing. I had blisters on my hands for a year but I sure learned how to plaster and stucco!"

In January 1953 she flew in the first plane. "The runway wasn't ready but I began operations because I had to get out of Barker Field. Frozen, the runway was OK, but it wasn't seeded and when spring came it was all mud. I broke a tail wheel landing in it. Joe Gerace over at Buttonville helped me out by allowing my students to fly out of Buttonville until I got my runway in shape." Another year passed before Marion had the airport operating the way she wanted. To celebrate and publicize the official opening of Maple Airport, she held an airshow on September 18, 1954. "It was no big deal, but it was fun.

Sally (Wagner), Helen and I put on a little airshow and Sally did some aerobatics. We also had spot landing contests and sky divers, and de Havilland demonstrated the Beaver and Otter. For a grand finale, two friends who were RCAF pilots roared over the field in their CF-100s."

Soon Marion had seven instructors and ten aircraft. Sally Kerton Wagner was one of the instructors and Helen Wilson, who held a commercial licence but no instructor's rating, dispatched and "passenger hopped." The school was a success, but the strain and hard work of the last seventeen years had exhausted her physically and mentally. "I just couldn't keep putting in eighteen hour days, which is what I had to do to keep the school going. It had gotten too big to handle myself. I

L *Marion Orr, Canada's first woman helicopter pilot and instructor, c. 1961.*

R *Marion in 1982. Still flying ten years after this picture was taken for the* Toronto Star, *she is one of Canada's longest-flying pilots.*

didn't want to take in a partner. I had done it all myself and was afraid of someone taking over. I decided to get out of flying altogether." In 1956 she sold Aero Activities and left Canada to live in Florida with her sister.

Flying soon lured her back. "I allowed myself to be talked into getting my American licences and before I knew it I was teaching six months of the year in Toronto and six months in Florida." In 1960 the Markham Airport Flying Club offered her the position of chief flying instructor at the newly-opened club. She accepted and returned permanently to Canada. "I was supposed to get the club on its feet. I did that and the next year the Board brought in some man who did not have my experience and I was relieved of my CFI position."

Shortly after, Vendaire Limited, wanting the publicity of having Canada's first woman helicopter pilot on staff, approached Marion and offered to subsidize her training if she would instruct and demonstrate helicopters for them. Marion accepted and in 1961 (Marion is unsure of the date), she became the first woman in Canada and the thirty-sixth woman in the world to hold a helicopter licence. A few months later she earned an instructor's rating (another first for Canadian women) and made newspaper headlines when the Ontario Provincial Police hired her to fly road patrol. "I did a few traffic trips; it was really just part of my job demonstrating and selling helicopters. I was showing the OPP how effective the helicopter would be in monitoring traffic. Most of my time was on the Brantley B-2. I called it an ice cream cone on skids; it was just a toy." Things were going well until an engine failure in 1961 almost brought her career as a pilot to an abrupt end. "The Brantley dropped hard" was how she described her descent. Her student was unhurt but she spent months in hospital with a broken back and to this day wears a back brace.

She recuperated at her sister's in Florida, returning to Toronto the next spring. "I flew at Joe Gerace's but the seats were so hard that I was in constant pain. It wasn't so bad if I was just doing circuits but if I was on a cross-country I'd have to get on my knees and lean over to relieve the pain. I finally had to quit." But Marion was born to fly. A few years later she was back instructing, part-time at first and then full-time in 1975 with Toronto Airways at Buttonville Airport. Although Marion was doing what she wanted she found that they were not good years. Back pain and financial worry were always present. "I didn't have a cent. I was really down. I flew a lot and often I had the highest number of hours of any instructor."

The final blow came when she was dismissed at age sixty-five. "I was devastated. Some people can retire and find other things to do, but all I wanted to do was fly." Desperate, she free-lanced until she found work at the Trenton Flying Club, which entailed driving a couple of hundred miles each day. On occasion she boarded with old friends, Vi and Arnold Warren in Colborne. When instructing at Trenton did not work out she returned to free-lancing, even giving free lessons because she wanted to fly so badly. In the fall of 1986 she was given a new lease on life when the flying club in Lindsay, Ontario asked her to be its manager and chief flying instructor. She was well qualified; a Class 1 instructor with a multi-IFR endorsement, a designated flight test examiner (DFTE), over 21,000 hours on 100 different types of aircraft, and experience in running a flying school. "It's great to be back at work. I feel just like a kid," she exclaimed. In 1988 Marion retired again, briefly, but in 1989 she was back in the air instructing. Still at it in 1992, she declared, "I'll never stop flying!"

MARION ORR'S RECORD of achievement is impressive. She was one of the first half dozen women in Canada to receive an instructor's rating, one of four Canadian women to serve with the Air Transport Auxiliary, the first to own and operate a flying school and an airfield, and the first Canadian woman to obtain commercial and instructor's ratings on helicopters. Perhaps her greatest achievement however is her almost fifty years of dedicated instructing. Through sheer determination and guts she made her own opportunities to achieve and in doing so carved out her own special niche in the aviation community.

In 1976 the First Canadian Chapter of the 99s, the International Organization of Women Pilots, awarded her the Amelia Earhart Medallion for her contributions to general aviation. In 1981 she was named a member of Canada's Aviation Hall of Fame with the following citation: "Her firm dedication to aviation from youth, her ability to impart knowledge and encouragement to students and her determination to succeed, have all been of benefit to Canadian aviation." In 1984 she was one of the pioneers in Canadian aviation honoured by Her Majesty Queen Elizabeth II at the dedication of the Western Canada Aviation Museum, in Winnipeg, Manitoba.

CHAPTER SIX

On the fringe

"I knew Trans-Canada Airlines wouldn't hire me but I applied anyway. I was called for an interview but was told right away that 'of course, we don't hire women.' It was all very pleasant — if being rejected can be enjoyable. When the TCA captain asked me why I had applied, I said, 'If women never apply you will never consider them.'" — *Pennie Naylor*

AT WAR'S END, the role of women reverted to the pre-war image. Their work in the productive economic sphere disappeared and household duties once again became the central feature of the idealized woman's life. Media recreated the all-pervasive stereotype of woman as the happy homemaker. It was taken for granted that when war ended and the men returned women would cheerfully surrender their newly acquired jobs and independence and return to their "proper place" in the home as wives and mothers. Most went home; home to anonymity and to men who did not understand the contradictory pressures that tore many of them apart.

Women pilots of the fifties and sixties remained on the fringe of aviation activity. For most, instructing, the lowest paid and the least prestigious of flying positions, remained the first and last rung of their career ladder. While the war had been a proving ground for women as commercial pilots, the traditional view that their proper place was in the home remained unchanged. The jobs available in the late forties were fiercely competed for by "the boys" who returned home. The old myths about women's unsuitability for flying were resurrected and the achievements of the women ferry pilots were conveniently overlooked by those in the aviation industry and were virtually unknown by the public as a whole.

However, discrimination and prevailing social assumptions were only partly to blame. There was also public opinion to be considered. Airline executives, like Grant McConachie, president of Canadian Pacific Air Lines in the forties, felt that the airlines could not afford to hire women pilots because the public would boycott the flight. According to Sheldon Luck, also of CP, some of the American carriers had conducted polls on passenger reaction to women pilots and confirmed this attitude.[6] There was no getting around the fact that the image of the pilot was male. Passengers felt safer flying with a man.

The attitude of the RCAF was much the same as the airlines' but more tied in with the male ego. As Group Captain (Ret) A. J. Bauer explained, "In the fifties we were the cocks of the walk.

ETHEL HARRIS DAVIES

Ethel Harris, of Vancouver, British Columbia, was a war widow and photographer when she enrolled for lessons to satisfy a long-held dream of flying. BC Aero Club manager (and Ethel's future husband), Wilf Davies, impressed with her skill or perhaps with her vivacious personality, told her that if she qualified for her commercial and instructor's licences he would hire her. As added enticement, he let her do check rides and ferry aircraft to build time. She earned both licences in 1947. "I loved flying so much that I gave up a good paying job for the insecurity of flying for a living."

Ethel instructed for the Aero Club on a part-time basis and took whatever else was available, such as demonstrating the Fleet Canuck and charter flying. "I flew for Roy Brett of B & B Logging Company. It was mostly flying loggers and parts. It was real rugged flying. Land Bay, for instance, was an unlicenced field. It was really just a logging road and regardless of the wind you came in over the trees from one direction only." One summer the club sent her to its satellite field at Powell River. "That was a 'hell hole,' I'll tell you. In those days a pilot was supposed to be a man and I sure had to prove myself there." Ethel logged about 2000 hours in her thirteen years of flying.

We had a tremendous wartime air force tradition to uphold. We were the top dogs as far as capability went. We were flying the top aircraft in NATO. It would have been a quantum leap for macho pilots to find one of their number was a woman. We were not ready for it." There were other factors as well, said Group Captain Bauer. "We could be sitting in an alert status for twenty-four hours. You have to consider the dynamics of the male/female situation. 'There's no goddamn way you're going to sit on alert with that girl' was what some wives would say."

Most women did not even bother to apply to the airlines or the RCAF because they knew they would be rejected. "Neither TCA nor CPA would have thought of taking on a woman pilot, dear me, no!" explained Bette Milburn Kerr. "I remember Helen Harrison applying to CPA and being turned down. If they rejected Helen with all her hours and experience I knew I didn't stand a chance."

Lethbridge Instructor Course, c. 1952, showing the usual ratio of men to women instructors. In the centre, from left, Eleanor Jones, Vera Strodl, Gretchen Matheson.

What was particularly galling for the women was knowing that there were plenty of jobs out there. World War II had accelerated the development of aviation in Canada. Aircraft manufacturing, the British Commonwealth Air Training Plan, and three joint Canadian/American projects (the Northwest Staging Route, the Canol Route, and the Crimson Route) resulted in vastly increased flying activity. New airports sprang up across the country. After the war Trans-Canada Airlines, Canada's national airline, grew to maturity and Canadian Pacific Air Lines consolidated its scattered routes and went international. The construction of the Dewline and the associated Mid-Canada Line in the fifties opened a new chapter to the aviation picture and helped to reshape the air transport industry. In the late sixties the intense search for oil in the Canadian Arctic offered more possibilities for the use of aircraft. The growth and expansion of the aviation industry were phenomenal and the effect on the carriers was far-reaching. Small bush companies evolved into regional carriers and, by 1966, five of them — Pacific Western Airlines (PWA), Transair, Nordair, Quebecair, and Eastern Provincial Airlines — were designated as "major" regional carriers by the Department of Transport. The heritage of the bush operator had come a long way, although bush flying remained a vital part of Canadian aviation.

The fifties also saw an expansion of charter services, contract flying, and specialty flying (flight training, aerial spraying, aerial photography) and the introduction of the helicopter. Indeed, chopper flying became one of the fastest growing sectors of the aviation economy. Okanagan Helicopters of British Columbia became a world leader in civilian helicopter services. There was even a revival of the flying club movement when war clouds appeared on the horizon in the early fifties and the clubs were seen as an important part of national defence.

Changes in the RCAF also affected civil aviation. Prior to

BETTE MILBURN KERR

"My family lived in Prince George, British Columbia and this was the centre for a great deal of pioneer aviation activity. Grant McConachie of CPA and Russ Baker of PWA both started out there. With all the flying going on, I decided I wanted to learn to fly too. I used to make model airplanes as a young girl. But we had no money; we were in the depths of the Great Depression."

Bette wanted to fly for the Air Transport Auxiliary and enrolled for lessons in 1942 but her instructor wouldn't allow any of the women in the class to solo. "I couldn't keep on taking lessons. I only earned sixty dollars a month and I soon ran out of money. I worked for Boeing Aircraft in Vancouver doing instrument installation in Cansos and Catalina Flying Boats." Once war ended Bette enrolled at the BC Aero Club and within the year obtained her private, commercial, and instructors. "I did a lot of instructing and ferrying on the Fleet 80 Canucks. I never did work full-time at flying; working as an instructor the hours were horrendous, dawn to dark, seven days a week and the basic pay was very poor, less than the men's. I worked part-time, mostly weekends when they were busiest. I received a lot of encouragement from the Club instructors, in particular from Rolie Barrett. I knew Rolie, Helen Harrison, Dawn Dawson, Eleanor Jones, Phyllis Drysdale, and Gretchen Matheson. Phyllis and I started 'Chisel Charter Service.'

Later Bette and her husband Mel Kerr moved to Kamloops, BC where, as a flying team, they organized a flying club and ran it for many years.

World War II the RCAF was a small force concerned mainly with civil operations. It expanded dramatically during the war to a purely military force and retained that role in peacetime, forcing the government to turn to the commercial operators for transportation and defence projects such as the Dewline. With all this increased activity there was an urgent need for pilots. But the old message was still clear: "Women need not apply."

Nevertheless they did apply — to the airlines and the military — and when rejected, they took what was available and used it to build their reputations. Not unexpectedly, the aviation world reacted slowly and uncertainly to the women's quiet persistence. The astonishing thing is that the women succeeded as well as they did and, despite the obstacles, a new generation of women pilots joined the ranks.

Only a few women licensed before or during World War II reappeared on the flight line at war's end. Rolie Moore Barrett, Margaret Littlewood, Marion Gillies, Helen Harrison, Marion Orr, Vera Strodl, Vi Milstead, Sally Wagner, Margaret Carson, Iva Coutts, and Elspeth Russell all spanned two distinct eras of aviation: the open cockpit biplane/helmets and goggles era, when women were often viewed as social butterflies, and the postwar period, when prewar planes were giving way to more sophisticated aircraft.

AS SOON AS CIVILIAN flying resumed after World War II, Rolie Moore Barrett (widowed by the war and with a youngster to support) quickly qualified for float, instructor's, and instrument ratings and in 1949 became the second Canadian woman to earn a Public Transport Licence. Rolie is Canada's first woman charter pilot. It was on a minor scale but it was charter flying nevertheless. Never pushy, her tactic was simply to be as qualified as possible and then let people know that she was available to fly.

Rolie began her post-war career by being "on call" — for Associated Air Taxi (flying charters) and for the BC Aero Club (doing check rides and instructing). For someone with a child to support this was a precarious way to make a living but it was the only option open to her. Breaking new ground, she knew it was necessary to prove herself. This was no problem for Rolie; an extremely skillful pilot with a pleasant unassuming manner, she fit in just fine and soon the BC Aero Club hired her full-

Rolie Moore Barrett.

time, giving her time off to fly for Associated Air Taxi when required. Asked to describe her experiences she said, "It was all float flying up and down the coast and it was always interesting. The one thing I could always be sure of was returning with wet feet!" Reticent, Rolie said nothing more, leaving unmentioned the sometimes dangerous weather conditions of the BC coast and the raised eyebrows she must have encountered when a passenger found his pilot to be a woman. Characteristically she also minimized her long working day. "I flew from 8:00 AM to dark, and then some, and fit everything else around flying."

Rolie remarried (a pilot) and continued flying until her retirement in the mid-fifties. All told she logged more than 1000 hours on a variety of aircraft and her logbook is sprinkled with such well-known aviation names as Terry Finney, Des Murphy, Hal Wilson, George Lothian, R. Carter-Guest, A. T. Cowley, and Art Sellers. While she adamantly stated that she suffered no discrimination it is possible that she never applied for a job that she knew she could not get and therefore never felt the impact of the door slammed in her face. However, what can be said with certainty was that Rolie Moore Barrett Pierce was a well-known and respected pilot and that she set a high standard of behaviour that smoothed the way for the women who followed her.

Rolie Moore Barrett with float-equipped Fleet Finch.

SOME, SUCH AS Margaret Littlewood, did not return to flying. After her wartime years of instructing on the Link Trainer, she gave up the idea of a flying career. "It was a painful decision because I loved it so much and had invested so much time in it. What I really wanted to do was fly with the airlines. At No. 2 Air Observer's School I discovered that I loved to fly instruments and multi-engine aircraft and I knew I wouldn't be happy going back to flying little single engine planes. Besides I didn't want to spend the rest of my life working twelve-hour days and that was what instructing was all about. I knew the airlines would never hire a woman and, of course, the RCAF had already proved that they wouldn't."

Although Margaret had quit flying, the idea of obtaining the coveted Public Transport Licence lured her back to the airport one more time in 1949. "It was the highest licence you could get and I decided I was going to get it simply to prove to myself that I had what it took to become an airline pilot. I couldn't have done it without the help of two of the instructors at the Edmonton Flying Club who devoted every moment of their spare time to teaching me. I found it hard work as I had been away from flying for more than five years. Most of the men regularly flew and got their transport licence by flying as first officers of heavy aircraft. With the exception of some training on the Cornell I could only afford to use light aircraft and I had to fit my flying in around my job. It took me a year of studying and saving and I only got it through sheer stubborness,

MARION GILLIES AITCHESON (1918-1964)

Marion often accompanied her father, Fred Gillies, a World War I pilot, on his barnstorming trips around the province. When he formed Gillies Flying Service at Barker Field in Toronto in 1938, he asked her to take flying lessons as a publicity gimmick. She agreed provided that he also teach her friend Margaret Littlewood. Marion received a private licence on August 3, 1939 and immediately went on to take her commercial and instructor's training. Marion was the first woman flying instructor in Canada.

When gasoline rationing closed the company, she was grounded for the rest of the war. According to Margaret Littlewood, Marion wanted to fly with the ATA but did not apply because her parents were afraid their only child might be killed. After the war Marion married one of her students, had two children, and continued to fly for her father's company, which eventually relocated to Buttonville Airport, outside Toronto. Apparently her husband was not happy with his wife working. According to their son Michael, "It was awkward, it caused a lot of friction. She lived in Langstaffe while our father farmed elsewhere. It was an unhappy time. She was always home at night but we had a babysitter during the day. She was very determined and often she and her father clashed, although he was very proud of her. My brother and I were also very proud of having such a talented mother." Marion instructed until her untimely death from blood poisoning.

Marion Gillies.

knowing I could never use it." Margaret received a Public Transport Licence in 1950, the third woman in Canada to earn it. "None of us could use it but I guess the others were as stubborn as me and wanted to see if they could earn the great airline pilot licence. The Edmonton Flying Club wanted me to renew my instructor's rating and teach part-time, but I was only interested in the airlines."

Once she reached her goal, she regretfully walked away from the airfield forever. "Had the airlines hired women pilots I would never have returned to secretarial work," said Margaret in 1979. "The only encouragement I received was for civilian instructing. None other. I felt banging on doors would be a

LUCILLE HALEY BASTER

Lucille Haley, of Tomahawk, Alberta, was one of the first women corporate pilots. Married at sixteen and separated two years later, she moved to Edmonton with her baby to complete her schooling and find work. Then she discovered flying and became determined to make that her career. "At the time I didn't realize I was trying to break into a profession that was not for women." To help cover the cost of training she drove a taxi in addition to her regular job of selling cosmetics.

Qualifying for a commercial licence in 1964 was easy; finding a job was not. She soon came to the realization that only instructing was open to her. She earned an instructor's rating in 1965 and eventually found work with the Castlegar Flying Club. Her goal however was the Edmonton Flying Club because she wanted to become known at Municipal Airport to be able to break out of instructing. "I just kept applying and they finally hired me. As far as I know I was the first woman instructor there. As soon as I was qualified they gave me the multi-IFR students and I began specializing in advanced training." That too was simply a means to an end but it was not to be; her dream of flying with the airlines was repeatedly dashed.

Her chance to leave instructing came when one of her former students, a corporate pilot, was hired by the airlines. He knew her goals and he so highly recommended her to his former boss that she was hired. Lucille had impeccable credentials: a Class 1 instrument rating, a Class 1 instructor's rating, an ATR, and 4000 hours experience. Veteran Transfer and Everall Construction's first woman corporate pilot was a knockout on any airport ramp; with her long blond hair and dressed in mini skirt and boots, there was no mistaking Lucille. She and her Beech Baron became a familiar sight at airports all over northern British Columbia,

waste of time and it appears after all these years I wasn't too far wrong, for women haven't progressed at any great speed in equality with men in the aviation industry."

After a few years of flying, newcomer Lorraine Cooper came to the same conclusion. "I decided I was wasting my time flying. I was just too early for the airlines and the military, and I was too energetic and ambitious to sit around waiting to fly the occasional charter. Although I ran into very little resentment or nastiness, more like wonder and amusement, and found most men very helpful, I doubt that I could have found a full-time flying job. I wouldn't have been happy if I couldn't have gone to the top."

No one likes marching to the rear and, as with many male pilots, becoming an airline pilot was the women's ultimate dream. Unattainable as this was, they nevertheless applied and re-applied, using a variety of strategies to be noticed. Some, like Lorraine Cooper and Dawn Dawson, who earned their licences in the early fifties, craftily used their initials when applying to the airlines. But the game was up when L. Cooper of Chinook Flying Service turned out to be a statuesque brunette. As

Alberta, Saskatchewan, Manitoba and the Northwest Territories, and much of the United States.

"I actually flew for two companies who shared a plane and a pilot. My job was to move crews from one job site to another and to fly company executives and project managers around. Only once did anyone refuse to fly with me. I just left him sitting." Neither did Lucille have any trouble when overnighting in small towns or camps. "There were usually female cooks and women's quarters. At first some of the wives were worried, until after they met me." Lucille was also not afraid to speak her mind. "Initially they pushed me to fly in bad weather or into places which I considered unsafe. I began to refuse some of the flights."

In 1975 Lucille remarried and made headlines when she and her husband-to-be (an air traffic controller) were married in a plane over Edmonton. She continued flying after her marriage but her career came to an abrupt halt in the early eighties when she suffered an aneurysm and lost her Category 1 medical. It was a bitter blow. However, with her usual optimism and determination she wasted no time feeling sorry for herself and, after logging more than 10,000 hours flying, soon rolled out on top in another career. She is now a well-known potter and her work, beautifully designed with images and colours inspired by her northern flying, has won her acclaim.

Lorraine explained, "My qualifications got me as far as an interview but when I walked in and they discovered that L. Cooper was a woman, that was it. The TCA captain said that he appreciated my eagerness but he did not think I had the necessary qualifications. When I pressed him to be more specific, he admitted that the main consideration was to be male. I didn't bother to apply to any others because I knew it would be the same old story."

Dawn Dawson had the same experience with CPA. "I got as far as the interview because personnel thought I was 'Don' Dawson. At the interview I was told that female pilots did not fit into the system because they would be incompatible in the cockpit, and overnights away from the base would be a problem. The fact that the stewardesses were women and also overnighted was ignored. CP did tell me that they would waive the nursing certificate requirement and hire me as a stewardess because of all my flying experience!"

Ten years later the situation had not changed one bit, although the excuses were a little more inventive. "I wanted to fly with the airlines," recalled Lucille Haley. "Once I passed the 1000 hour mark I began to apply. Their answers were all the same — all negative: they were not hiring, I was not tall enough, they had no uniform for a woman, or 'what would the passengers think.' At the 3000 hour mark I tried a different approach and began signing my initial and last name. Both Pacific Western Airlines and Canadian Pacific Air Lines called me for interviews. But when they found out that L. Haley was a woman they said I was not suitable. I found it very frustrating, especially when so many of my students with far less time were being hired."

Why did the women even try? Pennie Naylor of Montreal, who earned a commercial pilot's licence in 1952, explained. "I knew TCA wouldn't hire me but I applied anyway. I was called for an interview but was told right away that 'of course, we don't hire women.' It was all very pleasant — if being rejected can be enjoyable. When the TCA captain asked me why I had applied, I said, 'If women never apply you will never consider them.'"

In fact, one airline, which was really more "bush" than airline, did hire a woman but only because she came as part of the package. Nevertheless, history was in the making. For Dawn Dawson Connelly, it was a unique opportunity. In 1954

Pacific Western Air Lines hired the husband and wife team of Dawn and Ron Connelly; he to fly on the airline side and she to manage the flying school and fly charters. PWA even issued Dawn a seniority number and she felt as if she were halfway to her goal. Then, four and a half years later PWA withdrew her seniority number, telling Dawn she was no longer eligible to be on the seniority list. She was devastated but there was nothing she could do. PWA had begun its negotiations to join the Canadian Air Line Pilots Association and the Association told PWA: no women. "PWA was not strong enough to withstand pressure from the powerful Association and it did not want to fight one woman's battle," explained Dawn.

Even the small companies played it safe by hiring women only for instructing and the occasional "safe" charter. "When Dawn signed up for lessons we assumed that she would do her private licence and leave. When she finished her commercial

PENNIE NAYLOR

Pennie Naylor was one of the few professional women pilots in Quebec in the fifties and sixties. "I was always mad keen to fly and left school to get a job to pay for lessons," she recalled. Trained on a Fox Moth at Laurentide Aviation at Cartierville Airport, she received a private licence in 1951 and a commercial in 1952. "To cut costs I took friends flying and worked as a 'line boy' at Laurentide. The Scholefields let me ferry aircraft and they encouraged me to get my instructor's rating, saying they would hire me. After I got it in 1953 I thought it best to hold onto my other job until I saw how things went, so I only instructed part-time." In the meantime she started to work towards her night endorsement and multi-engine rating. "Obtaining my commercial and night licences gave me a taste of instrument flying. Flying the Cessna 310 and the Link Trainer made me realize that what I really wanted to do was fly sophisticated aircraft: in other words, fly with the airlines."

After she had accumulated a couple of thousand hours she applied to TCA and was politely refused. "I then tried to enlist in the RCAF for pilot training. I wasn't surprised when they told me they didn't take women. I had to accept that only instructing was open to me . . . but working only part-time meant that I had 'to take the tail of the dog.'" Pennie had an excellent position with Bell Telephone and the opportunity to move into a management position. She also had become used to a certain lifestyle: a home in the country and nice vacations. She instructed part-time until illness forced her to stop flying in the early seventies.

and instrument training and asked for a job, we were concerned about our customers. The opportunities for women have never been all that great," admitted Al Michaud of Vancouver U-Fly.[7]

The hiring of the Connellys illustrates another phenomenon of the times — women often required a male "sponsor" in order to be hired. It was one more indignity that women had to suffer. There were about a half dozen husband and wife teams flying in this period and when they went job hunting, it was usually the husband who received the choice bid and the wife who got the less desirable one of instructing. Vi (Milstead) and Arnold Warren, Lorna (Bray) and Dick DeBlicquy, Carole (Philips) and Barry Morris, Bette (Milburn) and Mel Kerr, and

IRENE COOPER

Irene Cooper, of Winnipeg, Manitoba took her training from Konnie Johanneson and received her private licence in 1946. "My father [Wing Commander Thomas Cooper] was so pleased that he bought me a Tiger Moth, which became known as 'Cooper's Folly Dammit All' because of the registration, 'CF-DAL.' I joined the Winnipeg Flying Club for its social and flying activities. It was a wild place in those days. I remember a couple of pilots, one of them an instructor, flying a plane out of the hangar. When Herb Taylor took over things settled down. We used to go on breakfast flights and cross-country rallies."

In 1953 Irene took her commercial training to improve her flying. The late Art Wallis of Transport Canada remembered Irene as the first person to be issued a commercial licence from the Winnipeg DOT office; before that, all licences were issued from Ottawa. "It was only after I had my commercial licence that I thought of flying as a career. I heard that Standard Aero Ltd. was looking for an executive pilot and applied there. I was given a flat 'no.' I then wrote to Okanagan Helicopters to see about a licence but they wrote back to say they wouldn't hire a woman. I didn't bother inquiring at the airlines or the RCAF because I knew they did not accept women. That left only instructing. When I asked Leo Hoffman of the Winnipeg Flying Club what my chances were of being hired, he told me he would give me the same consideration as anyone else." Taking that as an encouragement of sorts, Irene qualified for her instructor's rating in 1954, the first woman at the club to receive one. "I instructed part-time only because I didn't want to give up my office job. I was in a management position and knew I could go nowhere in flying. Instructing part-time gave me the best of two worlds."

Irene owned an Aeronca Chief, CF-DUP. Petite and blonde

Molly (Beall) and Jack Reilly all ran full tilt into this situation. The women had no choice but to be grateful for what they were offered. Characteristically, they did not waste time feeling sorry for themselves but simply used instructing to try to step up into bush and charter flying. Only a few however managed to slip into those traditional male fields and, almost without exception, they were sponsored by their husbands.

Though few and far between, some unrelated men also eased the way for women. Al Michaud of Vancouver U-Fly supported Dawn Dawson in a variety of ways and Lorraine Cooper received help from Franz McTavish of Chinook Air Service. "He allowed me to use Chinook's aircraft for passen-

she attracted the attention of reporters who regularly featured photographs of Irene and her plane. The Flying R Ranch at Clear Lake used Irene and her Chief for the cover of its brochure and in return Irene spent time at the ranch giving guests rides.

AUDREY STONEHOUSE PECK

Audrey Stonehouse was an accomplished horsewoman and stock car racer when her father, owner of Grand Valley Air Services at the Waterloo-Wellington Airport, urged her to take flying lessons. Taking her instruction from Terry Finney of Central Airways, she acquired a private licence in 1955, a commercial licence and multi-engine rating and a job with her father's company the following year. She flew charters on Cessna 172s and 180s, a Stinson 108, and a Czech-built twin-engine aircraft called a Balaero. She also married that year, joined the First Canadian Chapter of the 99s, and entered her first International Air Race. "I'll never forget that race. One of the contestants crashed and killed herself. I flew the Balaero with Lorna Nichols as my co-pilot. The course was from Washington, DC to Havana, Cuba. We received the 'Tail End Tony Award' for coming in last and made the centrefold of *LIFE* magazine."

The following year while pregnant she placed second in the Governor General's Cup Race in Toronto and gave birth three days later. "I remember all the teasing. The other contestants told me that because I had been pregnant I had broken the rule that contestants must fly solo."

Combining marriage, motherhood, and charter flying eventually proved too much and she gave up flying a few years later.

ger hopping and he also gave me ferry jobs and checkouts. In return I worked in the office, washed airplanes, and swept the hangar floor." And a few intrepid bush operators — Orville "Porky" Wieben, Hank and Keith Parsons, Lorne Andrews, and Bob Ferguson — hired women pilots, sponsor or no sponsor, because to them a qualified pilot was a qualified pilot.

Women pilots encountered other problems as well. It was not unusual for Department of Transport examiners to give women harder check rides than they would a man or even to refuse to give them one. When, in the early fifties, Dawn Dawson showed up for her instrument ride, examiner Bill Lavery rejected her application because he saw no point in wasting his time; after all, he said, what did she need an instrument rating for, no one would hire her. Al Michaud of Vancouver U-Fly ran interference for her. "There was a lot of shouting between Bill Lavery and Al Michaud," recalled Dawn. "Lavery stated that there was no way he would give a blankety blankety ride and if he did, there was no way he would blankety blankety pass me. I was determined to get my instrument ticket and wasn't going to back down. Al supported me and told Lavery he would report him. Lavery told me afterwards that he

PHYLLIS DRYSDALE

Born in Victoria, British Columbia, Phyllis said, "I can never recall being told that it wasn't for girls to do this or that. I was always told that ability would win out and it wasn't a problem what sex one was. I used to watch the mail planes fly overhead and thought what a great thing to do. My dad used to build gliders with a friend of his and one day he took me with him. That's how it all started."

When the Victoria Flying Club at Patricia Bay was formed, she enrolled for lessons and took instruction on Tiger Moths and Piper J3s, earning her private, commercial, and instructors licences by 1950. Phyllis related, "Bette Milburn and I used to fly together a lot and the airport jokers called the Tiger Moth we flew, 'Chisel Charter Service.' So we designed uniforms for ouselves. We thought we looked quite smart in a sort of RCAF blue."

Phyllis instructed for about ten years in British Columbia and Ontario on many types of aircraft, such as Fleet Canucks, Tiger Moths, Luscombes, Cessnas, Cornells, Stinsons, and Pipers. She also flew the Chipmunk, Seabee, and Harvard. Phyllis flew about 3000 hours in total but was never able to get any job other than instructing, ferrying aircraft, and doing the occasional charter.

'threw everything at me' and that it was one of the best rides he had ever given. We became friends after that." More harassment awaited her, however. When she went for her multi-engine ride the inspector refused to give her a DC-3 endorsement even though that was the aircraft used for her check ride. "He told me that he did not think I was strong enough to maintain control fully loaded with one engine out. I asked for a second ride under those conditions and another inspector. I got the ride and the endorsement, but not without fighting for it."

In some cases there was justification for not hiring a woman. Lorraine Cooper flew in the early fifties just as oil exploration

and all the associated activities were moving into high gear. She was no weakling but this is what she had to say. "Oil rig crews were astonished that I had brought the plane in with my own little pinkies. They just didn't expect a woman to be flying. I was expected to taxi right up to the oil rig and load or unload equipment. Some of the equipment, such as a box of cores, I

Bette Milburn and Phyllis Drysdale — "Chisel Charter Service."

couldn't lift without help. You needed to be strong. There was usually someone around who would give me a hand and I never found that people resented helping me. But the oil crew had its own work and I didn't like asking them for help. However, that experience made me realize my physical limitations and why companies were leery of hiring women."

THE WORKING HOURS were horrendous, dawn to dusk seven days a week, and the women's basic pay was less than men received. It was cheaper for clubs to hire women instructors part-time; $2 per hour for female instructors plus a small base pay was not unusual in the mid-sixties. Most men instructed only as a last resort and only to build their flying time quickly. Once they had acquired enough hours, they applied to the bush companies or the airlines. The women did not have this luxury of choice. They could instruct full-time (if they were offered full-time work) and face years of long hours seven days a week or instruct part-time, keeping their regular office jobs and instructing evenings and weekends. Many opted to go the latter route. As Pennie Naylor explained, "I

Eleanor Jones in a typical "posed shot" — looking at the engine of a Piper, c. 1954.

ELEANOR JONES

Born in Murrayville, British Columbia, Eleanor was "always fascinated with airplanes." She left school after grade ten to begin work and take flying lessons. "I took my instruction at U-Fly and I found Al and Lloyd Michaud very receptive to women, although women pilots at that time were always a bit of a curiosity." She trained on an Aeronca Chief, Cessnas 120 and 140 and had received her private, commercial, and instructors rating by 1952.

Eleanor kept her full-time position with BC Telephone and Art Sellers at Skyways in Langley, BC, offered her a part-time job instructing, a result of her passenger hopping and working the counter at Skyways after she received her commercial licence. "Once in awhile there were some raised

did not want to give up a secure well-paying job at Bell Telephone for the rotten hours, poor pay, and the insecurity of instructing. It would have been different if I could have moved out of instructing but that was a pretty remote possibility. I chose to remain with Bell and to instruct part-time at Laurentide Aviation."

Even when hired as "occasional" pilots their troubles were not over. "It was the same old story. The women had to be twice as good as the men and they had to prove themselves," said Chinook's Marjorie McTavish Stauffer. Dawn Dawson concurred. "Once you were known it was all right. When one of the presidents of an oil company found out that I was going to be his charter pilot he was not too happy. However, after an engine failure and a safe return he was only too happy to fly with me again. And once they had flown with a woman pilot they would take great delight in saying their pilot was female!"

Gordon Bartsch, Dawn's second husband, described another anomaly. "If a tough trip came up the attitude was, 'We must send a male pilot' but if all the men were out, then 'Send Dawn, she can do it.' Dawn didn't have the same level of experience because she didn't fly as much; yet she was expected to perform to the same level as the men even though she might not have had as many opportunities to fly" — the implication being that the women were, after all, capable of doing the job.

Sometimes women were the target of practical jokes, which they learned to grin and bear. "I'll never forget one of the jokes played on me," recalled Lorraine Cooper. "It was a day after a big blizzard and all of Chinook's pilots were busy dropping

eybrows about there being a woman instructor but it didn't really create a problem," she recalled. "As a woman in a male-dominated field you have to be better. You can't be average to be recognized in the first place. After that you are usually accepted on your ability: the ability to fly and the ability to get along with the people you work with. I believed in being feminine rather than being a feminist. I worked with men rather than competing with them. I never had a problem but you had to be prepared to be teased if you goofed."

Eleanor left flying in 1959, after she married. "I could have continued instructing but the hours were long, from dawn to dusk."

groceries and hay to snow-bound ranchers. One of the pilots asked me to pick up someone who needed treatment and I jumped at the chance. He gave me very explicit instructions and that should have tipped me off. Unsuspectingly I took off in the Champ on skis, landed, walked up to the farmhouse and asked where Mr. Stiff was. The man who answered the door looked at me a little strangely but said, 'There he is, over there.' All I saw was a canvas-wrapped bundle on the porch! I wanted to turn and run but I wasn't going to give the guys at Chinook that satisfaction. I had trouble getting the frozen corpse into the Champ and to make matters worse I had to fly with its feet resting on my shoulders because it would not fit into the back

CAROLE PHILIPS MORRIS

Carole Philips, of Victoria, British Columbia, was a qualified dental hygienist who could not shake the memory of a plane ride she had had when she was eight years old. In 1961 she finally gave in to her desire to fly and signed up for lessons. Within the year she earned private, commercial, and instructor's licences and a job. Shortly after, she married another pilot, Barry Morris, and they formed Morris Aviation at Revelstoke, British Columbia.

From a two aircraft, two pilot operation with a licence to fly to Mica Creek and offer flight training, the Morris's developed the company into a business with fourteen aircraft which provided service throughout the BC interior. Renamed Trans-Island Airlines in 1971, it flew the alpine route into Kamloops, Prince George, Nelson, and Mica Creek and provided air connections with the major airline terminals. In addition to a scheduled service it also offered a charter service, scenic tours, and flight training. Much of Carole's flying was for the Columbia Power project. "Until I became a familiar sight I learned to expect comments like, 'What's a little girl like you doing flying such a big plane?' No one, however, refused to fly with me."

Petite and attractive she made good news copy and, if the reporter exaggerated a little, well, it made a good story. "One Woman Airline . . . " stated one newspaper and then went on to say that the Morris's were one of the few flying husband and wife teams in commercial aviation in Canada. Carole raised some eyebrows in 1966 when she attended the Instructors' Refresher Course in Brandon, Manitoba and took her sixteen-month-old baby with her (and her sister-in-law to care for it). "Just because I had a baby didn't mean I was going to stop learning," she remarked. Carole had no problems retaining her Category 1 medical and commercial flying status with all three pregnancies.

seat! When I taxied up to the hangar I saw all the pilots at the window, waiting to see what I was going to do. All I said was, 'Hey guys, that was a good joke.' The practical jokes tapered off after that."

Like the aviatrixes of the earlier era, women pilots of the fifties and sixties were doggedly followed by reporters. A woman pilot finishing second in the Governor General's Cup Race in Toronto in the fifties was worth mentioning; a pregnant pilot placing second was worth a headline: "Flying Mother-to-be Comes Second in CNE Race." Three days later the pilot in question, Audrey Stonehouse Peck, gave birth to her baby and reporters and the newsreels at the movies fussed over the episode. Audrey was misquoted in Toronto newspapers as saying that she felt better flying while pregnant than not pregnant. What she had said was that she felt just as well pregnant as not. Once she was back working reporters were again on the scene. "Mother Pilots Air Taxi Between Kitchener and Toronto, Comforts Baby Between Flights" read the *Toronto Daily Star* headline on March 21, 1958, backed up with a picture of the babysitter handing the baby to Audrey who was seated in the plane. Let a man move from an office job into a flying one, no one cared; not so with a woman. When Felicity Bennett gave up teaching school to be a flying instructor, *The Kingstonaire* queried on May 25, 1953, "Is She a Flying School Teacher or Is She a Flying Teacher?" When Ruth Parsons left teaching for flying in 1956 the local paper reported it with this headline: "Quits City Teaching for Bush Job." Irene Cooper, a part-time instructor at the Winnipeg Flying Club became used to headlines such as, "Little blond pilot flies her own plane." The women found the publicity annoying.

WOMEN PILOTS OF THIS ERA made important progress. The single most striking fact was how firmly they

In the mid-seventies the Morris's moved to Toronto where Barry became a test pilot with de Havilland. Carole kept herself current by using the family Cessna 172 to fly to Victoria once a year and do some free-lance aerial photography for de Havilland. In 1983 she returned full-time to the aviation world when Carl Millard of Millardair (a freight airline in Toronto) hired her. He was looking for someone with a flying and business background and Carole, with over 4000 hours, fit the bill.

Gretchen Matheson c. 1953.

GRETCHEN MATHERS MATHESON

Gretchen Mathers, of Vancouver, British Columbia, worked one summer as a lab technician in a cannery. The company had a Seabee and after one flight in it Gretchen was hooked on flying. Although her goal to learn to fly was never far from her mind, she postponed taking lessons until after she had graduated from university and completed a business course. Along the way she also had a career as a professional model.

Gretchen enrolled at the Chilliwack Flying Club and received a private licence in 1952. "That was the beginning of the end. I didn't stop until I had my instructor's rating." Her first job was with Central Aviation in Wetaskiwin, Alberta, teaching air cadets. "That meant long days of flying

established themselves as dedicated and competent instructors. The importance of the instructor is easily lost in the more dramatic exploits of the military pilot or the glamour of the airline pilot, yet instructors are surely the backbone of the flying world. While instructing remained the bottom rung of the career ladder, women in this era raised that rung a few notches. Instructors like Gretchen Matheson, Felicity McKendry, Gina Jordan, Marion Orr, Lucille Haley, Helen Harrison, and Vera Strodl Dowling were so good that by the mid-seventies flying club managers were seeking out other women pilots. These women earned the respect and admiration of the aviation community. Students had fond memories of their women instructors and letters like the following, that Lucille Haley received after losing her medical, give an indication of the loyalty and trust they inspired.

> "I've had eighteen years of flying now, no accidents but I couldn't have gotten here without you. My founding education in the matters of stick and rudder were of the highest order. I thank you for your professionalism, the high standards you set for me, your patience and faith when I didn't understand and your caring. My hand is firm upon the stick (but gentle as you always told me). I remember to whom I owe so much. Thank you, Lucy. May your skies always be blue.
>
> — one of your students"

Many women demonstrated that they could combine flying with marriage and even a baby or two. "Old-timers" such as Vi Milstead and Elspeth Russell and newcomers, such as Bette Kerr, Carole Morris, Lorna DeBlicquy, Ruth Parsons, Felicity McKendry, and Gretchen Matheson refuted the old argument

and ground school. But I loved it. I knew I had found what I wanted to do." She also did some charter flying. Ferrying a Piper Colt from the factory in Hamilton to Wetaskiwin was an interesting experience. "I had never flown a Colt and I remember sitting with the instruction book on my lap and learning as I flew along."

Gretchen was competent and well liked and was soon appointed chief flying instructor. But her term was short; the following year she married one of her students (who is now chief pilot and supervisor of Westcoast Transmission). The couple moved first to Calgary and later to Vancouver. Three children initially caused Gretchen to instruct only enough to keep her licences current but for over thirty years she has alternated between part-time and full-time work.

Totally professional and with a particularly pleasant

that women do not take work seriously and that they leave for marriage and babies. Felicity McKendry and Gretchen Matheson, for instance, instructed for over thirty years; Felicity retired in 1988 and Gretchen is still flying. Along the way both women married, had children, qualified for the country's top licences, and became designated flight test examiners.

One of the key factors in managing flying, marriage, and family was a supportive husband, preferably one who was also in aviation. For instance, in 1955 Felicity Bennett married Spence McKendry, a pilot and air traffic controller, and began the tricky task of combining marriage and flying. "Spence was great. He supported me all the way and rarely complained about the meals I didn't cook for him because I was at the airport or the long hours I spent out there." Gretchen also married a pilot. She, however, initially fell prey to social expectations of what a "good wife" was. "For the first few months of my married life I worked in an office because I thought that as a wife I should be in a more traditional line of work. That lasted one winter. As soon as spring came I was back

disposition, Gretchen never had a problem finding work. Her philosophy was always to ignore "unhelpful comments." She chose instructing as a career because she felt it was more compatible with her home and family situation but, as she said, "I usually packed in the hours in the summer by taking on the air cadet program." She has been with the Pacific Flying Club since 1977 and its chief flying instructor since 1986.

In addition to flying, Gretchen has promoted aviation in general and women pilots in particular. A longtime member of the 99s, she is active in the BC Aviation Council (formerly co-chairman, now a member of the Training, Safety and General Aviation Committee). She has also been active in the Canadian Aeronautics and Space Institute (chairman of the Vancouver branch), and the Abbotsford International Airshow (a director). In 1990 she was elected a national director of the Canadian Owners and Pilots Association.

Her dedication to general aviation was recognized in 1981 when she received the Amelia Earhart Achievement Award from the International Northwest Aviation Council and in 1986 the safety programs she had organized were recognized by the BC Aviation Council with the Back & Bennington Safety Trophy. She currently holds a Class 1 instructor's rating and an airline transport rating, is a designated flight test examiner and has logged over 11,000 hours.

at the airport and flying. My husband understood. Never again did I worry about trying to fulfill an image of what a wife or mother should be."

Motherhood eventually caught up with many of these women and, as with marriage, they successfully juggled career and children. What is interesting is that, years later, women pilots of the seventies and eighties found themselves grounded as "medically unfit" when they became pregnant, while Gretchen, Felicity, and Carole Morris retained their Category 1 medicals and commercial flying status with all their pregnancies. Carole explained, "My doctor was a DOT doctor. If anyone should know if I were legal he should. But he never grounded me nor said I was 'unfit to fly.' My biggest problem when flying while pregnant was hand propping the J-3 on floats and then trying to squeeze around and back into the cabin with a big stomach!" Gretchen recalled that "Some of my students raised an eyebrow at having a pregnant instructor, but no one refused to fly with me and no one told me I was breaking any regulations. I maintained a Category 1 medical and commercial licence with all three pregnancies." When their children were young, these women flew just enough to keep themselves current and once the children were in school they returned to instructing, first on a part-time then a full-time basis. Only Ruth Parsons found herself grounded by DOT when she declared her pregnancy; apparently DOT doctors interpreted the regulations to suit their individual beliefs.

Gina Jordan, on the other hand, had a different outlook. "Marriage was never a part of my longterm plans. I didn't think that being a pilot was compatible with marriage, for a woman anyway. When you're in an aircraft you're used to being in command, not the best ingredient for a conventional marriage. I remain happily unmarried."

IF THE FIFTIES AND SIXTIES were not the time for the advancement of women in commercial aviation, they certainly made their mark in sport aviation. For this was the era of the all-women's air races. They were launched in the United States to promote flying skills and increase public awareness of aviation. After all, if a bunch of women could fly across the country then air transportation must be safe and easy! To play up the feminine angle, the women wore dresses or skirts; slacks and shorts were taboo. Many crews dressed alike, sometimes carrying a message. Dorothy Rungeling, a Canadian entry, remembered, "One year my co-pilot and I wore dresses and aprons on which we had embroidered 'To Hell With Housework.'"

Thus to the starting call of "Woman Your Planes" came the rustle of skirts and the click of heels as some fifty or more women climbed aboard their aircraft. Each pilot had to get the best out of her plane, the best out of the weather, and the best out of herself. According to Dorothy, weather and fatigue were the greatest hazards. "We'd go to bed at midnight and get up at 4:00 AM for a sunrise take-off and then battle thunderstorms, desert heat, and mountain ranges." The joy of meeting other women who loved flying, the challenge of competition, and the thrill of watching the first plane waved off or the last one to land were experiences never to be forgotten.

The most famous race was the All Women's Transcontinental Air Race better known as the "Powder Puff Derby." The

Gina Jordan in Tanzania with Mission Aviation Fellowship.

GINA JORDAN

Gina Jordan was the epitomy of the self-made "man." From a small farm near Saint John, New Brunswick, she left school at an early age to help out with family finances. As a child she had been fascinated with flying and kept a scrapbook on all historic flights. She never forgot her ambition to become a pilot and in 1954 she headed out to the Fundy Flying Club. "I fell in love with flying on my first flight. I came down walking on air." Unfortunately, because her salary was so desparately needed by her family it was another five years before she qualified for a commercial and instructor's licence. By 1963 she was restless. "I had gone as far as I could in the Maritimes. What I really wanted to do was get out of instructing and into charter or airline flying." There was little hope of her going anywhere in the Atlantic provinces. Realizing that she would have to use instructing as a springboard into something else, she decided to find a position with a school that emphasized advanced training. Only Margaret McTavish of Chinook Flying Service, Calgary, Alberta replied to her letter of inquiry and ultimately offered her a job.

By 1969 Gina was burned out and dissatisfied. "I regularly put in fourteen-hour-days seven days a week." Too ambitious to continue to work for someone else, she decided to operate her own flight school, and Chinook and Gina parted company. Although she had little formal education she had an innate business sense. Before making a move, she carefully assessed the situation in western Canada and

only race of its kind in the world, it was open to all qualified women pilots and crewed by women only. The aircraft had to be unmodified (stock), no more than 350 horsepower, and have a two-way radio. The object was to beat one's own handicap. "Powder Puff" was a gross misnomer since the derby was a gruelling race. It was flown during daylight hours over 2500 to 3000 miles of desert, mountains, and other inhospitable terrain. Official time clocks were set up at each of the nine to twelve airports designated as official refueling stops. Arrival and departure times were recorded by observers stationed at each clock. "Your prop had to be stopped and then you got out and ran to the time clock," explained Dorothy. "I remember one time I ran out of gas just as I was landing; so as not to be disqualified I got the airplane off the active runway, climbed out and ran to the clock!"

The first Powder Puff Derby was organized in 1947 and it

decided there was room for another school if it specialized in advanced training. Opposition to her plans came from other operators in the area and they held up her application for a licence for four years. Gina did not let the fact that she had no company, no office, no aircraft and no instructors, other than herself, stop her from earning a living. She freelanced, beginning with students who had their own aircraft. "Calgary was a rich town and there were plenty of flying farmers and businessmen who were aircraft owners. I had no problem finding business."

Jordan Flight Service was a respected name in the aviation community. Gina established herself as one of the best multi-FR instructors in the west. She was the first professional woman pilot to work in the Maritimes, the first woman to own and operate an advanced flight training centre, and the first woman to be appointed a designated flight test examiner in western Canada. She became good friends with Rosella Bjornson and was her mentor as she worked her way towards becoming Canada's first female airline pilot.

In 1980 she sold her business and went to follow another dream — to fly for Mission Aviation Fellowship (MAF) of Canada, an organization that Vera Strodl had told her about. Gina and Vera had met in the mid-sixties at an instructors refresher course and had kept in touch throughout the years, becoming good friends when Gina moved west. Gina currently lives in New Brunswick for six months of the year promoting MAF and the remainder of the year in Africa training MAF pilots.

was held annually until the seventies, when the cost of administering and flying it became too great. It was sponsored by the 99s, and financially supported with contributions from the aviation industry and cities and organizations at the start and finish points. American businessmen recognized its promotional value and provided cash prizes ranging from $800 for first prize to $200 for fourth prize plus other awards. The race was sanctioned by the National Aeronautical Association and conducted under the Rules and Regulations of the Federation Aeronautique Internationale. Because of the prohibitive cost, there was only the occasional Canadian entry; contestants were overwhelmingly American. "I was sorry to see it go," remarked Dorothy. "It was exciting to be a part of it all. I got goose bumps just watching the take-offs, which were every fifteen seconds. It was a thrill to match wits with Mother Nature. It was an endurance marathon and there was nothing else like it. We came from all walks of life: doctors, lawyers, scientists, teachers, mothers. But we all had two things in common: the love of flying and the challenge of a race.

"I never placed in the top ten in any of the Powder Puff races but I was satisfied with my performance. After all, I was flying against some of the most experienced pilots in the United States and I knew that I had given the races my best. I never flew a mile off course anywhere except to circumvent storms and I never goofed. I got a real feeling of satisfaction for finishing all the races I entered."

SALLY KERTON WAGNER (1915-1971)

Born in Toronto, Ontario, Sally earned her private licence on November 12, 1941. Grounded by gas rationing for the war years she resumed her training and received a commercial licence on October 21, 1945 and shortly after qualified for an instructor's rating. Working full-time as a cosmetician and part-time for Marion Orr, while also raising a son on her own, kept her life full.

Sally was best known as a show pilot. She took aerobatic instruction from Hal Wannamaker and became the co-owner of a polished aluminum de Havilland Chipmunk. With her silvery blond hair, she made an unforgettable sight striding out to her aircraft in a shimmery silver flight suit. She flew a smooth routine with variations of the roll, loop, spin, and hammerhead. She was one of less than two dozen pilots in Canada who performed regularly. In 1971 she died in the crash of her aircraft.

Another popular race of the era was the International Air Race, otherwise known as the "Angel Derby." It was conducted in much the same manner as the Powder Puff but had the distinction of starting and finishing in two different countries, such as Canada and the United States or the United States and Cuba. Since the race was shorter and less expensive than the Powder Puff, there were more Canadian entries. Felicity McKendry, Margaret Carson, Lorna DeBlicquy, Gina Jordan, Dorothy Rungeling, Audrey Peck, and Toni Ramsay were some of the regulars from Canada. Felicity recalled the heartbreak of being disqualified. "After flying 1400 miles we arrived over the finishing line twenty-four seconds after official night

and were disqualified. Ridiculous!" Dorothy's most memorable race was the 1955 Angel Derby from Washington, DC to Havana, Cuba. "It was like a B movie," she described, "out of twenty-five aircraft, seven dropped out along the way with engine problems; one woman flew into a mountain and was killed; and there was a 110 mile flight over water with the knowledge that an engine failure could mean death. The finish was a spectacular reception thrown by President Batista in his palace."

Canada had its own races as well, the most well known being the Governor General's Cup, held annually at the Canadian National Exhibition grounds in Toronto. A speed race around pylons, the six-leg course called for precise navigation

Sally Wagner, c. 1960, Canada's top woman "show" pilot.

and expert piloting. The route was kept secret until one hour before race time. As Dorothy described it, "We had to fly over each turning point in the 203 mile course, three of these intersections were mere backroads and very difficult to spot. It was a fun race and in no way compared to the Powder Puff."

Lucille Haley challenged her skill and her plane in another way. In January 1969 she set an altitude record in a Fleet Canuck. In -15°F weather, accompanied by an official observer and with oxygen tanks in place, she took an Edmonton Flying Club 85 horsepower Canuck up to 18,116 feet. "It took me two and a half hours to reach that height. On the way down I ran out of gas and had to do a dead stick landing." Another time

he aprons summed-up the at- des of those carefree days. othy Rungeling, right, and co-pilot an Koch celebrated their arrival Cuba at the end of the 1956 in- ternational race. They later former president Batista, presented him with a set of k made in Welland. —Photo by Jarvis Da

Newspaper clipping of International Air Race, the Angel Derby, 1956.

DOROTHY RUNGELING

Dorothy Rungeling, of Fenwick, Ontario, was Canada's most experienced air racer. The daughter of Canadian poet, Ethelwyn Wetherald, she drove motorcycles, enjoyed trap and skeet shooting, trained and rode horses, and judged horse shows before she discovered flying. Dorothy and her husband Charles owned an automotive and farm machinery business and, for an advertisment, Dorothy was photographed beside a car parked next to a small plane. After the photo session the pilot took Dorothy's husband and four-year old son for a flight and they insisted that she go too. Terrified yet fascinated, she agreed. "I was really annoyed with myself for being so afraid, so the next week I went out to the airport — just to look around and maybe sit in an airplane. That was the start of it all. I decided to take another flight just to prove to myself that fear did not rule me. Then I thought, why not take some lessons, just until I solo." Her instructor at the Welland Flying Club was not happy having a woman student and gave her "the works." Amazingly she went back for more, determined to conquer her fear. She soloed in 5 hours.

"I had intended to stop when I soloed, but I don't like to do things halfway, so I decided to get my licence. When I received it in 1949 I was in too deep to think of giving up flying. My husband bought me a Luscombe so I could take him flying." To build time for her commercial licence Dorothy flew to Havana, Cuba. "When I flew to Cuba I had only fifty hours or so and was supposed to be travelling with others, among them Carl Millard. But I became separated from them and flew most of the trip by myself. I sure learned how to navigate. I think it was that trip that led me into air racing." Over the next few years she earned a commercial licence, an instructor's rating, a senior commercial pilot's licence, and an ATR. She also bought a Cessna

Lucille and another instructor, Joe McGoldrick, ferried two Canucks from Goderich, Ontario to Edmonton as replacement for some of the aircraft lost in the 1967 flying club fire. "We flew 2100 miles in thirty-two flying hours over four days. We had no radios, the cabin heaters didn't work, the temperatures were below zero, we averaged sixty miles per hour and lived on frozen sandwiches and frozen milk. But it was fun."

Thus women continued to fly. "Certainly not for the money," laughed Ruth Parsons, "I guess for the love of it and the challenge it continually gave me." And Ethel Davies said, "My flying days were the best years of my life. At night, as soon as the hangar doors closed it was 'let's have a party.' The guys

170, then a Cessna 172, later a Piper Pacer, and finally a Beech Bonanza.

"I needed a reason to fly," she said. "Instructing part-time only partially satisfied me. When I heard of the Powder Puff and Angel Derby I knew that I had found what I wanted." In 1951 she entered the Angel Derby — a 1000 mile race from Orlando, Florida to Windsor, Ontario — with Lorna DeBlicquy as her co-pilot. The only other Canadian entry was Margaret Carson and Betty McCanse. In all, Dorothy competed in seven Angel Derbys, usually placing in the top ten. She also entered three Governor General's Cup races, twice flying off with first place against all-male fields and once coming in third.

In 1955 she decided she was ready to enter the Powder Puff Derby, the most gruelling of races. With Felicity McKendry as her co-pilot she flew a 2800-mile course from Long Beach, California to Springfield, Massachusetts. By the time they returned to Canada they had logged eighty-seven hours in eleven days and flown almost 9000 miles.

By 1958 Dorothy had qualified for every fixed wing licence there was, had participated in every air race open to her and was looking for another challenge. The opportunity came in the form of helicopter flying. A distributor asked her to write on rotary wing flying from a fixed wing point of view and offered free lessons to the solo stage on a Bell 47G-2. She soloed in 4 hours and 44 minutes and became, in 1958, the first Canadian woman to solo in a helicopter. From that experience she wrote an article titled "From Fixed Wing to Whirly Bird." The expense of further training with no prospect of a job deterred her from obtaining her licence.

Dorothy worked hard to promote general aviation. She helped organize the Canadian Section of the 99s and was one of its first governors. She actively supported air marking (painting the name of the airport on the runway or hangar roof) in Ontario and in 1959 was successful in having

Dorothy Rungeling, 1953 winner of the Governor General's Silver Cup.

were pretty good to us. They used to call us — Rolie Moore, Bette Milburn, and me — 'the three graces.' It was a great feeling to know that you belonged. Pilots are a rare breed; they have something in common that no one else has."

Sex roles in the forties and fifties remained clearcut; but, by the sixties, the feminist movement had begun to blur the lines between "what little girls did" and "what little boys did" — except in aviation. If women wanted to fly, they became stewardesses (flight attendants) or instructors. These jobs were consonant with women's so-called natural instincts: a caring or teaching role. The onus for change lay with the women. But career women were a rarity in all professions and they formed

Two Canadian teams on their way to the race, 1951. From the left, Dorothy Rungeling, Lorna Bray [DeBlicquy], Betty McCanse, and Margaret Carson.

Welland Airport air marked. She formed the Canadian Airplane Racing Association and wrote about the air transport industry in her aviation column in the Welland *Tribune* and in various Canadian aviation magazines. Twice, in 1953 and 1959, she won the Air Industries and Transportation Association of Canada Award for her writing on aviation topics. She was a well-known speaker and a popular guest at Rotary and Kinsmen functions.

Although she continued to fly during the sixties she did not have the same enthusiasm and in 1975, she allowed her licences to lapse. "Canada's Aviatrix of the Year," as the Toronto *Daily Star* dubbed her on May 17, 1956 or "Mrs. Good at Everything" as the local papers called her, needed new horizons and ultimately traded flying for sailing, celestial navigation, oil painting, and politics.

such a minuscule percentage of the work force that they had little impact on the dynamics of the workplace. As for women pilots, there were too few qualified to make a significant dent in attitudes. There were perhaps fifty professional women pilots in Canada compared with over 2800 men. Official figures do not include a male/female breakdown but the following approximation shows the discrepancy in the mid-fifties.

Licence	Male	Female
Private	4300	192
Commercial	1507	25
Instructor	378	22
Senior Commercial	335	2
Public Transport	587	2

The women's impact was further diffused because they were scattered across the country. Small pockets of women pilots in the Toronto-Ottawa, Lethbridge-Calgary-Edmonton, and Vancouver areas tried to band together as chapters of the 99s, the International Organization of Women Pilots. However, lack of numbers and the distances involved proved insurmountable and the chapters folded. They were revived in the late sixties and early seventies but they never proved to be particularly effective in furthering the cause of women pilots.

The problem of small numbers was compounded with the women's tactic of not making waves. "You must remember there were very few women pilots around and if we did have a job we tried very hard to keep it," explained Dawn Bartsch. And so, the women continued with the only option open to them. They waited. For another twenty-five years they waited, but it was not time wasted.

They established reputations as conscientious and skillful employees. Flying club managers liked them because they stayed, unlike the men who used instructing as a quick way to build time before moving onto something better. Often caught because of marriage and children, the women could not just pick up and go. So they remained and slowly earned the admiration of their male colleagues. Some, like the remarkable women whose stories follow, began to edge into the forbidden worlds of charter and bush flying.

MOLLY BEALL REILLY of Lindsay, Ontario wanted to be a pilot just like her brother and as soon as she completed high school in 1940 she tried to enlist in the RCAF. Indignant that her brother was accepted but not her, she decided to aim for the ATA instead; but gasoline rationing cut her flying lessons short. Determined to get airborne somehow, she joined the Women's Division of the RCAF and requested photographic duties, because that was the only trade open to women where flight time was possible. As soon as civilian schools re-opened, she enrolled at the Rockcliffe Flying Club. While still in uniform in 1946 she earned a private licence as well as an honourable discharge. She qualified for her commercial licence the next year.

Molly Beall Reilly, from the cover of The Legionaire, *July, 1948.*

With thousands of returning airmen hitting the job market, Molly knew that instructing was the only way to get her foot in the cockpit door. But when she applied to the Department of Veteran's Affairs (DVA) for permission to use her rehabilitation credits for her training, she received an emphatic "no." But Molly had already cooled her heels waiting for the end of the war and was not about to let another male government official keep her on the ground. Arguing that instructor training was in keeping with the spirit of the DVA Act, she finally received permission to proceed, provided that she first have a job guaranteed. She quickly convinced the Ottawa Flying Club to hire her. In an about-turn DVA then featured her on the July 1948 cover of *The Legionaire,* with the headline, "Rehabilitation Through Aviation." They boasted hers as "the most unusual request received by DVA." This was neither the first nor last time that Molly would make headlines. While training, she entered the 1947 Webster Trophy contest and was runner-up, losing by only three tenths of a point. Reporters made a big deal out of that fact as most of the contestants were male.

Molly's career with the Ottawa Flying Club lasted no more than five hours, just long enough to fulfill her committment to DVA. Molly knew that she had to become known; being hidden away in sleepy Ottawa was not the way to go about it. She wasn't remotely interested in a purely instructing environment and wasted no time convincing Jack Reilly of Leavens Brothers, Toronto to hire her as an instructor with the understanding that she could also fly charters. Neither did she remain complacent with her credentials. "She had an obsession with being perfect," recalled Jack, whom she later married. "During her six years with Leavens she constantly made deals to get free flight time and instruction. Three times she talked them into holding her job while she went elsewhere to obtain more training. She took an advanced instrument course at the Spartan School of Aeronautics, Tulsa, Oklahoma, where she received multi-engine and instrument ratings in the early fifties. She also took a seaplane course at Port Alberni, British Columbia and in 1953, travelled to England to qualify for her British commercial licence because she had heard that its course was more rigorous and complete than Canada's. She earned her Senior Commercial Licence and Public Transport Licence and when the Air Transport Rating (ATR) came out, she got that."

Molly Beall was just a little bit of a thing, barely five feet tall, but no one overlooked her. It was not that she bragged or fluttered her eyelashes. It was simply that she lived, breathed, and talked airplanes. "She had little time or interest in anything other than flying. Her intensity and dedication to learning and her skill as a pilot left an impression on everyone," said Jack. Valerie Cheltenham, one of Molly's students, described her as "serious and unflappable. I'll never forget the day I watched her bring in a Cessna Crane; the left engine was on fire and it was trailing smoke. Everyone was out on the field watching and expecting a panic-stricken woman to tumble out of the plane. Instead Molly climbed out, walked over to one of the mechanics and said, 'Better take a look at that engine' then sauntered

THE WINNERS—Mel Bradley and pretty Molly Beal, who place first and second in the Webster Memorial Trophy St. Lawrenc Zone eliminations at Hawkesbury Saturday, smile happily afte their victory. Both will compete in the Dominion finals to b held in Oshawa on September 5th and 6th.

—Photo by Bon Cairns

Molly Beall, c. 1947.

FELICITY BENNETT McKENDRY

Felicity Bennett, of Ottawa, grew up on a dairy farm in Spencerville, Ontario. "I used to play with model aircraft that I built myself and powered with rubber bands. During the war I was fascinated with the Harvards which were always flying over the farm on training flights. I was so keen on flying that I used the prize money I had won from the Rotary Club for raising the largest chicken, to pay for my first airplane ride when I was twelve." Felicity never thought of flying as a career but, after graduating from university in 1950 and securing a teaching job, she joined the Kingston Flying Club and earned a private licence in 1951.

In 1952 she represented the flying club in the Webster Trophy competition and, placing first, went on to the finals in Ottawa where she came in first in flying and third overall. By then she was so hooked on flying that her instructor, Doug Wagner, suggested that she obtain her commercial and instructor's licences. "With that encouragement I left my teaching job to concentrate full-time on flying. I worked on both licences simultaneously and qualified for both in May 1953. Doug hired me immediately. I was the first woman instructor at the club and the newspapers loved it." The *Whig Standard* noted she was one of only seven women instructors in Canada compared with approximately 400 men.

Felicity stayed with the club for three years, often putting in twelve- to fourteen-hour days. In return the club supported her racing ambitions, giving her time off and partially financing her trips. In 1955 she married Spence McKendry, a pilot and air traffic controller, and began the difficult task of combining marriage and flying. In 1956 he was transferred to Ottawa and she found work at Bradley Air Services at Carp Airport where, shortly after, she became chief flying instructor, one of the first women CFIs in Canada.

When Felicity became pregnant the following year

away. From that time on, Molly was known as 'the girl with the carburetor heart.'"

Molly also impressed fellow pilot/photographer Stuart Alexander. "As a photograhic pilot she was superb. She knew just where the lens would be pointing and I could count on her to give me just the angle I wanted, usually without words passing between us." He had only one complaint. "I rarely got a chance to fly! Whenever we got a job I'd say, 'Well Beall, what do you want to do, fly or take pictures?' Molly would inevitably answer, 'Oh, I'll fly.'"

Molly was still doing too much instructing for her liking so when Canadian Aircraft Renters of Toronto offered her the position of chief flying instructor and stand-by charter pilot in 1954, she took it, hoping for more charter work. In 1957 Molly finally put instructing behind her when Southern Provincial Airlines, a subsidiary of Canadian Aircraft Renters, hired her as a full-time charter pilot. They also promoted her to captain, the first Canadian woman to earn the title. Flying mainly Beech 18s, Lockheed Lodestars, and DC-3s, she hauled

neither Bradley Air nor the Department of Transport deemed it a problem and she flew until six weeks before the birth of her son. Back in the air soon after, she continued to fly full-time until the arrival of her daughter four years later, when she decided to spend less time away from home. Between 1958 and 1965 she flew just enough to keep herself current. In 1966 she resumed part-time instructing, working for Margaret Carson, then the Ottawa Flying Club and, from 1974 to 1986, with the Rockcliffe Flying Club. Over the years she continually upgraded her qualifications and when she retired in 1986 she held a Class 1 instructor's rating and an airline transport rating. With her retirement students lost a teacher whose calm and gentle manner, combined with her skill as a pilot and her dedication to instructing, made her one of the best-loved and respected instructors in the area.

L *Air racers Dorothy Rungeling, on the left, and Felicity McKendry, 1950s.*

R *Felicity Bennett McKendry, at the Brantford Flying Club Instructors' Course, 1953.*

people and freight all over eastern Canada, the northern States and the eastern Arctic. The first woman to fly professionally in the Arctic, she also logged many hours in a specially-equipped Cessna Crane on an air ambulance program. "It was Molly who convinced Canadian Aircraft Renters to buy the Crane because it had a special door suitable for handling stretchers. She then went to the health authorities and told them that the company was equipped to handle medevacs! Molly did most of the air ambulance trips," said Jack.

In 1959 Molly headed for Calgary. The lure was two-fold: a job as DC-3 co-captain for Peter Bawden Drilling Service and the chance to crew with Jack Reilly. Their paths had been crossing for ten years. From the start, big, boisterous, genial Jack Reilly had been impressed with the skill and intensity of little Molly Beall and when Peter Bawden hired him, he requested that she work with him. Molly happily accepted the

Margaret Carson.

MARGARET CARSON

Margaret Carson, of Ottawa, Ontario, took flying lessons to make herself more eligible for military pilot training. "As soon as I got my private licence in November 1940 I joined the Women's Division of the RCAF because I had been told that there was going to be a flying section. When it did not materialize I tried to get out so I could apply to the ATA. The RCAF would not release me as administrative officers were needed too badly."

After the war Margaret qualified for her commercial licence (1946) and during the next few years, she divided her time between running the family luggage business and flying. In the early fifties she formed Ottawa Aero Storage at Ottawa International Airport and also managed Cessna and Shell dealerships and a flight school and charter service. It was in this period that Margaret participated in the founding of the Canadian Owners and Pilots Association (COPA) "to present a united voice from the grassroots pilots of Canada to the bureaucratic offices of Ottawa." She served as secretary and was a director for many years.

Margaret was also one of the few Canadian women to participate in air racing. A member of the 99s, she entered and won its 1951 International Air Race (from Ontario to Florida).

Since 1978 Margaret, who commutes between Florida and Ottawa, has been associated with Operation Retrieval, a Florida-based operation which, explained Margaret, "has an international committee to look for aircraft which have been lost in the Caribbean or locked up by Castro."

job offer and Jack's proposal of marriage, and the legend of the "Flying Reillys" began.

Molly and Jack logged many trips together and, according to Jack, "We each recognized the other's ability. We had no trouble flying together and when we got home we closed the hangar doors." They flew into the Arctic, often in extremes of weather conditions and extensive periods of darkness. In those days there were few navaids and little radio communication. For five years they moved men and equipment to within 600 miles of the North Pole and to all the major oilfields in western Canada and the United States. "We flew a DC-3. We would leave Calgary at 10:00 PM for Edmonton, where we would put on the remainder of the load. Then we were off for Fort St. John, Fort Nelson, and Norman Wells. We'd refuel, put covers on the wings and the guys would off-load. Then onto Little Chicago, Fort Good Hope, and the Arctic Red River. It was a

RUTH CRIPPS

Ruth Cripps, of Toronto said, "I wanted to fly in the RCAF like my brothers, but when I applied they told me I couldn't join because I was a girl. I'd heard about the ATA and decided on that instead." Gasoline rationing ended her lessons however and she spent the rest of the war in an administrative position at the Air Observer's School at Malton. Once civilian flying resumed she signed up and received a private licence in 1946. "I began 'working the fence' in my spare time because I wanted to obtain my commercial licence. I met Molly Beall [Reilly] at Leavens and we were friends until her death." Two years later Ruth earned a commercial licence and, with that in hand, applied at Austin Airways, a bush company founded in 1934. She was hired as a secretary in the Toronto office.

She did her work well and, in her quiet way, reminded Jack Austin that she had a commercial licence. A few years later, he appointed her base manager for Sudbury. "I was responsible for scheduling the base's four pilots and aircraft, booking passengers and cargo, and doing anything else that had to be done. It was a seven-day a week job starting at 6:00 AM and finishing at 11:00 PM." Officially it was a ground position but Austin also checked her out on the Norseman, Beaver, and Stinson so that she could pinch-hit if a pilot were needed. Ruth remained at Austin Airways until 1959 when she chose to get out of aviation.

Her short career in aviation was a non-flying one but, like Eliane Roberge and Margaret Fane of the thirties, she helped forge a place for women pilots in the industry.

bleak place. We'd make three trips a week, hauling supplies, food, and drilling equipment. We would fly all night, grab a couple of hours sleep in the tool pushers shack." It was all very primitive but Molly never missed a day's work. "Even pregnancy didn't ground her. I don't think there was anything written [against flying while pregnant] but we kept the first one a secret. It's a wonder that Patrick wasn't born in a DC-3."

In 1965 the Reillys moved to Edmonton where Molly had accepted a job with Canadian Coachways. Shortly after, the company was absorbed by Canadian Utilities of Edmonton and Molly was made chief pilot, another milestone — the first woman corporate pilot in Canada. Molly flew a Beech Baron

and later, a Beech Duke, known as "Molly's Folly," all over North America. Because she had so much time on the Duke, Beechcraft asked her to do experimental flights in the north. She earned a personal commendation from Mrs. Beech. When illness forced Molly to stop flying she had more hours on the Duke than any other pilot in North America.

Molly Reilly was a remarkable woman. "She managed to do almost everything she wanted and to do it well," said Jack proudly. "Her standard in flying was nothing less than perfection and she never stopped trying to improve herself. There was no aircraft she could not handle and no job too lowly for her. She fueled planes in forty below weather, pushed 45 gallon drums about, and handled cargo herself when there was no one

L *Molly Reilly, up north, 1980.*

R *Molly with Edmonton Mayor Ivor Dent, at the first induction into Canada's Aviation Hall of Fame.*

to help. She never asked for special quarters, she simply threw her sleeping bag on the floor of a storeroom, and if that privacy was unavailable, she bunked in with the men." Added longtime friend Sara Johnson, "Her determination and intensity were so great that time and again she overcame the obstacle of being a woman in a man's world."

Molly Reilly logged more than 10,000 hours, all accident-free, a signal achievement by any standard. She was accepted and respected by the aviation community. Molly was made a Companion of the Order of Icarus and a Member of the Brotherhood of Silver Wings. In 1973 she was further honoured by being inducted into Canada's Aviation Hall of Fame.

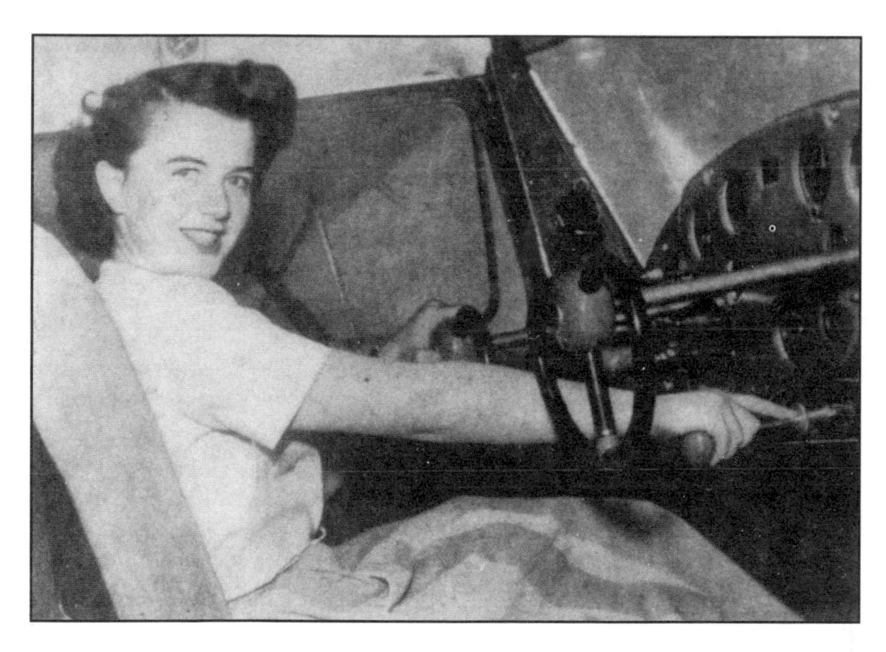

The respect and admiration that she evoked is perhaps best shown by the following excerpt from the memorial poem written for her funeral service in 1980.

> There passed a pilot, seen by God,
> Who marked her route across the blue,
> A chart for all to plan a course
> Where once an eagle flew.

LORNA BRAY NICHOLS DeBLICQUY of Ottawa, Ontario announced to her family at fourteen that she was going to learn to fly. Her brother, an RCAF pilot and later a bush pilot, had piqued her imagination with flying stories. A chance ride in a sporty little Globe Swift proved to be the clincher. "My

Lorna Bray, c. 1949.

parents were not pleased but did not stop me. They did, however, make three stipulations: they would not drive me to the airport; I had to come home right after my lessons because 'girls who hung around the airport were tough'; and I had to maintain a seventy-five percent average with no mark below sixty." To please her parents Lorna also attended university. "I had received a scholarship to Carleton University and wanted to take engineering but, in those days, girls were firmly discouraged from science and math. I took the easiest arts courses so that I would have more time for flying."

Her parents paid for the occasional lesson but Lorna financed most of her training working as a babysitter, theatre cashier, RCAF Reserve communications instructor and Girl Friday at the flying club. "It was hard to scrape the money together and often I could afford to fly only fifteen minutes at a time." Lorna received her private licence in 1948 from Atlas Aviation at Uplands Airport (now Ottawa International Airport), but not without difficulty.

Until 1948 the flight examiner stayed on the ground while the applicant soloed. Mentally prepared for that kind of flight test on December 11, 1947, Lorna was unnerved when the examiner climbed into the plane with her, following a new format that was due to be introduced in January of 1948. "I was very conscious of him watching my every move. I did fine on the first circuit and spot landing, and even the spin and forced approach over a farmer's field were okay. But when he suggested that I return to the airport all reason left. All the familiar landmarks disappeared, and after that, things deteriorated rapidly and the examiner had to take over the landing!" A devastated Lorna was not surprised to learn that she had failed. Not wanting to go through that experience again, she asked if she could be re-tested. A sympathetic Department of Transport official, Terry Saunderson, waived the thirty-day waiting period required for a second attempt and Lorna took her test "the old way" on December 27 confidently performing all the proper manoeuvres.

University, skydiving, and part-time jobs cut into her flying time and four more years passed before she acquired her commercial licence. She kept her hand in flying, however, by competing in a number of air races sponsored by the 99s. After graduating in 1953 she married Tony Nichols, a geologist, and moved to a drilling camp in northern Manitoba. Home at

Mystery Lake (Thompson, Manitoba) for the next two years was a roomy tent on skids, with a fur-covered toilet seat in the biffy house. To reach Thompson Lorna flew her Super Chief from Ottawa, a trip of roughly 1300 miles over rocky and mostly unsettled areas. Reporters heralded her journey with gut-wrenchers like "lone girl pilot who had only a kitten for company."

Eager to use her commercial licence, Lorna contacted Jock Hunter of Taylor Airways in Wabowden. "Hunter was amused that a woman had applied to fly a bush plane and word soon passed through the small town that a woman pilot had actually applied for a job," Lorna remembered. However, when his

Lorna Nichols, c. 1953 with the Waco Standard she flew for Taylor Airways, Wabowden, Manitoba.

replacement pilot did not show up, he was forced to hire Lorna to fulfill a contract. "My checkout in the Waco Standard, a five-place biplane, was very cursory. It was the first constant speed prop plane I had flown and I never did get the numbers the manual suggested. I was really 'an accident looking for a place to happen!'" Lorna was the first woman to fly professionally in northern Manitoba.

"I found most people looked a little surprised when they found out I was the pilot; but up north people generally take what they can get and only once did I run into someone who refused to fly with me. I solved the problem by leaving him, a government school inspector, behind. He waited three days, hoping that a male pilot would show up, before he reluctantly climbed into the plane with me." To reassure him she flew with exaggerated caution, remaining over the water after take-off far longer than usual before turning inland. She also landed far out in the lake, so he would not worry about her crashing into the rocks near the dock and then taxied in very slowly. "The next day I heard that he had told people that 'I did alright for a girl but I got lost easy and landed too far from the dock.'"

Lorna logged about 50 hours with Taylor Airways. "I acquired a mass of bruises on my shins from vaulting out the windows over bags of odiferous fish, grabbing heavy sharp objects just as some helpful soul was about to place them on the lower wing or lifting kicking children out of canoes into the arms of their anxious mothers." Besides flying natives and supplies into reserves, she flew diamond drillers, fishermen, and government inspectors. "My biggest problem was with the Indians who thought if they could squeeze ten in the plane that was okay. They were not concerned with weight and balance."

Lorna DeBlicquy, 1967, in a de Havilland Beaver.

In 1956 the Nichols moved to Sudbury. There Lorna kept herself busy with two jobs: one teaching full-time at the high school and the other, instructing part-time at Sudbury Aviation. "I had no problem getting a job because I was there, qualified, and able to work part-time, which meant they could pay me a lower salary than a full-time instructor. My students were mostly miners who did not always take kindly to a slip of a girl telling them what to do."

Lorna remained in Sudbury until 1962 when she left town and her husband. It was a bad time to be on her own. The aviation industry was in a slump and jobs were scarce. However, ready to try anything, she did a little barnstorming in an Aeronca Champ in backwoods Quebec and filled in as an instructor at Bradley Air Services at Carp, Ontario. While there she heard about an opening at the Kingston Flying Club. "I had no trouble getting the job because Felicity McKendry had left a good name for women instructors." Undoubtedly Doug Wagner, the CFI, was also pleased with the publicity his latest instructor generated. "New Kingston Flying Club Instructor Adds Glamorous Touches to Job" trumpeted the July 4, 1962 edition of the Kingston *Whig-Standard*.

The Kingston Flying Club did not keep Lorna for long,

because, as it turned out, she was carrying on a long-distance love affair with a pilot she had met at Bradley. Soon she and Dick DeBlicquy, [son of Michael DeBlicquy, the Winnipeg Flying Club's first flying instructor] were a twosome and leading a nomadic life between Canada and New Zealand. Dick, a fixed and rotary wing pilot, flew part of the year in New Zealand and the rest of the time for Weldy Phipps in the Arctic. Lorna, never one to sit at home filing her nails, kept her logbook open and added more planes, hours, and experience to an already varied career.

She instructed at the Wellington and Marlborough [New Zealand] aero clubs and flew sightseers for Sound Scenic Flights. "I flew in and out of little strips carved out of the sides of mountains and across the Cook Strait. One summer I rented an Auster and took a busman's holiday. I should have known that something would go wrong when I was told how to start the plane — if I couldn't get it going by hand propping, I was to remove the right engine cowl and bash the side of the magneto vigorously with any heavy metal object. I had every reason to believe that piece of advice because the dents in ZK-BDI's spare control column showed it was the heavy metal object most often used! Three days out the Auster began to vibrate. Within minutes the prop went spinning past the left wing tip to the hills below. I radioed 'Mayday' and landed in the only flat field about. My sightseeing was over."

Returning to Canada in 1968, Lorna took Spartan Air Services' twenty-five hour conversion course on helicopters and received her commercial rotary wing licence on a Bell 47. "I took up helicopter flying because in this game you can't stand still." When not travelling with Dick she worked as an instructor and over the next ten years, taught at the Kingston, Montreal, and Ottawa flying clubs and also flew charters for Georgian Bay Airways. Nineteen sixty-six was a busy year; she qualified for her senior commercial licence, worked in the Arctic, and had a baby. "I continued to fly. To my knowledge there was nothing in air regs that would have prevented me from flying."

In the summer of 1967 Lorna tucked the baby into the seat of an Apache and flew up to Resolute Bay on Cornwallis Island, near the Magnetic North Pole. Anxious to broaden her experience, she talked Texas Gulf, which was operating out of Strathcona Sound, into checking her out on the de Havilland

Beaver and Twin Otter. Her first line flight on the Beaver provided another memorable logbook entry. Her husband Dick, with Atlas Aviation, had become stranded, with one engine out on his Twin Otter, 5500 feet up on a glacier on Ellesmere Island. He radioed Resolute Bay to be picked up along with his five passengers, who were part of the RAF Mountain Rescue Team. They were due at Eureka in three days time and then were to fly to Thule to be met by Lord Shackleton himself. As Lorna said, "It would be poor PR for Atlas Aviation if the team were stuck on a glacier." The problem was there were no pilots at Resolute except for Lorna and the only aircraft suitable for landing at the rough strip at Tanquary was the Beaver on big tires. "I'd done all of three circuits in the Beaver and thought, 'no problem.' So I volunteered for the rescue mission. I was brave but stupid."

She made mistake number one by taking off in IFR (Instrument Flying Rules) weather. "I had some instrument training and the forecast called for improvement within the hour, so I barrelled off from foggy Resolute and into cloud." Two hours later, still with no visual ground contact and low on fuel, she had to admit that she was lost and becoming anxious. "Finally the clouds broke and mountains appeared, but the snowy peaks did not match those on my sectional [map]. All I could think about was that I was 'letting the side down.' A search for a man down in the Arctic was bad enough; a search for a female would be a blow for women pilots everywhere. I wanted to pass on a decent record to the next girl. Making a fool of myself 500 miles from the North Pole wasn't the way to do it." At last the weather cleared enough for her to pinpoint her position and an hour later she touched down at Eureka. "I sure learned a lesson about pushing weather and getting adequate checkouts." However, the story was not yet over. Because she had been out of radio contact for so long Resolute Bay had assumed she was lost. When she finally landed at Eureka, the station radioed her stranded husband that she was safe. "I didn't know she had been lost," he retorted.

During the next few years she flew right seat with her husband in the Twin Otter and spent a summer flying the Beaver as air support for the Department of National Defence Research Board's scientific program on Ellesmere Island. In 1970 she won an Amelia Earhart Award from the 99s and used it to finance a Class 1 instrument rating and airline transport rating (ATR). She also received a Class 1 instructor's rating and the President's Trophy from the Ottawa Flying Club in 1971. Further recognition of her skills came in 1974 when the Department of Transport (DOT) appointed her a designated flight test examiner, one of the first women to become one.

In 1975, deciding that she was long overdue for a change, she applied to the newly-formed Air Transit, a subsidiary of Air Canada formed to provide Twin Otter service between Ottawa and Montreal. "I had approximately 6000 hours and my ATR and I thought I was qualified. I wasn't even called for an interview, but two of my students were hired. When I asked why I had not been considered they gave me a bunch of excuses: I was too short, they could not design a uniform for me, or I had too much experience. I was so mad that I decided to 'go public' and charge Air Transit with discrimination. I'd always tried to ignore it but this time I objected that my taxes were being diverted to only half the population. I wrote a guest editorial for *Canadian Flight* and was interviewed on numerous radio talk shows. I also appealed to several government agencies; all of which accomplished sweet nothing."

Lorna had no choice but to wait for something else. That something, she thought, was a position in flight training standards and, when DOT held its next competition in 1976, she applied. "Someone with much less experience got the job," Lorna said. But she refused to let it slip by without a fight. "I wrote to DOT asking what their policy was for hiring people in flight training standards." She presented her case well but did not get the job. However, Lorna proved to be a catalyst for change in the government's hiring policy. A year later, she entered another competition for a civil aviation inspector. Unable to ignore her any longer, DOT broke with tradition and hired her. Lorna became Canada's first woman civil aviation inspector. "With one or two small exceptions I had few battles to fight once I was in the door. I knew many of the DOT officials and they ran interference for me. I was also older and therefore not considered a threat to others." Working out of the Toronto office, Lorna's responsibilities included categorization rides with instructors and flight testing at the private, commercial, and multi-engine levels. She held the position for two years, commuting each week between Toronto and her home in Ottawa. Since then she has continued to work for Transport Canada on what she calls a free-lance basis.

In 1985 Lorna added a DC-3 endorsement to her logbook and began flying Bradley-First Air's Ottawa to Syracuse run. "I found the DC-3 to be a delightful venerable aircraft. But I wasn't suitable for that operation as I held them up in the loading. It was a gold run and the poor Brinks guard had to load more than if I had been a young pilot." In 1986 she and Dick went to Ethiopia to fly Twin Otters on a famine relief project. Back in Canada by year end, Lorna returned to instructing and giving flight tests.

Lorna DeBlicquy's logbook reads like a travelogue, with entries from the Arctic, Northwest Territories, eastern Canada, the United States, New Zealand, and Ethiopia. Licenced for gliders, fixed wing, and rotary wing aircraft, she has flown as an instructor, barnstormer, charter pilot, bush pilot, air racer, and government examiner. The "Fiord Flying Momma," as the newspapers nicknamed her, was Canada's first woman "high latitude pilot" and she showed that bush pilots did not have to be hairy-chested males. That airline flying was not a part of her resumé was not for lack of trying. "I received no answer from Air Canada or CP Air and was told by the regionals that they did not hire women pilots." The normally forceful Lorna did not make a fuss. Indeed, for more than twenty years she quietly endured discrimination and patronizing comments. Too many times she was forced to watch in frustration as less qualified men were hired or promoted until finally, in the mid-seventies, she decided enough was enough. While her charges of discrimination made some women pilots shudder, they were effective. Lorna represented the first of her sex to enter the Department of Transport male compound and she brought with her a much needed grass roots component.

Notes
6 Sheldon Luck, letter, 1985.
7 Al Michaud, interview 26 November, 1986.

Bush flying

"Some thought it was great to be able to say they had flown with a woman pilot, or to have their picture taken with one — along with the fish they had caught." — *Ruth Parsons*

BUSH OPERATIONS remained a vital mode of transportation in the fifties. While aircraft were generally more sophisticated and better equipped, the essence of bush flying had not changed from pre-war days; it still embodied that continuous struggle with Canada's wilderness that airline flying did not.

Bush flying was tough. As Jim Lewington, former pilot with Eastern Provincial Airlines, said, "If a woman pilot had approached me in the fifties or sixties for a job in the bush, I would have expected her to drain the engine oil, lug it and the battery to a warm spot when overnighting away from base, spend an hour or two under an engine tent with a plumber's blow pot on a frosty morning, sail an aircraft with some precision in rough water, rig a gin pole or tripod to lift an aircraft up through the ice or an engine out of an airframe, manhandle 45 gallon drums of fuel. In short, if a woman pilot had applied to me for a job in the bush I would have looked at her with a skeptical if not jaundiced eye."

But women believed in their own capabilities. In the fifties and sixties they persisted in applying for work and, ever so slowly, they overcame the assumption that the bush was "no place for a lady." In some cases, they were helped by the bush operators themselves. Owners such as Orville "Porky" Wieben of Superior Airways of Fort William, Lorne Andrews of Nipawin Air Service, Hank Parsons of Parsons Airways Northern in Flin Flon, and Keith Parsons of Parsons Airways in Kenora gave women a chance. As Hank Parsons stated, "The right type of woman could carry on as well as a man."

Although bush operators were the first, outside of flying clubs, to open their doors to women, progress was excruciatingly slow, and legitimatizing their place was a hard-won battle for the women. The reception they received when seeking employment ranged from startled to downright chilly and whatever status they attained, they earned in spades. Their struggle to survive, to gain the freedom of the male experience, brought out their resourcefulness, but often cost them dearly in their personal lives.

Ruth Parsons, c. mid-fifties, with a Stinson 108.

Violet Milstead Warren, Canada's first woman bush pilot, had done much to allay men's fears that women could not cope away from modern conveniences. Ruth Parsons, Dawn Connelly Bartsch, the Studer sisters, Liz and Robbie Wieben, and Toni Ramsay continued in the fifties and sixties to blaze a trail for the women to follow.

RUTH PARSONS of Fort William, Ontario was the only girl in a family of boys. As she recalled, "I was born into a flying family. I always thought I was brought up conventionally, but I lived with flying. My father was a railway man and three of my brothers were pilots. We lived around freeze-up and break-up, when my brothers came home. I spent my summers in Kenora at Parsons Airways 'working the docks and catching airplanes.' It seemed only natural that I should choose flying as my career." Ruth trained at the Fort William Flying Club and received a private licence in 1952. "My mother hoped that I would find a job which kept me on the ground, so to please her I took my grade thirteen and teacher's college, but my heart was in the air. However, I promised her that I would teach long enough to get my permanent teacher's certificate." Ruth earned a commercial licence in 1954. "My father encouraged me to fly, but my brothers did not think it was a suitable occupation for a girl. Keith told me that when women came into the bush, he would go to Africa! When I got my commercial I reminded him of his remark. He just laughed and helped me out; they all did."

Ruth never asked for favours. "Keith treated me the same as the other pilots," she recalled. "If I was scheduled to fly when it was twenty or thirty below, I went. I had my fill of navigating in ice haze and forced landings and overnights in the bush." Ruth worked two summers for Parsons Airways, flying charters. She also flew for "Porky" Wieben who started her off flying a Fairchild 24, CF-FZQ, on sightseeing trips and then offered her the job of base manager at his Armstrong site. Tempted as she was she turned it down to fly for Barb Machin of Kenora.

Machin owned fishing camps in the Kenora and Shoal Lake areas and had just bought a Super Cub on floats to move guests and supplies. "It was a real dog of a plane; it just hung in the air," recalled Ruth. "I persuaded her to sell it for something more powerful and she bought a Stinson 108." On one of her first flights the plane's battery, located under the pilot's seat, shorted out and started a fire. Ruth quickly landed, put out the fire, and then proceeded on her way. Another demonstration of Ruth's cool-headedness occurred while she was flying a powerline patrol one winter day when a seal in the prop failed and oil sprayed the windshield, completely obscuring her vision. She flew back to Kenora by looking out the side windows and landed safely. "I led a charmed life," Ruth recalled. "Things happened but always I was close to help or I was over a lake where I could land." Her reputation as a capable pilot grew and many customers asked for her. As she remembered, "Some thought it was great to be able to say they had flown with a woman pilot or to have their picture taken with one — along with the fish they had caught."

Because business was slow in the winter Barb Machin and Ruth decided to start a flying school. Ruth obtained an instructor's rating in 1958 but, as it turned out, their request for a flying school was not granted. Her training was not wasted, however, because she married soon after and instructed at Red Lake, Ontario where her husband, a pilot with the provincial police, was based. Ruth instructed for five years until the Department of Transport grounded her when she became pregnant. More transfers and children eventually brought an end to her professional flying although she maintains a licence and continues to fly the family plane. Ruth proved that women could handle the heavier bush aircraft. Very likely her flying career influenced Parsons Airways Northern, which hired a number of women pilots over the next twenty years.

DAWN DAWSON CONNELLY BARTSCH of Osoyoos, British Columbia straddled the world of instructor, bush pilot, and co-owner/manager of a sophisticated bush company and proved beyond a doubt that women had a place in the aviation industry. Refused admission to the faculty of engineering at McGill University because of her gender, Dawn chose flying instead. She moved to Vancouver, and found work as a live-in babysitter, cleaning lady, and cook. Around 1950, having saved enough money to begin training, she enrolled at Vancouver U-Fly for lessons. Spending every free minute at the airport, Dawn earned private, commercial, seaplane, instrument, and instructor licences within eighteen months.

Despite these qualifications — which would have guaranteed a very good position for a male pilot — Dawn had trouble finding permanent work. She instructed for a few months at the Prince Rupert Aero Club, then dispatched for Bob Gayer of Associated Air Taxi of Vancouver until 1951, when he sent her to instruct and dispatch at Port Alberni Airways, which Associated had just purchased. Then, when Associated dropped the training section, it dropped her too. She found temporary work at the Chilliwack Flying Club and, in 1952, was hired by the Calgary Flying Club. There she met pilot Ron Connelly, the first of two men who would change the course of her life. They married in 1954 and moved to Whitehorse to new challenges.

"We had been hired by Pacific Western Airlines: Ron on the airline side and I to run PWA's flying school at Whitehorse and fly 'small' charters. I was given a seniority number and I wore their bush issue: leather jacket, tan shirt, and green slacks. PWA had inherited a flying school when it bought Yukon Flying Service and they gave me full control of it. I managed it for the next four and a half years." Although hired as part of a package deal, Dawn was well qualified, having earned a Class 1 instructor's rating and a transport licence. She did some charter work, using the Beaver, and even managed to obtain time on a rare bird, a Junkers W-34, CF-ATF. Her years with PWA were good ones but they ended on a sour note because PWA arbitrarily withdrew her seniority number when it began its negotiations with the Canadian Air Line Pilots Association. "I had always thought of myself as a PWA pilot and I was upset, to put it mildly. If we had remained at PWA I would have tried to keep my seniority number." However, Dawn and her husband left in November 1959 to live in Dawson City, Yukon where they had purchased the local charter service.

Dawn and Ron called their company Connelly-Dawson Airways. It had two Beavers and two Cessna 180s and operated two sked runs for mail and freight, and charters for the oil and mining companies. Dawn handled the books and dispatching and flew as required, and Ron oversaw the operations and flew. In 1960 they added a DC-3. "We were the first company in western Canada to use a DC-3 as a bush aircraft. We landed on sandbars during the summer and frozen lakes and rivers during the winter. We flew the it like the Beaver. It would get in and out of most small strips. We used the DC-3 primarily for fuel caching during the winter, for the summer geological camps and their helicopters." recalled Dawn. "Flying the DC-3 in the north was one of my most rewarding experiences. We took the travelling public everywhere in the Arctic. We would fly a hockey team one day and the next day transport a complete aircraft." Their first DC-3 trip into the north almost ended tragically. "People were not accustomed to seeing such a large aircraft," explained Dawn. "We landed on a very short sandbar and the Indians from the settlement came rushing out right into our path. They didn't realize that we needed more space to slow down. I wondered if we would be able to stop in time. We rolled to a stop,within inches of them."

DAWN DAWSON . . . at the controls

At the Airport

20-Year-Old Girl Has Job Of Training Pilots

By BILL DREVER

Calgary's airport isn't the best located in the Dominion and it certainly doesn't get the same publicity as many others—but don't sell it short. The traffic through

GIRL PILOT, Dawn Dawson, 19, faced winter storms and snowed-in landing fields to ferry new Piper Pacer plane 3000 miles from Ann Arbor, Michigan, to Vancouver for her company, Associated Air Taxi Limited. She is first girl to get her instrument rating in Canada, one of youngest female pilots on continent.

Dawn Dawson featured in various newspapers.

Dawn flew in the Yukon, the Northwest Territories, and Canada's last frontier, the Arctic islands. She hauled everything from fish to oil rig equipment, in Beavers, Otters, and DC-3s, and more than once spent an unplanned night in the bush because of weather or engine problems. "I rarely had any trouble. If I had to overnight in a camp of men I slept in the plane. I always flew with a rifle," she added, "in case of wild animals."

Despite technical advancements, flying in the bush was hard work. "On some of the aircraft we had to drain the oil every night and heat it again before we flew. If you were stuck out overnight it was the old blow pot, engine-tent routine for two or three hours to heat the engine. There was no up-to-date,

Typical load in a DC-3.

accurate weather so we learned to read the weather ourselves." There was also the problem of skis sticking to the snow or manoeuvring in tight spots. "You had to jump out, throw the rope over the ski, lock one ski to swing around, climb back, turn the aircraft, then jump out again and get the rope before you took off. Other times I landed only to be caught in a snowstorm. Then I had to tramp a runway with my snowshoes which took many exhausting hours." There were also gruelling hours spent loading and unloading. "It seemed that there was more of that than flying. If I were doing a fuel haul, especially up at a lake, there was usually no one there. I had to learn how to use my knees, not my back. Being female, you didn't complain. It kept me in pretty good shape."

Their flying was VFR. "There were no navaids and the maps weren't the greatest — the word 'unmapped' appeared more than once. We drew in lakes and rivers. I knew the country and I would always fly with our new pilots to show them the landmarks. They were used to flying on instruments and found it hard to navigate visually." In spite of the hard work Dawn said it was a great time to be flying up north. "There was still a kind of pioneering spirit and we felt like we were a part of the north's development." However, this segment of her life was drawing to a close.

In 1962 Dawn left Whitehorse and her husband. As a friend explained, "There had been a little chemistry happening between Dawn and one of the other pilots, Gordon Bartsch." Until Dawn was free to remarry, she worked for Cassidair, flying charters and running its flying school at Watson Lake in the Yukon. "I put hundreds of hours on the 180, Beaver, and DC-3 that year." A year later she married Gordon Bartsch. "We started our married life by flying fish hauls in a DC-3 in the Territories that winter." More than once they were weathered in. "One time there was Gordon and I and nine fishermen in a one room cabin with a dirt floor and one pot bellied stove. It took us six days to dig a 1500 foot runway."

Dawn Connelly in winter flying gear — Eagle Plains, Yukon, 1959.

Later the Bartschs moved to Calgary and formed Range Airways. They started with one Piper Apache and added another Apache and a Comanche within the year. Most of their work was charter flying and photographic work. "One of the most important contracts was an aerial survey between Churchill, Manitoba and Fort Nelson, British Columbia. I would be away weeks at a time. I spent two summers flying a Turbo Apache at high altitude (19,000 to 25,000 feet) on that job. Molly Reilly flew as my navigator on the northern Alberta section. It was really interesting flying. Precision and exactness were required. At the time most of the aerial photography was done by Kenting or Spartan, using World War II aircraft. An Apache had never been fixed up to do that type of work before. I remember an Air Canada DC-8 captain being very surprised to hear a female voice at that altitude, 'What are you doing up here?' he asked."

In 1965 they joined forces with John McMurchy, a photogrammetrist, to form Range Aerial Surveys and a year later they hooked up with Connelly-Dawson and Yukon Flying Services to form Great Northern Airways (GNA). The new company soon spread across the north connecting Dawson, Old Crow, Inuvik, Sachs Harbour, and points in the Arctic islands. It also took over CPA's Yukon schedules, flying the DC-3 between Whitehorse, Mayo, and Dawson City. GNA now had three main bases: Whitehorse, Inuvik, and their head office, Calgary, which was also home to most of the oil companies. The Prudhoe Bay oil discovery on the North Slope of Alaska doubled their business and, when GNA introduced oil tour flights for executives (the first airline to do so), sales increased again. The aggressive company adopted the slogan, "Nose around the North with GNA" and other catchy phrases as it continued to expand — "Go GNA The Big Dipper Way"

Liz Frost and a Cessna 206 at Tall Timber Lodge.

LIZ FROST SMITH

Liz Frost was a 1971 science graduate from McGill University who discovered flying in 1973 through her job at the Freshwater Institute in Winnipeg. She left a career as a scientist for one as a pilot and ultimately became one of the few women who owned and operated a bush company.

With the Freshwater Institute, Liz reported, "I spent summers in the field and transportation to the work sites in northern Manitoba was by helicopter. I enjoyed flying so much that I decided to take lessons. The closest school was the Winnipeg Flying Club and I spent the rest of the summer travelling 400 miles, 140 of them on gravel roads, in my Beetle every weekend." That summer she acquired her private, commercial, and float ratings. "Just for the heck of

or "The North is Now Country . . . GNA is its Action Airline!"

In 1966 when Air Canada's machinists went on strike the Air Transport Board granted permission to GNA to operate the DC-3 twice a day between Calgary and Vancouver. Two years later the Transport Board allowed GNA to enlarge its role to become a continent-wide aircraft charter organization. In 1969 GNA started a Whitehorse-Inuvik scheduled service, called the Arctic Trader Service, which linked by air two of the north's most active communities. At its peak GNA consisted of one hundred employees and twenty-four aircraft including Beavers, Otters, Twin Otters, DC-3s, F-27s and a DC-4. "GNA provided scheduled and charter services throughout the north; did contract hauling, aerial photography, and pipeline patrol throughout western Canada, and offered continent-wide charters. It was in direct competition with Pacific Western Airlines," said Gordon.

Dawn filled many positions: operations manager, traffic manager, executive assistant to the president and, at one time or other, she covered almost every aspect of operating an airline. She spent about half of her time in the north and the remainder at the head office in

it I thought I would see if I could find a job flying. I made the rounds of every company in Manitoba and northwestern Ontario. But no one wanted me. Finally I got a job for the summer with Tall Timber Lodge at Lac du Bonnet, Manitoba flying a Cessna 206 on floats."

Her first trip remains vividly etched in her memory. "I had been warned to hold the aircraft rope tightly when I docked. But the plane had so much momentum that it went gliding right by the dock, taking me with it and I landed in the water. I don't think my passengers were impressed." After the summer she obtained a multi-IFR and literally walked into a job with Aero Trades of Winnipeg flying an Apache to Jenpeg, a hydro project in central Manitoba. "I found the off-airport landings challenging. The strip at 8-Mile Channel, for instance, was only 1800 feet and had a

Fairchild F-27 turboprop of the newly formed Great Northern Airways, 1970.

Dawn Bartsch, 1986, with a Cessna 320.

power line at one end and another across the middle and it dropped off abruptly at the other end. You landed right the first time." As Aero Trades' first woman pilot, Liz caused a stir. "Most of the negative reactions disappeared when people realized I could do the job and was prepared to do my share of the work," said Liz. Unfortunately the job did not last. Laid off, she moved to Victoria, British Columbia and found work with Victoria Flying Services.

"I flew a beat-up Beaver and Aztec on floats. I'd go out every morning and shake the tail on the Beaver to make sure it was still attached. I wasn't happy with the maintenance but I knew if I complained too much I would be fired." In 1977, when the company went bankrupt, Liz decided it was time to move into the management-ownership end and she and four others bought the company, renaming it Cougar Air Inc. They dropped the school and concentrated on building up the charter operation. Liz was pilot, operations manager, bookkeeper, and dispatcher and

Calgary. "Even when I worked at a desk I still flew. I had the best of two worlds."

In 1969 GNA was in mid-stride in its dash for the top rung of the northern Canadian airline business ladder and was emerging as one of Canada's stronger third-level carriers. Oil and gas exploration throughout the Canadian north was the main reason for its rapid expansion and success. In four short years it had experienced phenomenal growth, but it had expanded too quickly. It had a run of bad luck and heavy losses on its newly-opened run from Whitehorse to Inuvik — three accidents involving the F-27s. These proved fatal to the company's financial state, already strained by the general tight money situation. In 1970 GNA went into receivership when the bank called a demand debenture and in the fall of 1971 the Bartschs lost their company.

Dawn and Gordon went to Hawaii to lick their wounds. They ended up staying and starting afresh, this time in the restaurant and pottery business. Successful, they sold out in 1986. Flying remains a part of their life and in 1992 they intend to tour the world in their Cessna 421.

NO STORY OF BUSH FLYING would be complete without mentioning Joan and Berna Studer, two of eight children born to a family who farmed, prospected, trapped, and fished in the bush of northern Saskatchewan. They grew up in a log cabin at Contact Lake, where the only access was by dog sled in

when two partners wanted out and the fourth became inactive, she found herself on call twenty-four hours a day. "The hours were pretty outrageous. I had no time for myself. I had no friends; no one wanted me — as soon as we would get together my beeper would buzz and off I would have to go." Nevertheless, Cougar Air grew, but not Liz's bank account or free time. "I ploughed all the profits back into the business. My pilots ate well but I didn't." After five years of working a seven day week, she decided to look for something less demanding.

"I applied to the airlines but they weren't hiring. Then in 1981 a friend suggested that I apply at Transport Canada. My initial reaction was, 'Good grief, that's not flying! I don't want to work for them.' But I applied anyway and got a job as a civil aviation inspector for Airport Licencing." With a university degree, a good solid civil aviation background, and approximately 5000 hours, she was well qualified. Liz is based in Vancouver.

winter, canoe in summer, or by aircraft. They were educated by correspondence courses until they went "out" to Prince Albert for high school. "As children they were fascinated with the aircraft that flew over, and if a plane landed they would pester the pilot for a ride or to sit in it. They loved to make model planes and would talk of the day they too would fly," wrote their mother. After high school, they qualified for their private and commercial licences (about 1954) but initially were unable to find flying jobs. Both worked in a bank, flying whenever they could.

In 1954 Mr. Studer helped Berna buy a Taylorcraft, CF-ENA, and she, often accompanied by Joan, flew all over northern Saskatchewan and Manitoba. In this way both became well known to miners, fishermen, and trappers and they

Toni Ramsay.

TONI RAMSAY

Toni Ramsay of Montreal, Quebec was married with two young children when she decided to fly in 1964 as an antidote to boredom and an unhappy marriage. Three years later she had her private, commercial, and instructor's licences and a part-time job at Laurentide Aviation where she had taken her training. Soon disillusioned with instructing, and her marriage, she headed west with her children to look for a job — anything except instructing. Luck was with her; when she reached Manitoba she was hired by Lorne Andrews of Nipawin Air Service. "I had no problem getting on there. Everyone was very satisfied with Joan Studer and was prepared to take a chance on another woman." Life as a bush pilot was not easy for the city-born Toni. Based in Pelican Narrows in the summer, she packed in the hours flying a Cessna 185 on floats. "The flying was pretty routine," said Toni, but she recalled being amused when she flew a group of American fishermen out. "Joan had flown them in. I remember one guy saying, 'What am I going to say to my wife. She lets me go on these trips only because there are no women and this time both pilots have been women!'"

After five years — and a lot of muscle wrestling with 45 gallon drums of fuel — Toni decided it was time for the children to return to civilization. Although well qualified, she found it difficult to get a good job. "I tried to get on with the Manitoba Government Air Service but my application was lost, on purpose, because the chief pilot did not want another woman. June Montgomery was already there." To pay the rent and buy the groceries, she flew highway patrols for the RCMP and then was a co-pilot for Aero

saw firsthand the growth of many mining communities. In 1958, for instance, they flew to Moak Lake in northern Manitoba, where there had been a new nickel discovery by Inco. "We landed at the drill site," wrote Berna, "and had dinner with the crew who pointed out a small lake (Cook's Lake) with six tents; that grew into the town of Thompson."

In 1958 Berna sold the T-Craft and bought a Cessna 170 on floats and that summer she made her first trip to the Northwest Territories. The next year Joan and Berna both flew to the Territories to look for gold, and the following year they flew down the Mackenzie River as far as Inuvik, near the Arctic Ocean. "Wherever they flew in the north they sought work," said their mother. "Always they were turned down with flimsy excuses." In 1964 Hank Parsons of Parsons Airways Northern

Trades, but the hours were unbelievably long. "Flying was consuming all my waking hours and energy and I was getting tired of waiting to get out of the right seat. When they told me I'd be flying six days a week, I quit. For awhile I free lanced. That was not profitable. My problem was that with two kids I couldn't just pick up and go."

She decided to return to the bush but to one of the larger bush companies. However, like Molly Beall Reilly earlier, Toni only got the job and slid into the co-pilot's seat with the recommendation of a male pilot. In 1980 Lambair of Manitoba hired Toni and her boyfriend, Norm McCrea. "I wouldn't have got the job on my own. Norm vouched for me and we were hired as a crew." To obtain the job, Toni also had to qualifiy for DC-3 and C-46 endorsements. "We were based at Thompson, Manitoba. The flying was okay but there was a lot of heavy loading, often 12,000 to 15,000 pounds. We quit after eight months because of poor maintenance; Lambair was already on the decline." They next worked for Barney Lamm of Ontario Central Airlines-Nunasi-Ilford Riverton and again, it was because of Norm that Toni was hired. "We were hired as a team to fly a DC-3 and C-46. We lived in Winnipeg but flew out of Thompson and Churchill." Retired from flying in 1985, she returned to it in 1988 and currently flies charter trips for Campbell Air, a Manitoba company.

Toni Ramsay is one of Canada's most experienced women bush pilots. Her flying spans two periods: the "holding pattern" era of the fifties and sixties and the progress of women pilots in the seventies and eighties. She has logged over 9000 hours, most of it on DC-3s and C-46s. She is likely one of the few women in the world to hold both C-46 (Curtiss Commando) and DC-3 endorsements.

in Flin Flon hired Berna, who by then had over 1000 hours of bush time. "Pilots with mechanical aptitude and ability to handle heavy freight were the usual rule with the company," Hank said. "Overnighting in the bush or stays in mining or drill camps was a common occurrence. I had some knowledge of Berna Studer before she was taken on the payroll. Her ability to live in the bush and look after any passengers in the event of a forced landing was one of the advantages we considered. Our male pilots had to accept Berna but I do not think they agreed with my decision 100 percent. Once Berna became known our customers seemed to accept her for what she was, a fully qualified bush pilot. She had an independent streak and when

SHE FLIES THE FRIGID BARRENS

Berna Studer is the only girl bush pilot north of the 55th parallel. She's so short she has to be propped up just to see out the cockpit, but don't let that fool you. She'll fly you into places the Indians can't reach Photography: Jorgen Halling

The day's flying in Northern Saskatchewan gets off to
start for pilot Berna Studer (top). A catalytic heater
photo) and a tarpaulin (above) have kept the plane's
from freezing during the 17-hour night, but it's 40
zero in the cabin and she has to wait there for 30
until the engine warms up and she can turn on the

she was laid off due to a reduction in staff she ended up with her own plane and some of our fish customers!" In his book, *Trail of the Wild Goose,* Parsons wrote that Berna "held her own under the handicap of all the male chauvinism around our base. It took real fortitude on her part to compete in what was looked on as a man's game . . . and we could all learn a lot about living in the bush from her."

Berna logged over 700 hours on a Cessna 180 in her first year. "I really learned to fly," she wrote, "I had to fly every day no matter what the weather was." Most of it was to service tourist and drill camps in the north, hauling groceries, supplies, and personnel. It was a hard way to make a living. She worked fourteen to eighteen hours a day, seven days a week. "A person

L *Berna Studer, c. 1965, publication source unknown.*

R *Joan Studer, flying a Beaver in the north, c. 1970.*

gets run-down from lack of food and sleep," she said. "You get hungry in the late afternoon, and realize that you have missed the noon meal. Sleep catches up to you and you catch yourself nodding off on the longer flights, especially when you see all three of your passengers dozing away . . . I ran into all kinds of weather conditions that even had the Arctic beat. As one old timer said, 'You bend down to pick up a stone and when you straighten up, the weather has changed.'" One such day was June 7, 1967, a fine 70°F when Berna arrived in Flin Flon with her passengers. But by the end of the day, when she was ready to take her people back, the temperature had already begun to drop and a strong northwest wind had come up. "It was a terribly bumpy ride back to Sandy Bay and really bad back to Pelican Narrows. About half way there I ran into a raging snowstorm and by the next morning there were six inches of snow."

She left Parsons Airways in 1968 and flew two seasons for Garry Thompson of Thompson's Camp at Otter Lake, about fifty miles north of La Ronge, Saskatchewan. It was while flying for him that she latched onto the idea of starting her own tourist camp. She settled upon McLennan Lake as the site and began building in 1970. Initially business was slow and Berna eked out a livelihood by helping Joan, who by then was flying for Nipawin Air Service. Eventually Tamarack Lodge became profitable and she and her husband, Gordon McCann, whom she married in 1973, now operate a thriving venture.

JOAN STUDER received her start in 1967 with Lorne Andrews of Nipawin Air Service. Based at Pelican Narrows, a native settlement of about 700 persons in northeastern Saskatchewan, she flew Cessna 180s and 185s, a Beaver, and an Otter. Passengers were mainly trappers and fishermen and the freight was mostly fish. Like Hank Parsons, Andrews knew that Joan was at home in the bush. She was also a proven commercial fisherman. "The previous summer she had taken her 180 and a canoe and had lived for weeks in the bush, coming in only to drop off fish at the plant at Pelican Narrows," described Toni Ramsay, another Nipawin Air Service pilot, who obtained her job because of Joan's track record. Lorne Andrews had high praise for Joan, "We always hired pilots by their capabilities and Joan Studer was one of the most capable, winter and summer. If the trip could be made she would do it. The whole North

Heather MacMillan.

HEATHER MacMILLAN

Heather MacMillan, a 1974 Fine Arts graduate from Dalhousie University in Halifax, Nova Scotia, turned a hobby into a career and became Labrador's first woman pilot. She earned her spurs in the bush with Labrador Airways. "It was no mickey mouse operation," described Heather. "It had two Twin Otters, two Queen Airs, a Beaver, a Turbo Beaver, and five single engine Otters and we provided passenger and mail service to the coastal communities of Labrador." Based in Goose Bay, she flew a scheduled run up and down the coast. "I found landing on the ocean exciting and challenging and loved every minute of the eight weeks that I was there."

Labrador Airways offered Heather a position for the next summer season. She looked for another job to carry her through the winter but found the excuses against hiring a woman endless. "Chief among them was what to do with me on overnights. They didn't want me sharing a room with the co-pilot, neither did they want the expense of another room. It was sort of silly. When I was finally hired I was on a courier run which meant that we left first thing in the morning and then spent a good four or five hours in a hotel room waiting for the return flight. If by chance we were weathered in then management insisted that we get two

knew her and respected her for her abilities. When flying the Otter she many times took loads of fuel drums to remote camps and offloaded them by herself. She knew the North like the back of her hand. Prospectors and Indians requested that she fly them; they all respected her. She would do contract flying and stay in the camps for months at a time. She knew the prospecting and trapline business and the customers respected her for it. If she had a problem she would make repairs and come to base for further repairs if necessary."

Joan Studer's career ended tragically in the early eighties when she was killed as she attempted to land her 185, knowing that one ski was disconnected and hanging perpendicular. The subsequent investigation absolved her of any pilot error.

BY THE SEVENTIES, the life of a bush pilot had changed considerably from the thirties — or even the sixties. There were more modern aircraft, improved radio communication, up-to-date weather reports, and more sophisticated navaids. Major northern urban areas used medium-range jet equipment and in the smaller communities, turbo-props were in service. Pilots

rooms. What they thought we might do at night that we couldn't do during the day, I don't know!"

She returned to Labrador Airways in the spring of 1980 with a senior commercial licence and a couple of thousand hours of multi-IFR time. The chief pilot made her captain on the Queen Air, over some of the older pilots who had less multi-IFR experience. "That caused some friction but the chief pilot backed me the whole way." She also found she was treated differently the second time around. "Many of the pilots now made a point of talking with me. Apparently 'mainlanders' had a reputation of not lasting and of coming in with a 'holier than thou' attitude. When I flew into the communities people called me by name, 'Hi Heather, glad you're back,' they'd say. It was then that I realized that while everyone had been polite they had never called me by my name. On one of my trips I had to overnight in one of the villages and when I mentioned to one of the old-time pilots that I had slept in the front room of Mrs. X's house he said, 'My dear, you're in like Flynn. If they didn't like you they would have told you there was no spare room in the community and you would have slept in the plane. You got the best room.'"

Flying in Labrador meant landing on a variety of runways. "I became good at doing all kinds of approaches. One airport was a 5000 foot gravel strip with no approach

usually flew into strips with support staff and returned to base each night. All of this meant that the old excuses — women's lack of strength and mechanical aptitude and the need to overnight away from base — were no longer valid and several companies inched their doors open to a few more persistent women.

Even in the smaller bush companies, where support staff was seldom available, the women were on a more or less equal footing with the men. As Bob Cameron of Trans North Turbo Air admitted, there were many men whose mechanical knowledge stopped at knowing that "there was a funny sound in the engine and who did not have the brawn to handle a 45 gallon fuel drum." In 1986 Bob Ferguson, new owner of Parsons Airways Northern, went so far as to say that if he could hire all women he would. "They listen better, they try harder, they're gentler with the aircraft and better with the customers. My only concern is that they can't always handle the cargo or paddle an Otter in a stiff wind; they're just not strong enough. But they make good pilots."

However, although bush flying no longer meant being out of touch with civilization and flying over unmapped territory,

lights, just runway lights. On a dark and stormy night it's hard to get a feel for depth and that strip was something else. At another community there was a 3000 foot asphalt strip with a VOR, but there was always a crosswind there to make things a little tricky. I also landed on the frozen ocean. That sounds easy but often we were landing in whiteout conditions." She found weather to be the biggest problem. "At times it seemed as if you were living in fog and if it was not fog, it was ice. My biggest fear was ice because it was a constant one. More than once I can remember sitting in the plane watching ice form and feeling the airspeed drop off. I would put the de-ice boots on and nothing would happen; I'd wait and sweat and eventually the boots would inflate and the ice would crack off. But it's a helpless feeling especially when you know that it's a no man's land below."

Bush flying could be lonely too, as Heather recalled. "I had to pick up a body from Churchill Falls . . . it had a sweet smell to it. I remember thinking, 'If only my mother could see me now.' There I was on a beautiful Sunday morning with only a corpse for company."

Heather eventually left the bush for a position with Transport Canada and became Canada's first woman accident investigator. She is now a civil aviation inspector for the Atlantic Region.

it was not an easy life. Bush pilots still flew fishermen and fish, loading and unloading cargo. While flying in the bush before joining Canadian Airlines International, pilot Paula Strilesky found out that the northern expression for co-pilot was a "grunt!" "On one of my first trips for Harbour Air I docked the aircraft and this guy comes out — he's real bush — and asks, 'Can she pack moose?'"

The flying was still tough — and it was certainly not glamorous. But Donna Hohle preferred the bush to the ease of airport-to-airport flying. "My husband talked me into flying and I liked it so much I just carried on. I instructed hard-rock miners in Thompson, Manitoba before I separated from my husband and moved with my three children to Leaf Rapids, Manitoba. There I formed RND Aviation with René le Brasseur. I mostly fly the Beaver, the Found, the Otter, or 185 on fish hauls, charters, or fire patrols," she said and continued, "You have to have muscles when you fly in the bush. It's no easy matter loading tubs of fish which can weigh up to eighty pounds each. You soon learn how to place them so you don't kill yourself." And, she added, "Bush flying is not like airline flying. You have to know how to handle people. If you have drunks or those who have not paid for their last trip, you have to be assertive. I have literally thrown people out of the airplane."

Donna is currently president and chief pilot of RND, with about 8000 hours of flying. Since 1985 she has also been involved with the Central Air Carrier Association; an organization of small carriers in Manitoba and Saskatchewan.

LEONA DUPONT also chose bush flying. Born, educated (science degree), and married in France, she and her husband moved to Edmonton in the mid-fifties. In 1971 her husband, who was taking flying lessons, asked her for help with ground school because of his poor English. Leona then completed the training herself and went on for the advanced ratings, eventually becoming a pilot for her husband's construction business.

Using a Cessna 206, Leona flew men and equipment all over northern Alberta. She also instructed, ferried airplanes, and was on contract with Pacific Western Airlines. She flew 120 to 140 hours a month, which, as she reported, caused her children to give her "the treatment: 'we never see you anymore.'" In 1978 Leona changed jobs. "From 1978 to 1983

I flew a Cessna 185 for an Edmonton construction company. It was the roughest and toughest kind of flying I had ever experienced. I got very good at landing on bush strips with trees in the middle or machinery scattered up and down. I often returned to Edmonton covered with mud and looking like I'd slept in the bush. But I love flying and I like being my own boss."

MARLENE CAMERON of Brooker Wheaton, Edmonton flew a Lear Jet and King Air 100, two sophisticated aircraft not normally associated with the bush, but her job was much the same. "I flew personnel, parts, and equipment all over the North. Often I'd be away a week at a time. I'd share a room with the others — one room with bunks. If it was winter I'd

ROBIN REID MacKINNON

Robin Reid was one woman who did not look upon bush flying simply as a means to build time but as a way of life. "I grew up in the wilds of Canada, about forty air miles southwest of Sudbury, Ontario. My father was a pilot and a trapper," recalled Robin. "We moved to Guelph in 1973 and lived right on the airport. Even though I had grown up around airplanes I had never thought of flying as a career until I saw a girl doing a walk-around check. I thought, 'Why not me?'" Within the year Robin acquired her private and commercial licences and she and her pilot husband, Al MacKinnon, began looking for a company that would hire them both. They were in luck. Bob Ferguson of Parsons Airways Northern hired them in 1976 to fly a 185 out of "Puk," (Pukatawagan), a native community in northern Manitoba.

"I started off by dispatching and doing the books and filling in for Al on the 185," Robin said. "The flying was no problem. I was used to the bush and found navigating easy. What I had to get used to was being the only white woman in the community. At first, there was a lot of door knocking late at night, especially if Al were away." Not all problems were related to flying or being female. "Puk was a dry community and the big thing was to haul in booze. It's tough to know what to do. If you suspect they're hauling liquor you're supposed to discourage it, yet it's really none of your business. You try and keep a low profile because if you make an issue they could make it difficult for you," explained Robin. "I always tried to make sure I didn't carry anyone who could cause trouble." Robin recalled one memorable passenger however, a drunk who fell asleep as

have to go out every few hours and start up the engines. It was considered a man's job; rough, tough, and dirty. At first, there were a lot of skeptical people. 'Well, where's the pilot?' they'd ask. A lot of men just came out and said I should be at home making babies. Some said, 'Give her a week and she won't come back' or 'she'll crumple the airplane.' Other men were good. Sometimes it was the wives who made my life miserable. I had to learn to ignore all of this, to be professional, develop a thick skin, and try not to let it bother me."

Marlene also came up against the pregnant pilot syndrome. "I found myself in that 'what do we do with her now' category." Brooker Wheaton solved the problem by taking her out of the left seat and plunking her in the right. "I tried to fight it but the company wouldn't let me fly as captain. I flew until

soon as they were airborne, then on the way, woke up and started hitting her on the shoulder with a paddle!

In 1977 Robin and Al were transferred to Pelican Narrows in Saskatchewan. "The living quarters were pretty primitive. There was no running water so we cut a hole in the ice. The flying was the same: hauling fish, mail, and Indians in a 185. You get strong flying in the bush. I've lifted and packed fifty to seventy-five pound tubs of fish myself. The 185 can carry nine tubs and it was the last tub that was hard to lift into place. You learn how to load a plane."

Generally Robin had no problems when she overnighted away from the base. "I'd usually stay with the cook in the kitchen; he was usually an okay guy. My tactic was to keep a low profile. If it was a matter of dropping off supplies and picking up freight and people and I had to wait, then I would usually stay with the plane. Sometimes I'd fish off the float rather than go up to where the men were — you could feel their eyes on you. I wore a big parka in the winter, it camouflaged the fact that I was female. I avoided trouble."

The next spring Robin and Al were transferred to the main base at Flin Flon and Robin began flying the Otter and Beaver and doing the occasional trip to Edmonton and Calgary on the Aero Commander. "I enjoyed the Beaver the best. It could haul anything and everything. I also did some fire fighting with it, dropping men and supplies. Fire fighting was high excitement: lots of pressure, it was go, go, go. When the wind switched we had to get the men out of the camp 'right now.' I remember calling in a helicopter for help and the fire had reached the dock just as I was pulling away with the last group of men."

Runway conditions in the north were always tricky. "Some were sand and clay and they could get very mucky if

I was six months pregnant. Considering the times, they were fair." Marlene, who in 1986 had about 6000 hours, now flies part-time.

LIZ AND ROBBIE WIEBEN, daughters of the late well-known bush pilot, Orville "Porky" Wieben of Fort William [now Thunder Bay] loved the bush. Their father had taught all five of his children to fly. According to Robbie, "He instilled a lot of independence in his children and he did not differentiate between his sons and daughters. As children we all sat on his lap and handled the controls of the plane. When we were teenagers we were taught to fly. We girls were expected to do the same hard physical work as the boys and face up to the bitter cold when on bush trips. We loved the outdoors and it never

Elizabeth Wieben.

wet. You had to be constantly asking yourself, 'Will I get off with this load?' You had to know where the potholes were and just where to land. On many you had to land on the last half of the runway. You learned to be very precise. When you're flying in the bush you have to do a lot of thinking yourself, no one is there to tell you what the wind is or where to land. However, navigation was a piece of cake if you knew what to look for."

Robin quickly learned to make things easier for herself when flying floats. "Currents, wind, and docking can be a challenge, especially in the 206 because the pilot's door is on the left and the cargo door is on the right. If the plane is loaded then you have to crawl up and go over the top." Once, she was trying to turn the airplane around and almost lost it. "There was no rope to hang onto and I had a passenger inside. I just managed to jump onto the stabilizer on the back before it floated away. Then it was a real challenge to jump from there to the float and go up and over and climb back in to restart. My passenger was a slight man from the Social Services and very gallant. He said, 'Jump, I'll catch you.' The problem was, I was bigger than he was."

In 1979, Robin and her pilot husband moved to Montreal. Loathe to give up bush flying, she returned to Parsons Airways for the summer season, a routine she continued even after the birth of her first child in 1981. Transferred to Winnipeg, Robin, then the mother of two, worked a season for Northway Aviation of Winnipeg. A third baby in 1986 cancelled her plans to fly that year but Robin soon returned to flying, first for Perimeter Airlines and recently for Ministic Air, both of Winnipeg.

occurred to either Liz or me to be anything else but bush pilots."

Liz, the oldest, learned to fly when she was sixteen. "Most of my hours are in the bush hauling construction materials, heating supplies, and so on to native settlements and flying prospectors, geologists, hunters, fishermen, and lumbermen into remote locations." Married twenty-six years and with four grown children, Liz has taught bush flying as a professor in the Aviation and Engineering Division of Confederation College in Thunder Bay, Ontario for the last five years. The intensive commercial training is primarily for civilian pilots, although some military officer-cadets also attend. Each student receives

twenty-five hours of concentrated float flying (all conditions) and much more "hands-on" instruction, as well as meteorology, navigation, and so on, which Liz also teaches.

Liz has taken survival courses, participated in searches and has herself been rescued by the Canadian Coast Guard. "I had lost an engine, so I landed but the water was very rough. I managed to sail my plane in close to one of the coves and then I took off my clothes, jumped into the water and pulled the plane into shore. I had used my CB to say I was down and the Coast Guard heard me, for they came around the corner and caught me just as I was climbing back onto the float, still naked. Now when people ask me how to get rescued, I say, 'Take off your clothes.'"

L *Elizabeth Wieben, 1990, on a fishing trip in her Citabria.*

R *Elizabeth Wieben and her sons, Colin Webster and Kenneth Webster, 1974.*

"I also fly the north shore of Lake Superior, both the islands and mainland, doing seaplane charter work. It's very demanding physically. I pump floats every morning and weigh every load. There is a lot of lifting and it's vital that you pack and store things in the aircraft properly. One time when I was hauling fish I allowed someone else to pack and didn't watch. I stopped fast and a load of fish landed down my neck and in my lap."

Liz, who also has degrees in business and economics, qualified for commercial licences in Canada, Australia, and the United States, and was the recipient of an Amelia Earhart Award for advanced flight training. She and her husband own a Citabria, which they keep on floats in summer and wheel/skis

MARIE MAZUR DANIELS

Marie Mazur began flying as a hobby in 1974 while taking geology at university but as time went on she began spending more time flying than studying and geology eventually lost the battle. A year later, qualified for her private, commercial, and multi-IFR she began work at Wondel Aviation at St. Hubert Airport, Montreal as a "line boy," fueling and washing airplanes. She next taught air cadets until Wondel hired her full-time in the fall of 1976. She instructed at Sept Îles, then became the chief flying instructor as well as flying charters on their Aztecs. Marie flew the upper north shore of the St. Lawrence River and north-eastern Quebec and became good friends with France Gravel who was with the same company.

After a year, Marie decided it was time to move on. "I really wanted to see the Arctic so I applied to most companies operating dewline equipment north of the sixtieth parallel. Northward Airlines hired me and in 1978 John Peacock, chief pilot, and I flew a Saunders aircraft from Peterborough, Ontario to Whitehorse."

From Whitehorse, Marie was transferred to Inuvik where she flew an Islander and then a Saunders and soon qualified as captain. Unfortunately Northward went into bankruptcy in 1979. Trans North Air took over most of the operation and Marie worked with them flying Cessna 310s, 404s, and Twin Otters until 1986 when Trans North Air shut down the fixed wing division. Shortly after, she returned to university and also to instructing and flying charters on a part-time basis for a small company in Whitehorse.

Marie, now a mother of two, continues to fly on a part-time basis. She is a designated flight test examiner for the Yukon region and does all the commercial and private pilot flight tests. With over 9000 hours she is one of Canada's most experienced women pilots.

in winter. "We are fortunate," wrote Liz, "to be able to land right at our house." She has flown some 6000 hours and continues to fly and to teach.

ROBBIE WIEBEN began flying when she was sixteen. "I worked for my father from 1965 to 1975 as pilot, operations manager, and chief flying instructor of Superior Airways. I flew charters for mining companies, government agencies, hunters, fishermen and hauled every kind of freight imaginable." After her marriage she continued to fly until she had three children, when she decided to stay at home. "I hated it and longed for the mental and physical stimulation that flying gave me. Encour-

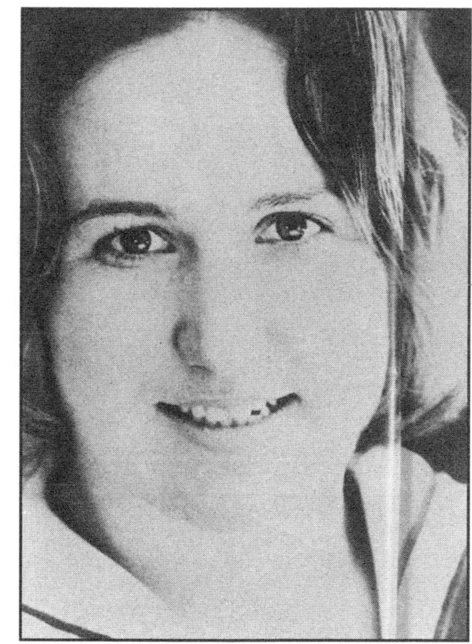

aged and supported by my husband Peter [Taylor] I returned to flying." In addition Robbie was a free-lance writer and active in civic affairs, serving on the Thunder Bay city council from 1972 to 1975. Her involvement in all these areas earned her the title of "Mrs. Chatelaine of Canada" in 1972 and an Amelia Earhart flying scholarship to upgrade her flying qualifications in 1977.

In 1978, after the death of her father, she and her husband, a pilot turned licenced aircraft mechanic, moved to Cranbrook, British Columbia, where they formed Taylor Aviation Ltd., a fuel sales and aircraft maintenance operation. There Robbie helped form the Canadian Rockies chapter of the 99s, became the area air chief for the BC Provincial Emergency Program,

L *Robbie Wieben Taylor in 1980, with the Beech Baron on which she completed her multi-engine rating.*

R *Robbie, 1972. This photo was used full page in* Chatelaine *magazine.*

Civilian Air Search and Rescue Program (1980-85), and between 1982-86 was under contract to the BC Forest Service for fire patrol. She was the first civilian woman pilot to take the Searchmaster's Course at CFB Comox. In 1986 Robbie began teaching at East Kootenay College, British Columbia. "I used my aviation background to teach pre-trade skills and career planning and life skills to women entering non-traditional occupations."

After 2000 hours of accident-free flying in about twenty types of aircraft, Robbie was injured as a passenger in a car and has not flown for two years. "Instead, I have been back at university completing my Bachelor of Social Work degree," she explained. She has been active with the Western Canada 99s — liaison to the Minister of Transport's Study on Substance Abuse in Transportation. Hardly "sitting still," Robbie hopes "to do industrial social work in the aviation sector" and plans on completing her Master's degree next year.

CHAPTER EIGHT

The winds of change

In 1928 Amelia Earhart said, "If enough of us keep flying we'll get someplace." Sixty years later her wish was beginning to come true. The once all-male front-end crews of the airlines and the military had a sprinkling of women pilots and more men than not said, "If she can do her job that's all that counts."

BY THE MID-SEVENTIES, the isolated efforts of the earlier women aviators began to produce results. Aided by the women's movement and technological advances in the aviation industry, women broke into areas previously closed to them. For the first time in Canadian history, women were flying with the major airlines, the military, and the government. More women were also being hired by the smaller companies, both fixed wing and helicopters.

The reasons for this ripple of change were diverse. For one thing, the number of women pilots had increased. For another, they were better qualified and not content to make instructing their ultimate goal. Most importantly, the women of the seventies and eighties came of age at the height of the women's movement, which promoted the belief that a woman's place was where she *chose* it to be and which helped to implement legislation forbidding discriminatory hiring policies. Thus armed, the women sought the heretofore forbidden flight decks. The recommendations of the Royal Commission on the Status of Women in 1971 and the promulgation of the Canadian Human Rights Act in 1978 forced the government, the military, and the airlines up against the wall. They *had* to reassess their hiring practices and the result was that Air Canada hired its first women pilots in 1978, the Canadian Forces admitted women for pilot training on a trial basis in 1979, and Transport Canada introduced the Equal Opportunity for Women program [EOW] in 1981.

Another happening of the seventies was the emergence of a small core of French-speaking women pilots in Quebec. For years, legislation and the Roman Catholic church had reinforced a woman's ties to the home and childbearing. However, as Quebec's "Quiet Revolution" took hold, social change began to evolve. "We started thinking about careers for ourselves, instead of early marriages and a baby every year," explained Rita Blanchet of Transport Canada. It was especially difficult for French-speaking Canadian women to break into

DEBBI ELDER WHITE

"Even as a little girl I was always more interested in fixing my doll carriage than in pushing it," Debbi explained. Debbi first intended to be a commercial pilot and qualified in 1968. However, she soon realized that there was little scope for women pilots. Quite happily she opted for aircraft maintenance instead. She and her husband, an aircraft mechanic, purchased a rundown skydiving operation at St. Andre Avellin and together they turned it into a successful fixed base operation called White's Aircraft Service.

In 1977 Debbi qualified as a licenced aircraft maintenance engineer, the first woman in Quebec and the third woman in Canada to hold an A Licence. "I did my apprenticeship at St. Andre Avellin and it was three years of twenty hour days. I had intended to qualify for my B licence but became so involved in the company, which just would not stop growing, that I put my time into learning to be a manager, a psychologist, an accountant, a computer programmer, a lobbyist, a correspondent, and whatever else you care to name."

Debbi was elected to the Board of Directors of the Air Transport Association of Canada in 1984 and the Aircraft Maintenance Engineers Association of Quebec in 1985: the first woman director for either group.

flying because all instruction, examinations, and radio transmissions were in English. It was not until the late seventies that French could be legally used in air traffic control in Quebec. As Janine Leclerc Harding of Montreal explained, "When I began my lessons I knew only three sentences in English. To learn English, I moved to Regina and worked as a 'line boy' at the flying club." Her hard work ultimately paid off. By 1971 she had her commercial, instructor's, multi-IFR, and ATR and began instructing at Wondel Aviation, Montreal. She soon established a reputation as one of the best multi-IFR instructors in Quebec. Married about this time, she and her husband operated a couple of air services in Quebec. In 1981 they bought ATL Air Tuteur at St. Hubert and four years later added the Montreal Flying Club to their holdings. Their companies were particularly open to hiring women pilots and gave pilots like Diane Desmarais their start in aviation. Janine, who has successfully combined marriage and children with flying, is chief pilot and handles most of the advanced training. She has logged over 11,500 hours. Appointed Quebec's first designated flight test examiner by Transport Canada, she is one of the most respected instructors in the province.

PROFESSIONAL WOMEN PILOTS were all but missing from the Maritime provinces. "For women in the Maritimes, aviation was a closed shop," explained Don McClure, longtime manager of the Moncton Flying Club. Comparatively little aviation activity meant limited career opportunities for anyone, male or female. Interestingly, of the first 100 women licensed in Canada, it appears there was no one from Nova Scotia. Long-standing conservative attitudes coupled with traditionally poor economic conditions were the main reasons why there was only one woman, Gina Jordan, who flew professionally until the seventies when Barbara Swyers and Heather MacMillan, both of Halifax, became the first two women pilots to secure positions other than instructing. Barbara went on to become one of the first five women pilots with Air Canada and Heather the first woman accident investigator with Transport Canada.

The situation in Newfoundland was even more dismal. While it was rich in aviation history — Phyllis Penney remembered the great excitement when planes were scheduled to stop; even school was dismissed so that the children could see history in the making — it seemed as if everyone landed there only to take off again and keep on going, explained Tom McGrath, longtime civil aviation official. Aviation — except for some bush flying and non-scheduled operations under primitive conditions — was hardly known before the mid-fifties when Eastern Provincial Airlines began a scheduled service in Newfoundland. Trans-Atlantic traffic had used Gander and Goose Bay airports as refueling stops as long as piston engine aircraft were operated. However, once the jets arrived, their high performance and longer range meant that Gander could be by-passed. Thus little aviation activity originated in or served the province itself and, with the exception of Eastern Provincial Airlines and TCA-Air Canada, no company lasted very long. While elsewhere in Canada women could usually gain a foothold with the flying clubs, this was not the case in Newfoundland. There, the small population, harsh terrain, scattered communities, and the poor economy hindered the development of the flying club movement as it had the aviation companies. The demand for instruction was limited and few clubs lasted more than a year or two. Longtime "Newfie" pilots cannot recall any women flying in the province prior to its joining Canada in 1949. That year Phyllis Penney became

Darlene Tripp-Simms, 1973.

PAULA BROOKS MATZ

Paula Brooks of Ottawa, Ontario, began flying in 1972 "just for fun" but soon abandoned her business studies for flying. "My goal was to fly for Air Canada even though no woman had ever been hired." She received her start at Bradley Air Services at Carp, Ontario where she had trained. "I didn't find out until later that there were some reservations about hiring a female instructor."

Paula began working for the government of Ontario's Nor'Ontair in 1976, eventually being promoted to captain on the Twin Otter, the first woman captain on a scheduled airline. By 1978 she had an ATR, 3000 hours, and was called by Air Canada for an interview — a welcome result of her years of applying. "The interview went well but I didn't pass the medical. I was devastated. It was hard to accept the fact that my goal had been snatched away for medical reasons, something over which I had no control."

In the meantime, her husband Roger had been hired by Nordair and was based in Montreal so Paula left Nor'Ontair. With her experience and the shortage of pilots at that time, she anticipated no problem finding work. "A friend from Innotech Aviation told me to apply there as I had all the

Newfoundland's first licenced woman pilot. However, thirty more years would pass before a commercial licence was granted to a woman from that province.

As it turned out, Ontario-born Darlene Tripp-Simms became Newfoundland's first professional woman pilot when the Gander Flying Club appointed her its chief flying instructor in 1979. "When I took over the club was in a slump," said Darlene. "The unpredictable weather, a poor economy, and the small population had taken its toll. The fast-changing weather in particular made hour-long lessons a dream. I had to get used to twenty minute flights between snow showers coming inland from the ocean. Between November and March I rarely saw the

Paula Brooks Matz, 1976, just prior to her promotion to captain, Nor'Ontair.

right qualifications: over 3000 hours, 2000 hours on turbines alone plus an ATR. However, Innotech turned me down flat and hired someone with a straight commercial and a bare instrument rating." She learned that the reason she was not hired was because some of the wives would not allow a woman in the cockpit with their husbands. "I was upset at that; I was married myself."

Paula then wrote her American transport licence exams and found work with Corporate Air of Hartford, Connecticut, flying a Beech Baron on a courier run from Dorval Airport to New York and Boston each night, Monday to Friday. "Going into those busy airports as a single IFR pilot was hard on the nerves. I'd be arriving at La Guardia at 11:30 PM and the controllers had to feed my little Baron into the flow of big jets. Often I would be number sixteen

sun. The terrain was also very inhospitable to pilots. Besides the trans-Canada highway there were very few places to land in an emergency. My students and I used to practise forced approaches over ice-covered lakes and bogs. Between Gander and Glenwood, the next little town, there was only one farmer's field and it had a hydro line right across the middle of it!" By 1989, Newfoundland had a grand total of four women who had flown professionally in the province.

In the seventies women also entered the world of helicopter flying, although they remained a rarity. In 1980, for example, there were 1429 men with a commercial helicopter licence and fifteen women. Six years later the situation was relatively

Captain Paula Brooks Matz, 1978.

with a 747 in front of me. They'd say, 'Keep your speed up' and I'd be going as fast as I could. I knew that others were missing their approaches because of me. I'd hear them roar over me."

After the quiet of northern Ontario and the mostly uncontrolled airspace, Paula found her new job very stressful. To make matters worse, the Baron did not have radar or an autopilot that worked; nor was it pressurized and she often ran into heavy thunderstorms which she could not get above. In addition the winds over the buildings in New York created a lot of turbulence. "I'd have full movement of controls, my speed would be going back and forth, and I could hardly take my hands off the wheel to handle the mike." If everything went well she would get back to Dorval at about 2:00 AM.

unchanged: 2297 men held commercial helicopter licences compared to twenty-four women.

Licence*	1982		1986		1990		1992	
	m	f	m	f	m	f	m	f
FIXED WING								
CPL	8032	267	7059	246	6570	279	7184	341
ATR	6134	57	6684	80	7407	113	8178	149
HELICOPTERS								
Private	135	6	160	4	205	5	215	8
Commercial	2058	18	2297	24	2379	38	2136	51

(*Licence: CPL=Commercial Pilot's Licence; ATR= Airline Transport Rating)
Statistics from Transport Canada

In the eighties women began to emerge as administrators and owner/operators of aviation companies although acceptance in these positions was by no means automatic. Elaine Parker, a 1976 graduate of the aviation program at Selkirk College in British Columbia, got her start with North Caribou Flying Service of Edmonton, Alberta. "I was only the third employee. I learned as the company grew. I was a dispatcher, training captain, safety officer, and so on. I was welcomed. I was someone to dump the dog of the fleet on. I started on the 206 and 337 and gradually moved into the rest of the fleet including captain on the DC-3." In 1982 she became base manager and in 1983, operations manager. Then, she related, "I bought shares in the company and became a junior partner. It was a tremendous difference to be an employee and an owner. Your perspective changes and your work seems endless."

First Officer Noreen Newton (left) and Captain Elaine Parker, first all-female DC-3 crew at Time Air, celebrating the 50th anniversary of the DC-3.

She remembered once cancelling the flight because everything on the coast was zero zero and there was no place to go for an alternate. "I phoned the guy at the courier place to tell him I was not going. He just tore me up and down, saying the former pilot, a man, never cancelled. I didn't sleep very well that night because I knew that he was implying that I was chicken because I was a woman."

The stress and the hours finally made her decide to resign and, as it turned out, she lost her Category 1 medical soon after. Unwilling to leave the aviation world, she became a flight services specialist and, from 1979 to 1986, worked in Timmins, Ontario where she and her husband lived. In the fall of 1986 they moved closer to Toronto where, for the first time in fourteen years, she was out of aviation and at home.

In the mid-eighties Time Air and North Caribou struck a deal and, in 1987, Elaine became manager of the Charter & Contract Operations for Time Air in Edmonton. Although she flew a desk more than a plane, she managed to log more than 7000 hours. "I guess you could say I broke new ground," said Elaine. "There are not very many women pilots around who were also into the administrative side of the airline business. Some men had trouble taking me seriously." In the late eighties Elaine became a civil aviation inspector with Transport Canada.

Janet Panteluk Keim is one of a few women pilots in Canada who owns and operates an aviation company. She initially intended to be an accountant and took flying lessons only to be

JAN KUZINA

Jan Kuzina, of Winnipeg, Manitoba recalled, "I wanted to be an astronaut but the Canadian Forces told me 'no women.' Neither would the air cadets accept girls. The only route I could go was to save my pennies and work my way through all the licences."

She enrolled at the Winnipeg Flying Club in 1972 and within two years had private, commercial, instructor's and multi-IFR licences and a job dispatching and instructing at the club. After that came a position with Aero Trades flying charters and pipeline patrol.

By 1977 Jan was flying DC-3s but a car accident made her realize how dependent her flying was on maintaining a Category 1 medical. "The astronaut thing was still at the back of my mind. When I checked into their qualifications and saw that they all had flying and university I decided to go to university." She graduated in 1982 from the University of Manitoba with an Honours degree in physics and spent the next two years with the National Research Council (NRC) doing aeronautical research. A scholarship from NRC and a Zonta Amelia Earhart Fellowship enabled her to complete a Masters degree in aeronautical engineering, the only woman in the program at Carleton University in Ottawa. "I still hadn't given up on the space program. I applied for the astronaut competition in 1983. I was in the top one hundred and made it through to the third cut and then was dropped.

"When I graduated [in December 1985] several companies called me. I didn't even have to send out resumés. I knew that the position of flight test coordinator at de Havilland was going to be open. I applied and got the job." Jan was the first woman aeronautical engineer hired by de Havilland Canada. As she explained, "They needed someone with both the engineering and flying background. Even though I was the first woman in that kind of a position, my

able to fly her father's plane. However, when she graduated from the University of Saskatchewan with a commerce degree, she had also acquired commercial and instructor's licences and a job instructing with Mitchinson's Flying Services, where she had taken her training. She also did their books and flew charters, mostly for Canadian Wildlife. "To this day," she related, "counting geese is one of the jobs I like best."

Her goal was a job with Air Canada, which she reached in 1979 when she was accepted for pilot training and successfully completed the rigorous program. However, just before going on line she decided that what she really wanted was to be her own boss and she left the airline. She returned to Mitchinson's and, with three silent partners, bought it. The company offers flight training, charter, rental and maintenance services. Now doing more paper work than flying, Janet reports that she misses instructing — except when it's cold!

THE WOMEN continued to prove themselves and even men who initially balked at hiring them occasionally recommended their promotion. Take the former chief pilot of Nor'Ontair. He did not want to hire Paula Brooks Matz who had been recommended for a job in 1976. "When I showed up for work, the look on his face said 'no way,'" recalled Paula. "He tried to discourage me by telling me I would have to lift baggage and freight. In fact, he put me to the test. We were

reception at de Havilland was great. Bob Fowler was a super person to work with."

To reach her goal Jan sacrificed her social life. "Everyone, including men, went on the back burner. Now I find I'm not too willing to compromise what I believe in or to give up my freedom. When I was in my twenties men shied away from me when they knew I had a Masters degree in aeronautical engineering. It's different now. Men in their thirties want an intelligent woman."

Janet Kuzina, pilot and aeronautical engineer, first female flight test engineer at de Havilland.

standing in the parking lot and he had his big flight case with him. 'Pick that up,' he said. I picked it up. Then he said, 'Put it on the hood of the car.' I did that. I kept waiting for his punch line. Then he said, 'Put it on the roof of the car.' By this time I thought I was being made a fool of. It was all pretty silly. He was in a bit of a huff because he thought he could refuse me with the excuse that I couldn't lift anything heavy." Oddly enough they eventually became friends and she proved to be so competent that he ended up promoting her to captain on the Twin Otter a few years later thus making Paula the first woman in Canada to fly as captain on a scheduled airline.

Although the promotion was appreciated the publicity that

KAREN BRYNELSEN MacGREGOR

Karen Brynelsen of Victoria, British Columbia, then a professional horsewoman, began flying as a hobby in 1967. "I just loved those instruments and knew that I wanted to fly with the airlines."

To build time she ferried aircraft. "Once I flew a Swearingen to Mexico and another time I flew a Bonanza to Lima, Peru, with a Peruvian first officer. I'll never forget that trip. It was getting dark and I was low on fuel and the airport was not where the map said it should be. Finally I saw another airplane so I followed it, figuring it had to land somewhere. When we landed a bunch of gendarmes came up to meet us, all the time yelling and pointing underneath the plane. Well I had one of those 'birds' (it's like a radar altimeter) underneath the plane, it looked like a big bullet. I was tired and feeling punchy and I said 'boom'. The next thing I knew they had arrested us and we spent the night in jail. After much explaining that we were not carrying a bomb, we were released. I learned never to speak out of turn, especially in a foreign country."

Karen flew as a corporate pilot for Woodward Stores and served as base manager in Edmonton for Flying Fireman of British Columbia. By 1972 she had an ATR and 2500 hours and decided it was time to apply to the airlines. "All I got were rejections with excuses." Discouraged and disillusioned, she nevertheless continued to upgrade her qualifications. "I got a DH 125 endorsement, wrote the Boeing 727 exams and my American transport licence exams and applied to the American airlines. But it was the same thing. I was too early." However, her time was right for the BC Air Services Branch, which hired her on April 24, 1973.

Like June Montgomery, who had been hired in 1973 by the Manitoba government, Karen found she had an upward struggle to gain acceptance. "I received a lot of publicity:

some of it good, some of it bad. I also got phone calls telling me that I had taken a job that belonged to a man. I'd say, 'I'm sorry, but I have to live too.'" Her biggest problem was trying to gain acceptance from the other pilots. "I was a thorn among roses. Some of the men were neutral while others tried to rattle me or set traps for me in the cockpit so I would mess up an instrument approach. I was often snubbed or made the butt of jokes. They rode me hard on check rides. Their aim was to humiliate me and wear me down. There were days when I wanted to quit." Being the first woman on staff also meant that she had no role model. "I started off being aloof and ultra professional and was told that if I ate a man for breakfast I was on my way for the day. I had to learn that I could retain my feminine qualities and still be a good pilot."

Karen Brynelsen MacGregor, captain of a Citation jet for B.C. Air Services, c.1987.

followed was not. Like the women of the earlier eras, the media were fascinated with them. When Paula became a captain, reporters sought her out. Being photogenic and cheerful, headlines like "Woman Pilot Making History" (*The Toronto Star*, May 29, 1978) began appearing. A few months later, when Captain Paula Matz and First Officer Jill Malkin flew together for Nor'Ontair they made history as Canada's first all-female aircrew on a scheduled airline. Reporters went wild photographing and misquoting the women, much to the chagrin of both who found the publicity embarrassing.

By the nineties only test flying remained closed to female pilots. While women have, in a sense, acted as test pilots it has been on aircraft that have already had the "bugs" worked out of them. According to Bob Fowler, former test pilot with de Havilland Canada, most women had not the technical expertise, the engineering degree, nor the flying experience to get them as far as an initial interview. In addition to these very real drawbacks, there were the usual unwritten arguments against

The role of the BC Air Services Branch, which had been formed shortly after World War II, was primarily that of air ambulance, although the Citation and King Air 200 were also used to fly government officials and VIPs, do aerial surveys, and provide a scheduled service from Victoria to Vancouver. Describing the flying, Karen said, "It seems that most medevacs occur in poor weather. When the urgency of a flight is added to the often challenging conditions of British Columbia — the ocean, mountains, rivers, and fog — and the many short strips in the interior, you can get sweaty pretty fast. The airstrip at Bella Coola is in a fiord and there are only two ways in. When we go there everyone is on their toes. There are four eyes searching for the mountains. The flight from Sidney to Inuvik is a real stress run. There are twenty-four radio transmissions in two minutes."

Karen nevertheless described the flying as "mostly routine" with the exception of two engine failures in the jet and the time the Beech 200 almost got away from her! "What happened was that the brakes had frozen and the minute I landed, the plane stopped rather rapidly and we blew three tires. I managed to keep the airplane right on the centre line. But you know what? The chief pilot asked the other pilot, 'Did she land with her feet on the brakes?' That's what you come to expect from some men when you're a woman. As long as things go well they'll leave you alone, but if anything goes wrong they condemn you before you even have the chance to prove your innocence."

hiring a female test pilot — woman's presumed lack of strength to handle the high G-forces, her female physiology (menstruation and pregnancy), which would limit her capabilities, and her commitment to a long-term career. Fowler, who learned to fly with Vi Milstead and was a longtime supporter of women pilots, hired Jan Kuzina of Winnipeg as a flight test coordinator in 1986 — the first woman to hold the position. With many years of flying experience as well as a Master of Aeronautical Engineering degree, Janet was well qualified and Bob Fowler had no qualms about hiring her. Who knows, a female test pilot may be aboard the next new aircraft off the drawing board.

Only a few of the "oldtimers" remained active in the seventies and eighties: Lorna DeBlicquy, Felicity McKendry, and Marion Orr in the east and Gretchen Matheson, Vera (Strodl) Dowling, Gina Jordan, Lucille (Haley) Baster, Molly Reilly, Toni Ramsay, and Joan and Berna Studer in the west. However, while the newcomers had the example and often the encouragement of the original pioneers, they still had the same

While being female got her the job, as part of a provincial initiative to enforce equal opportunities, it likely slowed her promotion to captain. "I expected to be in the left seat within three or four years. Instead it took nine years. I was bypassed for promotion six times. Each time I silently accepted the decision. But after the sixth competition, when I felt I had been unfairly ignored, I appealed. I lost the appeal and appealed again. Shortly after the chief pilot came to me and asked, 'Would you like to be captain?' 'You bet,' I replied." In 1982 Karen became the first woman in Canada to achieve the captaincy on the Citation 500 and 550. "Not everyone was happy with my promotion but I just let time take care of any hostility. Some time later I found a rose and a note of congratulations on my car. The note was signed, 'From someone who cares.' Finally, I thought, I'm accepted."

Karen loved her work and was proud to fly for the BC Air Services Branch. "Flying people who had been injured or women who had suddenly developed a pregnancy complication, especially in marginal weather, made me feel I'd contributed something."

In 1988 her course changed again when she married (another pilot) and applied to Transport Canada. Well qualified, she was hired as an air carrier inspector and aviation licencing inspector. In 1992 she will take on instrument standards inspection and, checked out on the DC-3, will be doing instrument flight tests.

old myths to dispel and the negative attitudes lived on. "Some airline captains at fifty-five were terrific while others at thirty-five were hard-core chauvinists," said Air Canada pilot Barb Swyers. Perhaps acceptance of women is a function of maturity. Many of the older pilots have grown out of what some women described as their "macho insecurity" and are more self-assured. Or, as some men admitted, "It's easy to be receptive to the women because they are so junior we will never have to fly with them in command nor will a woman ever be a threat to my job security." Fortunately, many of the younger ones were also supportive of the women.

HOSTILITY TOWARDS THE WOMEN was often more evident at government-run or government-established organizations, which had a long tradition of hiring only men. June Montgomery, the Manitoba Government Air Service's first woman pilot, discovered that situation. Her story also epitomizes what can happen when a woman is parachuted in without first "paying her dues."

Georgette Buch.

GEORGETTE BUCH

Georgette, daughter of an RCAF pilot, was one of the first French-Canadian women to fly professionally. "When my father left the RCAF he bought a flight school at Dorval and he asked my brother and I to help him run it," she explained. She began flying in 1967 and over the next ten years combined university and aviation, ultimately obtaining an ATR, a PhD (in linguistics), and a position, in 1978, with the federal government.

"Transport Canada was looking for someone who was bilingual, had a university degree, a teaching background, and an ATR. There were no men who could meet the requirements," said Georgette. "I took the job because it offered me the chance to use both my flying and academic backgrounds and my knowledge on student-instructor relationships and to apply it to the learning process in flying. Transport was looking into that facet and how it affected the student's learning ability."

Since then Georgette has become a well-known authority on the learning process in flying. She has written a manual on teaching techniques, given lectures on the subject at three international conferences, and worked closely with the American Federal Aviation Authority. In 1987 she was promoted into the senior management level at Transport Canada. Married with one daughter, she is currently director of Inspections, Engineering, Training & Development.

In 1973 an official of the Manitoba Government Air Service hired June. "I liked the look of her application," he explained. "She was a gold medalist, a graduate nurse, and had the flying skills I was looking for. Instead of putting her in Thompson, I brought her directly into Winnipeg to fly the MU-2, which we had just purchased. She had an ATR and a Class 1 instrument rating and I was so short of instrument pilots that she was more useful there than up north. Besides being qualified, she was female. The politicians were my bosses, the New Democrats (NDP) were in power and they wanted to give women more opportunities." Shortly after, June was given the plum posting of base superintendent of the Winnipeg IFR operation,

DIANE DESMARAIS

Diane Desmarais of Montreal was a Bachelor of Arts graduate and almost through a science degree when she fell in love with flying. She took flying lessons in the late seventies for pleasure, but, when her flight examiner told her that a private licence was as far as a woman should go, Diane saw red. "I was so insulted that I signed up for my commercial training with the examiner still standing there, just to prove him wrong." Within the year she was instructing and flying charters for Janine Leclerc of ATL Air Tuteurs.

In December 1984 she became a civil aviation inspector in Planning and Airports in Ottawa. Soon bored, she applied for another position and in July 1985 was accepted as an aviation safety investigator in Montreal, the third woman in Canada to hold this position. "I spend about one third of my time in the field. As an accident investigator I cover anything from ultra lights to 747s." It took about six months for her to be accepted. "They were afraid I might not understand the technical things . . . there is a lot of on-the-job-learning. Ideally you go out with a senior investigator but when I arrived we were short-staffed so I just followed one of the other investigators. On my second investigation he said, 'You handle, I'll follow.' On the third I was on my own. For an accident with a fatality both a pilot and a technician go out so that both aspects are thoroughly covered." People were often surprised to see a woman, Diane mentioned, "Some of them think you're the secretary. The first ten or fifteen minutes they look at you, wonder how much you know. Then they ask you if you have a licence. Sometimes it's an advantage to be a woman because people perceive you as more sensitive." Diane is now a Transport Canada civil aviation inspector in the Quebec Region.

even though she had not "served her time" in the north. "None of this went over well with the other pilots, many of whom were having problems getting an instrument rating. June was a real threat to them and they gave her a rough time. The check pilot was told to 'fail that bitch' but he couldn't. June was letter perfect." However, as June observed, "An over-zealous NDP government in its anxiety to promote women did me and other women no favours." In June 1978, after a change of government, those in power attempted to push June out by sending her to Thompson where all the new and non-instrument pilots began. Refusing to be banished to the hinterland, she resigned, and has since piloted on a free-lance basis, flying charters in western Canada.

The women were always under pressure to perform to a higher standard than the men because their actions would affect future women applicants. "If a guy screws up too many times he's fired and another guy is hired. If a woman messes up that company may never hire another woman," explained Noreen Newton of North Caribou Flying Service. And Georgette Buch of Transport Canada, who holds a PhD in languages and an ATR, said, "I always felt I had to try harder. I got every rating there was to make myself more credible and I use 'Dr.' instead of 'Mrs.' because it commands more respect."

By the eighties discrimination had become more subtle. Rejections such as "We don't hire women" were replaced by, "We're not hiring right now" — acceptable until a man is hired a week later. Another common excuse was that wives would object to their husbands flying with a woman. Some women found themselves constantly passed over for promotion. In 1979 a well-known company in Montreal hired Nicole Sauvé as first officer to fly the Citation and Lear Jet. However, nine years later she was still flying as co-pilot although she was captain-qualified and had approximately 6000 hours. As she said, "I've

Captain Nicole Sauvé and unidentified first officer, on the Boeing 757, January, 1992.

been passed over many times even though I have more than 3000 hours turbine and jet time alone. My last captain had no jet time, no high density airport time — I trained him!" However, Nicole's story ends on a happy note. In 1988 Nationair hired her as first officer on the DC-8. "The people are great and most are helpful and make me feel welcome." Nicole is now Captain Sauvé, the only woman among 131 Nationair pilots, and one of only two women in Canada to be in the left seat with a major company.

Husky Oil, on the other hand, promoted Lori Fitzgerald, its first woman pilot, to captain on the Citation 1 and 11 and HS-125 within two years of hiring her. A former architectural

MARIE ZUBRYCKYJ

Marie Zubryckyj of Edmonton, Alberta wanted to be a fighter pilot but was laughed out of the recruiting office. She went the civilian route and obtained her instructor's and multi-IFR ratings. In 1978, Marie began instructing on the side while working as an an assistant air traffic controller. For the next seven years she combined air traffic control, instructing, and charter flying. By 1981 she had over 1500 hours, an ATR, and a reputation as an able pilot who took good care of her passengers. "I always walked into a job as a pilot, not as a woman pilot. You have to let the guys know that you're there to fly, not to provide fringe benefits."

By 1983 she wanted to move on. "I wanted to be an executive pilot with Transport Canada. I knew that they wouldn't hire an unknown from Edmonton even though I had an ATR and over 3000 hours, most of it corporate flying, so I applied for the position of flight operations officer as my ticket into the system." Marie won the competition and became Transport Canada's first female flight operations officer. "It wasn't easy leaving the security of my work with ATC and my 'cushy' situation as a corporate pilot to move into a totally different atmosphere, especially one in which everyone else was male and seemed to be over fifty." She dispatched the Ministry of Transport fleet of Jetstars and Challengers, did the flight planning, selected the routes, put the crews together, and made all the flight and ground arrangements — a desk job.

"Then," she related, "in November 1984 the government decided that executive aircraft would be flown by military pilots and there went all my dreams." Not wanting to remain where she was she secured a transfer and in June 1985 became a civil aviation inspector in Instrument Standards in Montreal. Still in Instrument Standards, Marie is currently based in Ottawa.

technologist, who began flying in 1977 and was hired by Husky Oil in 1983 as co-pilot on the jet, Lori feels accepted. "No one complains about the smell of Nina-Ricci perfume mixed in with jet fuel odors and the hangar people refer to my cushion as my Maxi Pad."

Marriage and pregnancy continued as "trouble" areas. The airlines and military had long questioned a woman's commitment to a career and neither wanted to invest thousands of dollars in a woman who would not accept a transfer because her husband was not mobile or who lost her medical "intentionally" because she wanted to have a baby. Pregnancy, always a hot issue, reached the boiling point in the eighties when two airline pilots and two Canadian Forces pilots became mothers-to-be. At that time pregnancy meant an automatic loss of flying status, for the woman was assessed as "temporarily unfit." It could also mean loss of benefits, job security, and seniority. For the employer it could cause scheduling headaches. In the early

CATHERINE FLETCHER

Catherine Fletcher, a graduate of McMaster University, Hamilton, was a medical technologist when she began to fly. "I had always wanted to fly but felt I should wait until I was through university." An officer in the reserves, Catherine taught meteorology and aerodynamics to the air cadets. In 1978 she and her husband moved to Edmonton and Catherine quickly qualified for her commercial, instructor's, and multi-IFR ratings and had no problem being hired at the Edmonton Flying Club.

Officials were thrown for a loop when Cathy became pregnant in the early eighties and insisted she was medically fit to fly. With the backing of her doctor she applied for a waiver from the government. "The Ministry of Transport decided to use me as a test case in the Western Region and allowed me to retain my Category 1 medical status until I was six months pregnant provided that I was monitored by my doctor. I did not tell the flying club about my pregnant state for four and a half months. Some of the instructors were appalled that I had retained my medical. Some of my students were equally surprised when they found their instructor or flight examiner to be a pregnant lady." Cathy returned to flying four weeks after the birth of the baby.

Since December 1984 she has been a civil aviation inspector in Air Regulations, Transport Canada. She is also involved in Alberta's Stepping Stones program — going into schools to show children that non-traditional jobs are available to women.

eighties Transport Canada introduced a waiver which allowed a woman to fly while pregnant under certain conditions and provided that it was acceptable to management. However, this was not widely known among officials or the women themselves and, consequently, some women were grounded needlessly. Kim Sutherland Wheaton, for instance, the Alberta Government Air Services' first woman pilot, lost her flying status with her first pregnancy but argued against being grounded for her second. She partially won her case by being allowed to fly for as long she could squeeze into her uniform and returned to flying after the birth of her second child.

Initially, the Canadian Forces grounded a woman as soon as she declared her "delicate condition." However, according to Captain Micky Colton, by the 1990s there were "no restrictions. You officially stop flying when you and your medical officer feel the time is right."

In the United States the Federal Aviation Authority has not imposed any flying restrictions on pregnant women or predetermined that they are "unfit." It is up to the woman and her doctor to determine this. If her doctor assesses her medically fit and if she can fasten her seatbelt, the matter is between her and the company. Canada now appears to be moving towards this approach but only because a couple of women had the courage to fight for what they considered their rights.

Passenger reaction also remained a problem. The less passengers knew about flying, the less likely they were to accept a woman pilot. The women with the smaller companies received all sorts of ridiculous comments because many passengers have a distorted understanding about the skills required of a pilot. For them women do not fit the stereotype of the brave, strong, cool-headed captain. "There were always some who

Nancy Puttkemery, RCMP pilot.

CONSTABLE NANCY PUTTKEMERY

Nancy Puttkemery was raised in a flying family in Ontario. With her father and three brothers pilots, Nancy grew up wanting to fly but also very interested in police work. In the late sixties she reached her goal of being accepted by the Royal Canadian Mounted Police (RCMP). She applied for the Air Services in 1980, after she had qualified for a commercial licence and had gained experience as a flying instructor. In 1986 she became the RCMP's first woman pilot. Nancy was based in Edmonton flying an Otter when she was killed in an air crash.

didn't know quite what to think. It caught a few off guard when they showed up for a flight and found a female pilot," said Lori Fitzgerald of Husky Oil. "They expected some six foot five Greek Adonis with eyes parenthesized by crow's feet and some great square jaw. What they got was a five foot five blonde, blue-eyed girl who looked about fifteen years old and weighed only 115 pounds." Passenger reaction once took an unexpected twist as Barb Warwashawski Kahl found out when she was flying for Wilderness Airlines of British Columbia. "I was picking up some Forestry guys at a logging camp, about fifty miles from Bella Coola. When I was heading for the dock I knew something was up. They were all standing there with big grins on their faces. Then they all turned around and dropped their trousers. I was mooned! Well, I was laughing so hard I just about hit the dock."

Barb Warwashawski Kahl, 1986 — flying a Navajo.

Whatever the reaction, the women took it all in their stride, although, as Kelly Hepburn wistfully said, "I like the people who say nothing, just accept us as pilots. Some days I like the attention and the constant challenge, but some days I'd do anything to be just another deep voice on the radio."

FROM THEIR PROFESSIONAL PEERS the women of the seventies and eighties encountered various reactions. When Lorna DeBlicquy walked into the Toronto Department of Transport office in 1976 as a new civil aviation inspector, she broke one of Canada's longest-standing aviation traditions. Since the enactment of the Air Board Act in 1919 aviation officials were men and generally recruited from the ranks of the military. "Transport Canada was like an 'old boys school' and we were unwelcome intruders," agreed the women. If hiring one or two women pilots as inspectors made the men uneasy, inaugurating the Equal Opportunity for Women program made them downright ornery. "Transport Canada is taking all the losers now. Some fat-assed broads are coming," were the whispered comments that greeted one woman.

The Equal Opportunity for Women (EOW) program, begun in 1981, did nothing to help an already touchy situation. As Heather MacMillan explained, "All of a sudden there were women coming into the various regions. There was a lot of misinformation and you could understand their concern. Some of the guys were worried about being on the road with a woman — whether they could trust us or themselves. On one of my first trips with another inspector I heard one of the other guys ask, 'Hey, what do you do when you go back to the hotel?'" Added Heather, "I was hired under the Equal Opportunity program. I didn't think anything of it at the time. Now of course I would never recommend it for women who are already qualified because many of the men assumed I had little experience or the ratings for the job." When, in 1983, she became Canada's first woman accident investigator, the negative comments followed her again. "The stigma of EOW followed me. I was surprised at the hostility. Some of it was probably due to the fact that I came from headquarters but a lot was simply because I was a woman. One of the men actually told me that the office was not ready

JO HARRIS

Jo Harris of Edmonton, Alberta was content with her lot in life but at forty-one she decided to take flying lessons. "I wanted to do something for me, something unconnected with church, home, or community work, the frustrated housewife syndrome if you like. My husband supported my efforts but I think friends and relatives looked on my flying as a stage I was going through and they were looking forward to the day when I got over it. Women in aviation in 1976 were not common in Edmonton. My girlfriend and I were welcomed at the flying club but we were certainly considered an oddity — two married women with husbands and family at home."

Because of her age and background in teaching she opted for instructing. "I ran into some discrimination but the opportunities were excellent in the late seventies and I had no trouble getting a job as a flight instructor." Jo is now a civil aviation inspector in the Flight Training Standards Department of Transport Canada. Her job involves "responsibility for monitoring flying schools and small charter operations in Western Region, which means I do flight tests at all levels (private, commercial, IFR, instructor, multi, PPC's, etc.) and audits of schools to ensure safe operations. Western Region is huge — it covers all of the Yukon, half of the Northwest Territories, northern British Columbia, and all of Alberta, so we have our work cut out for us.

"The other area of the work that I really like is the educational aspect and I'm fortunate to be involved in that on a national level, which means having input on pilot decision-making material, enhancement material for the schools in the area of instructional techniques, ground schools, teaching multi-engine flying and so on." ATR qualified, Jo is a member of the 99s and a past winner of their Amelia Earhart Award.

for women! Others remarked that I got the job only because I was female. I was branded EOW, someone who had got into Transport with nothing. However, through it all my supervisor Jerry Saul supported me."

More pungent was Diane Klassen's assessment of the EOW program, "I was the first woman inspector in Central Region. At Winnipeg I was one of the boys. I came in the men's door and that gave me a lot of credibility. Others came in through EOW and that ruined it for the rest of us."

Most of the women with Transport Canada adopted a laid-back approach and did not even bother to challenge the accusations that were thrown at them. "At first they wouldn't

KAREN HIBBERD BURNETT

Karen Hibberd Burnett of Newmarket, Ontario was driving a car at age ten, motorcycles at age twelve, and racing power boats and motorcycles a few years later. "I liked anything that had a motor in it. Flying lessons were my sixteenth birthday present." Karen received her private pilots licence in 1972 but did not think about flying as a career until an airline pilot, who she had met at a local airport, told her there were no women pilots with the airline. "I decided then and there to pursue aviation as a career."

With her father's blessing and financial support, she qualified for her commercial and multi-IFR ratings the following year while attending university. "The day I obtained my multi-IFR I was hired by a small charter company in Toronto to fly right seat in a 690 Turbo Commander. Next I flew a MU-2 for Browndale. It was about that time that I became associated with the War Birds of America. I fell in love with the Mustang and I would have gone the airshow circuit as a career if three friends had not been killed in a crash."

Laid off from Browndale in 1977, she returned to university full-time. "The following summer I went to the Arctic on a fishing trip with my father and just for the heck of it I walked into the office of a company operating in the area and asked for a job. It had just lost its co-pilot an hour earlier and had a medevac to carry out and needed a co-pilot to make the trip legal. They were desperate and hired me! No, there were no problems if we had to overnight away from base. We stayed with Eskimo families." Karen remained there for the summer leaving only to return to university and to gain some pilot-in-command time.

The following year she earned her instructor's rating and applied to the airlines. "I had two interviews with Air Canada. It was a discouraging time for me as several of my

have believed you. One of the inspectors asked me how I ever got hired with only a few hundred hours. That was how the rumours flew. I told him that when I was hired I had an ATR and thousands of hours logged in the north flying as captain, plus a university degree. But he didn't want to hear that," said one. Another woman added, "But you learned to walk into the office smiling. If you had children who were sick you didn't mention it. You always pretended that everything was going smoothly. What I found hard to take was how vocal they were to my face and how far and wide they spread some of the talk." In the early years the public could be just as insensitive. As Madeleine Caouette recalled, "You had to get used to comments like 'I want to talk to a *real* inspector.'"

By 1992 there were thirty-two women standing firmly among the four hundred and eighty-five men of Transport Canada and most of the women felt part of the group . . . until they made a mistake. "Even after ten years our actions are closely watched," related one woman. "I dinged a nav light taxiing a DC-3 and all I heard for the next week was, 'Look at what you broads have done now!' Yet one of the men had recently smashed a wing and not a word was said. Fortunately, they're not all like that. One of them said to me, 'How did you stand all the crap we gave you?'"

SOME WOMEN PILOTS found their niche in specialty flying and made unique careers for themselves. Kelly Hepburn chose "ag flying" as her entry into the world of aviation. Rejected by Air Canada for flight attendant training in 1979 because of her impaired vision, Kelly took flying lessons instead. Her introduction to agricultural flying came when she became a "pointer pilot" on the Budworm Spray Project in New Brunswick. Anxious to become a qualified ag pilot herself, she went to Slaton Flying Services in Texas in October 1982 for their forty-hour ag course. The training paid off because she

male friends were being hired by airlines and they had the same or less time than me. Being female was a problem."

Next came a stint with Pemair on the Beech 99 and then a position with Air Atonabee. Karen, who by now had her transport licence was a first officer and then captain on the Saunders ST-27. In 1983 Transport Canada hired her as a civil aviation inspector in the Training and Examinations area and a few years later, she became Canada's second female accident investigator.

landed a job in June 1983 with Tony Bevan of Herschel Air Services in Saskatchewan, spraying herbicides and insecticides.

Spray or agricultural flying is one of the few areas left in aviation that is not inundated with automation. Pilots must maintain a high level of concentration because the slightest lapse can be deadly due to the low altitude at which they are flying. Commenting on whether ag flying was dangerous, Kelly said, "Well, the way I look at it, you have to work hard to keep it safe. You have to know your airplane really well, you have to make every turn at the end of the field as quickly and efficiently as possible without compromising safety. You have to be down in the field inches above the crop for maximum chemical

Kelly Hepburn, with crop spraying S2R Thrush Commander, Herschel, Saskatchewan, 1983.

MARIKO NAGATA

Mariko was a 1976 graduate of the aviation program at Trinity Western University in Langley, British Columbia. "I received commercial, multi-IFR, float, and instructor ratings. I took the instructing option because I was told I would never get any other job! I met Gretchen Matheson and she was my role model. I worked at Skyways Aviation at Langley and they loaned me back to Trinity as an instructor. I also typed, dispatched, and fueled aircraft. I invested two years of my life there and put up with a lot." Mariko next worked with other companies flying a Cheyenne and Turbo Commander but the memories were not good ones. "The second job was a courier run and the owner was the ops manager and captain. Safety was not a factor with him. There I was sitting as Joe co-pilot but I couldn't say a thing if I wanted the job. When the nosewheel fell off, investigation showed that it was corroded. I left and went back to Skyways and asked for an instructing job. All I got was a 'Ha, ha, we told you you should have stayed with instructing.' All they would give me was VFR instructing and I received less pay than before. I didn't stay."

In 1980 Mariko worked briefly for the Winnipeg Flying Club. "They desperately needed an IFR instructor and I was running on empty. I was booked solid. I also worked as a waitress." Then Transport Canada called. With about 2700 hours and an ATR and Class 1 instructor's rating, Mariko was soon in Flight Training Standards in the Atlantic Region working out of the Moncton office." She is currently a civil aviation inspector in the Ottawa office. "I believe that the stress factor is higher for a woman," Mariko said. "The trick is not to be bitter with some of the things that happen because you are a woman."

effectivness, you have to be constantly aware of wind conditions and drifting into susceptible crops, and you must use great caution with the poisonous chemicals which are used."

A job as co-pilot on a PBY-5A Canso on a lime dropping contract in northwestern Ontario with Rog-Air came next and that led into a full-time job with Frontier Air, where she became the senior base pilot in Kapuskasing and captain on the Navajo Chieftain and Beech King Air 100. "I pride myself in being the pilot-in-command of these airplanes as I have worked very hard to obtain this position," she said then. With an ATR, a Class 1 multi-IFR rating, and about 6500 hours, Kelly (now Kelly Scott, having married a Canadair test pilot) currently flies with

Montreal-based Execaire. The largest aviation management company in Canada, the firm operates aircraft for large corporations. Kelly mainly flies as captain on a Hawker Siddeley 125 for Bell Canada. She is expecting a baby in September 1992, but plans on returning to flying.

JUDY ADAMSON of Toronto, Ontario was a 1973 psychology graduate who turned a hobby into a career. She received her start in 1979 when Bob Ferguson of Parsons Airways Northern in Flin Flon, Manitoba hired her. "She was a really good girl, a good learner. She never made the same mistake twice," said Ferguson. "There was nothing glamorous about her job. She hauled smelly fish and flew people and equipment

Since leaving "ag flying" Kelly Hepburn flies as captain on this Hawker Siddeley 125 operated by Execaire.

into mining and fish camps. She always went out of her way to do her share. She was so proud that she hated to ask for help in case someone accused her of not being able to do the job."

By 1981, Judy had 2100 hours and a multi-IFR and felt it was time to move on. She got her break when Avalon Aviation, the water bombing section of Georgian Bay Airways, hired her. "I was based in Timmins and began on the amphibious 185 as a 'bird dog' pilot. My job was to circle the fire at about 200 feet above ground level, to keep in contact with the fire chief, and to fly the route the chief indicated. I would lead the water bombers in, pulling up sharply at the spot where they were to drop their load." Competent, she was soon checked out on the

The water-bomber Canso flown by Judy Adamson, 1981-1985.

Canso and CL-215, eventually becoming the first woman in Canada to be captain-qualified on these aircraft.

Flying the Canso and CL-215 brought Judy into a very special fraternity of aviators: the water-bomber pilots, who fly a hazardous mission — flames can leap a hundred feet into the air and the turbulence and wind currents associated with the fire can be treacherous. As Judy explained, "The water-bomber pilot, often flying at tree top level, must know when to ease off power so an up-draft will not carry the aircraft too high for the drop, and how much power to keep on to stay out of the flames if a down-draft catches the plane. Working a fire is physically and mentally exhausting for it means continuous landings and take-offs to scoop up and drop water. It means working in a smoke-filled environment, flying over flames which create their own weather, and keeping a constant watch for the bird dog pilot and the other water bombers."

After five years, in 1986, Judy joined Transport Canada as a civil aviation inspector, air carriers, in Moncton, New Brunswick. She is now a superintendent for the Ontario Region.

HELLA COMAT was Canada's top Canadian female aerobatic pilot. Born in Germany and raised in Canada, Hella was a school teacher when she began flying in 1977. "I had always wanted to fly and one day I saw a poster advertising aerobatic lessons, so I signed up." She received a private licence that year and went on for aerobatic instruction at Condor Aviation in Hamilton, Ontario. "The next year at Christmas my husband gave me a one hour flight in Gerry Younger's Pitts S-2A (two-seater). That cost $125. I began taking lessons from him the following spring." Younger, a professional aerobatic pilot charged $70/hour in his Ballanca Decathalon. "After ten hours I could do Cuban Ss, slow rolls, snap rolls, hammerheads, loops, Immelmans, and a Split S. I had begun aerobatics to gain confidence in my flying and for the sheer thrill of it. But then I found myself hooked by the precision required."

Judy Adamson is probably the first woman in the world to be captain on the Canadair CL 215 water bomber.

Hella was good; so good, in fact, that Younger and some of the other Aerobatics Canada pilots urged her to begin competing. In 1979 she earned her Sportsman Proficiency Award. "I was the only Canadian woman competing that year. I placed eleventh at the Michigan competition and seventh in the Canadian Nationals. Doing that well spurred me on. However, I realized that if I were to progress I would have to spend all my spare time practising. During the school year I went out most weekends and in the summer I flew five or six days a week." The next summer she entered the sportsman category and placed fourteenth out of thirty-six competitors at Fond du Lac,

Wisconsin, in the largest annual competition in North America. A few months later, she won first place at the Canadian Nationals and became the first woman to win a national aerobatic title in Canada.

"Nineteen-eighty gave me my first real taste of competitive flying. I learned what was meant by 'box pressure' the condition of pre-competition flight nerves. My way of coping was to enter as many competitions as I could afford to. I also realized that the Decathlon, while suitable for beginners like me, was no match for the Pitts Special or some of the other aircraft that the Americans or Europeans were flying. I knew that if I were going to get anywhere I would have to fly a Pitts."

Hella Comat.

COMPETITIVE AEROBATICS

Competitive Aerobatics is not a spectator sport. From the public's point of view the aircraft is flown too high; all that is visible is a moving dot in the sky. As a result, there is little public recognition and even less sponsorship. The Canadian Aerobatic Foundation, now known as Aerobatics Canada, was formed in 1969 to promote the sport but it has attracted little support. In the mid-eighties there were less than sixty active aerobatic pilots; about half of these were airshow performers. There has never been an all-female team and rarely have there been more than four or five women flying at any one time. Expense is the biggest drawback; few can afford to own and operate a $100,000 aircraft such as the Pitts Special. Time is another factor; a lot of it is needed to perfect manoeuvres and progress to the higher levels. Finally, current prohibitive public liability insurance rates have forced many in the sport to give it up.

Competitive aerobatic pilots must please judges and "precise" rather than "spectacular" defines the flying. The sequence of manoeuvres is flown in an "aerobatic box," an imaginary area 1000 metres on each side. Large markers on the ground outline the aerobatic box in the sky for the pilot, and electronic tracking equipment keeps track of the aircraft for the judges. If a pilot strays from the box he or she accumulates penalty points.

There are four aerobatic classifications: sportsman (novice), intermediate, advanced, and unlimited. In the sportsman stage the pilot flies basic aerobatic manoeuvres: loops, rolls, hammerheads, and spins, but no sustained inverted flight. In the intermediate category the pilot flies all of the above plus sustained inverted flight. In the advanced stage the pilot flies outside manoeuvres, such as the outside loop, which imposes negative Gs. For the unlimited, the pilot flies all of the above, with a high degree

Fully committed to aerobatic flying, Hella and seven other aerobatic pilots bought a Pitts S-1S, a single seater. "I took lessons from Gerry Younger in his two-place Pitts before I attempted to solo in mine. Adjusting to the tiny sensitive control movements in the air was nerve-wracking. I found approaches and landings especially difficult. Bringing in a small biplane weighing less than 1000 pounds at 90 knots in a side-slipping approach — to compensate for lack of flaps — knowing that the bottom wing is only a foot off the pavement at touch down, and keeping in mind the slightest amount of crosswind, all add up to a terrific degree of concentration in order to complete a smooth landing and roll out. But soloing the S-1

of precision. Each category is further defined by the height at which it is flown: the more advanced the level the closer to the ground the routine is flown. For instance, the pilot at the sportsman level flies between 1500 feet and 3500 feet AGL, and as low as 300 feet at the unlimited level.

Every pilot carries an Aresti card, which outlines the sequence of manoeuvres to be flown — the name comes from Count Aresti of Spain who developed a special language for aerobatic pilots to map out their particular flight. Competitive flying usually involves up to twenty-five separate manoeuvres and the pilot draws his or her sequences in "Aresti" on a card that is placed on the instrument panel; another card is used by the judges. Each pilot flies up to four different flights. Many things must be kept in mind, particularly the wind. As Jay Hunt of Aerobatics Canada explained, "You have that 1000 metre by 1000 metre box that you must stay in and if there is a strong crosswind component you can be pushed out of the box. Knowledge, planning, orientation, and timing are the keys to good aerobatic flying, with orientation probably being the most important factor."

The first World Aerobatic Championships were held in France in 1960 and have been held every second year since. Canadians, who were slow to adopt this new sport, did not compete internationally until 1976. The first national aerobatic competition was held in 1969. To begin with, they flew Harvards and Chipmunks, aircraft that were not designed for competitive aerobatics. But it was 1973 before the Department of Transport allowed homebuilt aircraft to be flown aerobatically. Only then did the highly manoeuverable Pitts Special roar into Canadian skies.

What makes a good aerobatic pilot? According to those who know: money, time, strength, drive, a competetive spirit, a strong ego, the ability to keep your wits about you and to use all your senses, and a lot of guts.

was one of the most thrilling experiences of my life. Its power, speed, and ability to climb almost vertically amazed me."

In 1981 Hella moved up to the intermediate level, designing a free-style program to include certain required manoeuvres. That year she finished second in the intermediate level at the Canadian Nationals. "I was encouraged to go immediately into the advanced category but as it is flown at lower altitudes and involves a lot of outside or negative G manoeuvres, I decided to gain more experience. I remember doing my first outside manoeuvres. After completing a hammerhead and heading vertically down, instead of pulling to level flight I pushed to inverted flight and then pushed forward on the controls to a vertical climb. All the way to level flight again was another experience etched in my memory. My most pressing thought was 'Have I done up the seat belts securely?' as the centrifugal force is pressing three to four times my weight against the belts." Her relentless schedule of practising and the change of aircraft paid off. In 1982 Hella was the first Canadian woman to place first at the intermediate level at the Canadian Nationals. The following year, she placed second in the advanced category at the Canadian Nationals and this was all the more remarkable because she was flying a borrowed plane. The same year — 1983 — Pat Cruchley, a medical doctor who had taken up aerobatics to improve her skill, entered and won her first competition in the sportsman category.

In 1985 Hella, who was then pregnant, withdrew from aerobatics. The Pitts S-1S was sold and she now flies Cessnas 152 and 172 for pleasure. Her goal though is to get back in a Pitts and continue aerobatic flying.

THEN THERE WERE the trans-Canada flights. In 1981 two young women from Newfoundland — Susan Davis and Tina Morgan — flew to British Columbia and back again:

Hella Comat and Pitts S-1S aerobatic plane, c. 1981.

perhaps the first Canadian women to do so. "Being on an island, especially one with few landing areas like Newfoundland, doesn't give you much incentive to fly cross-country. We wanted the challenge of a long flight," explained Susan. The flight was not considered record-setting because they had not sought approval from the Royal Canadian Flying Club Association, the official representative in Canada of the Federation Aeronautique Internationale (FAI). But, as Susan recalled, "We didn't do it for the sake of being the first. In fact, neither of us even thought of making if official and we never looked for any publicity. It was mostly to see if we could do it on our own." Susan was a medical technologist at Memorial University in St. John's and a part-time flying instructor with a bare 400 hours and almost no cross-country experience when she undertook the flight. Tina Morgan, a former "Newfie" and research assistant who was living in Moncton, New Brunswick, was a

HUGUETTE MENARD JENKOVICE

Huguette Menard Jenkovice of Montreal, Quebec remembered, "I was seven years old when I decided I wanted to fly. My parents tried to discourage me by saying that flying was for boys or for the very rich. My upbringing was a very traditional French-Canadian one and flying certainly did not figure into it." Huguette took her private licence in 1967 but could not afford further training. Next, marriage and children put flying on hold until 1978 when she obtained her commercial and instructor's ratings.

"Things were a little easier then. When I had taken my initial instruction at Wondel Aviation in St. Hubert I was considered a little odd. Some of the pilots were downright hostile and insulting, a few thought it was amusing that a girl should take up flying and a very few thought it was great. No one, however, encouraged me to go after the higher ratings. Women who wanted to go further were no longer thought of as women. They lost their feminine identity. The opportunities for women were almost nil then. If you really wanted to do something you had to force doors. It took a lot of guts and courage to even try. I really admire people like Janine Leclerc."

In 1981, she took special training to instruct aerobatics, becoming the first woman aerobatics instructor in Quebec. Huguette combined instructing at Aero Transmissions with collaborating with Ladislav Bezak, world champion aerobatic pilot, in writing a book on aerobatics. She has also had published *Entre ciel et terre,* her French translation of the primary manual for pilots, *From the Ground Up.*

private pilot with only 148 hours and no cross-country experience. They had met at Memorial and shared the dream of flying across Canada.

"It was very unusual for a woman to do something like that," explained Tina. "Women were very dominated by men in Newfoundland. At Aztec Aviation, where Susan instructed part-time, everyone thought it was a big joke." To keep costs down they stayed with friends, slept in airport terminals, or camped under the wing of the plane, a four-seater Cherokee 180, CF-AJY. The trip cost them $2500.

They ran into difficulties almost immediately. "The flight from Newfoundland to Nova Scotia was supposedly a fifteen

Susan Davis, left, and Tina Morgan with the Cherokee 180 they flew across Canada, 1981.

DEBBI HALL WARREN

Debbi Hall Warren of Renfrew, Ontario was working in Winnipeg as a public health inspector when, bored with her job, she began flying lessons. "I needed a challenge." She received her private and commercial licences. Then, she related, "It was Greg [Warren, her husband-to-be] who encouraged me to get my multi-IFR. He was with Perimeter Aviation. He was great. We'd get up at five in the morning and go to Perimeter to use the simulator. What a way to start off a marriage!" In March 1980 Debbi began working for Perimeter Aviation. "I had to be crazy to leave a secure and easy job at $20,000 for a $10,000 insecure flying job, which meant being at the airport at five every morning." After 1100 hours on the Fairchild Metroliner, Perimeter

minute hop," said Susan. "We got lost going over the Gulf! We lost our radio and navaids while enroute to Moncton from Stephenville via Sydney. By the time we realized we were lost we were over the Madeleine Islands. We then headed for Prince Edward Island but ended up on the coast of Nova Scotia and landed without radio at Port Hawkesbury — just before we ran out of fuel and just before a search and rescue operation was started! We then flew Nordo [no radio] into Moncton. The weather was very poor, the ILS [instrument landing system] was not working properly, the ADF [automatic direction finder] was not the best, and visibility was poor because of haze — anything that could go wrong did!"

Susan and Tina set out on June 5, 1981 and arrived at Victoria, British Columbia on June 23, nineteen days and 49.4 flying hours later. Consistently bad weather enroute slowed their progress and at one point forced them to divert south to

moved her to the aviation side of its operation to handle the multi-IFR instructing. "As senior instructor I expected to move into the next vacancy on the corporate jet, for that had been the trend. Instead I was by-passed. When I questioned the decision I was told that the chief pilot did not think that the wives of the business men would appreciate their husbands having a woman pilot!" In 1982 she applied to Transport Canada and was hired under the EOW program as a civil aviation inspector with Airways. "I needed a change. I had flown more than 3000 hours in a couple of years and had flown myself out. Also I wanted more normal hours, something more compatible with marriage. I was hired at the height of the publicity on EOW. I had an ATR, 3100 hours, and was only a few credits short of a science degree but some of the guys thought I was unqualified. They put you to the test. If you proved yourself, then it was okay. One man actually told me he did not look at me as a peer, but he didn't say it in an insulting manner!"

Debbi next fueled the flames of gossip when she became pregnant and wished to enter a competition for which she needed a current ATR — which she had automatically lost upon pregnancy. She eventually found out that she could apply for a waiver to maintain her Category 1 medical and that allowed her to apply for the position. "Generally I received support from my co-workers who thought I should apply for the job." In October 1985 Debbi was made a supervisor of Operational Requirements in Air Navigations Systems. Now acting director in Central Region, her tact and her ability have won her the admiration and respect of her fellow-workers.

Duluth, Minnesota. Over the Rockies they ran into sleet, snow, and hail and they took a week just to get across. The eastbound flight, on the other hand, took only 34.9 flying hours and was flown entirely over Canadian territory. As neither held an instrument rating, the entire trip was flown VFR (visual flight rules). Flying and navigating were equally shared. "On the final homeward-bound leg we stopped in Prince Edward Island so we could say we had landed in all ten provinces. Journey's end was at St. John's on June 30," said Tina.

After their cross-Canada adventure Susan continued to instruct part-time, the only woman flying instructor in Newfoundland. Now she has a Bachelor of Nursing degree and still flies — mainly search and rescue for the Canadian Forces. She is also part-owner of the Cherokee 180 that made the trans-Canada flight. Tina, now a widow and mother of two children, works for Bristow Helicopters in Scotland in an administrative position.

LILLIAN VARCOE of Vancouver was the first woman pilot to "officially" pilot a plane from coast to coast. "I used to build model aircraft as a child and I wanted to take Shops at

The crew of the trans-Atlantic flight, 1985. From the left, Adele Fogle, Daphne Schiff, and Margo McCutcheon.

A TRANS-ATLANTIC FLIGHT

In 1985, the International Rally Organization organized its first Trans-Atlantic Air Rally, New York to Paris. The rally, a competition to test pilots' flying and navigational skills, attracted seventy aircraft, ranging from single engines to business jets. There were nineteen entries from Canada, one of them crewed entirely by women. Sixty-six aircraft completed the over 4500 mile flight with the Canadian women coming in eleventh out of nineteen Canadian entries. The rally, which got off the ground in New York on June 14th, took nine days and approximately 25 hours flying time with stopovers in Montreal, Frobisher Bay, Greenland, Iceland, and Scotland. At each overnight stop each team was given a brown envelope with maps and instructions for the

school but in those days (early fifties) they wouldn't let a girl do that. What I really wanted to be was an aeronautical engineer." Currently a free-lance writer, Lillian began flying in 1979 and gained a commercial licence and a knowledge of restoration when she and her husband rebuilt their Cessna 180.

In 1983 Lillian heard that no Canadian woman had ever made an official trans-Canada flight, and she made up her mind to do it. As she recalled, "When I got down to the actual planning I was excited but at the same time embarrassed at attempting to make a record of such little consequence. Maybe that same self-conscious embarrassment is a sort of national trait that has prevented other Canadian women from making records. However, in this day and age of women jet pilots and women astronauts I can't help but see the humour of a Canadian woman pilot at the stick of a slow noisy 180 bumping along from lake to lake in an attempt to set a record!"

What made her flight different from Susan and Tina's was that she flew the complete west to east flight herself, with her husband navigating, and made her trip in a float plane — fifty-

next landing. Participants were graded on how well they completed tasks, such as judging fuel consumption and landing at precise times.

The all-female crew from Canada was composed of Adele Fogle, Margo McCutcheon, and Daphne Schiff, flying Margo's twin-engine Beech Baron. All three were experienced pilots with a minimum of a multi-IFR rating. Each had started flying as a hobby,had turned it into an adventure, and had flown light aircraft to the Yukon or the Northwest Territories. They saw the trans-Atlantic flight as another challenge. While each pilot took turns flying, the official work load split as follows: Margo was chief pilot; Adele, a flight instructor and manager of Maple Airport, was co-pilot; and Daphne, holder of a PhD and professor of natural science at York University, was the navigator.

There were a few embarrassing moments, such as when they did not realize their microphone switch was open and all the other pilots were treated to their personal, non-flying conversation. Or when fog forced them to stay overnight in Gothab, Greenland — the men were booked into Gothab's only hotel but the three women were billeted in a residence for transient sailors. Undaunted, they shared the joint showers with the sailors, although not at the same time. Daphne summed up the flight when she said, "A lot of time we were flying by the seat of our pants, and the seats are pretty worn out."

nine years after the first official seaplane flight across Canada. Since Lillian wanted the flight to be official she contacted the Royal Canadian Flying Club Association, which approved and monitored it.

According to Lillian, "The flight was no big deal, it was pretty uneventful. I left Tofino, British Columbia on June 6, 1984 and arrived at Paddy's Pond, Newfoundland on July 23. I had filled up a bottle with a little of the Pacific Ocean and when we arrived in Newfoundland, I emptied it as a symbolic gesture of blending east and west. It was a leisurely crossing with my husband in the right seat. I flew mostly at 500 to 1000 feet AGL [above ground level] using VOR [very high fre-

Deborah McGrath, captain of the GRHS Turbo Commander, 1987.

DEBORAH McGRATH

Born and raised in Corner Brook, Newfoundland and a graduate of Memorial University, St. John's, Deborah is Newfoundland's third professional woman pilot. She began flying in 1982, obtaining her commercial and multi-IFR in 1984 and her ATR in 1987.

Deborah did not go the usual route of building time by instructing. Instead she flew for the Grenfell Regional Health Services (GRHS) in St. Anthony, Newfoundland. She began as a volunteer co-pilot on a Navajo Chieftian; by 1986 she was salaried and flying right seat in the Commander, was captain in a year and later became chief pilot.

Describing her work in the late eighties, Deborah wrote: "We fly an average of six to eight hours per day covering over 1000 nautical miles, doing medivacs and transferring staff. GRHS owns and operates all of the nursing stations along the Labrador coast as far north as Nain. All of the landing strips along the coast are gravel and range in length from 2000 to 2500 feet, so we don't have a lot of room to work with. We also cover the Quebec south shore as far west as Chevery; Goose Bay; and on occasion Wabash and Churchill Falls. We also cover the island of Newfoundland and when the need arises we fly to Halifax, Montreal, Ottawa, or Toronto with special medivacs. We have four pilots in all and work a schedule of two weeks on and two off each month. The working conditions are excellent. I feel I have a situation not a job."

In May 1990 Deborah took a two year leave of absence to sail around the world and in 1992 she decided not to return to GRHS. "It was a terrific job in so many ways," she said, "but I feel it's time to move on and do other things." Deborah is presently delivering aircraft to Europe, Asia, and Africa. "It's equally as challenging as flying the Labrador coast in the Commander."

quency omni range] and ADF [automatic direction finder]. I wanted to see the contour of the land. We flew about four hours a day. The plane was very noisy, very bumpy, and it was very tiring. I tried to have someone sign my logbook at every take-off and landing but I flew over a lot of wilderness area where there was simply no one around. Fuel is only good if it is gurgling in your tank and that was my biggest worry as I was not flying into cities but following a more northerly route. It was a good experience and now you can say that a woman did fly across the country."

THE WOMEN who entered aviation in the seventies and eighties were strikingly similar to the aviatrixes of the earlier period: aggressive go-getters determined to be as educated and qualified as possible. Catherine Fletcher explained it best, "Flying became an obsession and I got that dreadful flying disease — I had to have my commercial licence, then my instructor's, then my multi-IFR, then my ATR." When Catherine, a graduate of McMaster University, began to fly, she was a medical technologist and an officer in the air reserves. "I taught meteorology and aerodynamics to the air cadets and wanted to know more about aviation. I was at the flying club all the time and my husband, who was very supportive, finally suggested that I leave hospital work and concentrate on flying so that I would have only one job and maybe then he might get to see me!"

The women's high energy levels and commitment to becoming as qualified as possible in the shortest possible time were impressive. Gwen Grant's pace was frantic. To pay for her flying she held three part-time jobs, including one on the ferry between the mainland and Vancouver Island. "My hours were wild as I juggled three jobs, university, and flying," she said. Her hard work and long hours paid off; Gwen was among the first five women to be hired as pilots by Air Canada.

Deborah McGrath — from a feature article in the April 1989 issue of The Canadian Aircraft Operator.

The woman who became the first female superintendent with Transport Canada had a more difficult balancing act. Diane Klassen of Winnipeg was married with three children, working towards a Masters degree in Sociology and commuting to Brandon University every Saturday morning where she lectured, when she discovered small planes in the fall of 1974. By the spring of 1975 she had earned not only her degree but a private pilots licence as well and, shortly after, added commercial, instructor's, and multi-IFR ratings. Over the next few years she juggled three part-time jobs, including instructing at a local flight school and lecturing at the University of Winnipeg, studying for her PhD, and trying to cope with three children as a single parent. Recalled Diane, "I was burned out by 1979 and realized that I would have to choose between an academic and flying career. Flying won out and I put all my

Diane Chudley Klassen, one of the first female managers with Transport Canada, c. 1988.

HEATHER WIENS

Heather Wiens of Calgary, Alberta recalled, "I began flying in 1974 because I had nothing better to do and I've never looked back since then." Instructing first with North American Air Training College, in 1978 Heather became a charter pilot with Springbank Aviation of Calgary, advancing to chief training officer and chief pilot. In 1981 Transport Canada hired her as a civil aviation inspector and instrument flight test examiner. Since then she has received a Cessna Citation and DC-3 endorsement and flies as captain on these aircraft. In 1985 she became the senior instrument standards inspector for southern Alberta and is now acting superintendent with Ontario Region.

GLENNA HENDERSON SHARRATT

Glenna Henderson Sharratt of Virden, Manitoba took flying lessons with her father in 1973. "I knew as soon as I began flying that that was what I wanted to do." Glenna qualified for her commercial and instructor's licences and literally walked into a job flying Cessnas 337 and 310 with a construction company in the vicinity. "Only once did I have someone who refused to fly with me because I was a woman. My boss told him — he was an architect — that if he didn't fly with me the company would find another architect!" Next Glenna flew with Perimeter Aviation flying charters and instructing. In 1980 Transport Canada hired her as a civil aviation inspector. Glenna, married with one child, is based in the Pacific Region.

efforts into acquiring my ATR." Diane instructed until May 1981 when Transport Canada hired her for a position in Flight Training Standards in Winnipeg, Manitoba. She is now regional director of the Western Region.

Diane's assertive personality has been known to ruffle some feathers but her qualifications make it hard for the system to overlook her. "Taking this job was a real challenge. There were fifteen years of someone with an autocratic military background, then a year of another person in an 'acting' capacity; then me, a female from out of the region. I never ran into the 'old boys club' until I came here." Diane had the stamina to "tough it out," however and in January 1986 she became the western regional director, Aviation Licencing, in Edmonton, Alberta, the first woman to hold this position.

TERESA O'FLAHERTY

Born in Edmonton, Alberta, Teresa said, "I've always been fascinated with how engines work. I like mechanical things. I'd tell my mom I wanted to be a stewardess but in my dreams I wanted to be a pilot. My dad always said I could be what I wanted to be."

In 1971 Teresa became the first woman to be accepted at Mount Royal College in Calgary for the two year aviation program. There she earned her private, commercial, and multi-IFR. "When I was accepted I made myself a promise that I would be one of the guys. You're with them on a competitive basis; you can't ask someone to open doors and do your walk around for you."

After graduation, Teresa qualified for her instructor's licence and then literally walked into the Calgary Flying Club and began teaching. "I told the club I could get customers for them. I had to convince them that I would be good for them. Then I went to Gina Jordan — I knew she was the best — and got my instrument rating in the fall of 1973."

Soon bored with instructing, Teresa " . . . put on a dress and went in to see Time Air. The chief pilot took me up in the King Air and did a couple of approaches. I was hired in 1974. After that, my father used to introduce me as, 'My daughter, the pilot.' I flew the Twin Otter and the Short. I wore a uniform — in those days, that really made people look at you."

In 1983 Teresa married, left flying and went into the parts department in a farm implement store. "I never left the mechanical field. I just went from aircraft to tractors."

Then there is Kathy Fox who, with her incredible energy, has had a variety of careers in aviation. "As a child I used to climb trees and pretend I was flying a helicopter. By the time I was ten I had made a mock-up of an instrument panel, which I kept in my bedroom and I knew the walk around inspection by heart and used to recite it to myself before falling asleep. I had my first ride when I was thirteen, in a Cessna 172, and I did not spiritually return to earth until several days later. After that I was determined to fly." Her uncle, Norm Bruce, known as the "Grandfather of Gliding in the West" paid for her lessons. Before she received her private licence her family moved to Montreal and her father made her choose between university and flying. Kathy opted for a university degree, reasoning that she could always fly later. Unable to afford flying, she joined the McGill University Skydiving Club, soon becoming its chief instructor. After graduating with a BSc in Mathematics in 1972, she taught school. Already a director for the Quebec Region of the Canadian Sport Parachuting Association, she was soon to make history in this 5000-strong membership by being elected president, the youngest ever and first woman in its twenty-five year history. In 1979 and 1980 she was Canada's representative in the World Championships held in France and China respectively.

MARIE-HELENE SIMARD

"I was hooked on flying at an early age," said Marie-Helene of Montreal, Quebec. Little wonder, since her father had an aviation business and her uncle was a pilot. She obtained a private licence in 1978 and her ATR in 1984.

In the early eighties, she and pilot Kathy Fox teamed up at Clamm Air, Marie-Helene becoming director of operations. Next, in 1982 she and Kathy formed Dynamaire Aviation at St. Jean Airport. Marie-Helene was the president, her husband (also a pilot) the vice-president, and Kathy, the secretary-treasurer. The company provides flying instruction, charter, and maintenance services. In 1992 it won a contract from Canadair to provide military training at the new training centre at Southport, the Portage la Prairie, Manitoba former Canadian Forces base.

In addition to her flying licences and over 5000 hours, she also holds an AME (aircraft maintenance engineer); has been a member of the Air Quebec Transport Association since 1985 and chairperson since 1990 and is also chairperson of the Board of International Aviation Management Institute. Marie-Helene is married with two children.

While her hobby presented an exciting life-style, her job did not. By 1979 Kathy was so bored that she applied for air traffic control (ATC) training. After graduating at the top of her class she spent the next three years in air traffic control in Baie Comeau and Sept Îles, Quebec where there was no skydiving. "Not being able to jump and having the time and the money to take flying lessons, I decided it was time to realize my life-long dream of learning to fly." She no sooner had her private licence when ATC transferred her to St. Hubert, then Canada's busiest airport. Even a hectic workday did not stop her from quickly qualifying for commercial, instructor's, and multi-IFR ratings *and* helping to form the first-ever flying co-operative (Clamm Air) in Quebec.

PATTY ABERSON SIMPSON

Born in Dauphin, Manitoba, Patty grew up in a flying family. "My father was a dairy farmer who began a crop spraying business and we belonged to the Flying Farmers. I received a scholarship from them and put that money towards my advanced training."

Patty received her private and commercial licences in 1974 and began working right away. "I flew a Luscombe 8A with a rotary sprayer. Then I bought a company and did mostly charter work and instructing. They were long days, from 6:00 AM until dark. "

In 1976, with about 1500 hours, she was hired by the Manitoba Government Air Service for fire detection, charter and air ambulance. Based in The Pas she flew the Cessna 337 and the Beaver. Laid off later in the year, she qualified for her instrument rating and was hired by Aero Trades for radar detection in cooperation with the RCMP.

In 1977 she married (another pilot) and was re-hired by the Air Service, this time based in Winnipeg doing charter and aerial photo survey, high level flying. After a second layoff in 1978 she and her husband returned to Dauphin where they became partners with her father in Dauphin Air Service. Since then Patty has had three sons but has managed to remain current. "During the years that the boys were not going to school, I alternated staying at home with them and bringing them to the airport with me. They became good back seat passengers when I was teaching an instructor's rating. I feel very privileged that I was able to continue flying and raise a family at the same time." By 1992 Patty was back on a more regular basis, doing more charter work and instructing as well as running the business and being the designated flight test examiner for the area.

It was about then that Kathy was asked to head up the air traffic control training program at St. Jean (Quebec) Community College. During that period she wrote "Tower Tips" for *Canadian General Aviation News,* returned to university to begin a Masters degree in Business Administration (completed in 1985) and in 1982, with two friends, formed Dynamaire Aviation, an aircraft leasing agency. Two years later they purchased Richel Air and established Dynamaire Enterprise at St. Jean Airport with the aim of being a fixed base operation, offering aircraft maintenance, instructing, and charter services. Kathy is the secretary-treasurer for both companies as well as Clamm Air. (The president and director of operations of Dynamaire is ATR pilot Marie-Helene Simard).

In addition, Kathy is a member of the Montreal Chapter of the 99s and on the Board of Directors of the Chamber of Commerce of St. Jean. She was tower supervisor at Dorval until October, 1989, then a controller at the Montreal Control Centre. In 1992 she was sent to Ottawa on a developmental assignment. As for her personal life, she is single with the explanation that "some day I hope to find someone who can keep up with my pace or who will make me want to slow down to his."

A CHARACTERISTIC common to the women was their perseverance in pursuing their goals. They refused to accept "no" for an answer. CP Air's second woman pilot Kathy Davenport Zokol's actions were not unique. "To make sure that CP Air knew how much I wanted to fly with them I made a point of personally taking in my up-date every eight weeks or so to Flight Ops. I think they hired me to keep me from coming in so often!" Nor was it unusual for the women to "fire off" a hundred or so resumés when job hunting, particularly in the economic slump years of the early eighties. No effort seemed too great for them.

Despite their intensity, most had a delightful and often offbeat sense of humour. To a passenger's blank look at discovering his pilot was a woman and his shocked, "How long have you been flying?" Air BC's Diane Rothberg, having been airborne for a short time, replied, "Oh, about fifteen minutes."

CHAPTER NINE

The helicopter pilots

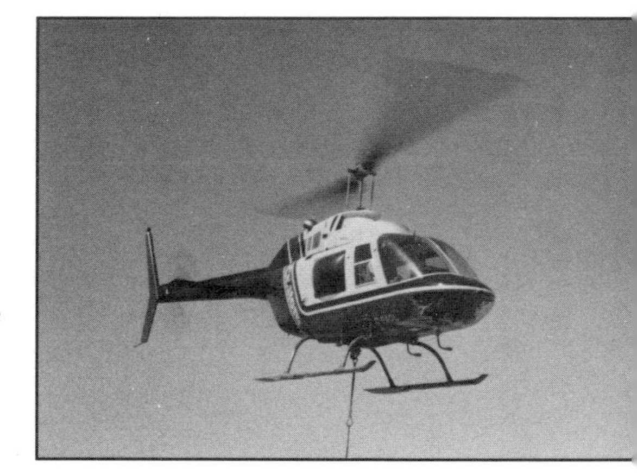

"Don't tell them you're sending a woman pilot, tell them you're sending a good pilot." — *Ruthanne Page*

DAWN DAWSON WANTED TO FLY helicopters. When, in the early fifties, she asked Carl Agar of Okanagan Helicopters about obtaining a helicopter licence he spoke for the aviation industry of the day when he said, "Don't waste your money. I won't hire you because most of the work is in the bush — no place for a lady."

The world of helicopter flying was one of the last masculine strongholds. Chopper pilots were part of a fraternity that jealously guarded its separateness and if their fixed wing counterparts were out in the cold, females were entirely out of the question! Women were so strongly discouraged that it was not until the seventies that there were more than two women flying at any one time. At $100 an hour rotary wing qualifications were a staggering expense and no woman was going to spend that kind of money knowing that no one would hire her.

Okanagan Helicopters (now Canadian Helicopters), incorporated in 1947, pioneered the first Canadian commercial use of helicopters. By 1956 it was the world's largest commercial helicopter operation with thirty-one helicopters and 105 employees. Thirty years later it was still the largest Canadian helicopter company and the third largest in the world.

Okanagan got its break in 1949 with the initial survey work on the Alcan project on the mountainous British Columbia coast. Having demonstrated its value there, it was soon called upon to handle topographical and aerial timber surveys and to provide support to prospectors and geologists. Mountain flying, game counts, fish releases, rig moves, crew shuttles, fire bucketing, cone clipping, logging, and spraying followed. Virtually all these operations were carried on in the bush. Former Okanagan engineer, Keith Rutledge, described the

Publicity shot of Dini Petty and the CKEY traffic helicopter.

DINI PETTY

Dini Petty of Toronto, Ontario was twenty-three when she landed in the world of helicopters. "I knew Gene Kirby, the program producer for CKEY, a Toronto radio station. He thought I would be just the person to pep up CKEY's image. There was a radio war going on and a number of stations had introduced traffic reports from a helicopter. CKEY wanted to steal the show by having a woman fly and broadcast. I was drifting and I thought flying a helicopter would be great. I auditioned and got the job."

CKEY picked up the $11,500 tab for her instruction on a Hughes 269A at Helisolair. "It was a terrific challenge especially when so many of the men kept telling me I would never be able to do it. There were days when I just wanted to quit but I wasn't going to give those guys the satisfaction." Dini received her commercial rotary wing licence in 1968 and from then on, she lived in a world of contrived rosiness as CKEY required her to wear a pink pant suit to match the pink helicopter. "I became known as the 'Pink Lady,' although ATC called me 'Pink Fluff, Pink Tiger,' or the 'Pink Dink!'" An instant hit with the Toronto public, the glamorous Dini's celebrity status expanded into the United States where reporters billed her as the first woman in the world to fly a helicopter and report on traffic. She appeared on TV shows such as "What's My Line" and "To Tell the Truth" and received hundreds of invitations to speak at schools and service clubs. An entertainer at heart, she enjoyed it all. A grateful sponsor even gave her a pink car.

While she handled the publicity with barely a flicker of an eyelash, she admitted that, "the flying was terrifying at first. It was hard trying to do everything at once: being in contact with the tower and the other CKEY helicopter, listening to the radio station so I wouldn't miss my cues and remembering to fly RGQ [the helicopter]. A bad day was

living conditions, "It was tent camps. There was no such thing as rotating crews as they have now. Once you went into a site you stayed until the work was done, even if it took six months."

Canada's first licenced woman helicopter pilot was Marion Orr, hired in the mid-sixties to instruct and demonstrate helicopters. An accident and resulting injury cut short her career flying helicopters. Dini Petty was the second to be licenced and she became famous as the first woman in the world to fly a helicopter as a traffic reporter on radio. In such "safe" areas companies capitalized on the novelty of women pilots and publicized their daring as if they were circus performers. "Real" helicopter flying remained confined to the bush for years. Bush camps spelled men, men whose only view of women for weeks on end were the ones tacked up on the walls. Management viewed women as disruptive and unsuitable in such a setting. For those women who wished to fly in the wilderness, operators told them the same old story — it was not safe for a woman alone in the bush or, worse still, in a camp full of men.

Paul Kristapovich, operations manager at Associated Helicopters (now Canadian Helicopters), explained that as recently as 1976 he would have been reluctant to hire a woman. Since

when the VHF was scratchy, the AM receiver was blaring, I had to fly the bird, watch for other aircraft, keep an eye on the ground traffic situation and my passenger was sick!" She covered metro Toronto weekdays and the freeways weekends, flying four hours a day, six days a week.

Dini dazzled Torontonians for almost four years before putting some of the Ontario aviation community into a tailspin. In 1972 she became pregnant and insisted on flying. "The Department of Transport wanted to ground me. 'What would you do if 'it' moved, they asked me. I told them the same thing that I would do if 'it' moved if I was driving down the parkway — 'nothing.' I said if they wanted to ground me they would have to shoot me down and then I would go to the press. They let me fly. My pregnancy never became a public issue and my passengers always assumed it was okay that I was still flying."

That battle won, she decided to end her flying career. "I resigned when I was eight months pregnant. I knew I didn't want to go back to flying after the baby was born. After 4000 hours I had become bored. Besides, I was really a broadcaster who became a helicopter pilot. I wanted to return to radio or TV." Dini has continued to be a well-known personality, currently hosting a national daily television show called, appropriately, *Dini Petty.*

then changing attitudes have made it easier to be a woman in a camp. As Lois Hill, a pilot in the Yukon, noted, "There were women in other non-traditional roles — geologists, diamond drillers — appearing in the bush." For their part, the women fortunate enough to get a flying job took without complaint whatever accommodation was provided, even if that meant a bunkhouse full of men.

In Quebec the James Bay project opened the door to women. "For the first time there were female cooks, truck drivers, geologists, and pilots," explained Mary Ellen Pauli, one of the first women to fly helicopters in northern Quebec. But, she added, "I've often stayed in camps where I was the only woman. There were never any separate accommodations for me. I've lived in tents, trailers and barracks."

Everyone but the women themselves thought there were problems. "We hired Ruthanne Page during the boom," said Paul Kristapovich, "when we had enough locations and a variety of jobs that a woman could fit into. We channelled her to those jobs with better accommodations. She lived in a tent camp at Baker Lake in the Northwest Territories and that was not too much of a problem. However . . . it can be difficult to put up extra accommodations; it's a monetary problem . . . a woman may not fit in because of the location . . . if she's small, handling fuel drums may be a problem." Kristapovich also explained, "I had a bigger problem with our male pilots

COLETTE LARIVIÈRE

Colette LaRivière of St. Roch, Quebec was the first French Canadian woman to receive a rotary wing licence. She wanted to be a bush pilot. "I chose helicopters instead of fixed wing because I knew bush operators would think I wasn't strong enough to do the work. With a helicopter it's different, it does the work." To learn English and earn enough money to take her instruction she moved to Ontario. In 1969, she began her training. "I found it hard going. My English was not as good as I thought. I found the textbooks very hard to understand and I couldn't really talk to the others." Finding a job was even more difficult. "I wrote to every helicopter company in Canada and received replies from less than half, all 'no.'"

Finally Trans-Quebec Helicopters hired her to fly a Bell 47G-2 on the James Bay project. Colette was based in Matagami, about 550 miles north of Montreal. "It was the last town before the bush. They only let me fly VIPs around

accepting her. In the IFR world there's *crewing* — captain and co-pilot — and some captains didn't want to accept a woman in the cockpit. Ruthanne, being a very strong individual, was fairly outspoken. The men didn't want to listen to a woman and they weren't used to having their authority questioned."

Customers also expressed concern. "I remember my boss forgot to tell the client that the pilot would be a woman," recalled Candace Wilson. "When I took my helmet off the customer almost fainted!" Suzanne Pomerleau was lucky; her boss was behind her. "At Baie James, the contractor didn't want a woman pilot and I was afraid my boss wouldn't let me go. I said, 'Sir, what time do I leave?' And he let me go. When I got there, they had to keep me because it was 2000 miles back home." Ruthanne Page's stock answer to an employer who was hesitant about hiring her because of customer reaction, was, "Don't tell them you're sending a woman pilot, tell them you're sending a good pilot."

For the first women helicopter pilots being hired did not mean being accepted. Dini Petty, whose job was to wear a pink flying outfit and fly a pink helicopter to report on traffic conditions in Toronto for a local radio station, recalled, "There were days when everything seemed to go wrong and the men would give me that 'I told you so' business. They were just looking for me to goof." And Ruthanne Page remembered, "When I began flying I got all the assignments that the men

and only short distances. They did not let me fly into the bush camps or to James Bay. They told me that some of the men had been in the bush for weeks or months and they thought it would be unsafe for me." A stocky woman with a no-nonsense manner, Colette was well-equipped to handle any over-amorous man, but Trans-Quebec took no chances. "They liked the idea of having a woman pilot. It was good PR for them. But I got bored sitting around waiting for 'safe flights' and I quit in June 1972."

Her limited experience made it difficult for her to find another job. A year passed before she found work with Trans-Canada Helicopters, flying a Hughes 269 on aerial photography. "The pay was poor and I could not make enough money to save anything. I couldn't find another job and it seemed as if everyone had the idea that women should not fly, so I finally left flying." Colette, continuing a non-traditional path, became a taxi driver and now owns her own taxi company.

didn't want but slowly, as I proved myself, I was given better jobs. Every lady in non-traditional jobs has had rough times for sure. So far I have found that the best policy when the unfairness or mean-heartedness or just plain unethical business dealings catch up to you, as they do occasionally, is to rage and scream and hurt for a while and then move on. Moving on — changing and growing — is very hard to do (and expensive) but when something absolutely has to change and the other side is firmly frozen in the ice age, it might as well be you." As Paul Kristapovich admitted, "What it comes down to is that the woman still has to work a lot harder in this industry than a man."

Diane Pepper, c. 1978.

DIANE PEPPER

Diane Pepper of Toronto followed Dini Petty into the seat of the CKEY helicopter. A model and fashion show commentator, she had never thought of flying until the radio station approached her. "A CKEY official heard my voice and thought I should be the next helicopter traffic reporter. I was hired on my voice quality alone," recalled Diane. She flew a Hughes 269A, a Hughes 500 (a jet) and then earned a fixed wing licence (at CKEY's request) and flew a Cessna 172. "It was a gift to learn to fly."

Diane left CKEY in 1980 to fly a Bell 212 for Toronto's Helicopter Air Ambulance. The helicopter, known as "Bandage One," operated from Toronto/Buttonville Airport. The crew, which consisted of pilot, co-pilot, and two paramedics, were on call twenty-four hours a day.

With Bandage One Diane ran into her first taste of prejudice against women pilots. "Until then all my instructors and co-workers had been supportive, but I found that there were still men around that felt women should either be in bed or in the kitchen, certainly not in a cockpit."

The worst thing about the job however was boredom. "My shift was from noon to midnight at the heliport. When no calls come through — twelve hours of television, washing cars, reading, or chatter could get to you." Diane left Bandage One after a year and, unable to find another job, left flying altogether. "I was tired of making a low salary, tired of the constant 'testing,' tired of smelling of jet fuel, and tired of proving that I was a good pilot. I loved flying but after almost nine years the hassles that went with it were not worth it."

Diane now works happily in real estate.

Despite employers being gencrally pleased with the job the women did, by 1988 there were less than thirty women flying helicopters compared to over two thousand men. The recession of the early eighties partly explained this, but the conditions under which most pilots worked were probably the main reasons why few women chose this career. In 1992 there were only fifty-one women with commercial helicopter licences compared to 2136 men. (See table, page 225.)

EXCEPT FOR URBAN or government work, helicopter flying is usually seasonal seven days a week at a remote location. Summer is generally the high season, except in the northern swampy "oil patch" where most of the work is done when the ground is frozen. This type of flying tends to attract people who love the outdoors and are independent and flexible regarding working conditions and scheduling. The pilot may be away six weeks at a time, usually on the move, often from one tent camp to another, with a lot of sitting around between. "You fly for a few hours and sit for a couple of days, waiting to move the crew and equipment to the next site. For a productive person, camp life can be boring," remarked Gera Megelink. It can be physically tiring too, as Candace Wilson reported. "When I was flying wildlife surveys it was eight to nine hours flying a day with only ten minute breaks throughout the day. The Robinson shudders and shakes and at the end of the day I was gone. I'd go straight to bed. It's a damn hard job."

Compared to fixed wing flying, helicopter flying can be a high-risk business and the pilot is constantly under pressure. A pilot may make twenty to forty landings a day, often in tight spots in marginal weather. Gera explained, "There are many elements to cope with. You must be watchful about weeds getting into the rotor. You're always trying to get into places not otherwise accessible and you're always thinking, 'Can I land there?' There can be many tense moments when doing high altitude landings and take-offs or when fighting forest fires, because the helicopter is usually loaded to capacity, and flying in turbulence or smoke can add to an already stressful situation." Suzanne Pomerleau agreed, "A helicopter becomes vulnerable near the ground. We work as tractors; it's not really flying, it's 'tractor working.' Most of the accidents happen when you're low and there is no way to land safely. You don't have the time."

Flying in the mountains may cause the adrenaline to flow, particularly if landing on a little platform of logs on the side of a mountain. Platform landing is a risky business and much depends upon understanding how aircraft performance is affected by changing combinations of wind, load, altitude, and temperature. Mountain flying can be almost psychological in that the pilot must be able to *sense* what is going to happen; the pilot and mountain must be in communication with each other.

"You must always be thinking," explained Ruthanne Page, as she described dropping geologists onto the side of a mountain. "The interesting part happens when you try to pick up these same people later. If it's a hot day the effective altitude may well be over 10,000 feet. There is a very good chance, if you are heavy with fuel, that 100 percent power may not be enough to hover and the darned thing won't even get off the ground. Or maybe it would but they don't tell you they loaded 200 pounds of rocks 'geological samples, my dear' in the baggage compartment. The situation is easy to fix, of course. You just get one person to wait until the next round — if you are not running out of daylight, gas, and weather."

Ruthanne elaborated, "The problem arises when you take off at lower altitude and have to land a heavy load up higher. If there happens to be any wind up on the top of the mountain or, heaven forbid, you figured it wrong and it is a 5 mph

SHARON ANN EWENS

Sharon Ann Ewens of Winnipeg, Manitoba is a pilot whose story is typical of those women who could not make a go of it. She grew up listening to stories about bush pilots from her father, a forest ranger. "I was intrigued with their exploits," recalled Sharon Ann, but travel and study beckoned. She completed a Bachelor of Arts degree in Classics in 1972 from the British School of Archaeology and worked for the Department of External Affairs in Saudia Arabia.

"However when I returned to Canada in the late seventies, the memory of my father's tales overcame my common sense and I decided to take helicopter lessons. I sold everything I had to pay for my lessons, which were $10,000. Falcon Helicopters was happy to have a woman pilot and after they trained me they hired me to demonstrate the Hughes 300." Unfortunately she was soon laid off and in the recession had difficulty finding another job. "I got a lot of negative comments, like 'women are not capable of being

tailwind — you will suddenly be faced with two options. One, falling out of the sky from five feet, which is good for bending skids, chopping off tail booms when the blades flex down in the crash, possibly bouncing and rolling over — which may be down the mountain, or two, pulling 110, 120, or 150 percent power, which will probably overtemp and kill your nice little $80,000 engine. Either one of these will leave you stranded on the mountain, until the cook remembers you didn't come home and calls someone to start a search."

Then there is slinging a load. Anything too big or awkward to fit inside a helicopter can be carried externally on a specially installed hook attached to a lanyard. This is usually a two to three hundred foot steel cable with a spring-loaded hook on one end and a steel ring on the other. "Slinging is potentially dangerous. It requires good judgment on the part of the pilot. It depends on the load and your crew. If they don't give you the right length of rope, the proper weight, or the load is too heavy for the aircraft, then you can be in trouble," explained Suzanne Pomerleau. After the load is delivered the pilot releases the lanyard and, as Ruthanne Page remarked, "it's important not to drop that steel on anybody's head!"

Women helicopter pilots have handled every conceivable job: traffic watch, highway patrol, air ambulance, pipeline patrol, forestry work, fire fighting, instructing, flying off oil rigs

pilots.'" She finally found work with Jeffco Aviation in Swan Hills, Alberta flying a Hughes 500.

When that company went bankrupt she searched unsuccessfully for another flying job. Forced to admit defeat she became a dispatcher with the Winnipeg Police Department until a job offer in 1982 in Hawaii lured her back into aviation. "I packed up again and headed for what I thought was going to be a dream job flying off a helipad on Waikiki Beach. Instead I found a company operating on a shoestring with little regard for safety. Even though much of our flying was over water, we had no floats or life jackets. There was no mechanic on staff and the maintenance was incredibly poor. There were so many engine problems that I lost confidence in the machine. I scared myself so many times that I decided to leave, even though I knew I probably couldn't find another job."

She was right. She ended up returning to the Winnipeg Police Department, where she intends to stay. But, she added, "I don't regret a moment or dollar that I spent on flying!"

in the Atlantic Ocean, and even doubling for movie stars. They have also hauled everything imaginable — from executives to structural steel.

Understandably being constantly on the move or away for weeks at a time makes it difficult for these woman to maintain friendships or even consider marriage and children. Although some women are married, for at least one, the hours away from home aggravated an already weak marriage and it eventually dissolved. With physically brutal working conditions and the social atmosphere of a pool hall, people may wonder why any woman would want to become a helicopter pilot. "It's so diversified and challenging," explained Suzanne Pomerleau, and Ruthanne Page agreed, "It's the continuous challenge of take-offs and landings, of slinging a load expertly, and working in less than ideal conditions. There is also the

MICHELE RIVEST

Michele Rivest of Rimouski, Quebec often accompanied her bush-pilot father. "I always kept in mind the beautiful sensation of flying over the earth. I always enjoyed operating any kind of machine and I used to tell people I would be a bush pilot when I grew up." Michele began her instruction in 1975 and within two years had completed her private, commercial, and instructor's licences at Wondel Aviation where she also worked as a line boy to help cover costs. She had logged about 1000 hours instructing when Helicraft at St. Hubert Airport offered to train her on helicopters if she would instruct for them. She agreed because she saw it as her chance to get into bush flying.

Barely five feet tall, Michele discovered that bush operators laughed at her when she applied for a job. She knew she stood a better chance flying in the bush if she were flying a helicopter where size and strength were not as critical. In late 1978 she obtained her commercial helicopter and instructor's licences and put in two years of instructing before she got a job in the bush with La Verendre Helicopters. Based in St. Clet, she flew a Hughes 300, 500, a Bell 206B, and an Enstrom. Michele initially ran into resistance from clients who would take one look at her and decide she couldn't be competent. "My boss backed me. He would say, 'Take her, I'm not giving you a male pilot.'"

Laid off in 1984 Michele went to work for Trans-Quebec Helicopters briefly until she was again laid off. She now teaches aircraft maintenance at Ecole Nationale D' Aerotechnique in Quebec. Michele has about 3000 hours; she retains her licences but does not fly.

enjoyment of meeting people who may smell of chain saw oil or carry a briefcase." And Lois Hill said, "I'm living where I want to, in the North, and doing what I love best, flying."

The early nineties are not promising for women helicopter pilots. With a surplus of highly qualified men, mixed opinions about women helicopter pilots still surface readily. As late as 1986 Georges Delaney, senior vice-president of Viking Helicopters of St. Clet, Quebec, said that while the two women pilots hired by Viking were "excellent on the technical side of flying, physical strength was definitely a problem in that we could not readily send them up on jobs where they had to refuel out of 45 gallon drums." And he also commented on sleeping accommodations, restrooms, and showers at bush camps "where all of the facilities have been planned for a total male camp" and the fact that "in certain cases, clients have shown a certain apprehension when a lady pilot arrived to perform services for them. I suppose some day this 'mental barrier' will be eliminated." Paul Kristapovich also heard comments such as "she may fly as well as a man but may not stay on the job as long because her interests may turn to marriage and children after she has conquered the challenge of flying."

On the whole women helicopter pilots were less successful in establishing a foothold than their fixed wing counterparts. Some, like Darlene Tripp-Simms, Gina St. Germaine, Valdine Berscheid, and Martine Germain earned licences but never found work. Valdine Berscheid of Winnipeg, licenced in 1979, explained what happened to her. "I moved to Calgary where I had received a tentative job offer but kept getting 'put-off' until they finally told me I wasn't needed. I would make the rounds every day, hoping that someone would need me. No one would say 'no' but they wouldn't say 'yes.' I was told that the only way to break into the industry was to find a real estate company which had a helicopter to take its customers out to sites — they might want a pretty pilot in a cute outfit. The whole year was a write-off. The next year Shirley Helicopters of Edmonton folded and that put many high-time pilots on the market. I knew then I would never get a job." Surprisingly, Valdine was not bitter. "From a business and practical point of view I can understand why they would want to go with a sure thing — a male pilot. Many of the companies did not want the hassles of hiring a female."

Others, such as Phurn Ball, Johanne Cosette, Sharon Ann

Ewens, Mary Garland, Susan McFarland, Michele Rivest, Kathy Stewart, Pat Vos, and Candace Wilson, while licenced, could not count on regular work.

The most successful women helicoper pilots, in terms of length of career, are Ruthanne Page, Lois Hill, Suzanne Pomerleau, Mary Ellen Pauli, and Mireille Samson.

RUTHANNE PAGE graduated in 1968 from the three-year electronic diploma course at the Northern Alberta Institute of Technology (NAIT), then she and her husband, also an electronics technician, set up an avionics shop at Calgary International Airport. "I did a lot of work for The Copter Shop:

L *Mireille Samson, helicopter stunt pilot, with Amy Madigan on the set of* Nowhere to Hide, *1987.*

R *Mireille at work with the Canadian Coast Guard, c. 1988.*

MIREILLE SAMSON

Mireille Samson, a registered nurse, entered aviation through sky diving in 1981. "I was a member of the Para Commando Sky Diving Club at St. Jean sur le Richilieu and a member of *Les Albatros,* a skydiving exhibition team. Her fascination with all things aviation led her to qualify for her commercial fixed and rotary wing licences (1983-84). Although she worked only briefly for Trans-Quebec and Trans-Canada Helicopters it was enough to qualify her for yet another career: stunt pilot for the movies. Films such as the 1987 *Nowhere to Hide,* in which she doubled for the female star, Amy Madigan, doing car chases in the helicopter and a simulated crash, seem to promise her a future in the movies.

maintenance and overhaul work on the Alouette II, III, Bell 206, Sikorsky-58, and Jet Ranger. I got lots of chances to go flying but I was a terrible passenger — too nervous. I decided to take lessons to overcome my fear and I ended up falling in love with flying." Ruthanne received her private licence in 1969 but did not proceed further until 1973, when she and her husband were divorced. Footloose and restless, she turned to flying and, within the year, obtained a commercial licence and instrument rating. However, flying for a living did not enter her mind until 1975 when a helicopter operator, who she was always helping, suggested she obtain her rotary wing licence. "Why not, I thought, besides, I liked the smell of the red hydraulic fluid."

Qualifying was relatively easy but finding a job was not. In her favour, however, was the fact that she was well known and could do her own maintenance. "I got my first job with Keen Industries because I had done some avionics work for them. It was just a summer job but with no experience, I couldn't be too fussy." Based at Fort Nelson, British Columbia, she flew and maintained a Bell Super G2 on the Dempster Highway construction project. "I lived in a hundred-man camp: the only woman. Most of the guys were as sweet as pie."

Her mechanical ability next got her a job with Northern Mountain Helicopter in Prince George, BC, flying Bell 47s and

In May 1988, Mireille became the first woman to fly helicopters with the Canadian Coast Guard. Her tasks include flying off an ice-breaker in the winter, doing ice patrols, escorting ships that take food to small villages, taking crews around the Arctic to do maintenance on all navaids, flying research geologists and all their equipment into the North, and occasional search and rescue or medical evacuation flights.

Married to a pilot, Mireille has about 3700 hours on helicopters — Bell Jet Ranger, Long Ranger, 212, and BO-105 — and is still doing stunt-pilot work for the film industry.

Ruthanne Page, Canada's most experienced helicopter pilot.

Jet Rangers. "With this job I became totally familiar with diamond drilling, geological exploration, and all aspects of the logging and lumber industry and became adept at 'slinging.' I also did all my own maintenance work." Next came a stint with Ed Darvill Copters at Grande Prairie, Alberta where she logged over 700 hours on SA 341 Gazelles and again did her own maintenance. "That was a seismic contract; I became very good with a long lanyard and learned about flying in -60°F."

Her break came in 1978 when she began working with Associated Helicopters of Edmonton. "When I started the Grande Prairie base I had no customers and only one helicopter. I expanded the operation into a rented hangar and then

Typical landing sites for a helicopter pilot.

CANDACE WILSON

Candace Wilson of Toronto, Ontario was a university student and had worked as a wine-taster in France when the idea of flying occurred to her. "It came to me out of the blue. I started on fixed wing but soon switched to rotary wing." She received her commercial helicopter licence in 1981 on a Robinson R-22 and — after some searching — found a job with a company in British Columbia flying forest fire patrol.

"The company consisted of one man with a couple of pilots. There was no maintenance in the field and no engineer on staff. They were a pretty carefree bunch — like using shoelaces to tie things together or strapping five gallons of fuel to the skids! I did three trips like that and

doubled business again and moved into a permanent hangar all within the year. The base did 1000 hours of flying, 600 of them mine." Constantly trying to overcome the perceived disadvantages of women pilots, Ruthanne was careful never to turn down an assignment. Consequently, she held the highest time at Associated Helicopters for mountain flying in 1984 and, in her words, "routinely had the highest time away from home in most of the companies I have worked for because I always made myself available for a job."

By 1986 Ruthanne appeared to have done it all. "I start out every year thinking that I've slung everything that could ever be hung under a helicopter, carried every last imaginable item, living or dead or half alive that could ever be stuffed into a helicopter only to prove myself wrong with some new challenge. I've become totally familiar with all aspects of the oil industry from legal surveying to trucking, drilling, testing, fracturing (lots of medevacs), production, and land reclamation. I've done thousands of miles of pipeline patrol, troubleshooting, and construction work. I've lived in tiny tents or trailors for months on end, in rig camps, logging camps, diamond drill camps, and seismic camps. I've dealt with smelly geologists, fire fighters, drunks, and a terrific number of really

when I complained I was told that since it was holding together 'we'll leave it!' I was appalled. I found the stress very severe, especially in bad weather. I was so terrified of the equipment that I finally quit. I decided I'd rather live!"

Back in Ontario with Ranger Lake Helicopters, Candace flew ferry trips to the States on the Robinson R-22. "One ferry trip took 26 hours flying time; it was across the desert and over the mountains at 11,000 feet — I was just skimming over the peaks. Other times I was flying only five feet off the ground. I had an engineer with me for the first part of the trip but we had engine problems right off and back we went to the factory. He went home on a commercial airline — he had bitten his fingers down to the quick, he was so worried about flying with a woman!"

Candace sent out resumés across the country but received only a few replies. Being a woman finally worked to her advantage for she was hired in a marketing role. As she explained, "I got to see anyone I wanted. 'Send her in,' they'd tell the secretary; they were curious to see me." Her last job was helping set up the heliport at Toronto International Airport before she finally packed it in as a helicopter pilot and set herself up in business in a different line of work.

great customers in every business. That's half the fun — meeting a diverse clientele from old skinners to PhDs."

In 1986 she added flying IFR off-shore on an oil rig to her list of accomplishments when Sealand Helicopters (now Canadian Helicopters) of St. John's, Newfoundland hired her to fly a Super Puma and, as she said then, "Sealand is a world class operator in the offshore business and I consider this job the best ever." The flying was unlike anything she had done before. Ocean survival and rig firefighting courses were a part of her training. "Everyone including the pilots wear 'immersion suits' to prevent instant hypothermia in the event of emergency ditchings. Life expectancy in the water is less than five minutes. Picture yourself in a one piece skidoo suit with the boots bonded on and a hood and wrists made of heavy, diver's suit-type rubber. We usually roll the hoods down on our shoulders and undo the big zipper as much as possible but in the sunny

GERA MEGELINK

Gera Megelink, born in Holland and raised in Toronto, was a 1977 Bachelor of Arts graduate in linguistics and psychology with no job when she moved out west to become a camp cook in the Northwest Territories. "It was there that I discovered helicopters and life in the bush. I decided that I wanted to do something totally different than I had ever done and chose flying a helicopter." Her interest had initially been sparked by her friendship with Darlene Tripp, a helicopter pilot turned fixed wing pilot; but it was her summer in the wilderness around helicopters that was the catalyst for her obtaining her licence.

By 1979 she had obtained her commercial and Class 1 IFR licences in helicopters at a cost of $20,000. "Kenting Helicopters [of Edmonton] hired me to fly a Jet Ranger 206 and a Bell 412 Twinstar out of Coppermine, Northwest Territories. I flew men and equipment into geology camps and oil rigs, flew pipe line control, and did forestry work. Fire fighting usually meant a ten hour day."

A big problem with contract flying was boredom. "There is a lot of sitting around in camps, waiting to move crews or parts to another site." Laid off by Kenting in 1983, and married with a baby by that time, she intended to return to flying once the slump was over. Asked why, in view of the conditions and the stress, Gera replied, "It's the flying, the challenge, that makes it all worthwhile. Helicopter flying is a high-risk job. You go into the mountains where there are many elements to cope with. You're constantly under pressure. But I like it."

cockpits they are horrendously hot in summer. Now I know how a baby feels when you take off a dripping wet diaper!"

Reflecting on her position in 1986 she said, "It took me fourteen years to get this far. There wasn't a moment or a breath or a trip in that whole time that was not done in the hopes of getting into a Puma for real. Now that I'm here I realize it isn't the end of the road. I don't know where the end of the road is anymore but it is awfully interesting and I hope to stay on it for as long as possible."

Ruthanne left Sealand in late 1988 to return to flying in western Canada. Working on a firefighting contract in 1991, she spent a "quiet" summer at Sioux Lookout — 200 hours on a Bell 205 — for the Ontario Ministry of Natural Resources.

LOIS HILL qualified for her fixed wing private licence in 1972. In 1978 she decided to combine flying with her love of the outdoors by becoming a helicopter pilot. She first obtained a fixed wing commercial licence and then a commercial helicopter rating, followed by a twenty-five hour mountain flying course and a field maintenance course on the Allison 250 C20B (the most common turbine engine installed on light helicopters). "I then wrote to every helicopter company in western Canada, about fifty in all. I received thirteen answers, twelve of them negative; the thirteenth offered me a job."

Having both fixed and rotary wing licences was an advantage because Terr Air at Ross River in the Yukon hired her to fly a Hughes 500D and a Cessna 206. "Our main business was

Lois Hill.

JILL PEMBERTON, DELORES GREENLAW AND SUSAN COLBERT

Helijet, a company which claims to be one of only two scheduled airline companies in the world using rotary wing aircraft, was established in 1986 and operates between Vancouver and Victoria in British Columbia. The firm has twenty-seven pilots, including Jill, Delores, and Susan, and five Sikorsky 76s, twin-engine state-of-the-art helicopters. Delores Greenlaw and Susan Colbert began as dispatchers with Helijet and worked their way into flying positions. Jill Pemberton, formerly with Canadian Helicopters and the most experienced of the women pilots, had over 2000 hours, earned mainly in the bush, when Helijet hired her in the late eighties. Although likely to be promoted to captain, according to chief pilot Gordon Jones, Jill left Helijet in mid-1992 to fly for KLM Airlines.

servicing the mining exploration companies. The job was seasonal, from April to September, and we had to take advantage of the good weather. We were on call twenty-four hours a day, seven days a week, and we had to be ready to go on a few minutes notice." Next she worked for Yukon Airways, again flying as a helicopter and fixed wing pilot, this time out of Whitehorse, Yukon. "This job took me all over BC and the Yukon and often I was away for weeks at a time. I lived at base camps or in tent camps pitched wherever the crews were going."

In 1980 Lois joined Okanagan Helicopters. "I wore a uniform, a man's uniform; only the tie fit." In 1985 Okanagan made her base manager at Norman Wells, one of the busiest in the company and for the past seven years she has worked " . . . seven days a week. It's oil patch. It's pretty exciting. My employers have always backed me one hundred percent. The funniest memories are probably the odd startled reaction by customers when they realize I'm the pilot as well as the 'coffee girl.'"

Suzanne Pomerleau, in Hydro Quebec helicopter, 1982.

Lois Hill is one of those fortunate people with complete job satisfaction. As she said, "I'm living where I want to, in the north, and doing what I want to, flying." A 1986 letter to the author illustrates this point: "Right now I'm sitting on top of a mountain twenty miles from Norman Wells at a Northwestel microwave site while a technician fixes our phones. I wish you could see the scene in front of me. I am parked above timberline on a fifty-mile long ridge which runs parallel to the Mackenzie River just north of town. So the river is stretched out in front of me, ice bound of course with five foot thick ice, and forty miles to the south the Mackenzie Mountains loom large. It is beautiful country. Flying is the *only* way to see it, as there are no roads . . . P.S. — PWA's 737 just flew by on its approach, at eyeball level from our perch on this ridge. Wish I'd had my camera. They didn't even have gear down yet, so were scooting right along. It looked great in the sunshine!" In 1992, after twenty years of nearly continuous flying, Lois is leaving aviation for other interests. She retires as one of Canada's most qualified and respected helicopter pilots.

SUZANNE POMERLEAU and her father took their private licences together. Suzanne then entered the aviation program at Le Collège General Enseignement et Professionel with the intention of becoming an airline pilot. After graduating in 1975 she worked for her father's company, Amos Aviation, and developed a taste for bush flying. "I liked the freedom and the non-regulated way of life and the idea of being in close contact with the passengers." A year later she discovered helicopters and decided that flying choppers was what she really wanted. "You live with your customers, you sleep and eat with them. You're a team. They can't do their job without you and you have no purpose without them."

Mary Ellen Pauli, helicopter pilot for Ontario Ministry of Natural Resources, Lake Superior, c. 1987.

Suzanne summed up her experiences by saying, "I never really had a problem. It's a question of people, personality, and circumstances. If someone said 'a girl!' I just ignored it. If your boss is behind you, then no problem." She had no qualms about accommodations. "In the camps you share the same bathroom. When they can provide it, you have a room to yourself. I found that the men take care of you and they take care of their manners. Some camps were designed for three hundred people; Hydro Quebec had permanent camps with mobile houses, usually one house for twelve people. In a small town you had to share a room with the men." Suzanne, an attractive woman with an easy charm, made it sound like the most natural thing in the world for her to have attained her position and her acceptance into a traditionally male environment.

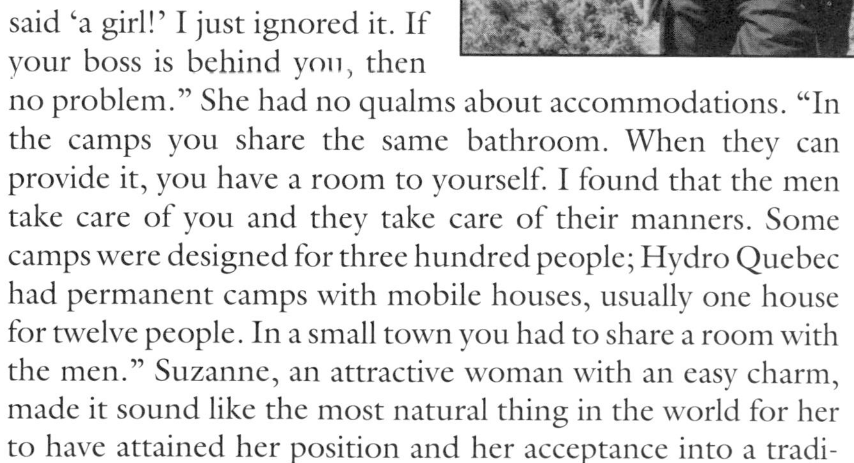

In 1984, having logged about 5000 hours, she traded life in the bush for the position of air carrier inspector, Helicopters, with Transport Canada. In the late eighties Suzanne left Transport Canada and now flies part time.

MARY ELLEN PAULI was raised in Matagami, Quebec. "I always wanted to fly. My father was base manager at Matagami for Fecteau Air Services. We lived right at the base. I knew what a bush pilot's life was all about and I also knew what it was like to live on the edge of civilization, because Matagami was the last town before the Baie James project. I wanted bush flying but not on a fixed wing. Flying a Beaver would have been hard work. I liked the idea of VFR flying on a chopper." And, as she remarked, "I did not want to become an Air Canada jockey. I enjoy the outdoors and the freedom that bush flying offers."

Mary Ellen flew first with Transport-Canada Helicopters and started in 1979 with Trans-Quebec Helicopters, becoming base manager of the Timmins operation. "I've hauled men and equipment for the Baie James project, fought forest fires, done power line patrols, and have carried or slung almost everything that can go on the hook of a helicopter. Most of my flying was into isolated areas and I've often stayed in camps where I was the only woman." Her husband, a geologist, is very supportive.

About flying, Mary Ellen said, "A white-out condition is one of the trickiest. If I'm flying a survey in hilly country, I'm going from one spot to the next and it's difficult if there are no trees. You need points of reference. We tend to push bad weather because we know we can stop and hover on a tree — we go from tree to tree but it's easy to get a skid caught."

Mary Ellen next went to work with the Ontario Ministry of Natural Resources. Grounded through two pregnancies by the Minister of Transport with the explanation that a rotary wing pilot has more stress on the job than a fixed wing pilot (her second child was expected in August 1992) she will return to work part-time — four days every two weeks. "I have the best of both worlds," she said. "I have encountered some discrimination as a flying mother as opposed to when I was a single woman or married with no children, and some of the older pilots still think that no woman can fly a CL-215, that it's a 'man's plane.'" There are approximately sixty pilots with the Ministry. Mary Ellen, with approximately 4500 hours, is the only woman pilot on staff.

CHAPTER TEN

Four stripes on the sleeve

"In 1973 I enrolled at the Brampton Flying Club and told them I wanted to be an airline pilot. They laughed at me! I ignored their advice not to waste my time taking lessons. Even before I earned a private pilot's licence I told Air Canada my intentions and I regularly kept them posted on my progress until I was hired. Sometimes I think they hired me to get rid of me. I wrote them every few months." — *Britt Ferst Irving.*

THE PRECEDENT for hiring women to fly the big jets was set in 1973 when Transair hired Rosella Bjornson. For five years she toughed it out as the only woman among 2800 male Canadian airline pilots. In 1978 Air Canada hired its first woman pilot, quickly followed by Nordair, with CP Air trailing a year later. While airlines officials insisted that nothing prompted them to take this "revolutionary" step, one retired Air Canada pilot, Captain René Giguere, called a spade a spade. "Politics forced Air Canada to hire girls." Nordair and CP Air sidestepped the issue by saying that until the late seventies no qualified woman had ever applied. Whatever the airlines' stated reasons, the hiring of the first women pilots coincided with the women's liberation movement and the employment boom of the late seventies. As Judy Cameron, Air Canada's first woman pilot, diplomatically explained, "In 1978 Air Canada was seriously considering women and within two years they hired over 500 pilots, five of them women. Essentially they hired all of the qualified women who applied."

The attitude of the airlines remained cautious, however, as airline hopeful Barb Warwashawski Kahl discovered. "I was told by CP that I had met all the requirements and would be on the next course *if* the woman they just hired proved satisfactory. That really made me mad." As she observed, that never would have been said to a male applicant.

In the seventies there were seven major and/or regional airlines: Air Canada, CP Air, Transair, Pacific Western Airlines, Eastern Provincial Airlines, Quebecair, Nordair, and a charter company, Wardair. Most of their pilots were recruited from the bush or the military and thus perpetuated the exclusivity of male pilots. With the exception of Transair, the catalysts for change were the Royal Commission on the Status of Women and the Human Rights Act.

In 1978 Canada's national carrier, Air Canada, realized it had to reassess its hiring practices. In its forty-one year history the airline had survived quite nicely without women pilots and it did not rush into changing its policy without first investigating possible problem areas. With approximately $1.5 million invested in training and maintaining each pilot over an average career span, Air Canada was not going to make any hasty decision. Keith Sanderson, director of flight operations, contacted then-Colonel Wendy Clay, M.D. of the Canadian Forces for information on absenteeism due to menstruation. Wendy Clay, now a brigadier general, an aviation medical specialist, and a pilot trained to wings standards, replied that "early motivation and early conditioning influences were probably quintessential influences on the successful career women's reaction to menstrual distress." Sanderson next asked pilot applicant Gwen Grant to take a 727 simulator ride. "Gwen gave a highly satisfactory simulator performance," reported Sanderson. Air Canada then gave two women applicants the Helix Screening Psychiatric tests. Its next step was to send a questionnaire to fifteen carriers in North America and Europe who had either hired women or who might hire women as pilots, asking about absenteeism, crew integration, motherhood (possible conflict with job), and marketing considerations (passenger reaction). The responses were all the same:

women pilots were not so different from the men. With these encouraging replies, Air Canada decided to hire women pilots. The die was cast.

Between 1978 and 1980 Air Canada received 1728 applications, twenty from women. Some 500 pilots were hired in this period, five of them women: Judy Cameron, Gwen Grant, Britt Ferst Irving, Glenys Olstad Robison, and Barbara Swyers. In the same time period, Nordair hired Stefanie Crampton and three years later added France Gravel and Lucie Chapdelaine to its crew. CP Air also took the plunge, hiring Sandra Lloyd in 1979 and Kathy Davenport Zokol in 1981. Wardair remained the only holdout. Rosella Bjornson was the only woman with Pacific Western Airlines, inherited in the take-over of Transair. By 1992 Air Canada had twenty women pilots and Canadian Airlines International (the result of various mergers between CP Air, Nordair, Eastern Provincial Airlines, Quebecair, and Pacific Western Airlines) had eight women pilots. Thus, in the sixty years since Canadian Airways Limited was created, only twenty-eight women made it to the flight deck as pilots with major carriers and only one of them, Rosella Bjornson, is wearing the fourth stripe of captain, which she received in 1990. Interestingly, newcomer Nationair promoted its only woman pilot, Nicole Sauvé, to captain in the same year.

THE INDUCTION OF WOMEN into the airlines has not been easy. While some pilots thought it was high time that women were admitted, others shook their heads in disgust and wondered aloud at what the airlines were coming to. The more fair-minded remained neutral, preferring to adopt a "wait and see" attitude. As one Air Canada pilot explained, "They have to beat down a lot of guys to get a job, they have to struggle harder for jobs because they are women, and they must be more dedicated. Most of all they have to overcome the image of the pilot as a man wearing a silk scarf and goggles!"

A man's age did not appear to affect how he perceived women. Some, like René Giguere, who began flying for TCA in 1937, claimed they had changed their minds. "I could fly with a woman now," he said. "As you become older you become more understanding. I don't think it would bother me any more than the time that I flew with a co-pilot who smoked."

Pregnancy and the supposed emotional instabiity of women

were still the biggest bugaboos for some men as evidenced by the following actual comments — heard often enough to be taken as generalizations.

"I can't understand why a woman would want a career and children."

"Women are different emotionally."

"If the fuel is low or the weather is down to minimums a woman is thinking about her baby, not the safety of the passengers."

"If they are tired or under stress they tend to cry."

"I think the women all do a good job but I wonder at their career commitment."

Some men even worried that women in the cockpit would stifle the joke-telling and "the farting and scratching that goes on" in an all-male environment. But, as Barbara Swyers, an easy-going woman, would say to the crew, "If I haven't heard it in the Maritimes then it hasn't been said."

All the women ran full tilt into discrimination and all glossed over it. "Yes, I had some problems," said one. "Sometimes I'm not sure if it's me, me as a female, or me as a second officer. I had some encouragement, others merely tolerated me, while others in good faith tried to discourage me. I always tried to do my best; I think I tried harder than a lot of the guys because I knew that people were watching me. In those first five years there were only five of us. We were something of an oddity, we always got stared at." Another said, "I was terribly naive. I believed I was there solely because of my ability; that got beaten out of me over the next two years. Some of the guys were terrific, others were just plain miserable. I used to book extra simulator time — at 12:00 AM — and some of the guys accused me of getting special treatment. That wasn't so."

Trying to present their arguments without sounding too strident was a problem for the women. "In the early days I often felt very isolated. There were still some men who couldn't accept a woman in any position other than wife or mother and they weren't very polite about letting me know how they felt about my being in a plane," explained one woman. However, ever mindful that their comments could hurt the chances of future women applicants, not to mention their own relationships with crews, none of the women wanted to be identified. "You try hard to blend in, knowing that you never will, and yet try and stick up for your rights," was how one woman put it.

BY 1987 THE WOMEN flying with the airlines had surmounted all of the obstacles, except one: maternity leave. No airline had come to grips with that issue. The two airlines faced with a pregnant pilot dealt with the situation on an ad hoc basis, which was not satisfactory to the women. As one said at the time, "We are left betwixt and between. I don't want to say too much except that the area of maternity leave is a problem. I myself do not see pregnancy as a reason to preclude women from a flying career but it is a hot issue."

The reaction of the men varied. Those who condemned a woman for taking a leave of absence to have a baby saw nothing wrong with a man taking a leave to attend university or taking sick leave because of a drinking problem. Similarly, the men who declared that a woman upset crew scheduling by becoming pregnant neglected to mention the problems caused by a man having a hernia operation or breaking a leg. The men argued that breaking a leg was an accident but having a baby was not. Pregnancy was looked upon as "a self-inflicted wound" over which the women had full control. Carl Millard of Millardair of Toronto likely spoke for many when he stated, "It's hard to keep a schedule with women. Marriage, pregnancy, menstruation — all mean a total interruption of performance. Look at that woman Judy Cameron (Air Canada pilot), her pregnancy — ludicrous as far as costs go. She is not a constant employee. An airline must look at what is efficient.[8]" Millard did not comment on the costs of rehabilitating alcoholic pilots or medical leaves for other reasons. On the other hand, some men were sympathetic and felt that women should not be penalized or forced to make the decision not to have children.

And there was the rumour mill. As one woman recalled, "The bongo drums started beating. The men had these crazy ideas of what we were asking; our requests were inflated out of all proportion. I even heard that we had asked for paternal leave!" The issue remains controversial.

Some male pilots, interviewed in 1991, indicated that they will probably always be uneasy flying with a woman. It was not a question of competence, they said, but a vague "they didn't fit in . . . it didn't feel right."

Still, sometimes good experiences overshadowed the bad and Glenys Robison could say, "There are a multitude of tales that I could tell about nervous male captains. It was a long training period all around. One has to realize that for the most part, they [the male pilots] were some fifteen years older than me and had never seen, let alone flown with, a female pilot. In my mind, the one incident that sums it all up occurred at Christmas 1981, when my captain that month, after several rum and eggnogs, gave me a playful punch on the shoulder and said, 'You know, when I found we had to spend Christmas together, I was disgusted, I figured you'd stay in your room and I'd be all alone. But you know something Glenys, you're not half bad.' The ultimate compliment."

As usual, the media were fascinated with these smart-looking women in uniform. Britt Irving, described by the press as a striking brunette, began her airline career as a flight attendant and became a favourite of the media when she moved from the "back end" to the "front end." In the kind of story that reporters thrive on, they wrote, "Stewardess earns her pilot's cap" and, erroneously, "It was a heroic walk out of the kitchen and into the driver's seat of an Air Canada DC-8." The *Toronto Star* (September 28, 1978) went on to say with distasteful sensationalism, "After 5 years of begging her boss for a promotion Britt-Marie Ferst finally pulled it off — the dramatic switch from stewardess to pilot for Air Canada."

Canada's current twenty-eight women airline pilots are based in Toronto, Montreal, Winnipeg, Edmonton, and Vancouver. Interestingly, despite their low numbers and concentration in a few cities, they are not a close-knit group and generally do not seek each other out on a regular basis. Perhaps this attitude harkens back to their early days in aviation when each found herself the only woman on staff and learned to fend for herself. They did, however, make a point of meeting each other. "I met Barb Swyers on my second day on the line. She introduced herself to me, said how nice it was to see me and for me to give her a call anytime. That really helped," recalled Glenys Robison.

Although few in number, they are living proof that all the sacrifices were worthwhile. They have shown themselves to be self-directed, highly disciplined women who thrived on challenges. Tough, smart, and confident, they persevered until they had the right credentials and then seized their opportunities. Their appearance on the flight decks is a vivid example of the changes aloft.

ROSELLA BJORNSON is the first woman in Canada to fly as captain with a major scheduled airline. Raised in Champion, Alberta, the eldest of three daughters, Rosella grew up flying. "I remember sitting on my father's knees holding the controls. My favourite playhouse was an old abandoned war surplus Anson Mark II. I flew regularly in my imagination." By the time she was sixteen she had logged many hours in the family plane and loved flying so much that her parents gave her lessons for her seventeenth birthday. That was only the beginning. "I knew that I wanted to be an airline pilot," she recalled, but except for her family she didn't receive much encouragement. "When I told my high school counsellor he just laughed and said that was impossible because I was a girl. I realized that I was going to have to have more than the minimum qualifications if I was going to overcome the hurdle of being female so I checked with Air Canada to see what they looked for in their pilots. When I found out that they favoured those who had a university degree I decided to go to university."

During the winters, Rosella pursued her Bachelor of Science degree at the University of Calgary and summers she flew, acquiring her commercial and instructor's licences. She also helped organize the University of Calgary Flying Club, the Alberta Flying Farmers Teen Chapter, and the Alberta chapter of the 99s. During this period she met Gina Jordan, owner of Jordan Flight Services, who became a close friend and mentor.

In 1969, with about 500 hours officially logged, Rosella began job hunting. "I knew that the only way I could build enough hours was by instructing. I didn't think that I could get a job as a charter or bush pilot. I wrote to all the flying clubs in Canada. Only one replied with a job offer — the Winnipeg Flying Club." René Giguere, then the flying club manager, remembered, "I hired her. She was a tall girl, very pleasant, someone who took her flying matter-of-factly. I thought she would be an ideal instructor. Some of the men were a little wary but she was so good that no one could complain." It was not easy, as Rosella remembered, "There was no base pay. We were paid only for the time we were in the air or teaching ground school. Consequently, I lived at the club from sun-up to sundown seven days a week. It seemed as if I never slept or ate. I was really thin in those days." In her spare time, she worked towards her multi-IFR and, as soon as she had her ATR, she began applying to the airlines. "I received the standard re-

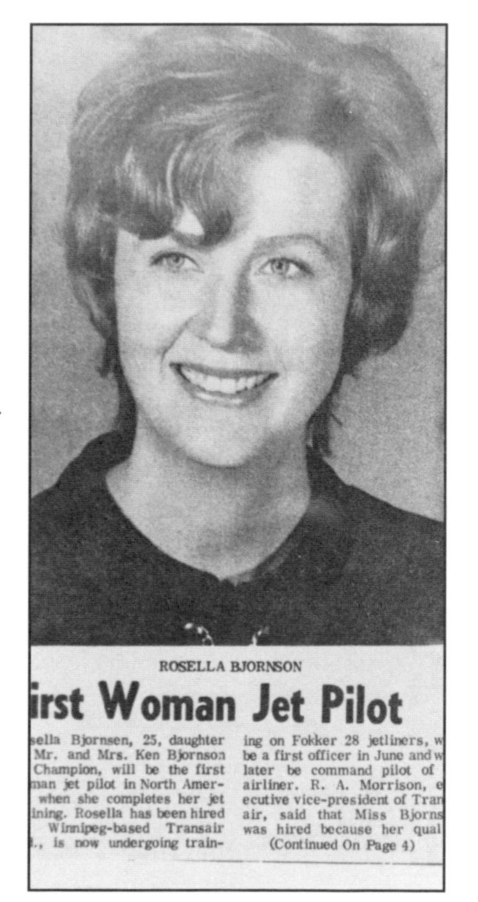
ROSELLA BJORNSON

irst Woman Jet Pilot

sella Bjornsen, 25, daughter Mr. and Mrs. Ken Bjornson Champion, will be the first man jet pilot in North Amer- when she completes her jet ining. Rosella has been hired Winnipeg-based Transair ., is now undergoing train- ing on Fokker 28 jetliners, w be a first officer in June and w later be command pilot of airliner. R. A. Morrison, e ecutive vice-president of Tran air, said that Miss Bjorns was hired because her qual

(Continued On Page 4)

Front page coverage from an unidentified Alberta newspaper.

sponse from Air Canada, no answer from CP Air, and PWA told me they did not hire women." Nevertheless, a glimmer of optimism came from an unexpected quarter — the Winnipeg Flying Club coffee shop.

"The club was at the international airport and its coffee shop and adjacent watering hole were favourite spots for off-duty pilots. I got to know many of the airline pilots because I was at the club so much. I asked them, 'Why don't you have a female pilot?' They had all kinds of answers. However, Doug Rose, Transair's chief pilot, pushed me to apply. He used to let me ride the jump seat of the 737. He told me that as long as I was qualified and could do the job he didn't care that I was female." When Rosella heard via the grapevine that Transair was hiring she went over to their office. "I just walked in without an appointment and asked to speak to the operations manager. I said to him, 'I want to fly for you.' He sat back — the look on his face said, 'What is she talking about?' — nevertheless, he handed me an application. I just got home when the phone rang. It was the ops manager asking me if I wanted to fly as first officer on the F-28 or captain on the Twin Otter! I chose F-28s."

When Transair hired Rosella in April 1973, she became the first woman airline pilot in Canada and the first jet-qualified female first officer in North America. Overnight she went from being an obscure instructor to a Canadian celebrity. Newspapers, radio and TV stations across the country carried the story of "Transair's Newest Bird" (*Winnipeg Free Press*, April 5, 1973) and they followed her progress avidly. When she finished her training three months later, reporters were hot on the scene of her first line flight. "First Woman Pilot Takes Off" was the *Winnipeg Free Press* headline on July 12, 1973. Everyone wanted to know all about her. By nature reserved, she nevertheless greeted reporters cheerfully; and her unassuming manner endeared the tall, slim, twenty-six-year-old to them.

What prompted Transair to hire her? Rosella explained, "The company was in a period of transition, moving away from its bush origins to more sophisticated aircraft. It had just got its second Fokker F-28, a turbo jet carrying sixty-five passengers, and needed about ten more instrument pilots. Transair was looking for pilots with an ATR and it was also pleased with my university background. The women's liberation movement was also a factor and, of course, having the backing of Doug Rose and some of the other pilots was a big help. I was definitely in the right place at the right time with the right qualifications. And at six foot they couldn't say I was too short!"

While Transair may have been pleased that it had scooped the other airlines by being the first to hire a woman pilot, some of its pilots were not enthusiastic over the turn of events. They complained that she had no bush experience, saying that her 3500 hours were useless and conveniently overlooking the fact that much of her time was multi-IFR, just what Transair was looking for. Others were jealous of the publicity she received, "What's so special about her?" they asked. Some resented her university education and others her relative youth. All of this

meant that her dramatic achievement had a darker side. She was the only woman pilot among approximately 2800 Canadian male airline pilots and that fact made it impossible for her to escape notice. The pressure on her was intense as everyone watched to see if she measured up.

Rosella simply bided her time. She neither tried to convert the anti-female faction nor did she complain. "I always tried to see their side of things and to keep things in perspective." Having a sense of humour was a definite help. "On one of my first flights into Toronto I was working the radio and ATC asked if Transair's first officer's jockey shorts were too tight since his voice was so high!" Some flattering comments softened the sting of the more derogatory remarks that came her

L *Transair's Fokker F-28.*

R *Rosella Bjornson, first officer, PWA.*

way. "We were just out of Winnipeg and I was asked to squawk 'Ident.' I did so and someone said, 'That wasn't a squawk; that was a sweet feminine voice.'" Another time a passenger asked the captain how he liked flying with a woman co-pilot and he answered, "I never think of her as a woman. She's my first officer.'"

Rosella was loathe to say anything negative about her first years with either Transair or Pacific Western, but admitted that there were some difficult times. "Most of the pilots were helpful. There was really only one, a check pilot, who deliberately gave me a hard time. Even when I was on line I felt I could not afford to make mistakes. Some of the captains were great,

Glenys Robison, Air Canada pilot.

GLENYS OLSTAD ROBISON

Glenys Olstad was born in New Norway, Alberta, a little town about sixty-five miles south of Edmonton. "As a child I was always doing things with my father. He taught me how to drive a car when I was nine and by ten I was going solo in farmers' fields. He taught me how to shoot a twenty-two and I carried the name of 'Dead Eye Dick' for many years." Glenys was no slouch academically either and intended to obtain a university degree and teach — until she discovered flying.

"It sounds corny but one beautiful summer evening in 1976 I happened to be watching a bird and thought, 'Wouldn't it be fun to fly.' I went to the Edmonton Flying Club the very next day, took a 'fam flight' and signed up for lessons. I was so inexorably hooked that I could think of nothing else but flying. At Awards Night I received my private pilot certificate along with the students I had taught!" she recalled. Glenys also won the Edmonton Flying Club Pilot of the Year Award for flying more than 1400 hours in a year and for training that year's top two private pilots and top two air cadets. "To do this I moved closer to the airport to cut down on travel time — I lived practically on the approach to one of the runways — and got two part-time jobs along with my full-time instructing job. I've always had a passion for work." Within eighteen months Glenys had her private, commercial, instructors, multi-IFR, and ATL.

Glenys credits Art Maskell, an instructor at the Edmonton Flying Club, with giving her good advice on how to handle herself. "One day I was in the Box [flight simulator] and having an awful time. I was beginning to exhibit the signs of a two-year old's impending temper tantrum. Art struggled with me for only a bit, then reached in, turned the machine off and told me to meet him in the coffee shop in ten minutes. When I was finally under control he laid life

while others were inclined to see any errors due to my being female, rather than being new on the aircraft." Her modest manner, her determination to "hang in" and her ability eventually won her acceptance as a crew member. When one of the captains turned to her and said, "I'd fly with you any day," Rosella knew that she had made it.

Rosella flew the F-28 until February 1979 when she moved to the YS-11. "We were based in Churchill a week at a time and we flew north to Rankin Inlet, Baker Lake, Pelly Bay to service the north. Things were going well. I had my life completely planned; or I thought I did. When I was in my early twenties I had decided I was going to be the totally modern woman and

Transair's YS-11.

on the line for me. He explained in the kindest yet toughest manner that I was different than the other pilots and would have to be stronger than I ever dreamed if I wanted to make it in aviation. I'd have to keep my emotions and my mouth under control. I grew up that day. This was a profession and I had to be a professional. Men were going to have trouble treating me like the rest of the pilots and I was going to have to rise to the occasion: be alert, competent, comfortable to be with, and the best pilot I could be."

Glenys instructed until she landed a corporate position flying a turbo-charged Navajo, which happened this way. "One day an old bush pilot walked into the Edmonton Flying Club and said his instrument rating had expired and he needed a pilot to make his trip to Grande Prairie legal. I said I was available but I didn't tell him my instrument rating

marriage and children were not in my plans. However, I met someone with whom I wanted to share my life. We were married in 1977. Two years later I became pregnant. I was quite upset and yet I really wanted the child. I was torn between flying and wanting to be a mother as well."

As soon as she declared her pregnancy, management promptly grounded her but then wrung their hands in despair. "What do we do with her?" they asked because there was nothing in her contract about maternity leave. Rosella suggested a leave of absence and also requested job security, no loss of seniority, and continuing health benefits. Unfortunately, the regulations stated that to retain these benefits she had to

was less than twelve hours old! Off we went in a brand new Navajo with me trying to act like I knew what I was doing. The weather was horrible; icing in clouds and stormy in Grande Prairie. I was quite out of my league. Anyway, we muddled through and when we got home, he offered me a job. He was tickled pink to have a woman pilot and whenever we landed at any of his construction camps, he always introduced me as the new company pilot. Of course, all good things must come to an end. Eventually he figured perhaps there could be even greater benefits in having a woman pilot and I simply had to move on. I was hired by Shirley Helicopters' fixed wing division to fly light twins, filled mostly with rig crews, into strips throughout Alberta. It was with Shirley Air that I gained invaluable time and experience dealing with the freezing temperatures and ice-covered wings that are the grief of a charter pilot's existence." Glenys worked with Shirley Air until Air Canada hired her at the end of the hiring boom in February 1980. She was twenty-two at the time.

"I was aware of about six other women flying where I was but we didn't chum together much. I preferred listening to, and emulating, the older male pilots, and spent hours in restaurants and bars listening to their tales and believing them to be the best that ever flew. I had never really made a decision to go airline. I was just caught up at the time the airlines were hiring. I had also tried to join the Canadian Forces in 1979 but a crusty old colonel at Namao said, 'As long as I'm alive there won't be any women in the air force.'" That was, perhaps, her only disappointment because Glenys was one of the few women who never experienced any problems finding work. She attributed this to the times, "I began flying at the height of the oil boom." By nature an optimist, Glenys always assumed that things would work out to her benefit. "I've never even considered that I might be unemployed, medically unfit, incapable, or discriminated

maintain a Category 1 medical, which she had lost upon becoming pregnant. On the other hand, if she asked for sick leave she could retain her benefits. Since Rosella did not consider pregnancy a sickness nor did she wish to pursue that line of thinking, she was caught in a void. Although she was not sick she lost her medical and without her medical she could not keep her privileges. To make matters worse, the situation hit the newspapers.

"Just at that point a *Winnipeg Free Press* reporter phoned, saying 'I have met you, admired what you have done, that sort of thing' — being sympathetic — and then he asked me how the pregnancy was going to affect my career. I was too vocal. I let him know! I didn't expect to see it on the front page. It was all blown out of proportion. My requests were made to seem unreasonable and I was made to look like a complaining bitch. Newspapers across Canada picked up the story and everyone was phoning me, asking questions. It got so I didn't even want to answer the phone." Complicating the pregnancy issue was the fact that at the time Pacific Western was negotiating to take over Transair. "No one knew who was in charge." recalled Rosella, "Transair tried to ignore the 'problem.' It took a while before it got sorted out. It was a pretty traumatic time for me. The same week I found out I was pregnant I was told that I was to start on course for the Boeing 737, just what I had been waiting for. In the end I took a personal leave of absence with no pay but I was allowed to retain my seniority and my job." Throughout it all, her husband Bill Pratt a former corporate

against. Even when I was hired by Air Canada I never dreamed that I'd be a second officer, only a first officer and sure enough, I was Air Canada's first female first officer on DC-9s for two glorious years." Glenys then became a second officer on the Boeing 727.

An outgoing fun-loving person with an incredible sense of humour, Glenys has won the acceptance of most of the pilots she has flown with and the heart of one, Jeff Robison, whom she married in 1982. "I could not have planned my life any better. Jeff is helpful and supportive; who else but another pilot could understand what really goes on up there at 35,000 feet or on a lonely layover across the country? We have close to the same seniority which means we'll likely never fly together. That suits us both fine."

Glenys is once again a first officer on DC-9s based in Toronto. She has also taken the time to complete a journalism course and is a staff reporter for a local paper.

pilot before joining Pacific Western, supported her fully.

On her return to flying eighteen months later, Pacific Western transferred her to Edmonton and then sent her to Vancouver for the 737 checkout. "It was not easy. I had been off flying for quite awhile and to go onto a new aircraft right away was difficult. I found it hard to leave the baby and Bill but even harder having to cope with a check pilot who seemed determined to make things difficult for me. He had his mind made up before I started that I wasn't going to make it. It was really the first time I had ever run into anyone so negative. But I was quite determined that I was going to make it." Naturally non-aggressive, Rosella nevertheless had a burning desire to

Barbara Swyers, one of the first five women pilots hired by Air Canada, c. 1988.

BARBARA SWYERS

Barbara Swyers was born in Halifax, Nova Scotia, the youngest of three daughters. "I was my father's last hope for a boy and, consequently, he took me under his wing," explained Barb. Intending to be a marine scientist she completed a Bachelor of Science degree in 1973 and a Master's in marine microbiology in 1976. However, her father's death that year so devastated her that she chose flying as an antidote to her grief.

What started as a diversion became an obsession. Within the year she obtained her private and commercial licences, her instructor's and multi-IFR ratings, and a job at the Moncton Flying Club, its first woman instructor. "I found Don McClure, the manager, to be supportive. He judged you by how hard you wanted to work, not by your sex." She instructed only a month before accepting a job with Forest Protection of New Brunswick for the budworm spray project. "My acceptance letter stated that I was responsible for my own clothes, survival gear, and shaving kit." Barb was the first woman pilot hired. As she reported, "The camps were just little dirt strips cut out of forests and the strips were hard to find. Living quarters were primitive; trailers and huts which were moved around to different sites. The walls of the huts were cardboard thin and sleeping right next to me on the other side of the wall was a man the pilots called 'the animal.' Every night he would say, 'Good night Barb' and I would say 'Good night' and hope he wouldn't put his fist through the wall and grab me!"

Describing the job of a pointer pilot, Barb said, "On the project there were about 100 pilots flying TBM Avengers and another 200 flying Cessna 172s. As an inexperienced pilot I flew the 172 as a bird dog pilot. It was my job to identify the area to be sprayed. We flew at roughly 100 AGL [above ground level] with the Avengers following at 20 to

achieve. "Course and line training took about six months and I commuted between Vancouver, Winnipeg, Peace River [where the baby was], and Edmonton. There were times when I wanted to quit but I knew that I couldn't because my actions would determine the company's policy about hiring other women."

Once back on line she found herself juggling her time as an airline pilot, mother, and wife. Besides coping on these fronts, she also had to prove herself to the whole new set of pilots. As a couple of them explained, "We thought we were a pretty macho bunch and any woman would have a hard time being accepted." But Rosella thought she had fair treatment. "The

50 feet. We followed a grid marked on the map and we laid out the path for the Avenger pilot. At the end of the 'block' we would do a wingover to mark where the Avenger must turn for the next section of the grid to be flown." Precision flying was not the only thing Barb remembered from that job. "I was the only woman among the 300 or so pilots and I guess the guys wanted to give me something to remember them by. On my first official flight the mechanics lined up at the end of the field and when I flew over and looked down I saw a row of bare bottoms poking up at me!"

After the Budworm project, Barb returned to the Moncton Flying Club until she found work with Atlantic Central Airways in Saint John, New Brunswick. Unfortunately the company went bankrupt within the year. Job hunting, she ran into the usual excuses — the wives would object to their husbands flying with a woman or she was not strong enough. "Once I didn't get the job because the chief pilot didn't think I could handle the fifty-pound mail bags. I was annoyed to learn later that a five foot puny-looking male got the job. I was bigger than he was." However, when her former Atlantic Central Airways boss became chief pilot with Eastern Flying Service he hired her. "I had to overcome management's objections and my own concerns about the propriety of my sharing a hotel room with the co pilot."

Barb flew left seat on courier and sked runs throughout the Maritimes. "I got really good experience with this company. We had lower limits than were approved by MOT. We often had problems going into Newfoundland — usually high winds, bad icing over the water. In the small aircraft we didn't have enough fuel to go to an alternate airport if the winds were too high; you made only one approach and you did it right the first time."

If those conditions didn't offer enough challenge, no doubt ferrying light twins across the Atlantic Ocean in her spare time did. "It was single pilot IFR. I was still too

fellows were great. I remember one captain. I guess he was kind of skeptical. After our first flight together he said, 'You don't fly any different from anyone else!' I know there were negative comments but that's to be expected. There were some captains I wasn't too sure about and I know there's one who absolutely refuses to fly with me — he doesn't want to spoil his reputation as a male chauvinist pig!" By 1983 she felt confident enough to say to one of the second officers, "Some day I'll be your captain." And he replied, "I'll fly anywhere with you Rose."

When Rosella again became pregnant in 1983, she hoped to stay airborne and applied to Transport Canada for a waiver. But the paper work was slow to be processed and she again found herself grounded for the complete pregnancy. On the plus side there was no fuss about her taking a leave and no publicity. "Most of the men I flew with were supportive of my wish to try and combine both career and family. They saw no reason for Bill and me not to have children just because I was a pilot." In fact, Pacific Western was quite happy to grant Rosella a leave as

ignorant to be frightened at what I was doing. I usually flew from Gander to the Azores because the winds were better in the south.

Interestingly, Barb never set herself the goal of airline flying. "I just assumed I was ineligible because I wore glasses. It was not until one of the Air Canada captains that I knew talked to me about applying that I did anything. He even went so far as to get an application for me and really pushed me to fill it out." Air Canada liked the look of Barb's application and called her for an interview. "It was on Friday the 13th, April 1979." She was hired for the October 1979 class: the fourth woman pilot to fly for Air Canada.

"I was the only woman in a class of sixteen. Even though I was older and female I had no problems and formed strong friendships with many of my classmates. Once on the line I found that the majority of the men were willing to help me and give me a chance. I ran into only one captain who was less than enthusiastic about my presence in the cockpit. 'Oh God, a woman' was how he greeted me on our first flight together. He thought I would go crazy at 'my time of the month.' For the men, the biggest problem seemed to be the language; they were always apologizing." However, her enthusiasm and earthy good humour soon overcame most resistance. A first officer on the DC-9 based in Toronto at time of writing, Barb has also been Air Canada's air medical chairman, Toronto, for the Canadian Air Line Pilots Association.

economy measures were forcing it to lay off pilots. In time, she too was placed on a lay-off status and by-passed five recalls to stay at home with the children. In late 1987 Rosella was back flying the 737. With over 11,000 hours logged she is Canada's most experienced woman airline pilot. In 1991, she received no less than three awards: the National Transportation Award of Achievement, the Manitoba Award of Achievement, and the Northern Alberta Transportation Personality of the Year Award. Most significant however, her struggles, set-backs, and day-to-day slugging were rewarded when Canadian Airlines International promoted her in late 1990 and she became Canada's first woman airline captain. The soft-spoken but very

LUCIE CHAPDELAINE

Lucie Chapdelaine, of Ste. Victorie, Quebec was fifteen when she had her first airplane ride. "One day my father took me to the airport for a ride and when I got back my whole licence was paid for. He saw me as a career pilot. He really pushed me."

Qualified for her commercial in 1973 Lucie thought of becoming an airline pilot but, as she explained, "I didn't think it was possible. I had never heard of a woman airline pilot, also I had no English. I knew I needed English to get through the books. My father paid for me to go to St. Boniface to learn English." After spending a year in Manitoba, pushing a mop at the St. Boniface Hospital and waiting tables, Lucie returned to Quebec and obtained her instructor's rating because she could not find any other type of work.

"The people were not used to seeing a woman flying. I also spent one month at Sioux Lookout flying Indians in a Navajo. On my first trip my passenger, an Indian, took a look at me and said, 'Anybody else?' When I shook my head he got out. After that I went to Condor Aviation in Hamilton for one year to learn my English well." In 1979 with 2500 hours and an ATR she applied to Air Canada. "Air Canada refused me because of my height, five foot four; they said I was not safe enough for the cockpit. I tried to get on with the Quebec Government flying the water bombers but every time I applied the chief pilot, Thomas Fecteau — he was about seventy years old — said I was not strong enough. I wish I had had a tape recorder with me because he never wrote that. His attitude was that women should be with the pans in the kitchen or making babies." However, in August 1982 Nordair called her for an interview and she began in January along with pilot France Gravel.

As a junior pilot Lucie began on the Fairchild 227 flying

Lucie Chapdelaine, first officer, Nordair.

competent Captain Rosella Bjornson moved gracefully into the left seat.

JUDY EVANS CAMERON was Air Canada's first woman pilot. An only child who was raised in Vancouver, British Columbia, Judy was attending university when a chance airplane ride in 1973 turned her life around. "I decided on the spot to become an airline pilot. I chose the two-year aviation program at Selkirk College in Castlegar, British Columbia as the most sensible way to go about it." Being the first and only woman in the aviation program was an eye-opener for her.

"I discovered for the first time in my life that women were not universally accepted in all fields and that flying was definitely considered to be for men only. Having been raised to believe that being qualified was what counted, not what sex you were, it was a shock to find that many of my classmates questioned my right to be there. I usually found myself alone; I had no one to study with or just to talk things over with." Judy graduated in June 1975 with a certificate in Aviation Technology, and commercial and multi-IFR licences. She was the first woman in Canada to obtain an aviation technology certificate.

No job was immediately available however, and it was some

Captain Rosella Bjornson, Canadian Airlines International.

in the Arctic. "I liked the experience. You have to see it, once, only once. God made that for the Eskimos and they can have it. You miss two weeks of your life every month. I think the accommodations were the same as in the fifties when the Dewline was built. There was only one shower room with no lock. I didn't expect them to change anything. If we want to be equal and want the job we have to live with it. Nordair had some concerns. They said to me, 'Are you going to be the first one to complain about accommodations?' 'What!' I said, 'Try me and see if I complain.' I think Nordair compared to the other airlines was the most open-minded — out of one hundred and fifty pilots they have three women. You maybe meet one or two that let you know they don't want you in the right seat and they take you only because they don't have any choice.

"There were twenty-five sites in 2500 miles. We flew food, parts, medevacs, and people six days a week, nine to five. When you were on a tour of two weeks you easily flew 100 hours. Sunday you were off unless you had an emergency. I could have become captain on the 227 but I didn't want to be locked up North especially with the change with CP." Lucie is now a first officer on the Boeing 737 for Canadian Airlines International.

time before BC Forest Products of Vancouver hired her to do all the jobs that no one else wanted. "They didn't really want to hire a female for full-time work. Most of my jobs were ground jobs — dispatching, office work, and doing an engine change on a DC-3. However, I did receive a Lear Jet endorsement and flew as copilot, although all I did was raise and lower the gear, handle the radio, and other copilot duties. In my three months with them I flew only 75 hours; usually I was waiting to fly." Her next job was not much better. She was an Air West reservations agent, ticket agent, clerk, flight attendant and if she were lucky, copilot on the Twin Otter or King Air. "When they needed a pilot I was there. Air West was a 'bushy' scheduled line and women pilots were definitely a rarity, but only once did I encounter a passenger who looked shocked to find the pilot was a woman. Not a word passed his lips; his face said it all! I logged more time on the phone than I did in the air but I certainly learned how to load the Twin Otter's tiny baggage compartment." Five months later Mike Vien of Bayview Air Service in Edmonton hired her.

Judy Cameron, first woman pilot hired by Air Canada, 1978.

"I think Mike hired me more out of curiosity than anything, but he gave me the break I needed. Bayview serviced the oil companies and provided charter and sked service. I was based in Slave Lake and most of my flying was in 180s and Aztecs in the Peace River and Rainbow Lake area. Once I got my DC-3 endorsement I went on the sked north from Edmonton. I got used to flying in thirty degrees below and loading and unloading cargo." Bayview not only introduced her to bush flying but also to the man she would marry. "It was on my first line indoctrination flight in the DC-3. The right engine noisily gave out in cruise and stranded us in Rainbow Lake, population 200. The engine change took three days and I had no choice but to notice the apprentice mechanic whom I later married." [Scott Cameron, a certified aircraft technician now with Air Canada]. Unfortunately, Bayview went bankrupt four months later and Judy began pounding the pavement again. Finding work was easier this time because she had some marketable skills: DC-3 and Lear Jet endorsements and 1000 hours, more than half logged in the bush. "Gateway Aviation needed a pilot and while the chief pilot told me he didn't want to hire a woman, he would because he knew that I wouldn't leave him for the airlines. 'Ha,' I thought, 'airline flying is my ultimate goal!'"

Gateway's main business was with the government and the

oil industry, and it serviced, among other things, the Dewline sites and Inuit and Native settlements. Based in Inuvik in the Northwest Territories, Judy flew as co-pilot on the DC-3. "Inuvik was an indefinite sentence because I was the most junior DC-3 pilot. I flew with a guy who did not communicate; he just grunted. I never knew when I would be flying or what leg I would be flying." As co-pilot Judy did all the fueling. "I got really good at leaping onto the wing of a DC-3. It seemed to take forever to fuel it, especially when you were up there with the mosquitoes. What I remember most were bugs and dust but it was really beautiful country."

Her position entailed more than flying. "We were on call

GWEN GRANT

Gwen Grant, a third year psychology student was walking across the University of British Columbia campus in 1972 and noticed a float plane overhead. "I decided then and there to begin flying lessons right away. I was going to become an airline pilot." As she explained, "I have six brothers and was always one of the boys. I didn't do the usual girl things. My father and two brothers were pilots and it never occurred to me that I might be considered strange if I took up flying."

Within a few months of her decision she obtained her private and commercial licences. "My instructor at Skyways at Langley Airport told me I was wasting my money because no one would hire a woman. I've never been terribly good about taking advice and besides you just have to say, 'I want that job,' and go for it." In 1973 she moved to Montreal to finish her Bachelor of Arts degree at McGill University and to begin looking for a flying position. "I made the rounds of all the companies at Dorval. No one wanted me so I got my instructor's rating at Laurentide Aviation to gain some experience."

Her first job offer came at 2:00 AM when the chief pilot of a small charter company phoned her and told her to be at Dorval at six that morning. "I flew right seat on an Aero Commander. After that I made a point of helping out in their office so I would be on the spot if they needed a pilot. I got quite a few hours on the Commander and a Beech 18." That winter she completed her degree and in her spare time she delivered fried chicken to pay the rent. "I also got a little flying in but it was mostly as a flight attendant on a DC-3 passing out biscuits in the back end."

Gwen's life was a confusing jumble of 100 hour weeks as she combined studying, flying, and her various jobs, making it impossible for her to have any personal life. She did,

twenty-four hours a day and often flew six trips a day, but more of our time was spent handling the cargo than in actual flying. What they really needed was someone who was six feet tall and covered with hair — loaders not pilots — I'm five foot seven. I think I pulled my weight but I could understand their concern about my strength. We carried drill parts, core samples, supplies to oil companies, and 45 gallon fuel drums — the DC-3 could take twenty-six. The captain unloaded them from the aircraft onto the ramp — I used to think he aimed them at me! I did most of the loading and unloading as my captain had just had his second hernia operation and was unable to lift anything heavy. Most of our work was freight. Passengers were a bonus; we didn't have to carry them. We often had 6000 pounds of cargo, which we had to load and unload. I wore coveralls and boots with steel toes. I worked as hard as I could. I didn't want anyone accusing me of not pulling my weight. To put it mildly, I got a lot of exercise. I put muscles on muscles."

however, find time to keep Air Canada informed of her progress. "Even before I had my commercial I applied. When I was in Montreal I regularly went into Flight Ops to up-date my resumé. Air Canada wasn't hiring but they were very encouraging and told me to keep on applying."

Gwen's return to Vancouver coincided with Air Canada's decision to consider hiring women pilots. "I just happened to walk into Flight Ops with an up-date when Keith Sanderson needed to find out whether women could cope with the 727 simulator. He asked me if I would be willing to fly it. I said 'sure' and away we went. He made all the systems fail. I wasn't great but we didn't crash," recalled Gwen. Air Canada did not forget her. When they began recruiting women pilots, she was the second woman hired. "There were twenty-five men on course and one other woman who failed. For me, the hardest part of the course was the pressure because my career rode on it."

Gwen's appearance in airport terminals still causes men's heads to turn. As for her personal life, she remains single. "When you tell a man, especially a non-pilot, that you are an airline pilot it tends to intimidate them. It's hard to establish a relationship when you work and study all the time. The woman pilots I know are aggressive go-getters. They are active physically and mentally. That can be hard for some men to accept."

At the time of writing Gwen was based in Vancouver and has flown some 4000 hours as second officer on the Lockheed 1011. In 1992 she was checked out as first officer on the Boeing 767.

Gwen Grant, one of the first five female Air Canada pilots.

Another job was the yearly "beer runs" into Fort McPherson for the Dewline. "We called it the Arctic Red River. On the first stop everyone in the village showed up to help unload. For the second load only about half the villagers appeared and on the last, it was just me and the captain unloading!" With a few exceptions the flying was routine. "One time we climbed only 100 feet a minute; we discovered that we were 2000 pounds overloaded. Another time I spent the whole trip trying to escape the advances of an amorous pilot, 'Just give me one kiss' he kept saying to me."

Being the only woman pilot flying in the western Arctic was a lonely existence. "I think most of the men accepted me because I was qualified and never tried to get out of doing my share of the work. There were a few that were hostile but I just had to learn to ignore their remarks. I was determined to stick with my job. The only women I had met were Karen Brynelsen [pilot with the BC Government Air Service], who came out to the college to meet me, and Lucille Haley, and I had heard of Rosella."

Britt Irving, one of the first five woman pilots hired by Air Canada, c. 1980.

In December 1976 Judy suffered a temporary setback when Gateway laid her off. "I applied at Aklavik Flying Serv-

BRITT FERST IRVING

Britt Ferst grew up in a Swedish fishing village. "My family did a lot of camping and sailing and I qualified for my Swedish master skippers licence, but what I really wanted to do was fly. However, in the socialist state of Sweden it was too expensive for the average civilian to become qualified. The only way to do it was through the military which was not open to me. So after one year of the Gymnasium (the equivalent of first year university), I left Sweden in 1971 for Canada. I'm a free spirit and I was looking for an alternative to socialism," recalled Britt. Fluent in Swedish, Danish, and German, with "passable" English, she became a flight attendant with Air Canada and, a little later, began sky diving and flying lessons.

ice and they hired me as a dispatcher. Gateway rehired me in February 1977 and based me in Edmonton. I was back on the DC-3 flying all over the north, landing anywhere there was enough length to land a DC-3 — frozen lakes or plateaus between mountains. It was spectacular country. Later that year I received a Hawker-Siddeley 748 endorsement. 'This is the big time,' I thought. I was flying a sked run from Edmonton north to Slave Lake, Peace River, and Rainbow Lake."

As it turned out, her time on the forty-eight passenger turbo-prop was limited because shortly after she was accepted by Air Canada. "I loved flying the Hawker-Siddeley so much that I almost asked Air Canada if I could go on their next course. I didn't realize then how important a couple of months could be to my seniority."

For Judy her dream was actually coming true. "I had applied with the airlines when I graduated and I had kept them up-dated, every 200 hours or so. I could always tell if they had

"I enrolled at the Brampton Flying Club in 1973 and told them I wanted to be an airline pilot. They laughed at me!" She earned her private, commercial, and instructor licences and soon was flying seventy-five hours a month as a flight attendant and another hundred hours a month as an instructor. "Once I began my multi-IFR training I knew I wanted the airlines because I like the precision of instrument flying. If the airlines hadn't taken me I would have tried the bush because I like the outdoors. I never considered the military."

Britt was hired by Air Canada in 1979 and flew as second officer on the DC-8 for about four years, and as second officer on the Boeing 727 until 1989. About flying as a cargo pilot on the DC-8, Britt recalled, "Cargo — it's a different type of operation; it's night flying. We have our own terminals. We're the midnight freighter pilots. We're not wimpy. There are no heaters; we freeze in the winter when they open the cargo doors. We're a class apart — lower — others hold their noses when we walk by!"

In 1981 Britt married, another pilot, and, on the side, manages Britt's Flight Institute, which she formed in 1981 — "I didn't want to waste my airline training and I remembered the poor training I received at the flying club and the confusion at the instrument stage, so I decided to teach it correctly." Britt also keeps busy on a farm she and her husband own, and flies a PA-11 for fun. With about 6000 hours, she is currently first officer on DC-9s, based in Toronto.

Air Canada DC-8 cargo plane.

read my letter when I got the reply beginning 'Dear Sir' and the 'Sir' was crossed out!"

However, there were problems being the first woman pilot hired by Canada's national airline, the major one being the publicity. "That added a lot of extra tension. By itself the Air Canada course can be pretty traumatizing. It's your one shot at the big time. Air Canada kept the media away from me, but I still got a lot of phone calls from newspapers, radio, and TV wanting interviews. Some resented the attention I was getting. The only way I got through was to pretend that I was the same as everyone else." Being the only woman in a class of twelve did not help either. The watchful eyes and snide remarks did not

Air Canada Boeing 767.

DIANE ROTHBERG

Diane Rothberg of Ottawa, Ontario was headed for a career in journalism (Bachelor of Journalism, 1974) when skydiving dropped her into the world of aviation. "I was bored at university and needed some inspiration so when I saw a poster advertising skydiving I signed up. The day my father discovered my parachute he was upset. 'But Daddy,' I said, 'you always told me not to be afraid of being different.' He was not amused. I think he would have preferred me to have taken up macramé." Two hundred and fifty jumps later Diane decided she needed a new challenge and took up flying instead. "Skydiving made me realize I could do anything I wanted as long as I was prepared to put the effort into it."

Never one to do things conventionally, Diane rejected 'the Cessna way' and took lessons on an aged Aeronca Champ in 1975. She obtained private, commercial, and instructor's licences and eventually an ATR. "Initially I had no intention of flying for a living, it was just that I like to hone my skills." In 1979 Diane, then a researcher with Transport Canada, was transferred to Vancouver. "I had come to a crossroads. I could either stay with the security of a government job or see if I had the guts to go out and make a living flying." She chose flying and during the next few years worked for Air West, Grey Beverages, and Air BC. When the position of editor of Transport Canada's *Aviation Safety Letter* became available in 1983, she applied. "It seemed made for me. They were looking for someone with a writing and flying background."

Two years later, in 1985, Air Canada offered her the position of second officer. "I had first applied in 1977. Yet again I had to weigh the pros and cons of a secure job with Transport Canada against the insecurity of the aviation industry. I was not married, had no dependents, and I knew

stop even after she went on line (as a second officer on 727s). There were some who suggested that she had been hired only because she was a woman. "There was no point in telling them that I had over 2000 hours, most of it gained in the bush on the DC-3. They didn't want to hear that." It was not just pilots who commented on her sex. "I remember when I was getting checked out on the DC-9. I was talking to Air Traffic Control and then I paused and someone came back with, 'What's the matter, getting your nerve up?'" Eventually her ability, good humour, and pleasant personality won her acceptance. Ever tactful, Judy remarked, "Flying with Air Canada has been a positive experience. The flight attendants have been very encouraging and supportive; they often defend me to the passengers. One passenger, when he saw me said, 'A woman pilot. Well, at least it keeps them off the roads!' Sometimes I think some of the captains felt a little left out with the attention that I've received. Most were pretty good."

Six years later, Judy again became the focus of attention. "I became pregnant. I was honest with Air Canada and told them. I was very upset to be the first to get pregnant. There was nothing in the contract about maternity leave and I realized I was in a difficult situation. I wondered how I would be treated. Most important to me was my seniority and pensionable time. The FAA has no ruling on pregnant pilots flying and I pointed this out to Air Canada. However, I did not want to make it so difficult for Air Canada that they wouldn't hire other women pilots. I applied for a waiver from the Ministry of Transport aviation doctor. I flew until the end of my fourth month. I didn't tell any of the guys because I was worried about their reaction. I just kept letting my pants out!" Three months after giving birth Judy was back on line, with the comment, "It would be fulfilling a lot of prophecies if I had a hundred children and never returned!"

that I would kick myself if I turned it down."

Diane was one of forty "new hires" taken on by Air Canada, two of them women. "I found the ground school course gruelling. I just stuck to studying. I had no time for anything else, hardly even for bodily functions." In April 1986 she was sent to Winnipeg on 727s, the first woman pilot to be based there. "Most of the crews were terrific to fly with", she said. Now based in Montreal, Diane is first officer on DC-9s.

Diane Rothberg, Air Canada.

Since Judy had her first child she has had two other children, although the second child, a son, died in infancy. "Things have changed dramatically since my first pregnancy," said Judy. "Now there is a plan in place. I was treated well with my last pregnancy." Judy is now first officer on the Boeing 767 and loving every minute of her flying.

CP Air, now Canadian Airlines International Ltd, was the third airline to hire women pilots. It was also Canada's oldest airline for its roots were in Western Canada Airways, formed in 1926 by James A. Richardson of Winnipeg. According to Jim McKeachie, Public Affairs, there was no change of policy to

Paula Venn Strilesky.

PAULA VENN STRILESKY

Paula Venn was a university student and professional figure skater when she began flying. "I heard a pilot describe the IFR environment and I liked the idea of an activity which combined both phyiscal and mental skills." She enrolled at the Edmonton Flying Club in December 1975 and squeezed in lessons between university and skating, eventually dropping out of university to concentrate on becoming qualified.

She taught skating in order to pay for her training and soon had her private, commercial, instructor's, multi-IFR, and 1500 hours. "I had no trouble getting hired by the Edmonton Flying Club. Vera Dowling and Lucille Haley had left a good name for women." However, instructing was only a stop-gap measure and she left when she was hired to fly a Turbo Commander for a charter company. In 1978 with an ATR and over 2000 hours she applied to the airlines.

"I was called for an interview by Air Canada. Everything looked good until I took the medical and failed because of my eyesight. I was devastated. I wasn't one to quit so I applied to Shirley Air Services in Edmonton. It had about fifteen aircraft, including a Cessna Citation, and it would give me a chance to move into sophisticated aircraft." The job was a good one and in 1980 she was promoted to director of flight operations and later placed in charge of all charter and scheduled operations. Soon she was putting in sixteen hour days.

In 1981 she decided to balance her professional and personal life a little more evenly. Married since 1979 to another pilot — "Who else would I have time to meet?" — and a mother the following year, she wanted more regular hours. "I applied to Transport Canada as that seemed to be one way I could combine my flying and administrative skills in a reasonable working day." She was hired in December

accommodate women pilots, it was simply that until 1979, when Sandra Lloyd was hired, no qualified women had applied.

SANDRA LLOYD of Vancouver, British Columbia took up flying " . . . because I had some money saved up and wanted to do something with it. I had met some airline pilots at the flying school and flying jets seemed exciting — remember, I was a teenager," explained Sandra, who earned her private licence in 1974 at the age of seventeen and her commercial and instructor's licences the following year. "I didn't know of any women airline pilots and I thought instructing would be a more realistic goal than airline flying. However, the more I learned about aviation — equipment, future opportunities, professional standards, working conditions, the more I came to the conclusion that airline flying was what I wanted."

Wanting more experience than instructing offered, she found a job in 1976 when Bob Ferguson of Parsons Airways

1981 as a civil aviation inspector in the Pacific Region but the bureaucracy got to her and she left in July 1985, having spent the previous year on unpaid maternity leave.

Her next job was with Air BC, which lasted only eight weeks. Hired to fly the Twin Otter and Dash 7, she found her probation abruptly terminated by the chief pilot. "Supposedly upper management had no idea that he had turfed twenty-three guys. It was that old game, only the favourites are promoted."

Finding another job, particularly with a husband and two children to consider, proved difficult. "Jobs in aviation are related to the economy and I heard comments like, 'We should give a job to a man because he has a family to provide for.'" Once she began flying again she found that attitudes had regressed. "Maybe it was a result of the economy. It was those little jokes again, 'Can you get us there?' and the raised eyebrows when they saw the pilot was a woman." Paula, with over 4000 hours, flew as co-pilot to a man who had 800 hours. "That was tough to take," she said bitterly. She also worked for Harbour Air flying fishermen up and down the coast. "That was real seat of the pants flying. I logged 500 hours that summer." In the fall of 1986 she was hired by Jet West to fly as captain on a Citation.

Finally, in September 1987, her dream of flying for the airlines came true when Canadian Airlines International hired her. She is currently based in Vancouver and flies as first officer on the Boeing 737.

Northern in Flin Flon hired her. Ferguson liked women pilots; Robin MacKinnon and Debbi King were already on staff. "It was good experience," recalled Sandra. "Most of my flying was on floats (Cessnas 206 and 185) although once I had my multi-IFR I also flew the Commander. During the winters I went back to British Columbia and instructed and flew charters with a Beaver."

Three years later CP Air called her for an interview. Sandra explained, "They had dropped their height requirements. When I had first applied you had to be at least five foot seven, I was five foot five. After my first interview they gave me a strength test. I found out later, that was not usual. I had about 2300 hours when they hired me as a second officer on the DC-8 in November 1979."

Reporters zeroed in on CP Air's first woman pilot and some were more concerned with sensational headlines than with accuracy. "The writer of one magazine article said that I packed my bag with bathing suits and sandals and barely left room for my aviation material," recalled Sandra indignantly.

Unfortunately life as an airline pilot came to an abrupt halt three years later when, in September 1982, she was laid off. "There were no jobs around so I enrolled at Simon Fraser University in Vancouver." She graduated in 1985 with a Bachelor of Business Administration. Still on lay-off status that September, she entered law school at the University of British Columbia. "The airlines were not hiring and it made sense to put aside any thoughts of resuming my airline career — easy to do when you have not sat at the controls of an aircraft for three years." Then CP Air recalled her one month later. "I was tired of being poor and seeing my flying friends wealthy. On the other hand, I really enjoyed law school — I just didn't know what to do." Sandra knew of pilots who had kept their airline jobs and gone to law school and that is the option she considered. She secured a leave of absence to finish her first year and in May 1986, returned to CP Air as a second officer on the DC-10 and in September 1987 went on the Boeing 737 as first officer. In 1988 she returned to university and obtained her law degree in 1990. She flew a reduced block to do her articling and was called to the bar in May 1991. Sandra initially stayed as an associate with her law firm but became too busy flying. At time of writing she was, as she said, " . . . only 'doing law' on an independent contract basis for other lawyers. In any case," she added, "I'm not leaving the airline; I'm enjoying the 737."

KATHY DAVENPORT ZOKOL was the second woman pilot hired by CP Air. Born and educated in Australia, where she graduated with a Bachelor of Education degree in 1968, Kathy decided to travel and flew to Vancouver in 1969 to begin her sightseeing. The flight was her first time in a plane and she was so entranced by flying that she abandoned her travel plans and signed up for flying lessons. She also enrolled at the University of British Columbia and obtained two part-time jobs to pay for her flying, one as a research assistant and the other as a high school teacher.

A fragile-looking woman with a soft voice, Kathy did not look tough enough to hold the work schedule that the next few years would bring. After graduating with a Bachelor of Arts degree in 1974 she set up a program for problem teenagers called High Adventure, structured on the lines of the Outward Bound program. She also managed the cafeteria at the community college where she taught. "By 1975 I found myself mentally and physically exhausted and decided to do something just for me."

Kathy Zokol, second woman pilot hired by CP Air.

The something was spending her time flying and thirteen months later Kathy had obtained her commercial, multi-IFR, and instructor's licences. "I still wasn't too sure just where I was heading. I took a leave of absence from the community college so that I could enroll full-time in the Masters degree program for Business Administration. I was also instructing part-time at Staran Flight, doing mostly multi-IFR."

Partway through her course Kathy received word that her father was very ill and she returned to Australia. The break helped her to resolve what she wanted to do and on her return to Canada, she opted for a career in flying. "I found work with Futura Aviation, a combination of working in the office and flying. It was not easy getting the job. I had to prove that I could handle flying a fairly sophisticated airplane — an Aero Commander, single pilot — and could hoist fifty to a hundred pound mail sacks. Yet I never tried to hide my femininity. Whenever I went for an interview I always dressed like a woman, in skirts and high heels." Kathy's philosophy was that she wanted to be treated like a pilot when she was flying but as a woman when out of the plane, although she discovered that could bring trouble.

"Sometimes I had to stay overnight in construction camps and there would be no separate accommodations and I would be the only woman. My way of dealing with it was to sleep with my jeans on so I could walk out of the room and into the plane."

Male/female problems were not the only difficulty. Kathy admitted that none of the men accepted her as an equal until she had an accident. "It was a crash that 'made' my reputation as a pilot!" she explained. "In October 1979 I had a double engine failure in the Turbo Commander. I had two passengers and was returning to Vancouver from Quesnel. I had climbed to about 4000 feet and was in a procedure turn about twenty miles south of the airport when I had a double engine failure, with the right engine blowing itself to pieces. I was in a valley that was ninety-nine percent treed and knew there was very little farm land around in which to do any sort of emergency landing. It didn't help that there was fog and the visibility was poor. I had almost decided to settle in some trees when I saw a small field, full of cows. I quickly 'dirtied up' the plane, dropping gear and flaps, and tried to land beyond the cows. Unfortunately the field was wet and I had no braking action. I had applied full rudder and tried to skid the plane sideways but I wiped out a fence, slid into a ditch, bounced back into the air, and then hit the trees at the far end of the field. The plane was a total write-off. Both passengers walked away but I was off work for the next six weeks."

Transport Canada accident investigators exonerated her. "Because I didn't panic in a stressful situation I gained a lot of respect from the other pilots. I also got a number of job offers. Because of the poor maintenance standards, I left the company in February 1980 and began flying with BCS Construction, flying a pressurized Cessna 210 and a Piper Cheyenne II. This was executive flying and I went all over British Columbia and the Yukon. It was fantastic. I stayed there until CP hired me in 1981 as a second officer on the DC-8."

Kathy had first applied to CP Air in the mid-seventies but her application had been misplaced. "To make sure that my next resumé was not lost I took it in myself. Unfortunately by then they had stopped hiring. To make sure that CP knew how much I wanted to fly with them I made a point of personally taking in my up-date every eight weeks or so to Flight Ops. I think they hired me to keep me from coming in so often."

Kathy was the only woman in the class of about a dozen

men. "I felt that my classmates accepted me. However, I thought that I was given harder simulator problems than the others and when I first went on the line there was a lot of 'testing' to see if I could handle the job. What was interesting was the fact that I found I was competing not just with the men but with Sandra [CP Air's first woman pilot] as well. She had set such a high standard and the men were always telling me how well Sandra had done."

Economic factors forced CP Air to lay her off in 1982, rehiring her in May 1986. In the interim she worked part-time as an executive pilot. She also remarried and had a baby. She is currently first officer on the Boeing 737 with Canadian Airlines International Ltd.

Stefanie Crampton, first woman pilot hired by Nordair.

STEFANIE SCHAUSS CRAMPTON was Nordair's first woman pilot. Like Transair, Pacific Western Airlines, and CP Air, Nordair's roots were in the bush and most of its pilots were former bush or military pilots. Stefanie was no exception, she was the first woman pilot to fly in the Arctic and, at nineteen, probably the youngest. Unable to find a job "down south" she applied to all the bush companies and, in 1976, was hired by Kenn Borek Air of Calgary to be a co-pilot on Twin Otters. Her base was Resolute Bay in the Northwest Territories. She found Arctic flying unlike any other kind of flying she had done — or has done since. "I'll never forget my first trip," Stefanie recalled. "It was IFR but totally different to what I had been used to down south. It was at night, snowing, and as we approached Strathcona Mines the captain told me to look out the window and tell him when I saw the shoreline. I thought, 'Is this instrument flying?'" She soon became accustomed to the over-sized Weldy Phipps tires on the Twin Otter and to landing where there was no runway and a minimum of navaids. Most of the flying was for the oil companies and was "off strip." Stefanie remembered the runway at Strathcona Mines was about 1800 feet on the top of a hill — "a hairy approach." Her flying included coping with Arctic weather. "You had to stay ahead of it. You could lose your alternate in a hurry if you were not careful. We would continuously check points to the west and stay ahead of any changes so that we didn't get boxed in."

Slim, blonde, and fragile-looking, Stefanie was the antithesis of what a bush pilot should look like, but handling the cargo was, as usual, part of the job. "At Resolute we had a forklift to load the heavy cargo but we were responsible for off-loading it and often there were fifty pound boxes of dynamite. For the heavier stuff I had to psyche myself up. I remember having to off-load those barrels of fuel. Thank heavens the plane was parked on a slight incline. I took a heck of a run at those barrels and just shoved them out the door. That was the hardest pushing I ever had to do.

"I found out later," Stefanie recalled, "that I was the first woman to stay at Strathcona Mines; even the nurses were not allowed to stay overnight. The mine provided the captain and me with a house. At the base on Cornwallis Island I was the only woman in the staffhouse among about thirty men. I had my own bedroom but I shared the showers and bathroom. They taped *HERS* on one of the bathrooms, which everyone continued to use anyways! I'd just yell, 'I'm coming in.' I never played the part of a shocked female if the language got a little coarse or with some of the pin-up pictures, although I noticed that the raunchier nudes quietly vanished from the dining room walls. I found most of the pilots friendly and helpful and they tended to treat me as a younger sister. I never had any trouble, but then I didn't look for any." Cheerful and soft-spoken, "Snow White," as she was nicknamed, found herself accepted by most.

Canadian Airlines International Boeing 767.

To pass the time when not flying, Stefanie took a correspondence course and read a lot. "The guys played a lot of poker but I stayed out of that. The north had a real mixture of pilots. Some like me were there to gain experience and others, in their forties, liked the Arctic and had made it their goal. The thing with the Arctic was that the pay was good and the time off was good — one month in and one month out."

After two years of Arctic flying — summed up as "I loved it" — Stefanie moved on to the airlines when she became Nordair's first woman pilot. After twelve years on the Boeing 737, Stefanie is now flying right seat on the Boeing 767 with Canadian Airlines International. "I'm finally getting to see the world out there. The routes our 767s operate on offer me a nice variety of destinations from Europe to South America to Vancouver and hopefully soon Hawaii." Now eligible to hold a captaincy on the 737 in Montreal, Stefanie is waiting out the present political conditions before considering a move. Besides, as she reported, she is thoroughly enjoying the 767.

FRANCE GRAVEL, who became Nordair's second woman pilot, grew up near Bagotville, Quebec, a military base. She loved to watch the fighters passing over her house and decided at the age of nine that she too was going to be a pilot. Knowing that there were very few women pilots, she believed that she should become as qualified as possible and chose the aviation program at CGEP [Le Collège General Enseignement et Professionel]. "Initially they rejected Suzanne Pomerleau's and my application because we were women. We kept on applying and once we were accepted all the instructors wanted to fly with us! Suzanne chose helicopters but I chose the airline course even though I knew of no women airline pilots. I thought, 'We have to start somewhere.'" When France graduated in September 1976, she had multi-IFR and commercial licences and 300 hours, as well as eighty jumps (sky dives) to her credit.

But jobs were scarce. Finally a sympathetic Andre Charette, the check pilot at Sol-Air Aviation in Rimouski, Quebec, told her she could fly the Cessna 206 on fire patrol, on condition that she be on time and do a good job! The job was short-lived however so France obtained an instructor's rating as a means to gain more experience. "I had no problem getting a job at Richel Air where I had learned. Janine Leclerc had established an excellent reputation for woman instructors."

France Gravel, one of the first three women pilots hired by Nordair.

Next came another season with Sol-Air on the 337 and then a job with Sept Îles Aeroclub flying charters on the North Shore. Once again, another woman pilot had paved the way. Marie Mazur was already there and had proven her competence so the company was prepared to take the chance on another woman. "It was a good experience," said France. "It was single pilot IFR flying an Aztec and we were on call twelve hours a day. At the beginning you scare yourself a little bit until you get used to flying in bad weather." France did not look like any bush pilot seen before in the Gaspé. "I could always feel the passengers' eyes watching me."

When that job ended she moved to Montreal to try to get on with one of the larger companies. She also applied to Air Canada, which told her she was too short and to the Canadian Forces, which said they did not accept women for pilot training. "I knew they had just opened the forces to women so I don't know why they said 'no' to me. I made many phone calls, I even went to Ottawa to see my MP but I soon realized I couldn't do anything."

When the chief pilot at Regionair offered her a job she accepted. "Regionair was a small airline but it was an airline. And the chance to fly a Hawker Siddeley 748 was too good to turn down even though it meant leaving Montreal again." France returned to Sept Îles and spent the next few years flying the Beech 99 and 748. "I was captain on the Beech 99 and first officer on the 748. It gave me excellent grounding for the airlines and in the summer of 1982 Nordair called me for an interview.

"When Nordair hired me in January 1983 I had 4000 hours and an ATR." With that kind of time and experience, no one could say that she was not qualified, although some voiced the opinion that she was hired only because she was a woman and a French Canadian one at that. Despite some of the negative reactions she encountered, she enjoyed Arctic flying—where all new pilots are assigned — and made sure she never made even a whisper of a complaint over accommodations. She began as first officer on the Fairchild 227. "The junior people go up north on the 227 for fifteen days. Nordair has two bases in the Arctic: in the west it's Cape Parry and in the east it's Hall Beach. Facilities in the west are better — I had my own washroom and shower. At Hall Beach the toilets and showers were all together. There were no flight attendants; normally we just carry freight."

What France remembered the most was the cold. "It was thirty to fifty degrees below and very dry — very hard to breathe outside, especially with a wind. There were always two aircraft up north; one in the east and the other in the west. In the west there was normally a stop every thirty minutes because there is a site every thirty minutes. In the east it was different because there were many mountains and the flying was longer. The job itself is not hard because it's just flying. We start early in the morning and finish late. The fifteen days pass quickly, except the last five days seem long."

In the spring of 1986 France could have bid captain on the 227 but, as she explained, "Nordair was very unstable then because of the merger with CP and I was afraid of a freeze on our positions — to be frozen up north would not be great. I'd rather be frozen in Montreal." France is now first officer on the Boeing 737 for Canadian Airlines International, and is based in Montreal.

Note
8 Carl Millard, interview, 30 January, 1985.

CHAPTER ELEVEN

Per ardua – through adversity

"Flying the CF-18 is like nothing you can imagine in your wildest dreams. It's a phenomenal aircraft."

— *Major Deanna Brasseur*

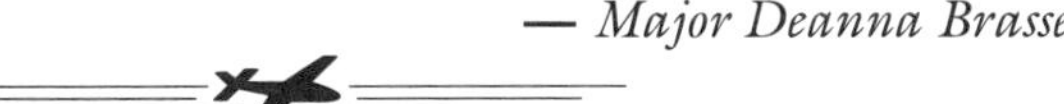

On November 8, 1979 the trial training of women pilots entered its first phase when four candidates showed up at 3 Canadian Forces Flight Training School (CFFTS) Portage. Captains Nora Bottomley, Deanna Brasseur, Leah Mosher, and Officer Cadet Kris Hummel were the female contingent of a class of forty-four trainees. Of this class three women and eighteen men graduated from Portage. While Hummel was unsuccessful, Bottomley, Brasseur, and Mosher went on to become the first women in the Canadian Forces (CF) to receive their wings for active duty.

These first four women were subjected to enormous pressures from both inside and outside the military and it was virtually impossible to blend in. "'It's one of them' was how the men talked about us," described Major Deanna (Dee) Brasseur. "We used to joke about the whiplash we caused when we walked anywhere in our flight suits. Our every action was noted. If one of us burped, Ottawa knew." Indeed, all twenty-one women who earned their wings under the trial program underwent extraordinary stresses. Although the military closed ranks around the women and reported throughout that the trials were progressing "satisfactorily," there were in fact many hurdles to overcome. The greatest was surmounting tradition: fifty-six years of the most exclusive boys' club in Canada. Emotions ran high amongst the men and the last all-male class to graduate was known as "LCWB" — "last class with balls." As one woman pilot sardonically remarked, "The trial was not whether women could fly but whether the men could accept us."

The program, known as the SWINTER (Service Women in Non-Traditional Roles) Trials, was to be run for five years because the military felt that that length of time was needed "to gain the necessary data, to design reasonable selection tests without lowering standards, to prepare and educate servicemen, and to assess the effectiveness of mixed units in operation." As one military official said, "It was a form of foot-dragging." The CF had no intention of moving quickly on what it knew would be a controversial project; the potential for resistance was great.

CANADIAN WOMEN have been in uniform since 1885 but their function has been limited primarily to nursing in wartime. In World War II their role was expanded to include employment in the communications, administrative, logistic, and medical support trades, but reduced again at war's end. With the outbreak of the Korean War in 1950 their numbers were increased and in 1951 Cabinet authorized the enrolment of women in the RCAF. But in the early sixties a changing defence policy and the introduction of more automated equipment, in the trades where women were concentrated, reduced the need for women. The result was that in 1965 their number was frozen at 1500 (about 1.8% of the total military force at that time) and they were restricted to support roles. While the 1968 unification of the army, navy, and air force to form the Canadian Forces included women, their future remained uncertain until 1971. Then, in response to the Royal Commission on the Status of Women, the military stated that there would be no limitations on their employment except that they could not be used in combat roles, on sea duty, or in remote locations. After eighty-six years of hovering uncertainly on the fringes, it seemed that there would be a permanent place for women after all and that the military trades were open to them. However, on closer examination women discovered that aircrew positions, such as pilot, were closed to them since pilot training fell into the first category. The three military colleges also remained off limits, the rationale being that their purpose was to train officers for sea, land, or air combat. Three factors finally prompted the military to re-evaluate these restrictions.

First, the CF recognized that women were seeking expanded employment opportunities. Second, it recognized that it would have to consider the Human Rights Act of 1978. Third, it foresaw that there was going to be a shortage of qualified male recruits in the eighties. In response to these findings the military reviewed its employment practices but decided that there was too little data to make a final decision and therefore recommended that it conduct a five-year trial program to assess the role of women in non-traditional areas. Accordingly, in January 1979, the Minister of National Defence, Barney Danson, declared that women would be employed on "a limited experimental basis in near combat roles on land, sea or in the air." Combat units would not be opened to women and the number of women to be trained to wings standard was to be limited to twenty.

The first three women to receive their wings for operational duty, CFB Portage, 1980. From left, Captains Nora Bottomley, Deanna Brasseur, Leah Mosher.

Despite this there was no sudden onslaught of women banging at the doors. In fact, much to the amazement of the military, of the 6000 women in the forces, only eleven applied. Indeed, during the entire six-year period that the trial was in progress, there were only 207 applicants, far less than the CF had hoped for. It was the opinion of some of the women that lack of publicity and misinformation at the recruiting offices were very much to blame. One woman said that she applied four different times before she was allowed to sign up for pilot training — "I was always told it was closed to women." Others, like Jane Van Ingen Schenau Foster, a fighter pilot, were unaware that flying was open to women. "I never saw any publicity on it. If I had known about it before, I would have joined earlier."

Those who made it past the recruiter's desk were selected in accordance with existing procedures and criteria for male aircrew candidates, except that the minimum acceptable height and weight for female aircrew were five foot two and a half and 113 pounds. Of the 207 women who applied, seventy-four made it to aircrew selection. Forty failed this screening, leaving only thirty-four to enter initial training at 3 CFFTS Portage. At this stage another ten women washed out, leaving a mere twenty-four to enter training at 2 CFFTS Moose Jaw. In all,

BRIGADIER GENERAL WENDY CLAY

While majors Nora Bottomley, Dee Brasseur, and Leah Mosher are usually touted as the first women in the CF to win their wings, in actual fact, Brigadier General Wendy Clay, a medical officer, was the first. The distinction being that Bottomley, Brasseur and Mosher were allowed to fly operationally and Clay was not.

When Wendy Clay of Fort St. John, British Columbia earned her medical degree in 1967 through the Medical Officer Training Plan, she unwittingly embarked on a path of "firsts." Wendy was the first female medical cadet officer in the CF; the first female officer cadet in the Royal Canadian Navy; the first woman to go through the subsidization plan since World War II; the first female general duty medical officer; and in 1974, the first woman to earn her military wings.

Flying never entered her mind until 1969 when, as part of the six-week flight surgeon's course, she took a high altitude indoctrination course at Trenton and a ride in a jet. "I so fell in love with flying that I joined the Trenton Flying Club a day later. Within the year, I had my private and commercial licences and began building time by flying skydivers." It soon became an open secret with the base commander that Wendy wanted to earn her wings. To do that she needed a posting to Moose Jaw, Saskatchewan. The precedent for doctors specializing in aviation medicine to receive flight training had already been set. "It was unofficially agreed that I could skip primary training at CFB Portage and go directly into jet aircraft." In November 1971 she was sent to Moose Jaw and was promoted to base surgeon, another first for a woman.

"As soon as I arrived I began training on the Tutor. I took a three-week leave of absence to attend ground school and then when the flying training began I returned to work full-

twenty-one women received their wings over the trial period: a mere drop in the bucket and too small, said some, to make a proper evaluation.

DESPITE AIR COMMAND'S declaration that the women were to be treated just like the men, that was almost impossible. The first group of women were constantly harangued by reporters. Air Command authorized media access to them only at designated intervals, but this directive did not stop persistent reporters from phoning. The calls, interviews, and special photo sessions disturbed the women and created jealousy within the class. To make matters worse they were often

time and fitted in the flying as best I could. Several of the instructors were very skeptical of the whole idea but it was made clear to them that even though I would not be an operational pilot I still had to attain the required standard." In July 1972, having logged 155 hours on jets, Wendy became the first woman in Canadian history to graduate from Basic Pilot Training. Now she was stuck. "To obtain wings standard I needed another hundred hours on T-33s, which was to be taken at Cold Lake. While the rest of the class went on to T-33s I remained at Moose Jaw. I was now on my own because none of the other flight surgeons had gone any further in their training." There was no precedent for her to point to and for a while it looked hopeless.

Wendy remained at Moose Jaw for another year and whenever she could she flew the Tutor to maintain her proficiency. In 1973 she was posted to Winnipeg for six months. While there she joined the Winnipeg Flying Club. Next came six months in England, where she attended the Royal Air Force Institute of Aviation Medicine at Farnborough and became the first woman in Canada or Great Britain to receive a degree in aviation medicine. With each step up the career ladder she seemed to be moving further away from her dream of obtaining her wings. "During this time I hadn't let anyone forget that I still wanted to finish my pilot training." As it happened, just when she returned to Canada, Moose Jaw was scheduled to hold its first advanced course on Tutors. "I was allowed to go to Moose Jaw long enough to finish my training, which consisted mainly of instrument work, formation flying, and aerobatics." Although long out of practice she was still so good that her CO wrote, "Her performance in the air was equal to and often exceeded the high standards that we impose on our professional pilots." In August 1974 she earned her wings and reporters publicized her achievement with headlines like, "Wings for Wendy" (*The Plainsman*, the Base newspaper

Major Wendy Clay, M.D., first woman to receive her wings — non-operational — for aviation medicine.

misquoted. Dee Brasseur recalled, "You had to be careful what you said for people remembered and often it was quoted out of context or blown out of proportion. I was haunted all through my training by something I said at the press interview in January 1980. They keep at you, find a line and twist it."

The first four women fit into the class with about as much ease as into a first-issue military uniform. The problem lay not only with their gender but also with their backgrounds and age. While the rest of the class consisted mainly of young recruits, the women were already ranking military officers. They knew many of the pilots and tended to gravitate towards their instructors and others of an equal rank in their off-duty time. A former (male) classmate observed, "We saw that as brown-nosing. We had our own problems trying to adjust to military life and worrying about washing out. Most of us saw them as 'those damn women.'" As Dee explained, "For some of the guys it was devastating to have older women who were actually going to get pilot training. The guys were keen but immature with sensitive egos. Many of them couldn't accept that we might do well on our own merits."

The women coped as best they could. A well-developed sense of humour turned out to be the best antidote. "We had code words," explained Dee, "that drove the guys crazy. 'How'd your flight go?' I'd ask Leah, and she'd answer, 'JFL.' (just f . . . ing lovely). Another time Nora started a rumour that we girls were going to be allowed to fly one of the Falcons that was to be posted temporarily at Moose Jaw. That really got the

on September 5, 1974) and "First Air Force Woman Pilot" (The *Vancouver Sun* on August 28, 1974).

Reserved by nature, she accepted the press gracefully as a small price to pay for being able to fly. As she explained, "My pilot training has allowed me to talk with pilots on an equal footing. I believe that a flight surgeon should be able to discuss all aspects of aerospace medicine and flying that might affect a pilot's capabilities. Being trained as a military pilot also improved my credibility and helped me to better understand the varied medical problems faced by pilots in their flying." Since receiving her wings she has continued to upgrade herself professionally, obtaining a Masters degree in community medicine. Now Brigadier General Wendy Clay, she was commandant, National Defence Medical Centre at the time of writing. In June of 1992 her position was to become Deputy Surgeon General of the National Defence Medical Centre.

guys wild." The women quickly learned to accept the amazed looks whenever they accomplished something. "I remember when Leah and I went on our first 'mutch' (mutual) together. We went to Cold Lake, which is a fighter-pilot base. When we climbed out one of the guys said, 'Where's your instructor?' 'Didn't bring one,' I answered. 'You flew it yourself?' he asked in astonishment. I nodded my head 'yes.' 'Very good.' he said."

Leah spoke of the stages they went through. "At first we were loners. If you had put us in a room with the men, you would have found one of us in each corner. As the stress of learning to fly and the hostility of some of the men increased, we turned to each other for moral support. Then it was 'united we stand.' As we became more confident and approached the end of our training, we were more than ready to go it alone. In fact, when we found out that they were going to post us all to Trenton, we objected. 'No way, do you think we're cry-babies that we can't survive by ourselves?' we asked." However, as Mary Bryant, a helicopter pilot, pointed out, "It would take a pretty hard-nosed individual to go it alone." For that reason the military tried to have at least two women in each class, although it was unrealistic to expect two women who are thrown together to hit it off just because they're women. As one woman reported, "I would have been better off on my own. The woman with me had applied just to prove that women could fly and she seemed to enjoy inciting the men. At first the guys thought I was the same."

While the path smoothed out for those who followed, there were still many deterrents to a complete integration of the women. Many men cynically assumed that the results of the trials were a foregone conclusion: that regardless of how they performed, women were going to be admitted permanently as pilots. To them, the term "trial" only served to emphasize the artificiality of the whole program. The trial concept was hard on the women too. "I did not like the feeling that when the trial was over I might be counting socks. I wondered about my job security," explained Herc pilot Micky Garner Colton. Long after the trial was over, in 1990, one of the women worried, "I'm being posted to CFB . . . as flight commander. I'm afraid that some will say it's only because I'm a woman."

The pressure was not limited to the women. Some instructors were torn between not being too hard on the women and, on the other hand, not letting any through who were not up to standards. One woman's opinion was that, "they were overly hard on us." While instructors tended to see the women as different, they also had difficulty viewing them as individuals. As late as 1984 the women remarked how some instructors harboured predetermined ideas on how women would perform. Liz Matchett Payette, who graduated from one of the last trial classes, explained. "If they had flown with a woman from one of the preceding classes and she had been good at formation flying, they seemed to assume that all women fell into the same groove. Even if they hadn't flown with a woman, they still couldn't look at us as individuals, each with our own skills. They seemed to think, 'now women are good at this and bad at that' and then they set up a cockpit situation to prove it. It was pretty discouraging at times." Another woman reported that one of her instructors "kept humming songs like, *Let's Get Physical* or *You're Having My Baby* to get a reaction out of me. I know that things were better for the women who graduated near the end of the trial. But we put up with a lot of shit and abuse."

The Canadair CT-114 Tutor.

On a more serious level, it was very frustrating for the women to hear men wondering if they deserved their wings. Even when Inge Plug won the Top Hat Award upon graduation, a fellow classmate told her she won it only because she was a woman. It obviously upset her a great deal because ten years later she reported, "It always ate at me. I thought he was a friend."

There were, of course, lighter moments. When Leah won the "jock strap challenge" for the student "who had the most screw-ups during training," the "double cup challenge" was introduced for the benefit of the women! "I won the Big 2 Bandit Award for the most unusual set of circumstances in the pre-solo phase of training. I was given a plaque on which was mounted the Bandit 2 crest and a set of wings on a bra," explained Leah.

Initially only Canadian Forces Base (CFB) Trenton was open to the women and it was considered to be one of the better postings. "We were always hearing, 'You women get all the best jobs,'" said Leah Mosher. "The men never stopped to think that maybe we might have liked some of the postings they got, but we couldn't request them. I used to say, 'How can three women jeopardize all you men?'" However, as Brenda Harder pointed out, "Trenton was being saturated with the women and it was resented by a lot of the men that the girls were being shoved down their throats. Also, Trenton was transport headquarters and had 'an old boys' school' attitude. We were always having to justify ourselves there." Once the women were allowed to spread out to other bases and take a greater share of the flying duties, much of the flack abated. And time eased tensions. "At 440 in Edmonton, for example, there was no problem," as Marlene Rudolph reported. "It was a young squadron with most people on their first tour and the women were more accepted." It helped too when some of the women were posted as instructors. Marlene noted that she "found most of the guys on the squadron receptive and the CO really nice. It was one of my students who picked me up at the airport and he said, 'Glad you're coming.' I had been dreading walking up to that squadron. I had been conditioned to thinking that Herc squadrons were jerks."

Robin Boutillier found that time and familiarity with the women eased much of the initial tension. "I was the first woman pilot at Summerside [Prince Edward Island, August 1983] and I was treated well *except* when the SWINTER survey was on. They asked the guys questions like, 'Do you like Robin?' or 'What do you think of women pilots?' The problem was there was only me. People tended to generalize too much about the women. But I never worried about blending in. Let's face it, it's more fun to work in a mixed gender situation. It was awkward at first — they were so used to acting in a certain way, they'd apologize if they swore, didn't know whether to help you or not. I kidded around a lot. I painted the women's washroom hot pink and was advocating hot pink flight suits." Micky Garner Colton summed up the acceptance factor, "Much had to do with the attitude of the CO and whether he could convince the rest of the squadron."

Most admitted that having another woman on the squadron helped, particularly if they "clicked." As Nora Bottomley said, "Cheryl Tardiff, the first female flight engineer in the CF, was on the Buffalo course with me. We hit it off and enjoyed doing silly things." Leah Mosher agreed, "After I made aircraft commander I sometimes flew with one of the female navigators. On one of our trips we decided to 'indoctrinate' our first officer, a man. We talked incessantly about shopping and clothes — not our usual cockpit chatter — then we made him go shopping with us."

Standard for the first few years was the tendency of some men to overlook the women even when they were aircraft commanders. "Especially if we were away from base I found that no one would think I was in charge. They would address their remarks to the men. People just weren't used to seeing a woman in a flight suit," recalled Leah. The women also had to get used to comments like, "You're a good pilot, for a woman." Rumours, of course, cropped up like dandelions. In the beginning they were mostly negative, "a lot of talk about some of the women being let through when they were borderline." However, when Dee Brasseur earned a "Good Show" for her handling of an engine failure at night in the Tutor, the rumour mill ground out accolades.

WHEN DEE, LEAH, AND NORA were first posted they found the reaction of the men mixed, everything from "it was high time that women were admitted," to a cautious wait-and-see, to "the military was going to pot." One jaundiced individual made sure everyone knew his point of view. "Ex Aircrew Earl Everson" as he signed himself, was quite explicit in a letter to the editor of the military newspaper, which they saw fit to print in 1981:

> "I sure don't go for the Air Force having these girl pilots . . . I don't feel too safe underneath with women pilots . . . You know what they'll be doing, don't you? All the time the aeroplane is trying to land, they'll be patting down their hair and pulling out their eyebrows and looking into their mirrors and putting on eye-makeup and all during the whole landing, that's what . . ."

Having no role models made it difficult for the women, and that was true for all twenty-one women because many were posted to squadrons that had never had women. Some tried too hard to be "one of the boys," out-drinking and out-swearing the guys or using language that even the men considered foul.

Others coped by secretly drinking and pretending outwardly that all was well. Still others adopted a formal attitude, afraid to socialize with the men or be too friendly in case someone misinterpreted their actions. Knowing that everything they did was observed by a thousand eyes affected whatever they tried. "It's a fishbowl effect," said a longtime woman pilot. "Everyone watches your every move. If you make a wrong move, you're made to suffer for a long time. I always made such an effort not to give anyone anything to talk about. I realized in the end you can't win." Those who fared best adopted a laidback approach, had a well-developed sense of humour, and a mentor, preferably a male pilot on squadron.

By 1986 the whole program was going more smoothly as an increasing number of men had occasion to fly with the women. But the last hold-outs were the fighter pilots. According to one aircraft commander, "It is the fighter squadrons who are the most chauvinistic and will give the greatest resistance. Once you have flown with a woman you are more likely to look favourably on them. My wife has 'educated' me and that really helped. A lot of the guys grow up in a military household, go to an all-male military college, and see no other world except one in which the man is dominant. It's no wonder they put the women down."

Many women noted that most younger men had a different mentality. "The young guys don't know what it was like before; whereas many of the older ones have idealized the 'old days.' Now the guys get the sexual harassment briefing before they hit the flight line. Students are so scared they don't do anything wrong," explained Robin Boutillier, who was instructing at Portage. "I remember one poor guy; it was just before his first spin and he was nervous. He was doing his pre-spin check for loose articles in the cockpit. He looks around and then says,

CAPTAIN MICHELLE GARNER COLTON

Michelle Garner of Kitchener, Ontario took a flight in a small plane on a dare and so loved it that she signed up for lessons immediately. "At about the 30 hour mark I realized that I could never afford to obtain all my licences. I was about ready to sell my soul to get money until someone told me about the Canadian Forces trial program for female pilots."

In March 1981 she reported to CFB Portage and later remembered incidents during her training. "My instructor and I flew to McCord Airforce Base. It was winter and I was a shapeless blob, dressed in mukluks, a 'bunny suit' (winter flying suit), a Mae West, and my helmet with the visor down. When I went to climb into the Tutor one of the Americans gave me a boost up and when he realized that I was a woman he was really embarrassed. 'Sorry ma'am,' he said. My instructor was in hysterics!"

Micky received her wings in June 1982 and was posted to 436 Squadron CFB Trenton to fly Hercs. "There were ten women at 436: five pilots and five navigators. I was the second woman on Hercs." Micky soon made her feminine presence felt. "I was sitting in the cockpit of the Herc trying to act very professional when I reached into one of the pockets of my flight suit to pull out my calculator. Instead, I yanked out a pile of tampons which fell all over the cockpit. I couldn't do anything but shrug my shoulders and laugh. The guys didn't let me forget that for awhile. Since then I've stayed in barracks with my crew, shared showers (not at the same time), used the 'can' on the Herc. You quickly learn to get over a lot of inhibitions."

Like the other women Micky ran into the usual startled reactions, and when she made aircraft commander the whole process repeated itself. "You the captain?" asked one of the men in amazement, when she landed in Shearwater.

'Anything loose on you ma'am?' I just cracked up. I knew he was thinking about doing the spin and hadn't realized what he was saying."

Often the men and women simply did not know how to treat each other. Social interplay between them had all the awkwardness of a high school prom. As Leah Mosher explained, "When I was posted to Trenton I started off trying to be 'one of the boys.' As I gained more confidence and experience I realized that I could still be feminine and treated as 'one of the crew' instead. At first it was awkward; if we were going to places where we didn't know anyone, it was the normal thing for the crew to go out for a meal together. For the most part I was expected to attend."

Neither did the men know whether they should be "gentlemen." Micky Garner Colton described a typical situation. "When I was in the plane and in the professional role of pilot I blended in. But when we all got out of the plane, especially if we were away from Trenton, some of the guys kind of stumbled over what they should do, like should they hold the door for

Captain Michelle Colton.

"You got it buddy," she retorted. A well-endowed woman with a wry sense of humour, Micky got along well with everyone, although she reported, "Often the guys just agreed with me, almost as if they couldn't be bothered to argue their point of view. I sometimes had the feeling that I was not getting straight answers from them — it would have helped if I did."

In June 1986 Micky was transferred to 429 Squadron at CFB Winnipeg, a transport squadron that supports the CF Air Navigation School. "I came in as an aircraft commander. That helped because I got more respect. 429 is a good squadron; it's like an extended family because it's so small. You get to know everyone faster and better than with the larger squadrons." When asked in 1986 what she thought about women flying combat, she replied, "I drool to fly the CF-18; it's quite the little beast. There will be resistance to women. It seems that fighter pilots have a definite mentality. Maybe it's just a myth perpetuated by the fighter jocks. Then again, they have to be macho because it's a very fast, dangerous form of flying."

Although Micky's commitment to the CF was up in August 1987 she extended her term. Stationed at 435 squadron in Edmonton, she flew C-130 Hercules until April 1990. With total flying time of 3679 hours, Micky is the area cadet officer, Air Command Detachment, Edmonton. She is married to a pilot and they have one child.

you? There's always a transition period. The guys see you in a flight suit, with your hair up and under a hat and earphones; and at the end of a long trip your boots aren't shiny, you're grubby, your flight suit doesn't do anything for you. Then you go to a hotel, have a shower, put on make-up, do your hair, maybe put on a dress. You come out and it's like night and day. And the guys think, 'Now what do we do with her. She's a pilot but . . .' When I'm in a flight suit I expect to be treated like a pilot, but when I'm off-duty I enjoy having someone open a door for me."

OFFICIALS SAW MARRIAGE as a potential problem area. In the past, wives followed their husbands. Now it was not so simple. If the wife were a pilot and the husband were also in the military, their postings might not mesh. If the husband were a civilian it was less likely that he would be mobile and able to follow his wife to wherever she was transferred. At least three women have married, two of whom subsequently were divorced. One of the women, Micky Garner Colton, elaborated in 1983 on some of the pitfalls. "I was married when I was still in training. It was a long distance love affair because my husband was also in the service and we were never on the same base. He eventually left the forces so that he would be more flexible and able to follow me on my transfers. I'm well aware of the sacrifices he made and I know that it is difficult to be the one who is left behind, thinking, 'Here I sit, there she goes having fun flying all over the countryside.' In 1987 they divorced. Micky is now remarried (to a pilot) and they have a family.

Some women expressed the same disappointment about the difficulty of combining the military and marriage and were less than generous in their assessment of what they perceived was the military's lack of cooperation. Others postponed any thoughts of marriage, believing that military flying and marriage were incompatible.

The pregnancy issue also elicited differing opinions. One woman felt that the military deliberately made it hard for women to combine flying and motherhood and cited the case of a navigator, "who told her career manager that she wanted to have a baby and asked for a ground posting. Instead, they posted her to a Boeing Squadron. Now she's pregnant and the squadron is pissed off. The military always need someone to man a desk between 8:00 and 4:30 and no one wants that job. The women are prepared to do it, plan their pregnancies so as not to totally inconvenience the squadron." Micky Colton summed up the views of many women, "It's a fact of life that women get pregnant and they don't do it alone. I think it's in the military's best interest to compromise — don't give her a flying job, put her in a desk position. If they're going to have women pilots — and they can't continue to ignore half the population — then something is going to have to be worked out."

But others felt differently. As one said, "The Canadian Forces doesn't owe you. You must not make demands. Maybe

CF helicopter pilots Captains Louise Neil, Mary Bryant, Inge Plug, c. 1988.

MARY BRYANT

Mary Bryant of Mission, British Columbia was a commercially licenced pilot (1976) who decided that she wanted to fly sophisticated aircraft and the military was the way to go. She began pilot training in January 1982 and halfway through the course at Moose Jaw she was asked if she wanted to fly helicopters. "I said 'yes.' I wanted to try it all." Training on a Jet Ranger, she graduated in April 1983, the second woman to receive her wings on a helicopter. After conversion on the Twin Huey, she was posted to 424 Squadron at Trenton.

About her experiences as a search and rescue pilot she said, "I've been on many searches, fewer rescues, and have arrived at search headquarters more than once with tragic

they could bend a little more but if I got pregnant I could foul up someone else's career progression. If the squadron is short a pilot it creates a problem." And another woman succinctly summed up the military point of view, "If you decide to marry while in the forces you must be aware that you could get separate postings. We have a job to do: 'operational readiness.' What some of the women are trying to do is put restraints on the job. You can't apply the same constraints as on civilian street. If you take off time to have a baby, someone else has to take up the load and the squadron suffers. I'd have no problem signing a document which said I would not get pregnant while on a fighter squadron."

Two women fulfilled the military's worst fear; they became pregnant while serving a flying tour. Elizabeth Matchett Payette and Robin Boutillier did the "unforgivable." Accord-

news. The rescues I performed were extremely rewarding. Smiles on the faces of the people we recovered far outweigh the inconvenience of any call-out. I have found many people drifting about the Great Lakes due to mechanical difficulties with their boat. People who have had a pleasant afternoon turn into a one- or two-day ordeal seem to re-evaluate life. A cup of coffee or a sandwich will never be taken for granted again."

In March 1986 Mary was posted to CFB Comox. A month later she was sent to the Sinai Desert for six months peace-keeping duties as part of Canada's commitment with the Multinational Force and Observers, three thousand or so military and civilian personnel from ten member countries manning checkpoints and observations posts to prevent any violations of the protocol signed by Egypt and Israel. Canada contributed 136 people and nine Twin Huey helicopters in a rotary wing unit and seven other staff officers. The first Canadian aviation unit arrived in March 1986.

Mary requested the Sinai posting. "The tour was considered to be in a 'hotter' area and there was some debate about whether I could go but because it was not a combat role there was no reason why not. Once there I encountered little resistance to my presence but people stared a lot and were surprised to see a female pilot." Duties entailed moving observers, providing VIP transportation, and doing search and rescue or medevacs. "We had to acclimatize ourselves to a desert environment; get used to temperatures that rose over 100°F and could be as high as 104°F on the tarmac. Our biggest problem was navigating around the sand — not much to use except the sand dunes. It was a challenge." Depth perception was also a problem because

ing to them and reports from others, there was no big fuss. "My squadron was great; it was very supportive. I was put on the desk and handled the phones [for search and rescue]," said Robin. Undoubtedly her bubbly personality helped to smooth out what could have been an extremely touchy situation and she initiated most of the jokes about her pregnancy. "I was huge, about 180 pounds. The normal call sign was Tusker Ops but the guys would call in and ask for Beluga Ops and I'd answer Harpoon Ops instead of Pontoon Ops." One of the few labour pains with the birthing of that baby was, according to rumour, that Robin had to assure her CO that the baby would not interfere with her duties. Retorted the woman who passed on that piece of information, "Do they ever ask a man if his child is going to interfere with his job?'" Elizabeth also reported that she found everyone positive about her pregnancy.

the terrain was very irregular and the sand was a uniform colour. And there were other hazards, beyond those natural to flying in the Sinai, such as land mines — more than three million of them were left behind from previous conflicts.

As for her place in 442 Squadron, she said in 1986, "I play the same role here as I did in Trenton except that I'm flying a Labrador. We're on twenty-four hour stand-by, 365 days of the year. Yes, things are definitely easier now than when I joined. More and more of the guys have trained with women and we're not faced with all the same prejudices as before."

After that duty tour Mary was posted to CFB Comox, flying the CH 113, until mid-1990. This was followed by a period as duty controller at the Rescue Coordination Centre at CFB Edmonton. She officially left the regular force in February 1992 having finished a posting to 408 Tactical Helicopter Squadron in Alberta, flying Bell 212 helicopters. At the time of writing Mary was finishing a course in business management studies at the Northern Alberta Institute of Technology and had begun a business that offers training in wilderness, arctic, and roadside survival. As Mary wrote, "This company, Outback Survival, also sells limited survival equipment and supplies lots of free advice." She also started flying a MMB BK 117 part-time for the air ambulance in southern Alberta and she expects to fly full-time when she completes her business courses. "I guess the bottom line is that now I am out of military the options seem endless and I am busier than ever. I do plan to remain in the aviation community as a pilot and to keep Outback Survival in the black."

"I told my CO right away. If there were any hostile comments I did not hear about them. I lost my flying status and was put into a ground position."

In October of 1985 the trial program came to an end. To all intents and purposes, the experiment "worked." Twenty-one women received their wings and performed satisfactorily in their squadrons. In some cases they did better than the men, probably because they worked harder. They disproved the myth that they were incapable of handling or commanding military aircraft. They toppled the popular masculine myth about the alleged shortcomings of women in a man's world. They met the standards and became good solid military pilots.

Lieutenant Inge Plug, first woman helicopter pilot in the military, receiving her wings.

IN RESPONSE to these findings Perrin Beatty, Minister of National Defence, announced on July 14, 1986 that women were eligible to serve as pilots, navigators, and flight engineers in the Boeing 707, the C-130 Hercules, and other transport aircraft; the CH-113 Labrador and CH-135 Twin Huey helicopters used for search and rescue; the CT-114 Tutor jet used for pilot training; and the T-33 Silver Star in the utility/ communications relay role. For the first time in Canada's history, they could serve regularly alongside men in all aircrew specialties in the training, tactical transport, search and rescue, strategic transport, utility, maritime reconnaissance, and long range anti-submarine roles.

Still outstanding, however, was the question of whether women would be employed in combat roles, in this instance, as fighter pilots. To address this question and others, a Charter Task Force was established in March 1986 by the Chief of Defence Staff to examine five areas of concern to the Forces, one of them "the policy on mixed-gender employment." Reporting in February 1987 it concluded "that there [was] insufficient positive evidence that mixed-gender employment could be further expanded without adverse impact on operational effectiveness . . . [but] sufficient additional evidence could be obtained from trials and experiences from other Armed Forces as well as from within the Canadian Forces, to re-examine all of the remaining single-gender male units in the next two years."

What that all boiled down to was another trial. True to form, the military reacted by not acting but by instituting an investigation that would allow it to move cautiously into what would be a controversial area. In fairness, it must be admitted that little was known about women in combat. For that matter, even the sociological impact of mixed units was still largely undetermined. Also the concept of "operational effectiveness" in the forces has aspects that do not normally appear in civilian activities. As the task force pointed out, "Members of the military must not only work together, but must often live together for twenty-four hours a day, in close confinement, with little or no privacy and with no choice of with whom they associate. In wartime, the military environment becomes even more intense and the problems even more difficult."

Major R.J. Butt, former information officer, CFB Winnipeg, elaborated, "There are a whole raft of options to look at. There are physical differences which can handicap training and the effectiveness of the unit. When Israel allowed women in combat roles [1948] it was found that the men protected the women — that's a way of life — and that was one of the reasons why Israeli women are no longer allowed in combat positions. Any change has to come logically and slowly. We cannot wave a wand." The strongest argument for allowing women into combat was that flexibility was fundamental because of the small size of the Canadian Air Force. As former Air Vice Marshall Leigh Stevenson caustically remarked, "It would never have occurred to us to train pilots for limited duties. All must be ready for combat." So, to examine the remaining restrictions on women a special Trials Office was established in February 1987.

What did the women want? "I'd love to fly fighters." exclaimed Jane Foster. Said Dee Brasseur, who had never made any secret of her desire to fly fighters, "I'm hoping that time is still on my side." And Susan Witchell declared, "If they ask me I'll say 'yes.' I'm not afraid of combat if that's what they're worried about." Not all of the women evinced interest in flying fighters, much less the possibility of being engaged in combat operations. To reassure them, the military stated that they would not be obliged to fulfill a combat role. That of course brought up the possibility that increased use of women beyond the traditional support areas could result in a decline in the number of women recruits. Indeed, this happened and the CF hopes to overcome it by a stepped-up publicity program.

Boeing-Vertol CH-113 Labrador.

In April 1987 Air Command said that the trial program for female fighter pilots would be composed of a total of ten women, five in each of the two Cold Lake squadrons. Just where these women would come from was the unanswered question. Dee Brasseur, who had instructed on Tutors and was then flying T-Birds, was the most likely, with Jane Foster, then a Tutor instructor, a close runner-up. However, whether there were sufficient women with wings who could qualify or wished to move into a fighter role was the question. There was already a problem of too few women candidates for pilot training and a concern by some that the trial would fold before it started. Then, in July 1987, without warning, the trial was cancelled and the CF announced that combat flying would be opened immediately to women. The last barricade was down. Dee jubilantly recalled, "I've been working toward this end for ten years. My ultimate design was to fly fighters." Two years later she and Jane Foster completed CF-5 and CF-18 training, becoming the first two combat-trained women jet fighter pilots in the world.

To all intents and purposes the introduction of women as military pilots is going along "just fine." Nevertheless, as with any minority, only time and more women will erase the traces of discrimination that are still alive. In 1989 one of the women had the opportunity to fly in Central America, in what was considered a near combat, if not combat, situation. However, a colonel overheard her saying she was going to apply and he retorted, "You can't. You're a woman!" Described the woman in question, "He tried to laugh it off and say he was just joking. But he wasn't; his comment was a gut reaction and one shared by most fighter pilots."

WHEN THE TRIAL program began CF pilot training and operational employment of aircrew were controlled by Air Command Headquarters, Winnipeg, including sixteen bases and twenty-four radar stations stretching from coast to coast. Pilot candidates first went to the Basic Officer Training Course at CFB Chilliwack. From there they went to 3 CFFTS Portage, which ran seven primary flying training courses a year, each comprised of forty-four students, for a total of three hundred and eight. With an expected attrition rate of thirty percent its aim was to graduate 216 students a year, of which thirty were from the Royal Netherlands Air Force. As pilot candidates they could expect the ten-week course at Portage to include ground school and twenty-seven flying hours on the Musketeer, which covered take-offs and landings, stalls, spins, emergencies, forced landings, and aerobatics. The course objective was to eliminate poor candidates quickly.

After Portage came high altitude indoctrination at CFB Winnipeg, land and sea survival training at CFB Edmonton and CFB Comox, and finally training on the Canadair CT-114 Tutor jet (the aircraft flown by the Snowbirds) at CFB Moose Jaw for about eleven months. At Moose Jaw students received more than 200 hours of ground school, an equal amount of flight training, simulator training, plus 180 hours of officer development. After about 140 hours on the Tutor, some were chosen for rotary wing training. Throughout all phases each candidate was continuously monitored and periodically tested.

After receiving their wings, pilots proceeded to different operational training units (OTU) across Canada for additional training on the type of aircraft they would fly in their postings.

It appears that the initial plan was to limit the women to CFB Trenton. When Dee Brasseur of the first group asked for an instructing posting at Moose Jaw, she was at first refused. Although the first women received their wings in March 1981, it was not until August 1983 that a woman, except Dee, was sent to a base other than Trenton. The Trials Office felt that if the women were scattered, with only one on each squadron, it would be too easy to work around them and the trial's results would be invalid.

Tactical airlift (TAL) was also off-limits to the first women although this restriction was soon relaxed when it became evident that squadron effectiveness would be impaired if the women were not TAL-trained. Neither was helicopter training permitted until Inge Plug made an effective appeal for rotary wing training. Inge received the "Top Hat" (best pilot) award in her graduating class and there was no rational reason for denying her rotary wing training. Two other women followed shortly after. By 1987 women were serving alongside men in all aircrew specialities and one woman had been on a United Nations peace-keeping mission in the Middle East.

Captain Nora Bottomley, c. 1980.

NORA BOTTOMLEY of Smithers, British Columbia, had no burning desire to join the CF much less become a pilot. "After grade twelve I didn't know what I wanted to do. One day I went past a recruiting centre, walked in and asked what was available for women. When I found out there was only administrative work, I turned around and walked out. A year later I walked into another recruiting centre. This time I was told I could be a teletype operator, a radar plotter or in administration. Being a radar plotter sounded interesting, so I joined. That was in 1970." After basic training, she was assigned to CF Station Shelbourne, Nova Scotia as an assistant watch officer. "I also flew as a radar plotter in the Argus and fell in love with flying. I knew that being a pilot had to be my ultimate goal."

For that she needed to be an officer. Never mind that she also needed to be a man. "Solve one problem at a time" was Nora's philosophy and she set about getting a recommendation for officer training. That was no trouble, but finding a trade that suited her was more difficult. Nora was not the rebellious type, yet rebel she did. In a gentle but obvious flouting of military expectations, she requested three positions that she knew were all closed to women.

"When I was recommended for commission I requested pilot training as my first choice, navigator as my second choice, and air weapons controller for my last choice. I was told that only nursing, administration, or pharmacy were available to women. I told them I wasn't qualified for two and didn't want the third. They asked me, 'Do you want to be an officer or not?' I asked for a little time to think about it but the very next day I learned that air weapons was open to women, so I took it and in 1973 received my commission [rank of Lieutenant] as an air weapons controller," the first woman in that trade.

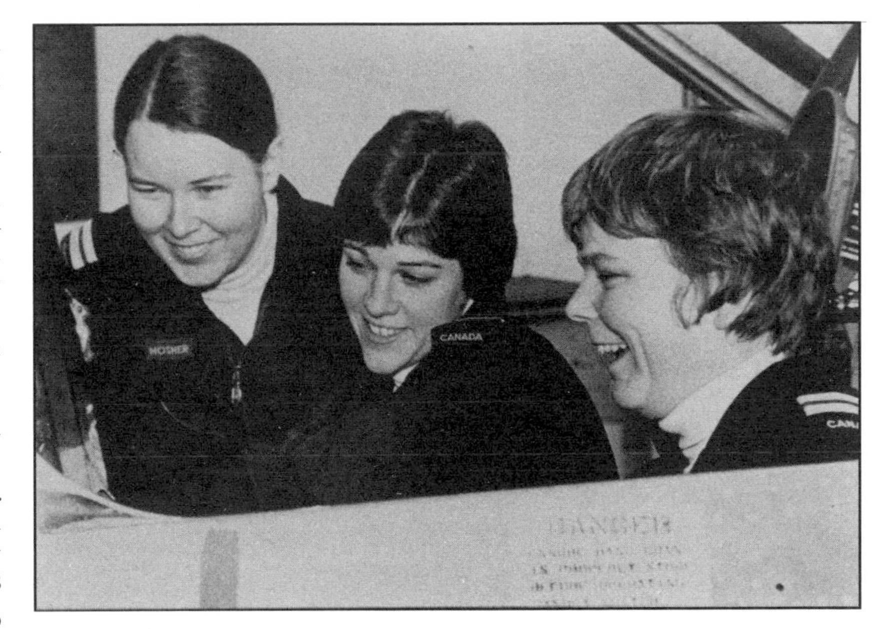

Captains Leah Mosher, Deanna Brasseur, and Nora Bottomley.

Posted to CFB North Bay and then to Great Falls, Montana, Nora seized every opportunity she could to fly. "I flew back seat in American T-33s on PACE (performance analysis by continuous evaluation) and target missions. On my own I qualified as an electronics countermeasures officer on the CF-100 and in 1976 I qualified for my private pilot's licence." That year she was also promoted to captain and became the first female senior director of Norad. She also reapplied each year for pilot training.

"The first year [1973] I formally applied for pilot training my CO put my application through to Ottawa in spite of the regulations saying that women were not eligible. After that my application never got further than the CO's desk. I applied just on principle. I was always careful not to make an issue over it but I wanted to make sure that the 'higher ups' knew what I wanted. If you want to make the military your career you don't make waves." For six years she waited. "Then one day in March 1979, my CO said, 'Nora, there's something of interest to you on my desk.' It was a memo advising that pilot training was open for a limited time to women in the Canadian Forces. Of course, I applied. I had good wishes from everyone. My co-workers just assumed that I would pass air crew selection and get my wings. From then on the pressure was on to succeed."

Nora, a quietly confident type of individual, was close-mouthed about the reception the women received, "Things were tense. I learned to let a lot roll off my back, to ignore the comments. My most difficult time was the day of the press conference on January 29, 1980. Leah Mosher and Dee Brasseur had both passed their final flight test. Kris had washed out and I was scheduled to take my test the next day. The reporters knew this and zeroed in, asking what would I do if I failed, would I get a second chance, and so on. All of this put a lot of pressure on me."

However, Nora remembered the lighter side as well. "It was just around solo time and my instructor and I were off for a clear hood trip," recalled Nora. "He was doing the walk around and I was climbing in to do the internal check when the toggle on my Mae West, which was worn under the parachute, got caught on the canopy rail of the Tutor. My Mae West inflated just as I was climbing in and threw me back against the side of the aircraft, leaving me suspended, feet off the ground, and gasping for breath. You're supposed to bleed off some of the pressure once you inflate a Mae West otherwise it can cut off your breathing. I was hanging there trying to yell 'Help' and my instructor couldn't hear me above all the other airport noise. Finally I remembered to release some of the pressure, grabbed the side of the aircraft and pulled myself up just as my instructor came around to my side looking for me. Everyone on base soon heard about that!"

Nora's first posting was to 424 Squadron CFB Trenton. "Search and Rescue [SAR] was my first choice. I had been in air defence playing war games and I never saw the result of what I was doing. I wanted a change and SAR offered that." However, life at 424 started off inauspiciously. "The aircraft commander, whether consciously or unconsciously, made my life miserable and I think it was because I was female. The flight was an 'up-down' one of short hops to eastern Canada and return. The weather was down to minimums, it was turbulent and there was thunderstorm activity. I felt he didn't give me too much consideration. He wanted me to handle everything, get the weather, work the radios, even though I was not fully familiar with them, do all the calculations even though we had a navigator, and fly all the approaches. I was swamped. He kept getting madder and madder at me because I was getting slower and slower. I became a total loss. On the return trip we stopped at Quebec City where he phoned the squadron to say he would not fly with me anymore. That really upset me. Thank heavens no one was there to take over and he had to fly back with me." However, his complaint meant a check ride for Nora with the base flight commander. Thoroughly shaken, she thought her flying career was over, but she flew satisfactorily. "He told me I was doing okay and not to worry, that I had just got hit with a bad first trip. I flew only a couple more trips with that aircraft commander before he was transferred out of the squadron."

When Nora arrived at 424 Squadron its primary duty was transport and tactical airlift, soon to be changed to search and rescue. "Before the change I got to fly some interesting flights. One of them was Air Patrol for the Ottawa Summit in July 1981. I remember that flight for two reasons. One, because we had a run-in with a helicopter and two because of the toilet facilities! In those days the Buffalo had just a can with a garbage bag behind a curtain. I had been flying for about nine hours and had to 'go,' but I didn't want to use that can, except I had no choice. I found it embarrassing. Now, none of that would bother me."

There was no such thing as a typical day. "The Buffs were tasked on very short notice. You could go in expecting to do nothing and then be gone for two weeks. We did a lot of transport flights, including an annual trainer around the world. The Buffalo had United Nations peace-keeping duties and we had to maintain our currency in Europe and throughout North America."

Search and Rescue crews consisted of two pilots, a flight engineer, a navigator, and two SAR technicians. "We were taught to do different types of search patterns. Each aircraft is assigned an area and the crew navigates visually along the lines

The de Havilland CC-115 Buffalo.

the navigator puts on the map. It is a very precise way of flying. We are taught different types of drops. The pilot has to learn the patterns, know how to set them up, keeping in mind the wind, terrain, weather, etc. I remember the first time I did a message drop. It was over the field at Trenton and I flew too high. The aircraft commander told me to go lower. I went lower. I was reading about 30 feet AGL. There was a guy on a lawnmower just off the runway, he ran for it. The aircraft commander said, 'Very good, but maybe a little higher next time.'"

Nora also described one of her first operational flights, which was a search for a missing boat on Lake Superior. "We had originally set out on a training flight but found the winds so high that we decided to return to base. On our way back we received a call to check out a boat which had been reported wallowing. All we could find were five life jackets floating. At this point a SAR helicopter joined us. We were bouncing all over the sky. I just concentrated on flying. We found out later that the surface winds were over 70 knots. When we reported that we were heading back because we were low on fuel, the helicopter pilot radioed, 'Don't leave me.' He was scared. When we landed at Hamilton and walked into the terminal we were asked, 'Where did you come from?' 'We just landed,' I said. 'How could you, three commercial airliners just overshot because of the turbulence.' 'Don't tell me,' I said, 'We've been working the last five hours at low level.' The crew was commended for the role we played in that search operation."

The Canadair F-5 Freedom Fighter.

In April 1983 Nora was upgraded to aircraft commander: the first woman aircraft commander in the CF. "There was no real press stuff. The CO came out to meet me after my first flight and the base photographer was on hand, that's all. I don't think there was any resentment. My squadron was positive." In July Nora achieved another first when she, as captain, was part of the CF's first all-female front-end crew. Later that year she received what she considered to be one of her most interesting and challenging assignments. "I was placed in charge of clearing the route for the cruise missile testing and given complete freedom on how I wanted to handle it. I was responsible for eighteen people. I set up headquarters at Fort Nelson and found out later that my ground crew used to tell the town folks that they had a great boss and the boss was a woman. I had terrific support from everyone."

Undoubtedly her down-to-earth personality and a well developed sense of humour helped to endear her to her crews. Her wit even cut through the tension of the American Air Traffic Controllers strike during an approach into Washington. As Nora recalled, "The controller was too busy to give each aircraft its altimeter setting individually, so he gave them all at once. 'Gentlemen,' he said, 'the altimeter settings for the following areas are . . . ' I couldn't resist saying when a lull came, 'New York Centre, do you have an altimeter setting for ladies or do I have to take the one for gentlemen?' The controller started laughing and said, 'You've made my day!'"

Nora had her share of mechanical problems with the Buffalo. "It got to be a standing joke that if you flew with me you packed a bag for two weeks because it seemed that every Buff I flew had something go wrong with it. A two-day trip to Bermuda lasted for two weeks because of multiple electrical malfunctions. We finally returned in the back end of a Herc. I had a windshield shatter on an overseas flight, three nose gear failures, and an engine failure. I think I had every emergency there was except a fire."

Nora spoke positively of the crews she flew with but found that five years of wearing pilot wings still did not ensure immunity against derogatory remarks. In February 1985 she was posted to Flight Instructors School (FIS) in Portage, where she washed out and was re-posted to another squadron, which caused some to say she received special treatment. "The Review Board recommended that in view of my past record I be posted back to transport flying. But some said I should have been grounded since I did not pass FIS," explained Nora. "What hurt was that there are a lot of guys who have flunked out of FIS but you don't hear anything negative about them."

In 1986 Nora became the first woman pilot to be posted to 440 Squadron, CFB Edmonton, a SAR and Transport squadron. She coordinated a program called CASARA (Civil Air

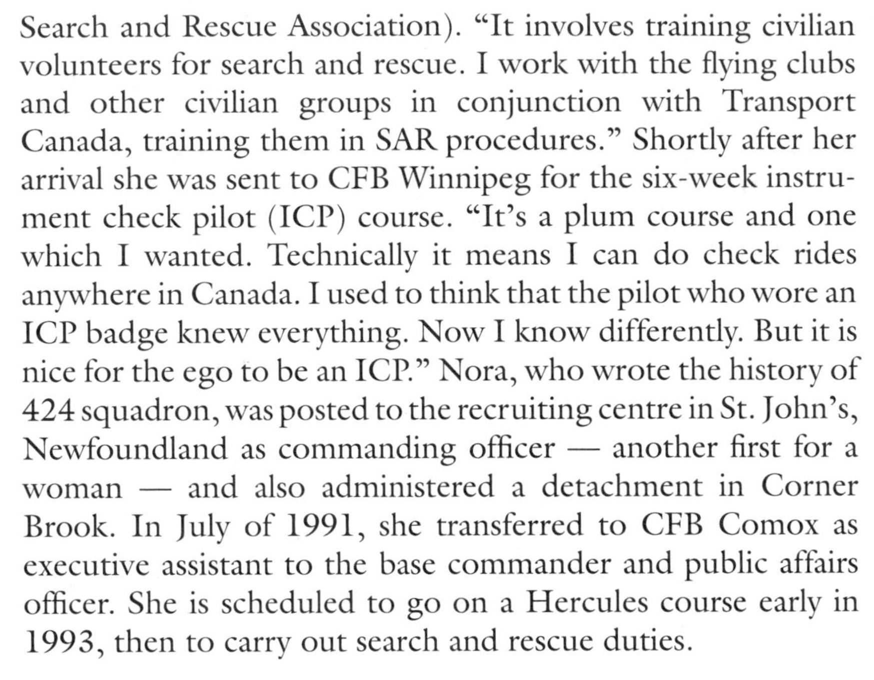

Search and Rescue Association). "It involves training civilian volunteers for search and rescue. I work with the flying clubs and other civilian groups in conjunction with Transport Canada, training them in SAR procedures." Shortly after her arrival she was sent to CFB Winnipeg for the six-week instrument check pilot (ICP) course. "It's a plum course and one which I wanted. Technically it means I can do check rides anywhere in Canada. I used to think that the pilot who wore an ICP badge knew everything. Now I know differently. But it is nice for the ego to be an ICP." Nora, who wrote the history of 424 squadron, was posted to the recruiting centre in St. John's, Newfoundland as commanding officer — another first for a woman — and also administered a detachment in Corner Brook. In July of 1991, she transferred to CFB Comox as executive assistant to the base commander and public affairs officer. She is scheduled to go on a Hercules course early in 1993, then to carry out search and rescue duties.

Captain Deanna Brasseur, c. 1980.

DEANNA BRASSEUR was born in Pembroke, Ontario, the oldest of three children. After grade twelve she enrolled for teacher training at Red Deer College, Alberta but left after a year to join the CF. "My father was an RCAF officer and I had the military and moving in my blood. I wanted to travel and I knew that the military would satisfy that need," she explained. Turning down her parents' suggestion that she enroll in the Regular Officer Training Program, Dee enlisted in September 1972 and emerged as an administrative clerk with the rank of private. "Within a short time I was so bored that I almost left the forces. My father suggested that I apply for a commission. This time I listened."

She was appointed an officer cadet in October 1973, commissioned with the rank of lieutenant and posted to North Bay as an air weapons controller, the second woman in this position. In 1977 she was sent to the headquarters of the 23rd Norad Region, Duluth, Minnesota, as officer in charge of the training program and the following year was promoted to captain. During this period she also attended university part-time and completed two years of a Bachelor of Arts degree.

Deciding that working days and studying nights was too much, Dee applied for basic officer's university training. But another idea was also occurring to her. "Working in air weapons control put me in close contact with pilots. I had taken a lot of 'fam' flights in the Voodoo and the T-Bird and had been allowed to take control. 'Hey, Dee, you should be a pilot,' a few of the guys said. That got me thinking and in 1978 I began my private pilot's licence. Up until then I had never thought of military flying. It was not until I met Nora [Bottomley], also in air weapons control, and learned of her wish to fly with the air force that I seriously began to think of pilot training for myself."

As soon as the trial program was announced Dee signed up and, shortly after, was told to report to Toronto for air crew selection. Then everything happened at once. She was simultaneously accepted for the trial program at RMC, the Royal Military College at Kingston, Ontario and informed that she had qualified for pilot training. "I had to choose. It was a tough decision to make. I wanted to finish university but I also wanted to fly. Flying won out because I felt that I could always complete university on my own, whereas I might never have another chance to fly in the military." In November 1979 she took her place in history as one of the first four women accepted by the military for pilot training.

Like the others, Dee said little about the "climate" at CFB Portage or Moose Jaw, except to allude to some of the name-calling that the women experienced. Her best memories centred on Major Clancy Sheldrup, their flight commander at Moose Jaw. "He was terrific," said Dee. "Both he and his wife were our friends. I was the first one in my course to solo at Moose Jaw and he was pleased because he wanted one of 'his girls' to be first. We became known as 'Clancy's Angels.'"

From the start Dee wanted to fly jets and eventually requested instructing or training on Tutors at Moose Jaw. The answer was "no." "Instructing was not open to women for their first tour. But I argued that the military was putting through 155 guys, in a situation riddled with rumour, and those guys

Captain Deanna Brasseur, initial training on a Beech Musketeer, c. 1980.

would carry on with the rumours. But if there were at least one female instructor then maybe the young guys would think that women had a right to be there. The other argument was that there was really no one that any of the women could turn to at Moose Jaw. I knew how frustrating it could be. If I could be there, as an instructor, there would be someone for other women to talk to." Articulate, logical, and forceful, Dee's request was granted.

"There were six guys on course with me and it was not easy. You could almost see their thought processes. We had seen those other instructors for the past eleven months as a student, now I was one of them. It took a good six months for me to feel comfortable with the flight group and as an instructor. I was always working harder. I knew the eyes in the other seat were really critical. No one wanted to fly with me. However, some had to and after a few flights they'd say, 'Hey, we'll have to do this again,' and it got better." The word got around that Dee was capable and soon she was treated as a member of the flight. "However, I often got the feeling that I didn't really belong. I'd walk into a strange Mess in a flight suit; people would stare at me and I'd get that insecure feeling. I'd think, 'Do I drink my beer and run or do I pretend I belong here and stay?' Eventually curiosity would win out and they'd walk over, 'So, you're one of them.' And then the questions would begin.

Major Deanna Brasseur, with the CF-18 Hornet.

"There seemed to be two types. From the first group of the old career guys there were those who were secure and confident about themselves and they were not threatened by us. They were usually the ones who would say, 'Hi, how are things going.' They were either a 'convert' or at least neutral and fairly well informed about the trial program. The others didn't want any change. They wanted the military to stay the same as it had been from the start. They were likely to say, 'What the hell are you trying to prove?' Then there were the younger guys. The eighteen-year-olds could be a problem. All of a sudden there was a girl who was as good as they were and they tried to transfer their frustrations to her. They could not follow a logical discussion. 'You girls take all the good postings,' they'd say, forgetting that we were limited in what we could choose and that maybe we wanted some of the postings that the guys got. As the program progressed some of the younger guys assumed that there had always been women and it was not such a problem."

Dee's manner was smart, tough, and confident, but as she admitted it was, in the early days, simply bravado. It took an engine failure in 1983 for her to be fully accepted. "I was on a night training session with a student. We were going to the outer traffic pattern and were on the downwind when I heard a loud thump. There was an odor of fried bird in the cockpit. 'Holy shit,' I thought, 'a bird's got sucked up in the engine.' Meanwhile my student was saying, 'Was that jet wash?' I said, 'Bird strike!' He eased off the bank, pulled up the nose slightly. I was watching the instruments and transmitting to the tower. Then I took control. 'I have control,' I told him, saying to myself, 'I'm thinking like an instructor' for I had let him handle the situation at first. The engine sounded like someone had thrown a bag of bolts in it. I thought, 'I really have lost my engine.' We had peaked out at 3800 feet ASL [about 2000 feet AGL]. We were already below the minimum recommended ejection altitude of 2500 feet. I didn't want to eject because that would have meant losing the plane and there were farm houses below. I elected to try and make it in. The DME showed four and a half miles from base. The Tutor manual claims good performance on the glide. 'Now I'll see if the book is right.' I thought, 'I could foul up if I put the gear down at the wrong time.' I could see the approach lights, I held my glide airspeed and we landed safely. 'Thanks, God,' I breathed. What a way to end a night trip." For her handling of the crippled jet, she received a "Good Show," an award given to pilots for an outstanding performance.

Dee spent four and a half good years at Moose Jaw. Then, much to her disgust, a ground posting and a French language course in Ottawa followed. She suffered through that for eight months before being assigned to be a part of the Charter Task Force studying the feasibility of women as fighter pilots. "It was a terrific introduction to staff headquarters. We looked at every country in the world, at every aspect, physical and medical. It was great to be in on the decision-making."

In 1986 her dream of flying fighters moved closer to reality when she was posted to CFB Cold Lake to fly T-33s. "I would like to have the opportunity to fly the CF-18. My biggest concern is that it won't happen. One of my reasons for coming out here is to be at the right place, waiting for a break," she said in February 1987. Before being posted to Cold Lake she went to CFB North Bay for a month's training on T-33s. "The conversion course for the T-Bird [T-33] was twenty-nine hours. I found it a challenge. It goes higher, faster and longer than the Tutor. It's pretty exciting to be flying by myself."

As she was the first woman to fly the T-Bird, there was a lot of press. "I wasn't even there four days before the reporters were out. Things like, 'From Clerk to Jet Jockey Now I Want to Fly F-18s' appeared in the papers. I told reporters I was too busy to give any interviews and I did the same when I arrived at Cold Lake. I was the first woman pilot there but there was no fanfare. I simply walked in and was just another pilot." In fact, Dee was more than just another pilot, she was the T-33 flight commander designate. "That was a real vote of confidence. There are twelve T-Birds and three helicopters at Cold Lake. Our primary role is local search and rescue, medevacs, primary support, flying PACE trips for the southern sites, target missions, towing banners for the F-18s to shoot at, GAT (ground

CAPTAIN SUSAN WEICKER

Sue Weicker is a relative newcomer to the military, having earned her wings (on the Jet Ranger) in October 1990. She was posted to 408 Squadron, Edmonton where she flies the CH 135 Twin Huey. "I like helicopters. I like to fly low and fast."

Beginning her military career almost a decade later than Bottomley, Brasseur, and Mosher, Sue reflected on her experiences compared to theirs. "The first three were the product of a different age. In an environment where there were no precedents, they had to try to conform. They were often treated badly by the male pilot community, some of whom even tried to make the women cry. *We* women now march to our own drums. I even bring my cross-stitch [embroidery] out to the field with me. What I do on my own time does not detract from my ability as a pilot. The earlier women couldn't have done that; any womanly characteristic was considered a weakness. However, the onus is still on us.

attack, low level). We also do administrative types of flying — support the squadrons here. It's a varied role. It's interesting and often fantastic — like when you're flying at 500 feet above ground at 450 knots with *Top Gun* on the radio!"

In October 1987 Dee went to CFB Winnipeg to take the instrument check pilot course. Everyone wanted her to take them for a ride in the T-Bird. "Talk about a turn-about in seven years," she recalled. "You knew it [acceptance] would happen sometime, but you wondered if there was enough time left." However, Dee seemed no closer to flying the CF-18 until suddenly, a few months later, she was told that she would begin fighter pilot training.

In June 1988 she and Jane Foster began a six-month training course on the CF-5, followed by six months on the CF-18. Recalled an excited Dee, "I've been working toward this end for ten years. My ultimate design was to fly fighters. I'm getting a challenge I should have had at nineteen. The toughest part for me is learning all about the aircraft. Those young guys just soak it up. Me, I study, study, study. One night I asked another retread, 'Do you think I'm too old?'"

Dee had flown the CF-18 a thousand times in her mind and she was not about to let her "advanced" age get her down, although another pressure weighing heavily on her mind was the knowledge that, if she failed, she would be letting down womankind. Dee did not fail the CF-18 check ride and could

We're *still* making inroads. There are *still* places we haven't gone. Some days we feel like an endangered species. We're not cocksure but we're sure of ourselves."

Sue also observed that most of the women now had a post-secondary education. "That helps. You're taken more seriously. However, the men have to take us on one at a time. They can't lump us all together; they must treat us as individuals. We're not 'those female pilots' — I hate that word [female]. It sounds like an animal species!"

Captain Sue Weicker is one of the first two women to do tactical helicopter work, providing support to the army with 408 Squadron. "There's fire bucketing, hoisting and slinging, bringing in supplies, air mobiles, insertions and extractions. There's a very army side to us. I carry a pistol and my kit — army green — has full chemical biological gear." It's tough work. As Sue says, "I take my share of the shitty missions. I work on weekends. I carry my own weight. I sleep in a tent. I can't lift the heavy loads but there are trade-offs. The guys on my squadron support me. I love my job."

say with delight, "Flying the CF-18 is like nothing you can imagine in your wildest dreams. It is a phenomenal aircraft. The thing that is the most challenging is not the flying but the systems. You're trying to navigate, drop bombs . . . the intensity is fierce and you don't really land until an hour after you land. You learn to think in micro-seconds because things happen in split seconds and either you make it in a split second or you don't." Promoted to major in October 1989, Dee flew CF-18s with the NATO-dedicated 416 Tactical Fighter Squadron. "My job," she explained matter-of-factly, "was to intercept invading nuclear bombers and engage their fighter escorts in individual dogfights or to rush to Europe, bombing and strafing Warsaw Pact ground forces."

Both she and Jane Foster have struggled to avoid media attention. "The more notoriety, the more potential for being diverted from the norm," Dee explained. "It's important to us that Canada did it. We're the first country to allow women to fly combat in an operational role. [In fact, the former USSR used women pilots in World War II.] We have to accept what's gone, pick up the torch and run with it. I have respect for the women before us, like Vera Strodl. Getting this far is my most significant achievement," she said in 1989. "A phenomenal turnaround in ten years. Jane and I did it as individuals; flying the CF-18 was something we wanted to do, not just for women's rights. We did it because we wanted to do it." In March of 1990, Dee was posted to National Defence Headquarters in Ottawa as director of flight safety.

Captain Leah Mosher, c. 1980.

LEAH MOSHER was born in Sydney, Nova Scotia and like Dee, the military was in her blood. "My mother had been a 'fighter cop' (fighter control operator) with the RCAF until marriage and so had my father." Joining the CF in 1973 Leah became a supply-technician until she was selected for officer's training two years later, at which time she returned to university, graduating with a Bachelor of Arts in history in 1976. After training in logistics and supply, she was posted to CFB Edmonton and Esquimalt as a supply officer. In 1978, she was promoted to captain.

"I enjoyed my work but I really dreamed of being a pilot. From my very first rides as a passenger in the Argus and the Herc, I knew that's what I wanted. As corny as it sounds I love viewing the world from above." She used to listen to the pilots talk about their trips and let it be known that she wanted to fly. "I knew there would be a day when pilot training would be open to women. To get a head start, I began flying lessons while stationed in Edmonton. When pilot training was offered I applied immediately."

"It was a blessing to have Nora, Dee, and Kris as it was tough going. There was so much emphasis placed on our not receiving special treatment that, unavoidably, we did. The camaraderie was between us girls. With the guys we only talked about neutral things. At first the negative comments hurt, but after awhile we all learned to ignore them, realizing that we couldn't please everyone and that the only way to survive was to please ourselves." She found life was not much easier at Moose Jaw. "There was still a lot of hostility. There was a wall at Moose Jaw with all the wings on it and when I was feeling down I'd go and look at them. They'd inspire me."

Upon receiving her own wings in March of 1981, Leah went to 424 Squadron for three months training on the Hercules before going to 436 Squadron at Trenton. "There was one month of ground school, local flying, simulator training and two long-range trips to get used to the radio work in different countries. We did a three-day trip to the States and a seven-day trip to Europe, the US and back to Canada." Leah's first trip with 436 was with a crusty old aircraft commander who was making his last trip and had scheduled it with her. "We were going to Thule and the weather was at limits. I was nervous, breathing heavily, and concentrating hard on the instruments. Everyone kidded me afterwards about all that heavy breathing in the cockpit!" Unfortunately the light-hearted comments were more the exception than the rule at this point in her career.

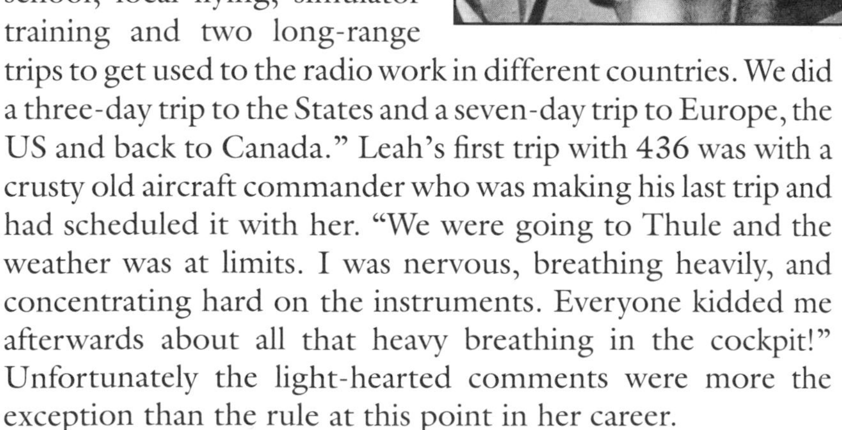

"The hostile attitudes were harder to handle than learning to fly the Herc. Things like accommodations away from base or the lack of a real toilet on the Herc were little problems in

Captain Leah Mosher, first woman aircraft commander on the Hercules, c. 1981.

Captain Jane Foster and Major Deanna Brasseur atop the twin engines of the CF-18.

comparison. Even as late as 1983 I still ran into comments like, 'I don't want no pregnant female beside me.'" Leah found it hard at first to know how to handle herself with the crew. "I guess I've run the gamut on a lot of things. At first I was very reserved in the cockpit. Then as I got to know the crew members and they me, there was some teasing, joke telling, a general easing of tension."

Leah enjoyed her time as a Herc pilot. "Our role was to travel around the world. We got used to high density traffic, high elevation airports, language problems and, as aircraft commander, being in charge of a crew. Then there was TAL [Tactical Airlift]. Initially I was not allowed to take the TAL course because it was considered to be training for combat. But my CO went to bat for the women and promoted the idea that we should be eligible." Used to support the army, TAL is a means of delivering troops and equipment to a drop zone, often an area where no runway or landing strip is available. "TAL is an exciting and exacting way to fly. It's low level flying combined with precise map reading," described Leah. "It can be flown day or night VFR or IFR and can be flown single ship, three- or six-plane formation or even twelve-plane formation." Herc pilots can also be trained in LAPES (Low Altitude Parachute Extraction System), which Leah succinctly summed up as, "The impressive one seen at airshows: The aircraft

CAPTAIN JANE CLEGG

Jane Clegg earned her wings on the Tutor in July 1990 and was posted to 412 Squadron in Ottawa to fly the Cosmopolitan. She was the first woman on this aircraft. The Cosmo has no hydraulic assists; it's a 60,000-pound aircraft that is controlled with cables and push rods. It's physically a hard aircraft to fly. "I asked for the Cosmo," said Jane. "I was a phys-ed grad and six foot tall and there was really no reason for the military not to give me a chance to fly it."

Describing how the women are treated in the 1990s, Jane said, "It's kind of like you're guilty until proven innocent. If you're a guy it's the reverse. There is a little bit of doubt [about ability] but once you've demonstrated that you can do the job, then it's okay. The people in my squadron have been excellent. I have more hassles with eighteen-year-olds who have seen *Top Gun* too many times!"

LIEUTENANT MARY CAMERON-KELLY

Mary Cameron-Kelly of Cape Breton joined the CF in 1981 and became an airframe technician on the Aurora. Ten years later, having qualified for her private pilots licence and won a number of awards at the Greenwood Flying Club on her own, she went on course and earned her wings on the Tutor in April 1991. Posted back to her beloved Maritimes, CFB Greenwood, Mary is the first woman to fly the Aurora.

"The Aurora is a long-range aircraft that patrols the eastern coast; it's a submarine hunter that also watches out for smuggling, does fisheries patrol, and some search and rescue. My trips can be of two- to three-weeks duration. I love the Aurora. I'm more 'a crew concept' person. I didn't want fighters." Mary is married to someone also in the CF who she describes as very supportive of her career.

Corporal Mary Cameron-Kelly, 1985.

approaches the landing zone, ramp and door are opened, the aircraft levels off at 5 feet above ground ideally, then the load is extracted by means of parachutes."

With 436 Squadron Leah travelled to thirty-three countries. "South America, Africa, Hawaii, Europe, India, Pakistan, the Arctic . . . of course, it is not always that exciting. It is a lot of living out of a suitcase and being in the air for long periods of time. My longest flight was 12.2 hours, Norway to Trenton non-stop. The Herc is a long range trainer and we supply embassies and engage in international exercises. We travel with two crews, about twenty people in all. Frequently I was the only woman. I liked the varied role and the travel."

The Lockheed C-130 Hercules, making a cargo drop.

CAPTAIN SUSAN WITCHEL

Sue Witchel of Toronto, Ontario was always interested in flying. She joined the air cadets and in 1978 she earned her glider's wings and then her private pilots licence. By then she was totally hooked on flying as a career and entered the CF in December 1981. On course with her were Sue Walker and Marlene Rudolph. Sue earned her wings on the Tutor in December 1983. One of the first women to be posted to a base other than Trenton, she went straight to CFB Summerside to 413 Squadron. There she flew the Buffalo primarily in search and rescue duties. "Robin Boutelier was the first woman at Summerside. She was there about three months before me and she 'broke the ground' for me. The

While the life sounded fascinating, Leah poignantly recalled that it was not without its down-side. "I remember one trip. I had just returned from Thule. Got into Trenton about 5:00 AM and drove home in the pre-dawn. I hauled out my Arctic kit, navigation gear, and suitcase and thought, 'How many other women in the world are doing this. My second thought was, 'How many want to do this?' My third thought was that the men were going home to a wife and kids and I was going home to an empty house."

In September 1985 Leah was a protocol officer at CFB Uplands and remained there until late summer of 1987 when she went on course for training on the Challenger — her dream.

guys were pretty friendly and I never felt I had to prove anything to anyone."

In July 1987 she was posted to 2 CFFTS Moose Jaw as an instructor on Tutors and in July 1991 to Flight Instructors School to teach pilots to become instructors on the Tutor. Although she admits that when she was a student she wanted to fly fighters — "At that time it was 'No' for women." — she has enjoyed all her postings and all the aircraft she has flown.

LIEUTENANT DIANE MacPHEE

A university graduate (Honours biology and chemistry), Diane earned her military wings in July 1991 and was posted to 2 CFFTS Moose Jaw. "There's probably twenty percent of the guys that think that women should not be near an aircraft. The older men are often better. Lieutenant Colonel "Yogi" Huyghebaert is super. The senior guys usually give you a chance to prove yourself and if you can fly, you're in. A big problem is wanting to fit in and being in danger of losing your femininity. I tried to change to please the guys but then I thought, 'I want to be me.'"

It appears that the CF women are now networking more. As Diane explained, "The guys have their own fraternity. Now we women are forming a network. I was the only woman on my course although there were other women at Moose Jaw. Now four of us keep in touch socially and we like that. We have started a "Girl's Night Out" once a month. It's nice to know that there are others who have gone through what you're going through. Besides," she added, "I was starving to talk to someone about nail polish!"

Diane's conclusion was that the good outweighs the bad, and she could say, "The military has given me the opportunity to fly jets. I love formation flying. Basically, I love my job."

Posted to 412 Squadron in Ottawa she flew the Challenger "for two glorious years" before being posted to Administration of Policy as the staff officer. Leah is currently director of recruiting services, National Defence Headquarters, Ottawa.

THE FUTURE of women pilots remains uncertain. Applicants are few. However, for those who have earned their wings and served their time, it has been said that as pilots they were as good and as bad as the men. Commanding officers have said that the performance of some has been stellar and their dedication unquestioned. Undoubtedly many of these self-assured and eloquent women, as skilled at flying a desk as an aircraft, have already been earmarked for further advancement.

CHAPTER TWELVE

Ad astra – to the stars

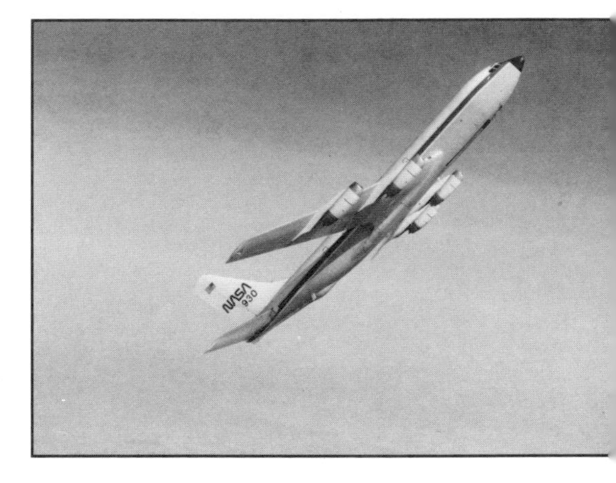

"Even as a child I wanted to fly into space and this was long before space travel was considered a reality . . . I have a picture of myself as a little child sitting on a star in space! That was my dream." — *Roberta Bondar*

THE BEGINNING of scheduled flights to and from earth by NASA's space shuttle in the eighties marked the coming of age of space travel. The space program had changed dramatically in twenty years. It was no longer a "because it's there" challenge; it had become a place to work. Travel to space had entered a utilitarian phase, an era of space exploitation rather then exploration. This was the context in which Canada's astronaut program was born. The National Research Council (NRC) viewed space as a place to do research and development.

When NRC went shopping for its astronauts, its prime consideration was to find people with relevant scientific and technical skills. While the individuals chosen are called "astronauts" this is a bit of a misnomer. There are now three distinct categories of astronaut: pilot-astronauts, mission specialists, and payload specialists. The pilot-astronauts are the test-pilot types, the inheritors of the early "right stuff" legacy. They are responsible for getting the space shuttle into and out of orbit, for controlling manoeuvres in space, and managing shuttle flight systems. Mission specialists are concerned with the technical and scientific goals of shuttle missions. Pilot-astronauts and mission specialists are NASA employees. Foreign nationals can only belong to the third category, the payload specialists. They are scientists or technically-qualified people who perform specific experiments on the shuttle. They are employed by a shuttle customer (either a company or a country) that has paid to fly a shuttle payload requiring special expertise.

The space shuttle is an aerospace vehicle that takes off like a rocket, manoeuvres in earth orbit like a spacecraft, and lands like an airplane. Preliminary testing for construction and manufacture in space is done aboard a scientific laboratory called a spacelab. Transported into orbit by the shuttle, the spacelab is adapted to operate in zero gravity and provides facilities for as many as four laboratory specialists to conduct experiments in such fields as medicine, manufacturing, astronomy, and pharmaceuticals. It remains attached to the shuttle and, like the shuttle itself, can be reused. While these payload specialists are scientists and technicians, rather than professional astronauts, they receive specialized training before going into space.

Thus when NRC placed its Help Wanted advertisement in Canadian newspapers in July 1983, they were not looking for jet jockeys or "Spam in a can," as Chuck Yeager called the early space test pilots. The ad generated 4300 applications and, from those hopefuls, six were chosen: Roberta Bondar, Marc Garneau, Steven MacLean, Ken Money, Robert Thirsk, and Bjarni Tryggvason. As Bondar quickly found out, the public and the media tended to divide the astronaut team into five men and a woman. Today, at the time of writing, Garneau, because he was the first Canadian in space, and Bondar, because she was the only woman, remain the best-known of the six.

ROBERTA BONDAR, born in Sault Ste. Marie, Ontario, was a neurologist at McMaster University's Medical Centre in Hamilton, Ontario when she learned she was one of the chosen. "Even as a child I had wanted to fly into space and this was long before space travel was considered a reality," recalled Roberta. "I have a picture of myself as a little child sitting on a star in space! That was my dream." Now that dream has become a reality. Roberta, who holds a PhD in neurobiology from the University of Toronto as well as a doctor of medicine degree (specializing in neurology) from McMaster University in Hamilton is also a licenced pilot and a former member of the Maple Leaf Chapter of the 99s.

Tom Wolfe wrote in his acclaimed book *The Right Stuff*, that being an astronaut in the sixties "seemed to be nothing less than manhood itself." However, when American astronaut Sally Ride was launched into space in June 1983 the "right stuff" suddenly included a feminine component. As Sally Ride became the role model for US women in space so has Roberta Bondar assumed this role in Canada. "I don't mind the publicity," she said in 1983, "what I don't like is the emphasis on my being a woman. I want to be seen as a highly-trained scientist, not someone who was chosen because she was female."

The 1986 *Challenger* disaster put Roberta's destiny on hold. Finally in 1989, her dream came another step closer to reality when she was named one of two candidates for the next experimental space trip. This immediately placed Roberta — and Ken Money — into a program of intensive training. Then, in 1990, NASA chose her as the payload specialist. In October 1991 the final countdown began. Three months later, on January 22, 1992 Roberta Bondar and six other astronauts climbed on board the US space shuttle *Discovery* and blasted off into space. Not only was Roberta the first Canadian woman to go into space, she is one of only two non-American astronauts to take part in a US space mission since 1985.

Roberta Bondar.

The *Discovery* flight was an eight-day mission to study, in simplified terms, the impact on humans of weightlessness in space. Roberta was a payload specialist for the International

Microgravity Laboratory 1 designed by the European Space Agency. She had already done a considerable amount of research with the Canadian Space Agency while in training. Much of it had taken place in a modified 707 tanker jet, nicknamed the "vomit comet" — the jet flies in a parabolic arc: straight up and then straight down and during the very few moments at the top of the arc an approximate microgravity environment is created; it also creates unbearable nausea. Roberta's performance was being continually assessed. As she said, "When women do something for the first time they are on trial. If one does something wrong then there is a tendency to generalize her actions to all other women; not so with a man."

Details of the mission can be found in many sources. What

EPILOGUE

Canadian women pilots did not set out to blaze trails or to look for glory; they simply wanted an equal opportunity to fly. In the twenties and thirties they were an oddity, a sensation based largely on their defiance of conventional notions of womanhood. They dared to make their mark when the perception of a heroine was a lacy vision of dependence and domesticity. Whatever prompted these women to climb into the cockpit, their desire and their determination were strong. The reception they received was curiously mixed: they were acclaimed as a novelty yet distrusted as interlopers.

Indifference and prejudice kept Canadian women from flying for their country during World War II, but the women of the ATA and WASPs demonstrated that women were physically, mentally, and psychologically able to fly high performance aircraft. Yet their real legacy was something less tangible; they disproved the time-honoured belief that military flying was for men only.

Economic and social forces kept most women "in their place" in the fifties and sixties, the golden years of the RCAF and the era of spectacular expansion of civil aviation. Women did not share in these achievements. Those determined to stay in aviation had few genuine options; there was instructing — take it or leave it — and only a few managed to progress beyond it. Women with brilliant wartime records were allowed to slip away, and relatively few capable women pilots — with a lot of perseverance — managed to work in their chosen field.

By the seventies, significant change was in the wind and each woman's accomplishment, no matter how meagre, fueled the advance. The old guard was beginning to move

is fascinating is to share in the excitement and sense of wonder felt by Roberta Bondar when, in space, she gazed at this green and lovely planet and the pride and gratitude she felt as a Canadian observing our vast share of the world.

AS A POSTSCRIPT it is interesting to note that another chapter of the Canadian Space Agency began soon after the *Discovery* flight. Four Canadians, one of them a woman, Julie Payette of Montreal, were chosen to carry on. And it was just "news" — neither amazing nor exceptional. Perhaps the future has arrived after all.

on and, by the eighties, the airlines, the military, and governments were adapting their thinking to the times. Feminist pressure, mainly from outside the military, forced change on one of the most tradition-loving institutions, the air force. Inside the military, despite years of rejection, were qualified and professional women. They had not asked for special privileges, only equality. Finally, in 1986, a new phase of military aviation history began when the government announced that women could apply for pilot training.

It was hard for the women who made a career in aviation. Eighty-hour work weeks were not unusual. Marriages broke up and friendships dissolved. So much emotional — and physical — energy went into flying that there was little left over for anything or anyone else. But women pilots had a certain spirit. They were self-directed, highly disciplined women who thrived on challenges, over-achievers with a singleminded preoccupation with being the best. They refused to see their sex as an obstacle.

The quiet patience and the dedication to excellence practised by women pilots up to the present has paid off. Perhaps their greatest legacy can be summed up in one word: persistence. They just pressed on and today's women pilots — and astronauts — are beneficiaries of their determination to stay the course. Without the past seventy years of women pilots' determination, it would have been unthinkable for Roberta Bondar to be considered, let alone be chosen, to travel into space.

The women who follow in aviation will face less discrimination and have fewer disappointments than those in the past; but the spirit, motivation, and love of flying will be shared with those who have gone before. One thing is certain: women will continue to follow their hearts to the sky.

Number	Name	Licence Number	Date of Issue	Notes (handwritten)
No. 1	Miss E.M. Vollick	77	Mar. 22, 1928	Ont
No. 2	Miss Eileen Magill	142	Oct. 24, 1928	
No. 3	Miss G. de la Vergne	157	Dec. 4, 1928	Alb
No. 4	Miss Dorothy Bell	220	Feb. 16, 1929	
No. 5	Miss L.J.C.M. Burka	243	Apr. 3, 1929	
No. 6	Miss J. MacBrien	325	Aug. 14, 1929	Hamilton
No. 7	Miss D.H. Paterson	327	Aug. 15, 1929	
No. 8	Mrs. G.C. Walker	372	Sept. 27, 1929	Edm.
No. 9	Miss N.I. Carson	384	Oct. 12, 1929	Sask
No. 10	Miss G.M. Hutchinson	387	Oct. 12, 1929	Sask.
No. 11	Miss E.M.C. MacLean	423	Nov. 14, 1929	Alb
No. 12	Miss E.S. Newlands	429	Nov. 19, 1929	Regina
No. 13	Mrs. J.A. Gilbert	479	Dec. 28, 1929	BC.
No. 14	Miss M.J. Chauvin	480	Dec. 28, 1929	
No. 15	Miss G.I.M. Goulding	495	Jan. 15, 1930	Ont
No. 16	Miss G. Thomson	500	Jan. 22, 1930	Ft. William
No. 17	Mrs. G. Samarow	512	Mar. 3, 1930	
No. 18	Miss A. Spencer	514	Mar. 5, 1930	
No. 19	Miss F.E. Webster	556	May 20, 1930	
No. 20	Mrs. J.C. Swaim	613	Aug. 15, 1930	
No. 21	Miss M. Roberge	678	Oct. 18, 1930	BC.
No. 22	Miss E.A. Hooker	694	Nov. 12, 1930	
No. 23	Miss C. Camm	755	Jan. 9, 1931	St Catharines
No. 24	Mrs. A.A. Rankin-Smith	811	Apr. 8, 1931	
No. 25	Miss M.Z. Jarvis	860	Aug. 21, 1931	Ont
No. 26	Miss J. Deb Norquay	928	Nov. 23, 1931	Alb
No. 27	Miss E. Flaherty	942	Dec. 19, 1931	BC.
No. 28	Miss E. Jenkins	973	Mar. 8, 1932	
No. 29	Mrs. L.M. Brodowich	1029	July 5, 1932	
No. 30	Mrs. W. Caldwell	1124	Oct. 24, 1932	
No. 31	Miss M. de N. Fane	1317	Oct. 12, 1933	Alb
32	Miss M. Secord	1322	Oct 12, 1933	
	Miss I. Freeman	[illegible]		Mont.

The author's starting point: the only list available from the Public Archives of Canada. Interestingly, the marital status of these women at time of licencing has been well documented.

APPENDIX ONE

FIRST WOMEN PILOTS

The lists that follow — of private, commercial, and public transport pilots' licences issued to women — are based on records obtained from the Public Archives of Canada. Only the names (and often only initials of given names) and dates of issue of licences were retained for the majority of the records. Information such as province licence was issued in, number of hours flown, home address, and so on were destroyed by either the Department of National Defence or the Public Archives of Canada. There are no official records in existence giving the dates of the instructor's ratings for the women.

The women whose names are preceded by an asterisk could not be located by the author.

In order, the first 100 licenced women pilots, 1928-1945

NAME PROVINCE DATE OF ISSUE

Eileen M. Vollick
Ontario March 22 1928
Eileen Magill
Manitoba October 24 1928
Gertrude de la Vergne
Alberta December 4 1928
Dorothy Bell
Manitoba February 16 1929
* Louise Burka
April 3 1929
* J. MacBrien
August 14 1929
Daphne Paterson
Quebec August 15 1929
Gladys Graves Walker (Mrs)
Alberta September 27 1929
Nellie Carson
Saskatchewan October 12 1929
Grayce Hutchinson
Saskatchewan October 12 1929
Elsie MacLean
Alberta November 12 1929
Edina Newlands
Saskatchewan November 19 1929
Jeanne Genier Gilbert (Mrs)
British Columbia December 28 1929
Marjorie Chauvin
Alberta December 28 1929
Grace "Tib" Goulding
Ontario January 15 1930
* G. Thomson (Mrs)
January 22 1930
* Alix Samarow
Ontario March 3 1930
* F.E. Spencer
May 5 1930
* J.C. Webster (Mrs)
May 20 1930
* M. Swaim
August 15 1930
Eliane Roberge
Quebec October 18 1930
* C. Hooker
November 12 1930
* A.A. Camm (Mrs)
January 9 1931
Margaret Rankin-Smith
Ontario April 8 1931
Jessica Jarvis
Ontario August 21 1931
Enid Norquay
Alberta November 23 1931
Betsy Flaherty (Mrs E.)
British Columbia December 19 1931
Louise M. Jenkins (Mrs)
Prince Edward Island March 8 1932
* Wanda Brodowich
Manitoba July 5 1932
* M. de N. Caldwell
October 24 1932
Margaret Fane
Alberta October 12 1933
Isobel Secord
Alberta October 12 1933
* Edith Freeman
October 12 1933
* F.E. Lundon
October 12 1933
* J.T. O'Brien-Saint (Mrs)
October 27 1933
Isobel Whitaker
British Columbia December 7 1933
Alma Gaudrau Gilbert
British Columbia April 7 1933
* E.H. Vance
May 10 1933
* E.M. Hall
September 26 1934
Margaret Clements
Saskatchewan October 9 1934
* M.A.M. Weber
October 22 1934
Dorothy Renton
Saskatchewan June 7 1935
Rolie Moore British Columbia October 7 1935
* A.E. Blake
October 18 1935
* A.L. McNeill
October 18 1935
* R. Campbell
November 16 1935
Joan Bonisteel
Ontario January 3 1936
Jean Pike
British Columbia February 4 1936
Tosca Trasolini
British Columbia August 12 1936
* M.A. Canfield (Mrs)
October 7 1936
Joyce Bond
Saskatchewan December 8 1936
* M. Skrypnyk
December 18 1936
* M.E. Holmes
January 14 1937
* M.C. Yates
March 17 1937
* Doris Manewell
May 14 1937
* M.M. Roberts (Mrs)
July 14 1937
Mary Spearing
Ontario June 29 1938

* L.N. Riffer
July 19 1938
* C.E. Stock
August 2 1938
* A. Sinkins
August 3 1938
Margaret Littlewood
Ontario August 3 1938
Marion Gillies
Ontario August 3 1938
Connie Culver
Ontario February 21 1939
Iva J. Coutts
Manitoba June 6 1939
Joyce A. Reid
June 24 1939
* R.A. Fitzgerald
July 12 1939
* M. McQueen
August 2 1939
* M. Munn
August 24 1939
Ethel Higdon
Alberta August 29 1939
M.E. Treau de Coeli
September 28 1939
* E. Fletcher
October 24 1939
Florence Elliott
Ontario November 16 1939
Violet Milstead
Ontario January 3 1940
Marion Powell
Ontario January 5 1940
Gladys Smirle
January 15 1940
* Helen Julia Cowan
January 20 1940
* V.E. Harris
June 4 1940
* K.E. Kinman
June 20 1940
* M.A. Richards
August 13 1940
* M. Honsinger
September 18 1940
Beryl Armstrong
October 21 1940
* H.J. Walker
October 31 1940
Margaret Carson
Ontario November 4 1940
* M. Maxwell
January 9 1941
* L. Rashaw
April 7 1941
Elspeth Russell Quebec
June 30 1941
* C. Connon
September 16 1941
* P. Hecker
September 23 1941
* P.A. Gray
September 25 1941
* L.L. Treble
September 25 1941
Sally Kerton
Ontario October 29 1941
* L. Richards
November 12 1941
* I.M. Collins
November 27 1941
* M.B. Lang
January 28 1942
* C.F. Williams
February 19 1942
M.B. MacLeod
April 30 1942
Gloria Large
Prince Edward Island June 4 1942
* O.M. Leach
October 3 1942
* M.L. Morkin
Manitoba October 30 1942
* E.C. Dawson
Manitoba November 26 1945

In order, first twenty commercial pilot's licences issued to women in Canada, 1928-1945

NAME PROVINCE DATE OF ISSUE

* Mrs Miller (American)
February 5 1930
Daphne Paterson Shelfoon
Quebec March 24 1930
* F.E. Spencer
July 2 1930
Eliane Roberge
Quebec October 27 1932
Jessica Jarvis
Ontario August 23 1934
Margaret Fane
Alberta August 28 1935
Rolie Moore
British Columbia July 19 1939
Helen Harrison
Ontario July 20 1939
Ethel Higdon
Alberta January 8 1940
Marion Gillies
Ontario January 26 1940
Iva Coutts
Manitoba February 29 1940
Violet Milstead
Ontario April 9 1940
Connie Culver
Ontario May 17 1940
Margaret Littlewood
Ontario October 31 1940
Florence Elliott
Ontario November 13 1940
Alma Gaudrau Gilbert
British Columbia September 26 1941
Marion Powell Orr
Ontario December 12 1941
* D.R. Fury
February 3 1942
* M.B. Lang
August 12 1944
Sally Kerton Wagner
Ontario October 21 1945

In order, first ten instructor's ratings for women (author's research)

Marion Gillies c.1940
Helen Harrison c.1940
Margaret Littlewood c.1940
Violet Milstead c.1941
Marion Orr c.1942
Daphne Paterson Shelfoon c.1942
Elspeth Russell Burnett c.1946
Molly Beall Reilly c.1946
Rolie Moore Pierce c.1946
Sally Kerton Wagner c.1949

In order, first four public transport pilot's licence (now airline transport licence)

Daphne Paterson Shelfoon 1938
Rolie Moore Barrett 1949
Margaret Littlewood 1949
Molly Beall Reilly c.1954

APPENDIX TWO

CANADIAN WOMEN PILOTS

The following list represents women pilots from 1928 to 1992 that the author was able to locate and/or research. The individual stories of all of the women researched have contributed greatly to the whole of *No Place For a Lady.* It was not practical to mention every woman pilot in the book however, and in many cases hard choices had to be made; those not mentioned in the text are afforded a brief biography here.

Any list of women is necessarily complicated by changes to their last names. Whether or not a woman has flown under two (or more) names she may be known to friends and associates by one name only. In this listing birth last names (when known) are in italics, married last name(s) follow. Each woman is listed under each known name.

Aberson Simpson, Patty. See index
Adamson, Judy. See index
Aitcheson, Marion *Gillies*. See index
Allanson, Sally *Ross*. See index
Allen, Shirley. Ontario; 99s; commercial, multi-IFR; initiated aviation seminars, coordinated Operation Skywatch, a program of pollution control by aerial surveillance
Almeida, Captain Cheryl. CF, earned wings on Tutor 1984 under trial program; CFB Trenton on Hercules until 1988; currently CFB Edmonton on Hercules.
Anderson, Sandy. ATR; charter pilot for Perimeter Airlines; currently Canadian Airlines International pilot
Appleton, Laurie *Sutherland*. See Sutherland.
Armour, Captain Karen *O'Mahony*. CF, earned wings on Tutor 1983 under trial program; flying positions until late 1980s; currently Director General Manpower Utilization, Ottawa
Armstrong, Jill M*alkin*. See index

Baerg, Barbara. Air Canada pilot
Baggaley, Major Inge *Plug*. See index
Bailey, Eleanor. Alberta, 99s, member of Western Warbirds
Bailey MD, Dr. Karen. Alberta, 99s; daughter of Eleanor Bailey; combines flying and medical skills.
Ball, Phurn. PPL 1970, commercial & helicopter licences 1973 on Bell 47, flew briefly for Niagara Helicopter; unable to find another job.
Barrett Pierce, Rolie *Moore*. See index
Bartsch, Dawn *Dawson* Connelly. See index
Baster, Lucille *Haley*. See index
Bates, Sue. ATR, pilot in 1980s for Air BC, Time Air; current status unknown.
Baxter James, Shirley. New Brunswick; first woman to receive PPL in Saint John; trained at the Fundy Flying Club; "I was at an airshow when I was a little girl and a yellow airplane made such an impression on me that I knew I wanted to learn to fly," recalled Shirley in 1984. "I earned $7.00 a week as a telegraph operator and it cost me $10.00 an hour to rent an airplane."
Beall Reilly, Molly. See index
Beament, Grace "Tib" *Goulding*. See index
Beamish, Mildred. Alberta 99s, Flying Farmers, known as the "flying grandmother."
Bell Richardson, Dorothy. See index
Bennett McKendry, Felicity. See index
Bereznay, Brigitte. Began flying 1977, ATR; instructor, flew RCMP highway patrol, charters; 3000 hours, not accepted by airlines; left aviation.
Berscheid Kalinsky, Valdine. Manitoba, helicopter licence 1979, unable to obtain a job.
Bjornson, Rosella. See index
Blanchet, Rita. Quebec, began flying in 1970, ATR; instructor, charter pilot; Transport Canada civil aviation inspector 1979 to present.
Bond, Joyce. See index
Bondar, Roberta. See index
Bonisteel, Joan. See index
Bourdon, Diane. Air Canada pilot
Booth Flemming Campbell, Betty. See Flemming
Bottomley, Major Nora. See index
Bourgeois, Lieutenant Nathalie. CF, earned wings on Tutor 1990; 440 Sqn Edmonton on Twin Otters
Boutilier, Captain Robin. See index
Bradbury, Elaine. Air Canada pilot
Brasseur, Major Deanna. See index
Bray Nicols DeBlicquy, Lorna. See index
Bristol, Helen *Harrison*. See index
Brooks Matz, Paula. See index
Brown, Kathleen. Ontario, 1980s flying instructor
Bryant, Captain Mary. See index
Brynelsen MacGregor, Karen. See index
Buch, Georgette *De Bagheera*. See index
Bulger, Karen. Ontario, Transport Canada civil aviation inspector.
Burleson, Debbie. Nova Scotia; 1980s, ATR, DFTE, glider licence, instructor, towed banners, aerobatic pilot
Burnett, Elspeth *Russell*. See index

Burnett, Karen *Hibberd*. Ontario, began flying in 1970s, ATR, instructor, charter pilot with Pemair Ltd, Air Atonabee, captain on Saunders ST-27; Transport Canada civil aviation inspector; note: Karen was second woman accident investigator in Canada.

Butler, Cheryl Lynn M*eunier*. Quebec, began flying 1970, fire detection for Ministry of Natural Resources; stopped flying 1982.

Cameron, Judy Eva*ns*. See index

Cameron, Marlene. See index

Cameron-Kelly, Lieutenant Mary. See index

Campbell, Peggy. British Columbia, Transport Canada Supervisor.

Caouette, Madeleine. ATR. fixed wing instructor and charter pilot in Quebec; also helicopter pilot; Transport Canada civil aviation inspector in 1980s, currently a Superintendent.

Cardinal, Blanche. PPL 1947, Vancouver, BC.

Carscadden, Joy. Became interested in aviation in 1955 when husband became a pilot in the RCAF. "I studied along with him through Chipmunk, Harvard and Expediter stages." Joy earned private licence in 1964, commercial in 1969, instructors in 1970 and began instructing that year at the Trenton Flying Club; earned multi-IFR, was CFI at various flying clubs in Canada; owned PA-11, a DFTE, has over 8000 hours flying time, currently the manager of the Calgary Flying Club, member of the Board of the Calgary Transportation Authority and a director of the Alberta Aviation Council.

Carson, Margaret. See index

Carson, Nellie. See index

Cera, Eileen *Magill*. See index

Chauven Herity, Marjorie. See index

Chapdelaine, Lucie. See index

Cheltenham, Valerie. See index. Ontario; earned private and commercial licences in early 1950s but other than ferrying positions could find no other work; left flying mid 50s.

Clay, Brigadier General Wendy. See index

Clegg, Lieutenant Jane. See index

Clements, Margaret. See index

Cody, Joan. Private pilot in the Maritimes

Colbert, Susan. See index. British Columbia; helicopter licence in mid 1980s; first officer on Sikorsky 76s for Helijet of Vancouver, BC.

Colton, Michelle "Micky" Ga*rner*. See index

Comat, Hella. See index

Connelly Bartsch, Dawn *Dawson*. See index

Cook, Ruth *Wilson*. Not licenced but said to be the first woman student at Moncton Flying Club in 1929; newspaper clipping asserts that Ruth, a naturalized Canadian citizen, held an Engineering Certificate in Aeronautics, took flying instruction from Walter Fowler and Dick Cully of International Airways Training School in conjunction with the Moncton Flying Club.

Cooper, Irene. See index

Cooper, Lorraine. See index

Cossette, Johanne. Quebec, earned helicopter licence 1980 at CGEP; worked for Air Alma on Bell 47 & 206 flying pipeline patrol, forestry and James Bay project.

Coutts, Iva. See index

Crampton, Stefanie *Schauss*. See index

Cripps, Ruth. See index

Cruchley, Pat. See index

Cubitt, Connie *Culver*. See index

Culver Cubbitt, Connie. See index

Currie, Ethel *Higdon*. See index

Daniels, Marie *Mazur*. See index

Davenport Zokol, Kathy. See index

Davies, Ethel *Harris*. See index

Davis, Susan. See index

Dawson Connelly Bartsch, Dawn. See index

Daynard, Dorothy *Renton*. Saskatchewan; learned to fly from Dick Ryan of Moose Jaw Flying Club 1935; member of Flying Seven

DeBagheera Buch, Georgette. See index

DeBlicquy, Lorna *Bray* Nicols. See index

De La Vergne Tanner, Gertrude. See index

Denis, Lorraine. Ontario; began flying 1975; ATR; instructor and charter pilot with West Coast Air Service (1979) on Twin Otter, City Express (1985) on Dash 7. Stunt pilot: played Sharon Stone's double in the sequel to Police Academy; now lives in Caribbean, flying Beech 18s for Antigua Air Service.

Derepentigny, Captain Marie. CF, earned wings on Jet Ranger 1986; 403 Sqn Gagetown on CH 135 Twin Huey helicopter.

Desmarais, Diane. See index

Dharamsi, "Shenys" Shehnoor. Graduate of Mount Royal College's aviation program 1981; bush pilot in Africa & Fiji; Air Canada pilot since 1986 although currently not on flying status

Dionne, Leola. New Brunswick; instructor and charter pilot since mid 1970s for Dionne's Flying Service (husband's company), Grand Falls, NB.

Doerr, Virginia Lee *Warren*. See index

Dowling, Vera *Strodl*. See index

Drysdale Lindsay, Phyllis. See index

Dugal, Gertrude. See index. First French Canadian woman born in Quebec to receive her licence in Quebec (1947); took instruction from Jack Scholefield at Laurentide Aviation

Duke, Grace. Saskatchewan; currently flying for Ministry of Natural Resources, Ontario. Arts and Law degrees plus 5000 hours, ATR, Class I instructor.

Dupont, Leona. See index

Dutit, Marie. Instructor at Dionne's Flying Service, Grand Falls, New Brunswick

Elliott Whyard, Florence. See index

Elliot, Oonagh. Ontario; Transport Canada civil aviation inspector

Enright, Mary *Spearing*. See index

Etzkorn, Jane. Began flying 1979, wanted to be a bush pilot; flew for Parsons Airways Northern, Manitoba Government Air Services, currently flying with Wilderness Air in BC.

Evans Cameron, Judy. See index

Ewen, Sharon-Ann. See index

Fane Rutledge, Margaret. See index

Fitzgerald, Lori. See index

Flaherty, Betsy. See index

Fletcher, Catherine. See index

Flemming, Betty *Booth* Campbell. British Columbia; built and earned glider and private pilots licences 1946; BSc 1947 (Math & Physics); worked for NRC in physics dept; Spartan Air Services as aerial photographer; Energy Mines & Resources as technical officer with Canadian Topographical Survey 1966; first woman to win an award from the American Society of Photogrammetry

Fogle, Adele. See index

Foster, Captain Jane *Van Ingen Schenau*. See index

Fothergill, Jeanne *Genier* Gilbert. See index

Fox, Kathy. See index

Fraser, Cathy. Air Canada pilot

Frogley, Suzanne. Ontario; ATR; married with children and had just completed Masters Degree in Economics and working for Statistics Canada when she began to fly "for fun" in 1976; instructor; currently Transport Canada civil aviation inspector.

Frost Smith, Elizabeth. See index

Garland, Mary. Ontario; helicopter pilot in the 1980s

Gaudrau Gilbert, Alma. See index

Gaul, Phyllis *Penney*. See index

Genier Gilbert Fothergill, Jeanne. See index

Germain, Martine. Helicopter pilot in 1980s

Gilbert, Alma *Gaudrau*. See index

Gilbert, Isobel *Whitaker*. See index

Gilbert Fothergill, Jeanne *Genier*. See index

Gillies Aitchison, Marion. See index

Goodwin, Shirley Goldring. Ontario, private pilot in late 1940s; began an all girls flying club under YWCA "umbrella;" moved to Alberta, earned glider licence; 99s.

Gordon, Captain Joan. CF, earned wings on Jet Ranger 1984 under trial program; SAR at: CFB Summerside on CH 113 Labrador until 1987; CFB Trenton on Labrador until 1990; CFB Comox on Labrador 1990 to present. Currently an instructor on the Operational Training Flight for the Labrador helicopter.

Goulding Beament, Grace "Tib." See index

Graham, Madge. (not licenced) See index

Grant, Gwen. See index

Gravel, France. See index

Graves Walker, Gladys. See index

Greenlaw, Dolores. See index. Commercial helicopter licence in 1986, ATR; flying for Helijet since 1987; approximately 3000 hours

Gregg, Lynda. Manitoba; ATR; married with children when she began flying in 1981; charter pilot for Perimeter Airlines

Grondin, Frances. Registered Nurse certificate in 1953; PPL (1960), CPL (1966), first woman to earn a commercial from Moncton Flying Club; woman pilot of the year at Moncton Flying Club; however, no jobs so took law degree in 1982

Halle, Therese. (not licenced) Married when began flying lessons in 1930 from Arthur Fecteau in Quebec City; instructor left area before she completed training

Haley Baster, Lucille. See index

Hall Warren, Deborah "Debbie." See index

Harder, Captain Brenda. CF, earned wings 1982 under trial program; 436 Sqd CFB Trenton on Hercules; 1986 to 440 Sqd Edmonton SAR on Twin Otters

Harding, Janine *Leclerc*. See index

Harris Davies, Ethel. See index

Harris, Jo. See index

Harrison Bristol, Helen. See index

Hegstrom, Kerri. ATR; began flying 1978; flew for City Express (1986); part of a 1986 flight that had a all-women crew and all women passengers: known as the "Petticoat Run"

Hems, Helen Wil*son*. Ontario; commercial licence in early 1950s, dispatched for Marion Orr at Maple Airport

Henderson, Pennie *Naylor*. See index

Henderson Sharratt, Glenna. See index

Henderson, Suzanne. Air Canada pilot

Henley, Irene *La Chance*. Alberta; ATR, instructor, civil aviation inspector with Transport Canada in mid 1980s; now in Australia

Hepburn Scott, Kelly. See index

Herity, Marjorie *Chauvin*. See index

Hibberd Burnett, Karen. See Burnett for biography

Higdon Currie, Ethel. See index

Hill, Lois. See index

Hohle, Donna. See index

Holiday, Sandra. Began flying in 1977, graduated from avition program from Selkirk College, BC; instructor and charter pilot, currently with Air Canada
Hunt, Jessica *Jarvis*. See index
Hutchinson Stewart, Grayce Sandra. See index

Ireland, Beatrice. Ontario; private pilot in the 1960s
Irving, Britt *Ferst*. See index

James, Shirley *Baxter*. See Baxter
Jarvis Hunt, Jessica. See index
Jenkins, Louise. See index
Jenkevice, Huguette *Menard*. See index
Jonasson, Sylvia. Private pilot in 1940s
Jones Powers, Eleanor. See index
Jordan, Regina "Gina." See index
Jozwiak, Nanette. Air Canada pilot

Kahl, Barb *Warwashawski*. See index
Keim, Janet *Panteluk*. See index
Keogh, Janet. Flies as captain on tracker aircraft for Saskatchewan Government Northern Air Operations.
Kerr, Bette *Milburn*. See index
Kerton Wagner, Sally. See index
King, Debbie. See index
Klassen, Diane *Chudley*. See index
Krygsveld, Lieutenant Lisa. CF, earned wings on Jet Ranger 1992
Kuzina, Jan. See index

LaFreniere, Carole. Ontario; Transport Canada civil aviation inspector
LaJoie, Aline. Air Canada pilot
Large Walker, Kathleen Gloria. See index
La Riviere, Colette. See index
Law, Beverley *Gerand*. Private pilot in British Columbia in late 1940s; helped organized BC 99s
Laws, Marjorie. New Brunswick; second woman to receive PPL (1948) from Moncton Flying Club; won Webster Trophy zone competition in 1949
LeClerc Harding, Janine. See index
Lindsay, Phyllis *Drysdale*. See index
Littlewood, Margaret. See index
Lloyd, Sandra. See index
Lush, Sheila. Manitoba; private pilot mid 1940

MacAuley, Libby. Private pilot in Manitoba
MacBrian, Julia. Ontario; received PPL in 1929; father was General MacBrian, former Chief of General Staff, DND and one of the directors of International Airways Ltd of Hamilton
MacFarlane, Elsie *MacLean*. See index
MacGregor, Karen *Brynelsen*. See index
MacKinnon, Robin. See index
MacLean MacFarlane, Elsie. See index
MacLeod, Marion. New Brunswick; first woman to receive PPL (1940) from Moncton Flying Club; instructor was Al Lilly—"He was terrific. However, in a place like Moncton, flying was a 'no no' for a girl. When you soloed you bought a case of beer but you couldn't join the party," recalled Marion.
MacMillan, Heather. See index
MacPhee, Lieutenant Diane. See index
Magill Cera, Eileen. See index
Malkin Armstrong, Jill. See index
Mannix, Gloria Jean. Ontario; received helicopter licence in 1979 and worked in helicopter sales
Mathers Matheson, Gretchen. See index
Maussenet, Corinne. Quebec; Transport Canada civil aviation inspector
Matchett Payette, Captain Elizabeth. See index
Matheson, Gretchen *Mathers*. See index
Matz, Paula *Brooks*. See index
Mazur Daniels, Marie Daniels. See index
McCann, Berna *Studer*. See index
McCanse, Betty. See index
McCutcheon, Margo. See index
McDonald, Enid *Norquay*. See index
McFarland, Susan. Helicopter pilot in 1980s
McGrath, Deborah. See index
McGraw, Maureen. Ontario; EAA member, building a triplane; formed Wings & Wire 1982 to tow banners
McKendry, Felicity *Bennett*. See index
McQuin, Margaret *Rankin-Smith*. See index
McTavish Stauffer, Marjorie. See index
Megelink, Gera. See index
Milburn Kerr, Bette. See index
Mills, Dr. June. MD. 99s; formerly of Saskatchewan; interested in aviation medicine and flying; 1976 earned diploma in aviation medicine from Institute of Aviation Medicine, Farnborough, England.
Milstead Warren, Violet. See index
Montgomery, June. See index
Moore Barrett Pierce, Rolie. See index
Moore, Ruth *Parsons*. See index
Morgan, Tina. See index
Morris, Carole *Phillips*. See index
Morris, Lieutenant Katherine. CF, earned wings on Jet Ranger 1992
Mosher, Major Leah. See index

Nagata, Mariko. See index
Naylor Henderson, Pennie. See index
Neil, Captain Louise. CF, earned wings on Jet Ranger 1985; CFB Comox, on CH 113 Labrador until 1990; currently Staff Officer, Northern Region HQ Yellowknife; qualified on Twin Otter
Nelson, Lenora. British Columbia, Transport Canada, civil aviation inspector.
Newlands, Edina. See index. Saskatchewan; daughter of Lieutenant-Governor of Saskatchewan, Edina obtained instruction from Roland Groome of the Regina Flying Club on a Cirrus Moth; received PPL 1929.

Newton, Noreen. See index. British Columbia; began flying in 1978; flew for North Caribou Flying Service; was first officer on first Canadian all-female crew on a DC-3 flight with Elaine Parker as captain and Helen Towne as flight engineer in 1986.

Norquay McDonald, Enid. See index

O'Flaherty Uzelman, Teresa. See index

O'Mahony Armour, Captain Karen. CF, earned wings on Tutor 1983 under trial progra; instructor at Moose Jaw; currently DGMU Ottawa

Olson, Janet. Air Canada pilot

Olstad Robison, Glenys. See index

Orr, Marion *Powell.* See index

Paddon, Lieutenant Blythe. CF, earned wings on Jet Ranger 1991; 423 Sqn 1991 CFB Shearwater on CH 124 Sea King helicopter; first woman on the Sea King, which is often away for weeks or months at a time.

Page, Ruthanne. See index

Parker, Elaine. See index

Parsons Moore, Ruth. See index

Paterson Shelfoon, Daphne. See index

Pauli, Mary Ellen. See index

Pawluk, Lieutenant Debbie. CF, earned wings on Jet Ranger 1991; currently CFB Moose Jaw, base rescue on helicopters

Payette, Lieutenant Elizabeth *Matchett.* See index

Peck, Audrey *Stonehouse.* See index

Pemberton, Jill. See index

Penney Gaul, Phyllis. See index

Pepper, Diane. See index

Petty, Dini. See index

Phillips Morris, Carole. See index

Piche, Danielle. Quebec; began flying in 1973, charter pilot with Air Dorval, civil aviation inspector with Transport Canada since 1984.

Pierce, Rolie *Moore* Barrett. See index

Piette, Michelle. Air Canada pilot

Pike, Jean. See index

Pilon, Carole. Ontario, Transport Canada civil aviation inspector

Plonka, Peggy. Alberta, Transport Canada civil aviation inspector

Plug Baggaley, Major Inge. See index

Pomerleau, Suzanne. See index

Powers, Eleanor *Jones.* See index

Purdy, Captain. Former Canadian Forces pilot; no other information available.

Puttkemery, Nancy. See index

Ramsay, Toni. See index

Rankin-Smith McQuin, Margaret. See index

Reid, Lieutenant Kim. CF, earned wings on Tutor 1990; posted to fighters December 1990; qualified on CF-18 December 1991; posted to Cold Lake to fly CF-18; the only operational woman fighter pilot in Canada.

Reilly, Molly Bea*ll.* See index

Renton Daynard, Dorothy. See index

Ricard Standring, Peggy Ethel. (not licenced) See index

Richardson, Dorothy *Bell.* See index

Richter, Kathleen. Ontario, Transport Canada civil aviation inspector

Rivest, Michele. See index

Roberge Schlachter, Eliane. See index

Robertson-Reid, Lola. Began flying in 1979, instructor; first officer on Twin Otter for Bearskin Lake Air Services; left Bearskin to return to university because "getting nowhere" in aviation

Robison, Glenys Ol*stad.* See index

Rogers, Rita. 99s, former owner/manager of Markham Airport

Ross Allanson, Sally. (not licenced) See index

Rothberg, Diane. See index

Rudolph, Captain Mary. See index. CF, earned wings 1983; instructor on CT134 Sundowner, CFB Portage; 435 Sqd Edmonton on Hercules 1987-91; instructor at Chilliwack 1991 to present. "I just love what I'm doing. It's a great career." Married.

Rungeling, Dorothy. See index

Russell Burnett, Elspeth. See index

Rutledge, Margaret *Fane.* See index

Samson, Mireille. See index

Sauvé, Nicole. See index

Saxby, Judy. Commercial licence in 1970s, owner/operator, with husband Bob May, of Keewatin Air Limited

Schauss Crampton, Stefanie. See index

Schermerhorn, Betty Jane. Ontario; began flying in 1970, commercial, multi-IFR, instructors; 99s, Governor of Eastern Canada Section, International Treasurer 99s; represented the 99s at many international functions such as the International Aerospace Education Congress; worked with DOT on personnel licensing. Powder Puff contestant with Lorna DeBlicquy

Schiff, Daphne. See index

Scolefield, Jacqueline, "Jacquie". Daughter of Jack Scolefield, one of the founders of Laurentide Aviation. Began flying in 1978, ATR; flown with Air Creebec, Capital Aviation, Air Alliance; currently with Laurentide Aviation

Scott, Kelly Hep*burn.* See index

Secord, Isobel. See index

Seehagel, Val. Transport Canada civil aviation inspector

Sharratt, Glenna *Henderson.* See index

Shaw, Lynn. Married with children when she began to fly in 1974; instructed at Pultz Aviation Training, Saskatoon; she and husband then began own company: Professional Flight Services, sold out in 1980; became CFI at Regina Flying Club until 1984; free-lance pilot.

Shelfoon, Daphne *Paterson.* See index

Sifton, Heather. Ontario, 99s, serves as chairman of the Board of Directors for the Canadian 99s Award in Aviation; owns and operaates "The Prop Shop" at Buttonville Airport; began flying in 1967, commercial, multi-IFR
Simard, Marie-Helen. See index
Simms, Darlene *Tripp*. See index
Simpson, Patty *Aberson*. See index
Smith, Elizabeth *Frost*. See index
Spearing Enright, Mary. Ontario; PPL 1938 from Leavens Brothers, owned a Taylorcraft.
Standring, Peggy Ethel *Ricard*. (not licenced) See index
Stauffer, Marjorie *McTavish*. See index
St. Germaine, Gina. Helicopter pilot in the 1980s
Ste Marie, Nicole. Quebec, began flying in 1965 with father's company: Ste Marie Air Service at Bellefeuille airport; earned commercial 1969; however, with no prospects of a job, Nicole eventually stopped flying
Stonehouse Peck, Audrey. See index
Strilesky, Paula *Venn*. See index
Strodl Dowling, Vera. See index
Studer, Joan. See index
Studer McCann, Berna. See index
Sutherland, Kim *Wheaton*. 1976 university graduate who began flying in 1977; hired by Alberta Government Air Services in 1979
Sutherland Appelton, Laurie. Alberta; began flying in 1976. Second woman hired by Time Air (1979), flew for Time Air for 4 1/2 years on Dash 7 and Twin Otter.
Swyers, Barbara. See index
Sykes, Laura. Air Canada pilot

Tanner, Gertrude *De la Vergne*. See index
Taylor, Debbie. Ontario, Transport Canada civil aviation inspector
Taylor, Jennifer. Ontario, Transport Canada civil aviation inspector
Taylor, Roberta, "Robbie" *Wieben*. See index
Tenoff, Tosca *Trasolini*. See index
Trasolini Tenoff, Tosca. See index
Tripp Simms, Darlene. See index

Uzelman, Teresa *O'Flaherty*. See index

Van Ingen Schenau Foster, Captain Jane. See index
Varcoe, Lillian. See index
Venn Strilesky, Paula. See index
Vincent, Mary. Montreal, Quebec, began flying in late 1970s; hired by Transport Canada in early 1980s as a civil aviation inspector; left in 1985 because of lack of flying.

Vollick, Eileen. See index
Vos, Pat. Keg River, Alberta; 1974 BSc Degree whose work with Environment Canada brought her into contact with helicopters and she decided to qualify for her commercial helicopter licence. Unfortunately the recession meant no job.

Wagner, Sally *Kerton*. See index
Walker, Gladys *Graves*. See index
Walker, Gloria Kathleen *Large*. See index
Walker, Captain Susan. CF, earned wings on Jet Ranger 1984 under trial program; 413 Sqn Summerside on CH 113 Labrador helicopter; 1987-89 CFB Portage to instruct on CH 139 Jet Ranger; posted to Flight Instructors School, CFB Portage to instruct on Jet Ranger 89-91; CFB Toronto as Deputy Flight Safety Officer 1991 to present.

Warren, Debbie. Air Canada pilot
Warren, Debbie *Hall*. See index
Warren, Violet *Milstead*. See index
Warren Doerr, Virginia Lee. See index
Weber, Maureen. Ontario, Transport Canada civil aviation inspector
Webster, Elizabeth *Wieben*. See index
Weicker, Captain Susan. See index
Weissenborn, Lieutenant Jennifer. CF, earned wings on Jet Ranger 1988; CFB Gander flying CH 113 Labrador
Whitaker Gilbert, Isabel. See index
White, Debbie. See index
Whyard, Florence *Elliot*. See index
Wieben Webster, Elizabeth. See index
Wieben Taylor, Roberta "Robbie." See index
Wiens, Heather. Calgary, Alberta; instructor, charter pilot for Springbank Aviation, Calgary 1978; hired by Transport Canada in 1981 as a civil aviation inspector; flies Citation and DC-3; 1985 Heather became the Senior Instrument Standards Inspector for southern Alberta.
Wilson, Candace. See index
Witchell, Susan. See index
Wilson Hems, Helen. See index

Yaeger, Barbara. Private pilot, post World War II

Zokol, Kathy *Davenport*. See index
Zubryckyj, Marie. See index

APPENDIX THREE

WOMEN PILOTS EMPLOYED BY MAJOR AIRLINES, MILITARY, AND TRANSPORT CANADA.

Names are in alphabetical order and were compiled with the assistance of the following organizations.

AIR CANADA

Barbara Baerg
First Officer DC-9
Diane Bourdon
Second Officer B-727
Elaine Bradbury
Second Officer B-727
Judy Cameron
First Officer B-767
Shenys Dharmasi
Second Officer
Cathy Fraser
Second Officer B-727
Gwen Grant
First Officer B-767
Suzanne Henderson
Second Officer B-727
Sandra Holiday
Second Officer B-727
Britt Irving
First Officer DC-9
Nanette Jozwiak
Second Officer B-727
Aline Lajoie
First Officer DC-9
Karen Mundell
Second Officer B-727
Janet Olson
Second Officer B-727
Michelle Piette
First Officer DC-9
Glenys Robison
First Officer DC-9
Diane Rothberg
First Officer DC-9
Barbara Swyers
First Officer DC-9
Laura Sykes
First Officer DC-9
Deborah Warren
Second Officer B-727

CANADIAN AIRLINES INTERNATIONAL

Sandra Anderson
First Officer B-737
Rosella Bjornson
Captain B-737
Lucie Chapdelaine
First Officer B-737
Stefanie Crampton
First Officer B-767
France Gravel
First Officer 737
Sandra Lloyd
First Officer B-737
Paula Strilesky
First Officer B-737
Kathy Zokol
First Officer B-737

WOMEN PILOTS WITH THE CANADIAN ARMED FORCES

Captain Cheryl Almeida
Captain Karen Armour
Major Inge Baggaley
Captain Robin Boutilier
Captain Mary Bryant
Major Nora Bottomley
Lieutenant Nathalie Bourgeois
Major Deanna Brasseur
Lieutenant Mary Cameron-Kelly
Lieutenant Jane Clegg
Captain Michelle Colton
Captain Marie Derepentigny
Captain Jane Foster
Captain Joan Gordon
Captain Brenda Harder
Lieutenant Lisa Krygsveld
Lieutenant Diane MacPhee
Lieutenant Katherine Morris
Major Leah Mosher
Captain Louise Neil
Lieutenant Blythe Paddon
Lieutenant Debbie Pawluk
Captain Elizabeth Payette
Captain Purdy
Lieutenant Kim Reid
Captain Mary Rudolph
Captain Susan Walker
Captain Susan Weicker
Lieutenant Jennifer Weissenborn
Captain Susanne Witchel

WOMEN INSPECTORS — TRANSPORT CANADA

Judy Adamson
Superintendent
Rita Blanchet
Inspector
Georgette Buch
Inspector
Karen Bulger
Inspector
Karen Burnett
Inspector
Peggy Campbell
Supervisor
Madeleine Caouette
Superintendent
Diane Desmarais
Inspector
Oonagh Elliott
Inspector
Catherine Fletcher
Inspector
Suzanne Frogley
Inspector
Jo Harris
Inspector
Diane Klassen
Regional Director
Corinne Maussenet
Supervisor
Karen MacGregor
Inspector
Heather MacMillan
Inspector
Mariko Nagata
Inspector
Lenora Nelson
Inspector
Elaine Parker
Inspector
Carole Pilon
Inspector
Peggy Plonka
Inspector
Kathleen Richter
Inspector
Val Seehagel
Inspector
Glenna Sharratt
Inspector
Elizabeth Smith
Inspector
Debbie Taylor
Regional Director
Jennifer Taylor
Supervisor
Debbie Warren
A/Director
Maureen Weber
Superintendent
Heather Wiens
A/Superintendent
Marie Zubryckyj
Inspector

APPENDIX FOUR

AIRCRAFT FERRIED BY AIR TRANSPORT AUXILIARY PILOTS DURING WORLD WAR II

Aircraft were classified in order of difficulty and ATA Ferry Pilots were classified according to the types of aircraft they had been cleared to fly.

Class 1 — light single-engined

Magister
D. H. Moths
Fairchild Argus
Auster
Proctor
Tutor
Whitney Straight
Wicko
Hart Variants
Swordfish
Gladiator
Messenger

Class 2 — advanced single-engined
Section I covers the more important types, listed in order of difficulty. Section II covers older types, listed alphabetically.

SECTION I
Harvard I, II, III
Spitfire I, II, IV, V, VI, VII, VIII, IX, X, XI, XIII, XVI
Seafire I, II, III
Reliant I
Albacore
Master I, II, III
Martinet I
Hurricane I, II, III
Sea Hurricane I, II
Defiant I, II, III
Fulmar I, II
Mustang I, II, III, IV
Firefly I, II
Lysander I, II, III
Barracuda I, II, III
Traveller I
Wildcat I, II, III, IV, V, VI
Hellcat I, II
Avenger I, II, III
Spitfire XII, XIV, XVIII, XIX, 21, 23
Seafire XV, 45, XVII
Typhoon I
Tempest II, V
Vengeance I, II, III
Corsair I, II, III, IV
Firebrand I, II, III
Walrus I, II
Sea Otter (after Walrus experience)

SECTION II
Airacobra
Battle
Bermuda
Chesapeake
Dauntless
Helldiver
Henley
Kingfisher
Kittyhawk
Mohawk
Roc
Seamew
Skua
Tomahawk
Vigilant

Class 3 — light twin-engined

Oxford I, II
Anson I, X, XI, XII
Dominie I, II

Class 4 — advanced twin-engined

SECTION I
* Hudson I, II, III, IV, V, VI
* Albermarle I, II, V, VI
Blenheim I, IV, V
Wellington I, II, III, IV, VIII, X, XI, XII, XIII, XIV, XV, XVI, XVII, XVIII
* Whitley I, II, IV, V, VII
* Ventura
Expediter I
Warwick I, II, III, V
Beaufighter I, II, VI, X, XI
Beaufort I, II
Welkin I
DB.7 Variants
Mosquito I, II, III, IV, VI, VIII, IX, XII, XIII, XVI, XVII, XVIII, XIX, 25, 26, 30, 34, 35, 36
+ Dakota I, III, IV
+ Mitchell I, II, III
Buckmaster I
Buckingham I
Meteor III

SECTION II
Botha
Hampden
Hereford
Manchester
Maryland
Whirlwind

Class 5 — four-engined

* Halifax I, II, III, V, VI, VII, VIII
Class 5 pilots with ten or more Halifax deliveries could be authorized by the Ferry Pool commanding officer to ferry the following:
* Lancaster I, II, III, VI, VII, X
* Lancastrian
* Stirling I, III, IV, V
+ Fortress II, III
+ Liberator II, III, V, VI, VII, VIII
+ York I
+ Lincoln I, II
+ Skymaster I

Class 6 — sea planes (with crew)

Catalina
Sunderland
Walrus (on water)
Sea Otter (on water)

* Pilot's assistant to be carried.
+ ATA Flight Engineer to be carried.

Source — Appendix 7, *The Forgotten Pilots* (op cit)

SOURCES

Abbreviations for provinces
AB: Alberta
BC: British Columbia
MB: Manitoba
NB: New Brunswick
NF: Newfoundland
NS: Nova Scotia
NT: Northwest Territories
ON: Ontario
PEI: Prince Edward Island
PQ: Quebec
SK: Saskatchewan
YT: Yukon

PRIMARY SOURCES

All interviews were conducted by the author and all letters were addressed to the author unless otherwise indicated. The author was also given access to much personal memorabilia (letters, photographs, newspaper clippings, scrapbooks, flying club instruction sheets, log books and other pertinent data). Unless otherwise identified all sources listed are women pilots.

Interviews & Letters

Adamson, Judy. Personal interview 30 January 1985, Toronto, ON; letters 1985-86.

Aitchison, Michael. (son of Marion Gillies Aitchison) Telephone interview 3 November 1986.

Alexander, Mel. (World War I pilot, early president of Toronto Flying Club) Personal interview 25 May 1984, Winnipeg, MB at World War I Flyers Reunion.

Allanson, Mike. (son of Sally Ross) Personal interview 3 November 1983, Vancouver, BC.

Allen, Shirley. Personal interview 4 November 1986, Toronto, ON.

Anderson, Sandy. Personal interview 11 October 1986, Winnipeg, MB.

Andrews, Lorne. (owner of Nipawin Air Services) Letter 23 October 1985.

Appleton, Laurie Sutherland. Letter December 1986.

Attenbring, Charles. (longtime member of Winnipeg Flying Club) Telephone interview 2 March 1980.

Austin, Peter. Letter 27 September 1985.

Aylen, Bess. (sister of pilot Enid Norquay, longtime friend of pilot Isobel Secord) Personal interview 27 July 1984, Winnipeg, MB.

Baggaley, Major Inge Plug. Personal interview, Winnipeg, MB.

Bailey, Eleanor. Personal interview 1 April 1984, Calgary, AB.

Ball, Phurn. Personal interview 25 June 1986, Winnipeg, MB.

Ballentine, Gordon. (glider instructor of Sally Ross) Telephone interview 2 November 1983.

Baltzer, Al. (Atlantic Canada Aviation Museum Society) Personal interview 17 October 1984, Halifax, NS.

Bartsch, Dawn Dawson Connelly. Personal interview 5 January 1987, Kona, Hawaii; telephone interview December 1986; letters 1985-87, 6 April 1992.

Baster, Lucille Haley. Personal interviews 2 April 1984, Edmonton, AB, 24 November 1986, Stony Plain, AB; letters 1984-86.

Bates, Sue. Personal interview 16 November 1984, Sidney, BC.

Bauer, Group Captain Arnie J. Ret'd (RCAF) Personal interview 4 November 1986, Hamilton, ON.

Baxter, James, Shirley. Telephone interview 15 October 1984.

Beament, Grace "Tib" Goulding. Personal interview 4 October 1983, Orillia, ON; letters 1983-84.

Bereznay, Brigitte. Telephone interview 28 April 1990.

Berscheid, Valdine. Personal interview 24 June 1986, Winnipeg, MB.

Best, Frederick. (World War I pilot) Personal interview 19 May 1983, Edmonton, AB at World War I Flyers Reunion.

Bisson, Captain Louis. (early Arctic pilot) Letters 1983-86.

Bjornson, Rosella. Personal interviews 1980-1991, Winnipeg, MB; Edmonton, AB; Langley, BC; letters 1981-1992.

Blackey, David. (re pilot Joan Bonisteel) Letter 8 December 1983.

Blanchet, Rita. Personal interview, 23 April 1985, Montreal, PQ.

Boffa, Ernie. (former bush pilot) Letter 1 June 1985.

Bond, Joyce. Personal interview 4 November 1981, Winnipeg, MB; letters 1981-86.

Bondar, Roberta. Personal interview 28 January 1985, Ottawa, ON, ten minute personal interview 21 April 1992 Winnipeg, MB; telephone interviews 22 June 1984, 20 April 1985.

Bonisteel, Gail. (re stepsister of pilot Joan Bonisteel) Telephone interview 25 November 1983.

Booth, Betty Flemming Campbell. Personal interview 25 January 1984, Ottawa, ON.

Booth, John. (Canadian Pacific Airlines). Letters 1985.

Bottomley, Major Nora. Personal interviews 28 January 1980, CFB Portage; 14 November 1983, Toronto, ON; 23 March 1986, Winnipeg, MB; telephone interview 9 February 1987; letter 18 June 1992.

Boutilier, Captain Robin. Personal interview 22 January 1987, Winnipeg, MB.

Bradbury, Elaine. Telephone interview 26 July 1991.

Branca, Judge. (longtime employer of Tosca Trasolini) Telephone interview 2 November 1983.

Brasseur, Major Deanna. Personal interviews 28 January 1980 CFB Portage, 27 September 1983, 6 December 1985, 6 September 1987, 20 March 1988, 10 November 1989, Winnipeg, MB, 7 August 1991 Langley, BC; telephone interviews 1986-1991; letters 1980-1991.

Bredenhof, Lloyd. (RCMP Air Section, Edmonton, AB) Telephone interview 24 November 1986.

Brown, Kathleen, Letter 16 September 1986.

Bryant, Jan. (daughter of Elizabeth Pease) Personal interview 2 November 1983, Vancouver, BC.

Bryant, Captain Mary. Personal interview 19 November 1983, Trenton, ON; telephone interview 10 February 1987, 25 March 1992; letter 25 March 1992.

Buch, Georgette de Bagheera. Personal interview 23 January 1984, Ottawa, ON; telephone interviews 31 October 1986, 28 April 1992.

Buckingham, "Buck." (World War I flyer). 19 May 1983, Edmonton, AB at World War I Flyers Reunion.

Burgess, E. G. (Alpine Helicopters Ltd) Letter 11 July 1986.

Burke, Fraser. (son of Carl Burke, founder of Maritime Central Airways) Telephone interview 5 January 1984.

Burleson, Debbie. Telephone interview 18 October 1984.

Burnett, Karen Hibberd. Personal interview 21 January 1984, Ottawa, ON.

Burnett, Gerry. (husband of Elspeth Russell Burnett) Personal interview 15 November 1983, Matane, PQ; letters 1982-86, 1992.

Butler, Cheryl Lynn Meunier. Letters 1984-86.

Butt, Major R.J. (senior information officer, DND Office of Information CFB Winnipeg) Personal interview 23 January 1987, Winipeg, MB.

Cameron, James. Letter 14 December 1984.

Cameron, Judy Evans. Personal interviews 23 November 1983, 1 November 1986, Oakville, ON; telephone interviews 1 February 1985, 20 February 1988, June 1992.

Cameron, Marlene. Telephone interview 25 November 1986.

Cameron, Bob. (pilot, Trans North Turbo Air) Letter 13 November 1983.

Cameron-Kelly, Lieutenant Mary, Telephone interview 10 February 1992.

Cardinal, Blanche. Personal interview 31 October 1983, Vancouver, BC.

Caouette, Madeleine. Telephone interview 27 October 1986.

Carscadden, Joy. Letter 29 January 1992.

Carson, Margaret. Telephone interviews 1984-1986.

Catto, J. M. (World War I pilot) Personal interview 28 May 1982, Ottawa, ON at World War I Flyers Reunion.

Cera, Robert. (son of Eileen Magill Cera) Telephone interview 24 November 1983.

Chapdelaine, Lucie. Personal interview 28 October 1986, Montreal, PQ; letters 1986-1991.

Cheltenham, Valerie. Personal interview 2 November 1983, Vancouver, BC.

Clay, Brigadier General Wendy. Personal interview 21 January 1985, Ottawa, ON; telephone interview 13 June 1987; letter 18 March 1992.

Clegg, Lieutenant Jane. Telephone interview 10 January 1992.

Cody, Joan. (early private pilot in Maritimes) Letter 17 October 1983.

Comat, Hella. Personal interview 31 January 1985, Oakville, ON; letter 12 January 1992.

Connelly, Ron. (pilot re Dawn Dawson Connelly Bartsch) Telephone interview 25 January 1986.

Cossette, Johanne. Letters 1984-85.

Colton, Captain Michelle "Micky" Garner. Personal interviews 19 November 1983, Trenton, ON; 4 October 1986, Winnipeg, MB; 7 August 1991, Langley, BC; telephone interview 22 February 1987; letters 1983-92.

Cooper, Irene. Personal interview 13 November 1984, Vancouver, BC

Cooper, Lorraine. Personal interview 31 October 1983, Vancouver, BC.

Cooper, Richard. (journalist) letter 21 October 1984.

Cooper, R. (longtime Newfoundland pilot) Letter 21 November 1984.

Coutts, Iva. Personal interview 25 March 1983, 21 October 1984, Winnipeg, MB

Crampton, Stefanie Schwauss. Personal interview 28 November 1984, 28 Marach 1986, Winnipeg, MB; letters 1984-1992.

Craton, Doug. (former DOT inspector) Telephone interview 21 March 1980.

Cripps, Ruth. Personal interview 12 November 1984, Calgary, AB.

Croll, Ethel. (sister of Margaret Clements) Personal interivew 30 October 1983, Victoria, BC.

Crone, Ray. (Saskatchewan aviation historian) Personal interview 11 November 1984, Regina, SK.

Cruchley, Pat. Telephone interview 31 January 1985.

Cubitt, Connie Culver. Personal interview 21 November 1983, Kitchener, ON.

Currie, Ethel Higdon. Letter 25 June 1983.

Curtis, Mildred. (sister of pilot Jeanne Genier Gilbert Fothergill) telephone interviews & letters 1980-1991.

Dalgleish, Keith. (Time Air) Telephone interview 26 September 1986.

Daniels, Marie Mazur. Telephone interview 22 October 1984; letters 1986, 26 March 1992.

Davies, Ethel. Personal interview 26 October 1983, Vancouver, BC; telephone interview with Ethel & Wilf 26 November 1986.

Davis, Susan. Telephone interviews 16 October 1984 , 24 May 1992.

Delaney, J. Georges. (senior vice-president of Viking Helicopters Ltd.) Letter 4 August 1986.

Del Begio, Bill. (owner of early airways company in Winnipeg MB) Personal interview 15 February 1984, Winnipeg, MB.

DeBlicquy, Lorna Bray Nichols. Personal interview 21, 24 January 1984, 31 October 1986, Ottawa, ON; letter 16 January 1992.

Denard, Dorothy Renton. Personal interview 24 October 1983, Vancouver, BC.

Denis, Lorraine. Personal interview 3 November 1986, Toronto, ON; telephone interviews 19 December 1987, 21 February 1992; letters 1988-1990.

Desmarais, Diane. Personal interview 29 January 1985, Ottawa, ON; telephone interview 28 October 1986; letters 1985-1992.

Dharamsi, "Shenys" Shehnoor. Telephone interview 28 October 1986; letter 1984.

Dickins, C. H. "Punch." (World War I pilot; bush pilot & district manager with Western Canada Airways-Canadian Airways Limited; vice-president and general manager of Canadian Pacific Air Lines; senior executive with de Havilland Canada) Personal interviews 1980-86; telephone interviews 1980-90; letters 1986-91.

Dionne, Leola. Telephone interview 15 October 1984; letter 20 January 1992.

Doerr, Virginia Lee Warren. Personal interview 19 April 1984; tape recording Lee to author May 1986; letters 1983-87.

Doherty, Marjorie. (sister of Eileen Vollick) Personal interview 22 November 1983, Brantford, ON.

Donovan, Donald. (early Maritimes pilot). Letter 16 October 1984.

Douglas, Dr. W.A.B. (directorate of history, Department of National Defence Headquarters) Letters 1982-84.

Dowling, Vera Strodl. Personal interview 20 May 1983; 3 April, 17 November 1984, Edmonton, AB; 7 August 1991, Langley, BC; letters 1980-86.

Duff, Dan. (aviation enthusiast) Letters 1984.

Dugal, Gertrude. Personal interview 22 April 1985, Montreal, PQ; letters 1985.

Duke, Doris. (mother of Grace Duke) Telephone interview 24 July 1992.

Duncan, Dave. (former RCAF, former flying instructor) Telephone interview 3 November 1983; letters 1983-86.

Dupont, Leona. Personal interview. 3 April 1984, Edmonton, AB.

Dyson, Sarah. (daughter of pilot Barb Yaeger) 5 January 1984.

Edward, Gathen. (flying instructor of Louise Jenkins, TCA-Air Canada pilot) Letter re Louise Jenkins to Dorothy Renwick 25 February 1975.

Edward, Isabella. (wife of pilot Gathen Edward) Telephone interview 23 April 1985.

Edwards, A.J. "Spunky". (early flying instructor) Telephone interview 14 November 1984.

Etzkorn, Jane. Telephone interviews 20 June 1987, 23 February 1992.

Ewen, Sharon-Ann. Telephone interviews 21 October 1984, 15 June 1985.

Farrington, Harold. (early bush pilot) Personal interview 11 May 1982, Red Lake, ON.

Ferguson, Bob. (owner/operator of Parsons Airways Northern) Personal interview 9 January 1986, Winnipeg, MB.

Fitzgerald, Lori. Personal interview 30 November 1986, Calgary, AB; letters 1985-86.

Fletcher, Catherine. Personal interview 17 November 1984, Edmonton, AB; letters 1984-86; telephone interview February 1992.

Foster, Captain Jane Van Ingen Schenau. Telephone interview 17 February 1987.

Fowler, Bob. (former chief test pilot at de Havilland) Personal interview 20 November 1983, Toronto, ON; telephone interview 10 November 1983.

Fowler, Walter. (bush pilot with Canadian Airways Limited, pilot with TCA) Personal interview 16 October 1984, Moncton, NB; letter 15 January 1984.

Fox, Kathy. Telephone interviews 23 October 1985, 28 October 1986; letter 13 May 1984, 15 January 1992.

Frogley, Suzanne. Personal interview 21 April 1985, Toronto, ON.

Fuller, Bill. (early pilot) Letters 1978-84.

Gareau, Ray. (longtime pilot) Letters 1984-86.

Garland, Mary. Telephone interview 5 January 1985.

Gaul, Phyllis Penney. Personal interview 22 April 1985, Montreal, PQ.

Gilbert, Alma Gaudrau. Personal interview 26 October 1983, Vancouver, BC; letter 1984.

Gilbert, Nicholas. (son of Isobel Whitaker Gilbert) Telephone interview 30 October 1983.

Goodwin, Ley (Shirley Goldring) Personal interview 22 September 1984, Winnipeg, MB.

Gowans, Bruce. (Alberta aviation historian) Personal interview 12 November 1984, Calgary, AB; letters 1984-86.

Graham, Robert. (son of Madge Graham) Personal interview 23 January 1984; letters 1983-85.

Grant, Gwen. Personal interview 1 November 1983, Vancouver, BC. letters 1984-86, 21 April 1992.

Grant, Robert. (pilot & aviation writer) Telephone interviews 1984-86.

Grantham, Robert. (Atlantic Canada Aviation Museum Society) Telephone interview 17 October 1984.

Gravel, France. Personal interviews 13 November 1984, Winnipeg, MB, 27 October 1986 Montreal, PQ; letters 1984-86; telephone interview 7 November 1991.

Greenlaw, Dolores. Telephone interview 15 July 1992.

Greenough, George. (Maritimes aviation historian) Letters 1983-87.

Gregg, Lynda. Personal interview 11 May 1987, Winnipeg, MB; telephone interviews 1985-87; letters 1989-92.

Grondin, Frances. Personal interview 2 April 1984, Moncton, NB.

Halle, Therese. Personal interview 24 April 1985, Quebec City, PQ; letters 1984-85.

Harder, Captain Brenda. Personal interview 19 November 1983, Trenton, ON; telephone interview 10 February 1987.

Harding, Janine Leclerc. Personal interview 22 April 1985, Montreal, PQ; letters 1984-87, 19 January 1992.

Harris, Jo. Personal interview 2 April 1984, Edmonton, AB; letters 1984, 11 January 1992.

Harris, Ormond. (World War l pilot) Personal interview. 19 May 1983, Ottawa, ON at World War l Flyers Reunion.

Harrison Bristol, Helen. Personal interviews 28, 29 October 1983, 30 November 1986 Point Roberts, Washington.

Hatch, George. (World War I pilot) Personal interview 19 May 1983, Ottawa, ON at World War I Flyers Reunion.

Hegstrom, Kerri. Personal interview 4 November 1986, Hamilton, ON.

Hellstrom, Colonel Sheila A. (director women personnel, Department of National Defence) Personal interview 24 January 1984, Ottawa, ON; letter 21 January 1985.

Hems, Helen Wilson. Personal interview 4 October 1983, Orillia, ON.

Henderson, Pennie Naylor. Personal interview 22 april 1985, Montreal, PQ; letters 1984-85. 1992.

Henderson, Glenna Sharratt. Telephone interview 8 May 1984; personal interview 7 August 1991, Langley, BC.

Henderson, Suzanne. Telephone interview 25 July 1991.

Henley, Irene La France. Personal interviews 2 May 1984, 10 October 1986, Winnipeg, MB.

Henry, Walter. (editor of Canadian Aviation Historical Society's newsletter, Outbound) Letters 1983-85.

Hepburn, (Scott), Kelly. Telephone interview 1 August 1984, 22 June 1992; letters 1985-86, 25 June 1992.

Herity, Jack. (husband of pilot Marjorie Chauvin) Personal interview 17 November 1983, Toronto, ON.

Hohle, Donna. Personal interview 26 March 1986, Winnipeg, MB; letters 8 November 1986, 7 January 1992.

Holley, Brian. (RCAF pilot & son of WW I pilot Gil Holley) Personal interview 25 May 1984, Winnipeg, MB at World War I Flyers Reunion.

Holley, Gil. (World War I pilot) Personal interview 25 May 1984, Winnipeg, MB at World War I Flyers Reunion.

Holman, Rock. (World War I pilot) Personal interview 22 May 1983, Edmonton, AB at World War I Flyers Reunion.

Holiday, Sandra. Personal interview 14 November 1984, Vancouver, BC.

Hotson, Fred. (aviation historian) Letter 8 December 1983.

Hill, Lois. (personal interview) 24 December 1984, Headingley, MB; letters 1984-87, 3 February 1992.

Hoffman, Leo. (former flying instructor & DOT inspector) Personal interview 11 March 1980, Winnipeg, MB.

Humphrey, W. Letter 21 November 1983.

Hunt, Jarvis Jessica. Personal interview 19 October 1984, Toronto, ON; telephone interview 25 November 1983; tape recording Jessica to author January 1985; letters 1983-87.

Hunt, Jay. (former president Aerobatics Canada) Personal interview 30 January 1985, Ottawa, ON.

Hunter, John. (executive secretary of Western Canada Airways) Telephone interview 19 December 1982.

Ireland, Beatrice. Personal interview 22 November 1983, Brantford, ON.

Irving, Britt Ferst. Personal interviews 17 November 1983, Toronto, ON, 11 July 1991, Winnipeg, MB.

Jenkins, Jack. (son of pilot Louise Jenkins) Telephone interview 24 November 1983.

Jenkins, Louise. Personal interview 1 October 1983, Old Lyme, Connecticut.

Jenkevice, Huguette Menard. Personal interview 22 April 1985, Montreal; letters 1984-86, 12 March 1992.

Jonasson, Sylvia. Telephone interview 4 May 1984.

Jones, Gordon. (chief pilot, Helijet). Telephone interview 15 July 1992.

Jordan, Gina. Personal interview 31 March 1984, Calgary, AB; Telephone interviews 1988, 24 March 1992.

Judge, Terry. (Canadian Aviation Historical Society) Letter 16 April 1990.

Kahl, Barb Warwashawski. Personal interview 29 November 1986, Vancouver, BC; letters 1986-88.

Keddy, Larry. (Atlantic Canada Aviation Museum Society) Personal interview 17 October 1984, Halifax, NS; letters 1984-85.

Keim, Janet. Letters 26 November 1985, May 1992.

Kerr, Bette Milburn. Letters 1983-84.

Klassen, Diane Chudley. Personal interviews 19 January 1980, Winnipeg, MB, 23 November 1986, Edmonton, AB; telephone interview 1992.

Kristapovich, Paul. (Associated Helicopters Ltd.) Telephone interview 25 November 1986; letter 8 December 1986.

Kuzina, Jan. Personal interview 12 June 1987, Winnipeg, MB; telephone interviews 1 November 1986, 1991.

LaRiviere, Colette. Personal interview 24 April 1985, Montreal, PQ.

Latremoulle, Austin. (longtime Norduuyn Aircraft employee & executive [vice-president & general manager]) Telephone interview 18 December 1984.

Lavery, Bill. (former DOT inspector) Telephone interview 14 October 1984.

Law, Beverley. Personal interview 30 October 1983, Victoria, BC.

Laws, Marjorie. Telephone interview 15 October 1984; letter 29 September 1984.

Leigh, Z. Lewis. (flying instructor, early bush pilot [Canadian Airways Limited], TCA pilot, RCAF) Personal interview 22 November 1983, Grimsby, ON.

Lewington, Jim. (longtime pilot in Newfoundland & executive with Eastern Provincial Airlines) Letters 1984-86.

Lilly, Alexander J. (flying instructor, Ferry Command, Maritime Central Airways, Canadair test pilot) Personal interview 15 October 1984, Moncton, NB; letters 1984-85.

Lindsay, Marie Crevits. Letter from Mr. Lindsay, husband, November 1983.

Lindsay, Phyllis Drysdale. Personal interview 16 November 1984, Sidney, BC; telephone interview 2 November 1983.

Littlewood, Margaret. Personal interview 1 April 1984, Edmonton, AB; letters 1980-1992.

Lloyd, Sandra. Personal interview 13 November 1984, Vancouver, BC; letters 1984-87, 13 October 1991.

Luck, Sheldon. (bush pilot with Yukon Southern Air Transport, executive with Canadian Pacific Airlines) Letters 1984-86.

Lush, Sheila. Letter November 1983.

MacAulay, Libby. Personal interview 23 November 1983, Oakville, ON.

MacFarlane, Elsie MacLean. Personal interview 27 October 1983, White Rock, BC.

MacGillivray, Father. (re Louise Jenkins) Telephone interview 15 November 1983; letters 1983-84.

MacGregor, Karen Brynelsen. Personal interviews 29 October 1983, 16 November 1984, Sidney, BC; 7 August 1991, Langley, BC; telephone interview 15 March 1988; letters 1983-87; 30 March 1992.

MacKinnon, Robin. Personal interview 7 June 1986 Oakbank, MB.

MacLaren, Donald. (WW I pilot, pilot with Western Canada Airways-Canadian Airways, Trans Canada Airlines) Telephone interview 2 November 1983.

MacLeod, Marion. Personal interview. 15 October 1984, Moncton, NB.

MacMillan Heather. Personal interviews 13 June 1984, 12 April 1986, Winnipeg, MB.

MacNeil, Don. (former flying instructor in Maritimes) Letter 18 October 1984.

MacRitchie, W. A. (early bush pilot, WW II pilot, instructor) Letter 7 March 1985.

Magill, Edward. (brother of pilot Eileen Magill Cera) 7 March 1980, Winnipeg, MB.

Malkin, Armstrong, Jill. Personal interview 31 January 1985, Toronto, ON; letter 5 January 1985.

Mannix, Gloria Jean. Telephone interview 8 January 1985.

Matchett, Captain Elizabeth Payette. Personal interview 13 January 1987, Winnipeg, MB.

Matheson, Gretchen Mathers. Personal interview 31 October 1983, Vancouver, BC; letters 1983-88, 10 January 1992.

Matz, Paula Brooks. Personal interview 4 March 1985, 29 January 1987, Winnipeg, MB.

McClure, Don. (longtime manager of Moncton Flying Club) Personal interview 15 October 1984, Moncton, NB.

McDonald, John. (MB Government Air Service) Telephone interview 24 January 1986.

McDonald, Enid Norquay. Personal interview 27 July 1984, Winnipeg, MB.

McGrath, Deborah. Telephone interview 15 October 1984, 17 January 1992; letters 1984-87, 9 January 1992.

McGrath, Tom. (longtime aviation official in Newfoundland, former DOT inspector) letter 16 December 1984.

McGraw, Maureen. Telephone interview 6 November 1985.

McGregor, Maurice. (former TCA pilot & friend of Margaret Clements) Telephone interview 31 October 1983.

McKeachie, Jim. (director public relations CP Air). Telephone interview 15 November 1984.

McKendry, Felicity Bennett. Personal interview 20 January 1984, Ottawa, ON; letters 1983-86, 1992.

McLeod, Earl. (World War I pilot). Personal interview at 25 May 1983, Edmdonton, AB at World War I Flyers Reunion.

McLeod, Max. (aviation enthusiast of Maritimes aviation history) Personal interview 18 October 1984, Halifax, NS; letters 1983-86.

McMillan, Stan. (early bush pilot, Mackenzie Air Service.) Personal interview 17 May 1985, Edmonton, AB.

McNaughton, George. (World War I pilot) Personal interview 28 May 1982, Ottawa, ON at World War I Flyers Reunion.

McPhee, Lieutenant Diane. Personal interview 12 January 1992, Winnipeg, MB.

McQuin F. Hollister. (husband of pilot Margaret Rankin-Smith) Telephone interview 21 March 1984; letters 1984-87.

McVicar, Don.(World War II pilot, aviation author) Letter 5 October 1984.

Meagher, Pierre. (President Newfounland Labrador Air Transport Ltd.) Letter 30 June 1986.

Megelink, Gera. Personal interview 12 November 1984, Calgary, AB.

Michaud, Al. (former owner of Vancouver U-Fly) Telephone interview 26 November 1986.

Milberry, Larry. (aviation historian) Telephone interview 4 September 1984.

Millard, Carl. (president Millardair) Personal interview 30 January 1985, Toronto, ON.

Miller, Don. (flying friend of Nellie Carson) Letter 21 March 1984.

Molson, Ken. (aviation historian) Personal interview 3 July 1985, Kenora, ON.

Montgomery, June. Personal interview 1 May 1984, Winnipeg, MB.

Moore, Cathy. Letter 9 March 1992.

Moore, Lois. Letter 21 November 1984.

Moore, Phyllis. Letter 3 October 1984.

Moore, Ruth Parsons. Personal interview 6 August 1984, Kenora, ON.

Morgan, Tina. Personal interview 15 October 1984, Moncton, NB; letter 6 June 1992.

Morkin, Mary Lou. Telephone interview 18 May 1984.

Morris, Carole Philips. Personal interview 30 January 1985, Toronto, ON; letters 1984-85.

Morris, Ted. (director public affairs Air Canada) Telephone interview 20 June 1988.

Mosher, Major Leah. Personal interviews 28 January 1980, CFB Portage, MB; 19 November 1983, Trenton, ON; 31 October 1986, Ottawa, ON; telephone interview 9 February 1987; letters 1980-87, 31 March 1992.

Mutch, Jim. (Canadian Pacific Airlines executive & re Dawn Bartsch) Telephone interview 28 December 1985.

Nagata, Mariko. Personal interview 30 October 1986, Ottawa, ON.

Newlands, Edina. Letter 30 November 1984.

Newton, Noreen. Personal interview 28 November 1986, Victoria, BC; letter 23 October 1984.

Nielsen, Erik. (former Canadian deputy prime minister, pilot and friend of Dawn Bartsch) Letter 21 December 1986.

Norman, Ron. (World War I pilot) Personal interview 28 May 1982, Ottawa, ON at World War I Flyers Reunion.

Oakes, Stan L. (former student of Helen Harrison) Letter 15 October 1983.

Ogilvie, Joyce Reid. Personal interview 22 November 1983, Grimsby, ON.

Oliver, W. R. J. (early Quebec pilot) Letter 24 January 1984.

Olson, Captain Keith. (former bush pilot and Air Canada pilot) Personal interviews 4 March, 20 April 1986, Winnipeg, MB.

O'Mahony, Captain Karen. Telephone interview 17 February 1987.

Orr, Bill, (longtime flying instructor at Halifax Flying Club) personal interview 17 October 1984, Halifax, NS.

Orr, Marion Powell. Personal interviews 21 May 1979, Winnipeg, MB; 7 October 1983, Toronto, ON; 3 November 1986, Richmond Hill, ON; letters 1978-1991; telephone interview 1 June 1992.

Page, Ruthanne. Personal interviews 12 April 1984, Edmonton, AB; 18 April 1988, Winnipeg, MB; letters 1984-1992.

Paige, Lois. Letter November 1983.

Parker, Elaine. Personal interview 24 November 1986, Edmonton, AB; letters 1985-86.

Parsons, Hank. (owner of Parsons Airways Northern) Letter 6 November 1986.

Patchett, Sally. Letter November 1983.

Paterson, Jane. Telephone interview 10 November 1983.

Paterson Shelfoon, Daphne. Letters Daphne to Dorothy Renwick 1975-78.

Paton, Terry. (former manager Winnipeg Flying Club) Personal interview 4 May 1984, St Andrews, MB.
Pauli, Mary Ellen. Personal interview 24 March 1985, Winnipeg, MB; letters 1985-92.
Paxton, Lawrie. (Air Canada pilot) Letter 10 October 1984.
Paxton, Lindsay. (Air Canada pilot) Personal interview 14 November 1984, Vancouver, BC.
Peck, Audrey Stonehouse. Telephone interview 3 November 1983; letter 2 December 1983.
Pengelly, Don. (City Express) Letter.
Pepper, Diane. Letter 6 February 1986.
Petty, Dini. Personal interview 30 January 1985, Toronto, ON.
Piche, Danielle. Personal interview 23 April 1985, Montreal, PQ.
Pickler, Ron. (former bush pilot, Canadair) letter 26 November 1984.
Pierce, Rolie Moore Barrett. Personal interview 25 October 1983, Port Coquitlam, BC; letters 1981-87.
Piette, Michelle. Telephone interview 19 September 1991.
Pinch, Liuetenant F. C. (director personnel selection, Research & Second Careers, Department of National Defence) Personal interview 24 January 1984, Ottawa, ON.
Pomerleau, Suzanne. Personal interview 23 April 1985, Montreal, PQ; telephone interview 29 October 1986; letter 1987.
Porter, Edna. (cousin of pilot Daphne Paterson) Telephone interview 30 November 1983.
Powers, Eleanor Jones. Personal interview 25 October 1983, Langley, BC.
Puttkemery, Nancy. Telephone interview 24 November 1986; letter 17 December 1985.
Ramsay, Toni. Personal interviews 11 April, 1984, Selkirk, MB; 15 March 1992, Winnipeg, MB; telephone interviews 1984-92.
Reilly, Jack. (husband of pilot Molly Beall Reilly, also RCAF pilot, corporate pilot) Personal interviews 22 May 1983, 23 November 1986, Stony Plain, AB.
Reny, Jean. (assistant chief pilot, flight operations, Quebecair) Letter 25 July 1986.
Ricard, Peggy Standring. Letter 7 October 1984; CBC tape recording 2 February 1977.
Richardson, Dorothy Bell. Personal interview 29 October 1983, Victoria, BC.
Richardson, Kathleen. (cousin of pilot Dorothy Bell Richardson) Telephone interview 15 March 1980.
Richardson, Ross. Letter 11 November 1984.
Richardson, Sheila. Letter 2 november 1983.
Riley, George. (World War I pilot) Personal interview 20 May 1983, Edmonton, AB at World War l Flyers Reunion.
Rivart, Jacques. (Quebec aviation historian) Telephone interview 23 April 1985; letter 15 November 1984.
Rivest, Michele. Personal interview 23 April 1985, Montreal, PQ; letters 1984-86, 30 March 1992.
Robertson-Reid, Lola. Letters 1985-86.
Robinson, Elsie. (sister of pilot Nellie Carson) Letter 8 December 1983.
Robison, Glenys Olstad. Personal interview 14 November 1984, Vancouver, BC; telephone interview 19 January 1992; letters 1984-86.
Rogerson, Loyde. (president, Frontier Air-Rog-Air Ltd.) Letter 28 July 1986.
Rothberg, Diane. Personal interviews 22 January 1984, Ottawa, ON; 20 July 1986, Winnipeg, MB; telephone interviews & letters 1986-1991.
Rudolph, Captain Marlene. Personal interview 13 January 1987, Winnipeg, MB.
Rungeling, Dorothy. Personal interview 6 October 1983, Fonthill, ON; letters 1980-86. May 1992.
Russell, Frank. (chief engineer 1940-60 and superintendent of maintenance 1960-75, Austin Airways) Letter 9 December 1986.
Rutledge, Keith. (former engineer with Okanagan Helicopters, husband of pilot Margaret Fane Rutledge) Personal interview 14 November 1984, Vancouver, BC.
Rutledge, Margaret Fane. Personal interviews 17, 21 September 1982, Winnipeg, MB; 24, 26 October 1983; 14 November 1984; 29 November 1986 Vancouver, BC; letters 1981-1992.
Ryan, Dick. (early flying instructor at Moose Jaw Flying Club, bush pilot with Prairie Airways, executive vice-president of Canadian Pacific Airlines) Telephone interview & letters 1984-87.

Samson, Mireille. Personal interview 23 April 1983, Montreal, PQ; letters 1986-87; telephone interview 8 June 1992.
Sanderson, Captain Keith. (director of flight operations, Air Canada) Personal interview 13 November 1984, Vancouver, BC.
Sauve, Nicole. Personal interview 23 April 1985, Montreal, PQ; telephone interview 28 October 1986; letters 1984-91.
Schlachter, Fred. (husband of pilot Eliane Roberge Schlachter) Personal interview25 October 1983, Vancouver, BC.
Schiff, Daphne. Letter 6 October 1986 re trans-Atlantic flight with Margo McCutcheon and Adele Fogele.
Scolefield, Jacqueline. Telephone interview 21 April 1985.

Scolefield, Jack and Ann. (parents of Jacqueline; Jack, owner of Laurentide Aviation) Letter Jack to author 11 April 1984; letter mother to author 1992.
Secord, Isabel. Personal interview 16 November 1984, Edmonton, AB.
Shaw Lynn. Letter 25 November 1983.
Shorthill, Murray. Letters 1983.
Simard, Marie Helen. Telephone interviews 23 April 1985, 14 January 1992.
Simpson, Patty Aberson. Personal interview 28 January 1984, Winnipeg, MB; letter 23 January 1992.
Sitler, Thelma. Tape recording Thelma to author 23 January 1984.
Smith, Elizabeth Frost. Personal interviews 30 October 1983, Sidney, BC; 7 August 1991, Langley, BC; telephone interview 29 November 1985; letters 1983-88.
Smith, Captain J.L. (Nordair pilot) Telephone interview 23 April 1985; letter 25 June 1986 from J. Smith to Stefanie Crampton on behalf of author regarding number of women pilots with Nordair.
Soulsby, John. (son of Elsie MacGill Soulsby, Canada's first woman aeronautical engineer) Personal interview 3 November 1981, Winnipeg, MB.
Spearing, Mary. Telephone interview 13 October 1983; letter 14 Mary 1984.
Steeves, Barb. (re Peggy Ricard Standring) Letter 25 May 1984 to author.
Ste Marie, Nicole. Personal interview 24 April 1985, Montreal, PQ; letter 12 November 1985.
Stephenson, Joan "Tony." (daughter of Louise Jenkins) Personal interview 1 October 1983, Old Lyme, Connecticut.
Stevenson, Air Vice Marshall Leigh. (World War I pilot, RCAF) Personal interview 26 May 1994, Winnipeg, MB at World War I Flyers Reunion.
Stewart, Grace Sandra Hutchinson. Personal interview 9 June 1981, Thunder Bay, ON; 22 September 1983, Winnipeg, MB; letters 1981-85.
Strilesky, Paula Venn. Personal interviews 1 November 1983, 27 November 1986, Vancouver, BC; letter 1987.
Studer, Lina. (mother of pilots Joan and Berna Studer). Letter 26 June 1980; 22 October 1985 in which she enclosed article written by Berna Studer McCann.
Supper, Huguette. Letter 21 January 1984.
Sutherland, Kim Wheaton. Personal interview 24 November 1986, Edmonton, AB.
Swyers, Barbara. Personal interviews 24 November 1983, Toronto, ON; 14 November 1986, Winnipeg, MB; telephone interview 1 February 1985; letters 1983-1992.
Sykes, Laura. Personal interview 11 October 1987, Winnipeg, MB.

Tanner, Gertrude de la Vergne. Personal interview 24 October 1983, Vancouver, BC.
Taylor, Roberta "Robbie" Wieben. Personal interviews 1979-1992; letters 1979-1991.
Towne, Helen. Personal interview 12 November 1984, Calgary, AB.
Tenhoff, Tosca Trasolini. Telephone interviews 8 May 1981, 20 September 1983.
Trasolini, Norm. (brother of pilot Tosca Trasolini). Letter 10 December 1983.
Trasolini, Elmo (brother of pilot Tosca Traslini). Telephone interview 7 June 1992.
Tripp-Simms, Darlene. Tape recording & letter 4 August 1985.
Trenholm, Marion. Letter 31 January 1984.

Uzelman, Teresa O'Flaherty. Personal interview 25 November 1986, Edmonton, AB; letter 15 October 1986.

Vachon, Georgette. (wife of early bush pilot, Romeo Vachon) Letters September-November 1983.
Varcoe, Lillian. Personal interview 14 November 1984, Vancouver, BC.
Vollick, Roy. (brother of pilot Eileen Vollick) Telephone interview 23 November 1983.
Vincent, Marie. Letters 1984-86.
Vos, Pat. Personal interview 12 November 1984, Calgary, AB; letter 31 January 1992.

Wadden, Brian. (Newfoundland Aviation Society) Letters 1983-84.
Wagner, Stan U. (early bush pilot, Transair) Personal interviews 1985-86, Winnipeg, MB.
Walker, Kathleen Gloria Large. Personal interview 17 October 1984, Stellarton, NS; letter 5 February 1980.
Walker, Peter. (former DOT) Letter 15 December 1984.
Warren, Debbie Hall. Personal interview 15 April 1986, Winnipeg, MB; telephone interview 14 February 1992.
Warren, Arnold. (husband of pilot Violet Milstead Warren) Personal interviews 20 November 1983, 2 November 1986, Colborne, ON; letters 1980-87.
Warren, Violet Milstead. Personal interviews 20 November 1983, 2 November 1986, Colborne, ON.
Watson, E.P. (early flying instructor in Maritimes) Telephone interview 16 October 1984.
Weicker, Sue. Telephone interview 18 February 1992.
Wheeler, Tom Jr. (Wheeler Airlines, one of the oldest aviation companies in Canada established 1929). Letter with comments from Tom Wheeler Sr 18 September 1985.

White, Debbi. Letter 19 February 1985.
Whyard, Florence Elliott. Personal interview 16 May 1984, Winnipeg, MB; letter 3 February 1980.
Wieben, Elizabeth. Personal interviews 1979-86; letters 1979-92.
Wiens, Heather. Personal interview 30 November 1986, Calgary,
AB; letters 1984-86, 30 April 1992.
Wilkin, Carolyn. (widow of early bush pilot Leigh Brintnell of Western Canada Airways, Mackenzie Air Service). Personal interview 1 April 1984, Edmonton, AB.
Wilson, Candace. Telephone interview 3 November 1986.
Williams, Tom. (World War I pilot, held flying licences until 1980s) Personal interview 28 May 1982, Ottawa, ON at World War I Flyers Reunion.
Witchell, Susan. Telephone interview 13 February 1987; 11 January 1992.
Witt, Reg. (early flying instructor) Telephone interview 1 November 1983.
Wrathall, Tom. (World War I pilot and early flying instructor at Montreal Light Aeroplane Club) Personal interview 28 May 1982, Ottawa, ON at World War I Flyers Reunion; telephone interview 25 April 1985.

Zokol, Kathy Davenport. Personal interviews 1 November 1983, 15 November 1984, Vancouver, BC; telephone interview 26 November 1986.
Zubryckyj, Marie. Personal interview 30 March 1986, Winnipeg, MB.

SECONDARY SOURCES

Archives

Civil Aviation Authority, London, England
Glenbow Museum Archives
Provincial Archives (all provinces)
Public Archives of Canada
Western Canada Aviation Museum

Aviation Colleges

Mount Royal College
Seneca College of Applied Arts and Technology
The Confederation College of Applied Arts and Technology

Flying Clubs

Edmonton Flying Club
Fredericton Flying club
Halifax Flying Club
Moncton Flying Club
Montreal Flying Club
Winnipeg Flying Club

Libraries

Metropolitan Toronto Library Board
Newfoundland Public Library Services
Regina Public Library
Winnipeg Public Library

Unpublished Articles

Backgrounder. "Women in the Canadian forces." n.d. c 1986.
Backgrounder. "Charter Task Force Final Report." n.d. c 1987.
Canadian Armed Forces. "The Employment of Women in Non-Traditional Roles in the Canadian Armed Forces." Canadian Armed Forces, "No. 2 Canadian Forces Flying Training School." February 1981.
DND Report on Civil Aviation and Civil Government Air Operators 1936. Printer to Kings Most Excellent Majesty, Ottawa.
"Fact Sheet on Aircrew Evaluations." Annex D, 30 November 1983.
"History of Quebecair." n.d.
News Release. "Beatty Announces Women Aircrew." 14 July 1986.
"Pacific Western/Transair History." n.d.
Report on Civil Aviation 1923-1931. DND Ottawa.
"Report of the Attitude Surveys On Women In Combat Roles and Isolated Postings." Sugey Report June 1978. Directorate Personnel Development Studies.
"Summary of Surveys on Women in Combat and Isolated Postings." June 1978. Directorate Personnel Development Studies.
Transair Limited. "The Golden Way." n.d.

Forestell, Lieutenant Diane G. "The Victorian Legacy. A Social Historical Analysis of Attitudes Toward Women in the Canadian Forces." CF Personnel Applied Research Unit Toronto. n.d.
Haakonson, Major N.H.; Major V.A. McKee. "Medical Considerations For Employment of Women in the Canadian Military." DPM Report No. 1/78 Directorate of Preventive Medicine Surgeon General Branch, DND.
Neikamp, Dorothy. "Women & Flight, 1910-1978: An Annotated Bibliography." July 1980.
Orr, Bill. "History of the Halifax Flying Club."
Park, Captain R. E. "Factors Influencing The Final Conclusions of the Canadian Forces Trial Employment of Servicewomen In Non-Traditional Environments and Roles." Canadian Forces Personnel Applied Research Unit. 1983.

Park, Captain R. E. and Lieutenant D.G. Forestell. "Notes on Specific Issues Related to the Employment of Women in the Canadian Forces" presented at the 19th International Applied Military Psychology Symposium Meeting, Copenhagen, Denmark, 7 June 1983.

Prociuk, Terry J. "Women At Canadian Military Colleges: A Survey of Attitudes (1980)." Departmental manuscript 80-1 July 1980. Department of Military Leadership and Management.

Resch, Major Gerald D. "Servicewomen in Non-Traditional Roles and Environments: An Overview of Canadian Projects and Cross National Similarities." Social & Behavioral Science Advisor HQ CF Europe. Prepared for the 18th international Applied Military Psychology Symposium, London, England, June 1982.

Simpson, Captain Suzanne, Major Doris Toole, Cindy Player. "Women in the Canadian Forces: Past, Present and Future."

Strother Lt.Colonel Dougherty USAF Reserve. "The W.A.S.P. Program: An Historical Synopsis." April 1972 & "The W.A.S.P. Training Program: An Historical Synopsis." January 1973.

Published Articles & Books

Journals

Canadian Aviation

Canadian Aviation Historical Society Journal

Newspapers

Aviation articles too numerous to list, 1974-1992.

The Citizen Ottawa

The Evening Telegram

The Gazette Montreal

The Hamilton Spectator

The Journal Edmonton

Northern Miner

The Toronto Sun

The Winnipeg Free Press

The Vancouver Sun

Articles

Allen, Peter. "Aerobatics." *Airborne*. June 1980.

Barker, Ralph. "Aviator Extraordinary, The Sidney Cotton Story." title of journal missing.

DeBlicquy, Lorna. "When The Flight Examiner Stayed On the Ground." *Canadian Aviation*. December 1974. pp 22-23.

Clarke, Basil. "The Epic of the ATA." *History of Aviation*. New English Library. n.d.

"Four Stripes and Female." *Flight International*. 17 November 1984.

Feldman, Gail. "The Only Child As a Separate Entity." *Psychology Report*. 1978. Vol. 42: pp 107-110.

Horowitz, Milton W. "For Men Only?" *Flying*. August 1965. pp 30-33.

Lindert, Peter H. "Sibling Position and Achievement." *The Journal of Human Resources*. Spring 1977. pp 198-219.

Meaney, J. T. "The New Newfoundland Airport." *The Book of Newfoundland*. pp 152-3.

Meaney, J. T. "Aviation in Newfoundland." *The Book of Newfoundland*. pp 141-152.

Novello, Joseph R & Zakhour I. Youssef. "Abstract Psycho-Social Studies in General Aviation 11. Personality Profile of Female Pilots" in letter Novello to author 11 November 1983.

Pierson, Ruth and Beth Light. "Women in the Teaching and Writing of Canadian History." *The History and Social Science Teacher* Special Issue, Re-Appraising Canadian History. Vol 17. No. 2. Winter 1982.

Silverman, Eliane Leslau. "Writing Canadian Women's History, 1970-82: An Historiographical Analysis." *The Canadian Historical Review* pp 513-533.

Strong-Boag, Veronica. "Raising Clio's Consciousness: Women's History and Archives in Canada." *Archivaria* 1978. pp 70-82.

Vollick, Eileen. "How I Became Canada's First Licensed Woman Pilot." *Canadian Air Review*. June 1928. pp 14, 42.

Zajonc, R. B. & Gregory B. Markus "Birth Order and Intellectual Development." *Psychological Review*. 1975. Vol 82. pp 74-88.

Books

Acton, Janice, Penny Goldsmith, Bonnie Shepard. *"Women at work, ON 1850-1930*. Toronto: Canadian Women's Education Press. 1974.

Boase, Wendy. *The Sky's The Limit, Women Pioneers in Aviation*. London: Osprey Publishing. 1979.

Boyd, Monica. ed. *Canadian Attitudes Toward Women: Thirty Years of Change 1954-1984*. Prepared for the Women's Bureau, Labour Canada. Minister of Supply and Services. Canada 1984.

Cheesman, E. C. *Brief Glory, The Story of the A.T.A.* Leicester: Harborough Publishing. 1946.

Cochran, Jacqueline. *The Stars at Noon*. n.d. no pub.

Curtis, Lettice. *The Forgotten Pilots, Air Transport Auxiliary, 1939-1945*. London: C. Arthur Pearson. 1945.

Douglas, W. A. B. *The Creation of a National Air Force. The Official History of the Royal Canadian Air Force*. Vol. II. University of Toronto Press in co-operation with DND and the Canadian Govt Publishing Centre, Supply and Services, Canada. 1986.

Ellis, Frank H. *Canada's Flying Heritage*. University of Toronto Press. 1954.

Fuller, G.A., J.A. Griffin, Ken Molson. *125 Years of Canadian Aeronautics, A Chronology 1840-1965*. Willowdale, ON: Canadian Aviation Historical Society. n.d.

King, Allison. *Golden Wings, The Story of Some of the Women Ferry Pilots of the Air Transport Auxiliary.* London: C. Arthur Pearson. 1945.

Langevin, Liane. *Women in Canadian Federal Politics.* Advisory Council on the Status of Women. March 1977.

Lefrancois, Guy R. *Of Humans: Introductory Psychology.* California: Brooks/Cole Publishing. 1974.

Lothian, George. *Flight Deck, Memoirs of an Airline Pilot.* McGraw-Hill Ryerson. 1979.

McGrath, Tom. *History of Canadian Airports, Airports and Construction in Canada.* Ministry of Supply & Service. 1984.

Milberry, Larry. *Austin Airways, Canada's Oldest Airline.* Toronto: Canav Books, 1985.

——. *Aviation in Canada.* Toronto: McGraw-Hill Ryerson, 1979.

Ministry of Industry, Trade & Commerce. *Aviation in Canada 1971. A Statistical Handbook of Canadian Civil Aviation.* Ottawa: Statistics Canada. February 1972.

Molson, K.M. and H.A. Taylor. *Canadian Aircraft Since 1909.* Stittsville, ON: Canada's Wings. 1982.

Molson, K.M. *Pioneering in Canadian Air Transport.* Altona, MB: D. W. Friesen & Sons. 1974.

Ostry, Sylvia. *The Female Worker in Canada.* Ottawa: Dominion Bureau of Statistics. 1968.

Ryan, Dick. *From Box Kite to Board Room.* Moose Jaw, SK: The Grande Valley Press. 1986.

Scharr, Adela Riek. *Sisters in the Sky.* Vol. I, The WAFS. Gerald, MO: The Patrice Press. 1986.

Smith, Philip. *It Seems Like Only Yesterday, Air Canada, The First 50 Years.* Toronto: McClelland and Stewart. 1986.

Stephenson, Marylee ed. *Women in Canada.* Toronto: General Publishing. 1977.

Stevenson, Garth. *The Politics of Canada's Airlines from Diefenbaker to Mulroney.* Toronto: University of Toronto Press. 1987.

Stromberg, Ann H. ed. *Women Working.* University of Kansas Mayfield Publishing. 1978.

Yeager, General Chuck & Leo Janos. *Yaeger: An Autobiography.* New York: Bantam Books. 1985.

INDEX

Women are indexed under their most commonly used pilot name. Cross-referencing is provided.